Controlling Public Expenditure

Controlling Public Expenditure

The Changing Roles of Central Budget Agencies – Better Guardians?

Edited by

John Wanna

Professor, School of Politics and Public Policy and Deputy Director, Centre for Governance and Public Policy, Griffith University, Australia

Lotte Jensen

Associate Professor of Public Administration, Institute of Political Science, University of Copenhagen, Denmark

Jouke de Vries

Professor of Public Administration and Scientific Director, Leiden University, The Hague, The Netherlands

Edward Elgar
Cheltenham, UK • Northampton, MA, USA

Published by
Edward Elgar Publishing Limited
Glensanda House
Montpellier Parade
Cheltenham
Glos GL50 1UA
UK

Edward Elgar Publishing, Inc.
136 West Street
Suite 202
Northampton
Massachusetts 01060
USA

A catalogue record for this book
is available from the British Library

Library of Congress Cataloguing in Publication Data

Controlling public expenditure: the changing roles of central
    budget agencies – better guardians?/edited by John Wanna,
    Lotte Jensen, Jouke de Vries.
        p. cm.
    Includes bibliographical references and index.
    1. Budget process. 2. Expenditures, public. I. Wanna, John.
    II. Jensen, Lotte. III. Vries, J. de, Dr.
    HJ2009.C665   2003
    352.4'8—dc21

                                                2003047765

ISBN 1 84376 043 6

Printed and bound in Great Britain by MPG Books Ltd, Bodmin, Cornwall

Contents

Figures

Tables

Contributors

Stephen Bartos
Budget Group, Department of Finance and Administration, Australia

Stephen Bartos heads the Australian government's principal budgeting and resource management group in the Finance Department. He led the introduction of the first outcomes–outputs–accruals-based Commonwealth budget in 1999–2000. He previously held positions in the Department of Transport and Communications, the Public Service Board and Andersen Consulting, and has published widely in professional and academic journals. He holds a BA (Hons) from the Australian National University and is currently completing doctoral studies on public sector institutions and budgeting.

K.C. Cheung
Department of Management, Hong Kong Polytechnic University, Hong Kong

Kai-chee Cheung is Associate Professor in the Department of Management at the Hong Kong Polytechnic University. His PhD thesis investigated central–local tensions in the Chinese budgetary system. His main research interests are in budgetary reform in China, environmental governance, and public sector management in China and Hong Kong. His recent publications have appeared *in Public Administration Review, The China Quarterly*, and *Public Administration and Development.*

Nicholas Deakin
Centre for Civil Society, London School of Economics, UK

Formerly a civil servant, Nicholas Deakin was Professor of Social Policy and Administration at the University of Birmingham (1980–98) and is now a Visiting Professor at the Centre for Civil Society, London School of Economics. In 1995–96 he chaired the Independent Commission on the Future of the Voluntary Sector in England. Among his recent research projects has been a review of inner city policy under the Conservatives, case studies of local authority–voluntary sector relations, and a study of *The Treasury and Social Policy* (with Richard Parry, 2000).

Jouke de Vries

Department of Management, Leiden University, The Hague Campus, The Netherlands

Jouke de Vries is Professor of Public Administration and Scientific Director of Leiden University at The Hague. He studied political science at the University of Amsterdam, and specializes in political administrative relations and the functioning of the Dutch political system. Recent publications include: 'Core Executives and Party Politics: Privatisation in the Netherlands', *West European Politics* (with K. Yesilkagit 1999); 'A Trojan Horse in the Dutch Ministry of Agriculture', in M. Thompson *et al.* (eds), *Cultural Theory as Political Science* (1999); and 'The Netherlands: Fragmenting Pillars, Fading Colours', in R.A.W. Rhodes and P. Weller, *The Changing World of Top Officials: Mandarins or Valets* (2001).

Arlene Holen

Congressional Budget Office, USA

Arlene Holen is an Associate Director of the Congressional Budget Office, Washington. She manages the agency's review process including budget reports, research papers, and testimony. She previously headed a division at CBO that conducts studies of budget concepts and process, accounting and financial management, and general government. Before joining CBO, she chaired the Federal Mine Safety and Health Review Commission. Under Presidents Reagan and Bush, she served as Associate Director in the Office of Management and Budget responsible for budget policy for the departments of Health and Human Services, Education, Labor, and Veterans Affairs. Prior to this she served as a senior staff economist for the Council of Economic Advisers, specializing in labour and health issues. She holds a bachelor's degree from Smith College, and an advanced degree in economics from Columbia University. She has published articles on labour markets, occupational licensing, immigration, and accident rates.

Gwenda Jensen

School of Accountancy, Victoria University of Wellington, New Zealand

Gwenda Jensen is a lecturer in accountancy at Victoria University of Wellington, New Zealand. Previously, she worked as a senior analyst in the Budget Management Branch of the New Zealand Treasury (from 1998 to 2001). She has also developed policies for the NZ Office of the Controller and Auditor-General, and the departments of Internal Affairs and Corrections on contemporary issues of accounting, financial management, budgeting, and contracting. Her research interests and publications include accounting for infrastructure assets and resourcing government policy obligations.

Lotte Jensen
Department of Government, Copenhagen University, Denmark

Lotte Jensen is an Associate Professor of Public Administration in the Institute of Political Science at the University of Copenhagen. Her research interests and publications cover urban politics, social science methodology and central government. She has authored a number of publications on the Finance Ministry including: 'Finansministeriet', in Tim Knudsen (ed.), *Regering og EMbedsmænd* (2000); 'Etik, kultur og værdier i Finansministeriet', in Anders Berg-Sørensen (ed.), *Etik til debat* (2001); and 'Images of Accountability in Danish Public Sector Reform', in James Guthrie *et al.* (eds), *Learning from International Public Management Reform* (2000).

Joanne Kelly
Treasury Board Secretariat, Canada

Joanne Kelly has been a visiting post-doctoral scholar at the Treasury Board Secretariat in Canada since September 1999 and currently holds the Reisman Fellowship. Her research focuses on the politics and processes of government budgeting and public expenditure control from a comparative perspective. Joanne has published academic articles on these topics, and written discussion papers for the government of Canada. She is co-author of *Managing Public Expenditure in Australia* with John Wanna and John Forster and is currently writing *The Art of Budgetary Control: Public Expenditure in Australia and Canada* with John Wanna.

Evert Lindquist
School of Administration, University of Victoria, Canada

Evert Lindquist is Director of the School of Public Administration, University of Victoria, and a former Treasury Board Secretariat Visiting Fellow. He has written on government transitions, cabinet decision-making, budgetary processes, capacity for policy innovation, alternative service delivery, business planning and performance reporting, think tanks and policy networks. He edited *Government Restructuring and Career Public Service in Canada* and *The Co-op Alternative: Civil Society and the Future of Public Services*. Recent chapters include: 'Reconceiving the Center', in *Government of the Future*; 'How Ottawa Plans', in *How Ottawa Spends 2001–02*; and 'Culture, Control or Capacity?', in *New Players, Partners and Processes*.

Markus M. Müller
Economics Ministry of Baden-Württemberg, Germany

Markus M. Müller holds a PhD in political science from Erlangen University and an MA from Tübingen University. He lectured at Erlangen University from 1996–2001, and in 2002 was appointed head of the policy division at the Economics Ministry of Baden-Württemberg. His research interests include: comparative political economy; American politics; and German politics. His major publications are *The New Regulatory State in Germany* (2002); *Haushaltsausgleich durch Verfassungspolitik?* (1997); and *Regulierung und Deregulierung im wirtschaftlichen Transformationsprozess* (with Roland Sturm *et al.* 2000).

June O'Neill
Baruch College, City University of New York, USA

June O'Neill is Wollman Professor of Economics and Director of the Center for the Study of Business and Government at Baruch College, City University of New York, and also an Adjunct Scholar of the American Enterprise Institute in Washington. Between 1995 and 1999 she was Director of the Congressional Budget Office in Washington. Prior to this she was Director of Policy and Research at the US Commission on Civil Rights, senior economist on the President's Council of Economic Advisers, senior research associate at the Urban Institute and research associate at the Brookings Institution. She received her PhD in economics from Columbia University and was elected Vice President of the American Economic Association in 1998. She has published books and articles on labour markets, determinants of wage and income differentials, welfare and welfare reform, social security, tax issues and health insurance.

Richard Parry
School of Social and Political Studies, University of Edinburgh, Scotland

Richard Parry is Senior Lecturer in the School of Social and Political Studies at the University of Edinburgh where his main interests are public management and resource allocation. With Nicholas Deakin he is the author of a major study into *The Treasury and Social Policy* (2000) and his recent research has been on the impact on the civil service of the establishment of devolved government in Scotland, Wales and Northern Ireland.

Gert Paulsson

School of Economics and Management, Lund University, Sweden

Gert Paulsson holds a PhD in Business Administration and is currently an Assistant Professor in the School of Economics and Management at Lund University in Sweden. His research has focused on public management reforms and institutional budgetary adaptation in Sweden. He has also held positions as a senior analyst at the Swedish National Audit Office, a senior economic advisor at the Budget Department in the Ministry of Finance and a political advisor on economic affairs in the Prime Minister's Office.

Roland Sturm

Department of Political Science, University of Erlangen-Nuremberg, Germany

Roland Sturm is Professor and Head of the Department of Political Science at the University of Erlangen-Nuremberg. He has studied or held academic positions in many universities including: Berlin (Free University), Sheffield, Heidelberg, Stanford and Hamburg. His research interests include regional policies; politics of European integration; German and comparative politics; comparative public policy; and economic policy. His publications include: *Der Haushaltsausschuß des Deutschen Bundestages* (1988); *Public Deficits: a Comparative Study of their Economic and Political Consequences in Britain, Canada, Germany and the United States* (1998); *The Information Society and the Regions in Europe: an Anglo-German Comparison* (with Georg Weinmann 2000); and *Rediscovering Competition: Competition Policy in East Central Europe in Comparative Perspective* (with Jürgen Dieringer and Markus M. Müller 2001).

Susan Tanaka

Policy Analyst, Washington, USA

Susan Tanaka directs PolicySite.org, a web site on US public policy. She previously held positions as Associate Director for Communications and senior analyst in the US Congressional Budget Office, budget examiner for the US Office of Management and Budget, and was Vice President of the Committee for a Responsible Federal Budget (a bi-partisan, non-profit educational organization). She holds an MBA from the Yale School of Management, an MA from the Fletcher School of Law and Diplomacy, and a BA from Antioch College.

Kurt Thurmaier
Department of Public Administration, University of Kansas, USA

Kurt Thurmaier is Associate Professor of Public Administration at the University of Kansas. His research interests focus on decision-making by budget analysts in state and local budget offices. He has also researched budgetary reform in local self-governments in Poland and the Ukraine. Before joining the University of Kansas, he was a budget and policy analyst in the Wisconsin State Budget Office from 1984–87. His publications include articles in *Public Administration Review, Public Budgeting and Finance*, the *Journal of Public Administration Review, Public and Society*, and *State and Local Government Review.*

John Wanna
School of Politics and Public Policy, Griffith University, Australia

John Wanna is a Professor in the School of Politics and Public Policy and principal researcher in the Centre for Australian Public Sector Management at Griffith University. He has written a number of books on public policy, public sector management and government budgeting including: *Budgetary Management and Control* (with John Forster 1990); *Managing Public Expenditure in Australia* (with Joanne Kelly and John Forster 2000); and *From Accounting to Accountability* (with Chris Ryan and Chew Ng 2001). His research interests include the budgeting and management of public expenditure, government–business relations and Australian politics.

Kutsal Yesilkagit
School of Governance, Utrecht University, The Netherlands

Kutsal Yesilkagit holds a PhD from the University of Leiden and is senior researcher at the Utrecht School of Governance. His research interests include civil-military relationships, public policy change, and Turkish politics. Currently he is working on public management reforms and the changing relationships between politicians and bureaucrats. His most recent publication on 'Core Executives and Party Politics: Privatisation in the Netherlands' appears in *West European Politics* (with J. de Vries 1999).

Preface

The words 'mystique', 'centre of power', 'adversarial' and 'all-powerful' are used in some form to describe and define virtually all the central budget agencies (CBA) in this study. The very mention of the words Ministry of Finance provokes a range of emotion from fear to exasperation in the press, the public and, most importantly, in the government's spending departments. While the real power of the CBA is more subtle, the rise in prominence and strength of a country's central budget agency has been a near universal event. As governments grew in size and scope they needed powerful central authorities to provide command and control over the executive's budget. As government spending outstripped the will to tax, an even stronger CBA was needed to control total spending.

An omnipotent CBA has helped contain spending, it has, however, not necessarily proven successful at making government more efficient and more effective. Many countries including many of those that are members of the Organization for Economic Cooperation and Development (OECD) are now looking to make government more effective by focusing on results and performance. A revolution is under way as governments attempt to link the input of the budget with the government's outputs and outcomes; in short to make the public sector look more like the private sector.

The performance revolution is forcing the greatest change on the role of the centre or core executive. While unique to each country, the new budget process will generally be a more top-down process. Aggregate spending will be defined for each ministry who will receive, in return, the flexibility to achieve goals agreed to with the legislature and their minister. The centre (through the CBA) in turn must change from policeman to partner. In a performance oriented budget the CBA must become a policy advisor to support coherence, but to stand off and respect the decisions made by ministries. It will need to evolve and adapt both the forward-looking budget functions with which they are comfortable as well as a backward-looking audit and evaluation function.

There are a myriad of questions in need of answers as CBAs oversee this shift to performance. For example, will these changes require a fundamental shift in the focus of the CBA or will it simply add on a layer of complexity to an already difficult job? Will the employees of the modern CBA need a new skill set? Is there a continuing need for a Central Budget Agency?

Despite the importance of the CBA, there is precious little international comparative information and research to explain and help guide the performance revolution. The research presented here is a good first step in filling that void. The chapters explore a range of countries, including those that have been among the most innovative and successful in reforming their public service. They answer the important questions of how CBAs have evolved and how the governance context in which they work is changing. Yet, the value of the research lies beyond a simple description of the budget process. The analysis of the staff, the management, their background, and their view of the work and organizational culture offers unique insights into challenges that policy-makers face as they move forward with reform. In a world with many theories and few facts, this book is a welcome addition and an important resource for academics, citizens and their governments that seek to understand and improve their policies.

Michael Ruffner
Administrator, Public Management Service
Organization for Economic Cooperation and Development

Acknowledgements

This project would not have been possible without the collaboration of a number of research active organisations. In particular we wish to acknowledge the support of the Department of Management at The Hague Campus, Leiden University (the Netherlands); the School of Politics and Public Policy, Griffith University (Australia); the Department of Government, University of Copenhagen (Denmark); The Danish Ministry of Finance; the Canadian Treasury Board Secretariat; and the Swedish Ministry of Finance. We also wish to thank the Public Management Service of the Organisation for Economic Cooperation and Development for their involvement in this project. They all assisted in important ways in producing the research for this book.

We would particularly like to thank the many practising finance and budgetary officials who participated in the project – some of whom appear as joint authors of chapters, but others were equally important in providing access, information and comment. In most cases their commitment to scholarly research meant that assistance with this project was added to their many other duties and responsibilities. The editors wish to thank them for their commitment and time, in particular: Steven Bartos (Department of Finance, Australia), Ton Bestebreur (Dutch Ministry of Finance), Arlene Holen (CBO, United States), Gwenda Jensen (formerly New Zealand Treasury), Mike Joyce (TBS, Canada), Marcus Muller (Economics Ministry, Baden-Württemburg, Germany), Gert Paulsson (formerly Ministry of Finance, Sweden), Mogens Pedersen (Danish Ministry of Finance) and Susan Tanaka (formerly CBO, United States). Other officials generously assisted with interviews or with feedback – some of whom are acknowledged in individual chapters.

Leiden University's Department of Management hosted a two-day seminar in The Hague that brought together academics and practitioners from around the globe. Their hospitality and organisational prowess was crucial to the success of the project and the resulting publication. We appreciate the input of those who participated at the seminar especially those who provided commentary and discussion on the drafts presented. Special thanks go to Mogens Pedersen, Denise Fantone (GAO, USA), Ton Bestebreur, Frans Journa (Leiden University), Oliver James (Exeter University), Charles Broughton (Finance, Australia), Michael Ruffner (OECD) and Patrick Weller (Griffith University, Australia). We wish to acknowledge the involvement or encouragement of Michael Ruffner, Adam Wolfe and Alex Matheson from the OECD. Their interest in this project was greatly appreciated, as well as Michael Ruffner's participation at a seminar in The Hague. The Danish Ministry of Finance also provided support in 2001 for the editors to edit the final manuscript and finalise conclusions.

In Australia the Australian Research Council provided funding for this research, while the Department of Management at Leiden University met most of the costs of the seminar.

We wish to acknowledge the research assistance provided by Margriet van Sisseren (Leiden), Charles Broughton, Mikkel Havelund (Copenhagen) and Alexander Gash (Griffith). They all gave invaluable support at various stages of the project and we wish to acknowledge their efforts. Thanks are also due to Olwen Schubert of the School of Politics and Public Policy, Griffith University, for transforming the files of final chapters into camera-ready copy.

Finally, editors and contributors would like to extend their appreciation to Edward Elgar Publishing for encouraging research publications in this field. We feel this project makes an important contribution to the gaining of a better understanding of public sector finance, and we thank Edward Elgar and Dymphna Evans for their interest in this project.

John Wanna, Lotte Jansen and Jouke de Vries
Brisbane, Copenhagen and The Hague

Abbreviations

AA	Audit Administration (China)
AAU	Agency Advice Unit within the Dept. of Finance (Aust)
AIMS	Accrual Information Management System (Aust)
AME	Annually Managed Expenditure (UK)
ARLU	Annual Reference Level Update (Canada)
BBA	*Balanced Budget Act of 1997* (US)
BD	Budget Department (in Ministry of Finance, Sweden)
BEA	*Budget Enforcement Act of 1990* (US)
BMB	Budget Management Branch (NZ)
BMD	Budget Management Department (Ministry of Finance, China)
BOB	Bureau of the Budget (US)
CBA	Central Budget Agency
CBICA	*Congressional Budget and Impoundment Control Act of 1974* (US)
CBO	Congressional Budget Office (US)
CCP	Chinese Communist Party (China)
CEO	Chief Executive Officer
CEO	Chief Executive Officer (Aust)
CEO	Departmental Chief Executive Officers (Canada)
CFELG	Central Finance and Economic Leading Group (China)
CFO	Chief Finance Officer (Aust)
CPI	Consumer Price Index
CSRs	Comprehensive Spending Reviews (UK)
DoF	Department of Finance
DoFA	Department of Finance and Administration (Aust)
DM	Deutsche Marks (Germany)
DSL	Departmental Spending Limits (UK)
DURD	Department of Urban and Regional Development (Aust)
EC	Economic Committee (Denmark)
EDX	Public Expenditure Committee (UK)
EMU	European Monetary Union
EPB	Environmental Protection Bureau (China)

ERC	Expenditure Review Committee of Cabinet (Aust)
ESO	Expert Group of Public Finance (Sweden)
EXOP	Executive Office of the President (US)
EU	European Union
FEC	Finance and Expenditure Committee (NZ)
FER	Fundamental Expenditure Review (UK)
Finance	Department of Finance (Canada)
FIS	Financial Information Systems (Canada)
FMA Act	*Financial Management and Accountability Act 1997* (Aust)
FNV	Federatie Nederlandse Vakbeweging (Dutch Federation of Unions)
GAAP	Generally Accepted Accounting Practice
GAO	General Accounting Office
GBE	Government Business Enterprises (Aust)
GDP	Gross Domestic Product
GDR	German Democratic Republic
GPRA	*Government Performance and Results Act of 1993 (US)*
GST	Goods and Services Tax
IGCP	Interdepartmental Guidance Committee for Privatization (Netherlands)
ILSBA	Illinois State Budget Agency (US)
IRF	Office of the State Budget Inspectors (Netherlands)
KRA	Key Results Areas (NZ)
MC	Memorandum to Cabinet (Canada)
MMP	Mixed Member Proportional electoral system (NZ)
MoF	Ministry of Finance
MYEFO	Mid-Year Economic and Fiscal Outlook (Aust)
NASBO	National Association of State Budget Officers (US)
NEC	National Economic Council (US)
NPC	National People's Congress (China)
NPM	New Public Management
NPR	National Performance Review (US)
OCG	Office of the Comptroller General (Canada)
OECD	Organisation for Economic Cooperation and Development
OFFM	Office of Federal Financial Management (US)
OFPP	Office of Federal Procurement Policy (US)

OIRA	Office of Information and Regulatory Affairs (US)
OMB	Office of Management and Budget (US)
PAD	Program Associate Directors (US)
PAYGO	Pay-as-you-go (US)
PCO	Privy Council Office (Canada)
PEMS	Policy and Expenditure Management System (Canada)
PESC	Public Expenditure Survey Committee (UK)
PFC	Parliamentary Finance Committee (Denmark)
PIU	Performance and Innovation Unit (UK)
PMO	Prime Minister's Office (Canada)
PMO	Prime Minister's Office (Denmark)
PPBS	Planning, Programming and Budgeting System
PRC	People's Republic of China
PSA	Public Service Agreements (UK)
PSBR	Public Sector Borrowing Requirements
PSX	Public Expenditure and Public Services Committee (UK)
PvdA	Partij van de Arbeid (Labour Party, Netherlands)
RCM	Regulations of the Council of Ministers (Netherlands)
RMOs	Resource Management Offices (US)
SBA	State Budget Agency (US)
SDPC	State Development and Planning Commission (China)
SOE	State Owned Enterprise
SPC	State Planning Commission (China)
SRA	Strategic Results Areas (NZ)
SSC	State Services Commission (NZ)
TBS	Treasury Board Secretariat (Canada)
VAT	Value Added Tax
VBTB	Van Beleidsbegroting tot Beleidsverantwoording (From Policy Budgeting to Policy Accounting) (Netherlands)
VVD	Volkspartij voor Vrijheid en Democracie (Conservative Liberal Party, Netherlands)
Y2K	Year 2000

Introduction: the Changing Role of Central Budget Agencies

John Wanna

One of the most important functions of modern government is to marshal and deploy resources to achieve desired objectives and outcomes. Taxing, spending and the control of public expenditure are fundamental to this function. Responsibility for controlling and allocating expenditure is usually entrusted to a relatively small group of budgetary actors at the centre of the institutional framework of national government. Politicians who flit on and off the political stage have typically consigned significant authority to their budgetary actors, and often charged them with unilateral responsibility for operating budgetary procedures and providing financial and resourcing advice. It was often argued that resource decisions were too important and politically charged to be left to a plethora of (potentially self-interested) institutional actors or budget 'claimants'.[1] Hence, central budget agencies (CBAs) have emerged to help frame the spending plans of governments and administer their financial affairs. These central budget agencies (either as single entities or in multiple combinations) exercise predominant responsibility for the shaping of resource decisions and superintendence of public finance. Their institutional and procedural position is important and often strategic; yet, the roles they play are often shrouded in mystique and the changes in their culture not adequately appreciated.

Control over resources makes central budget agencies powerful institutions – at least according to certain measures of influence and forms of power. Their power is expressed in the name of 'collective decision-making' principally through the non-market allocation of public resources to authorised purposes of government, meeting the expenses of administration and reallocating funds back to the community. Guardianship over the public purse (including various off-budget reserves or separate government-established funds) is exercised through institutional roles, procedural arrangements and administrative cultures. Guardian-spender relations involve 'big picture' issues, emerging agendas, the cut and thrust of micro politics, unspoken assumptions, the clash of behavioural incentives and inevitable gaming possibilities. The annual round of budget formulation, in most cases leading to the presentation of budget estimates of expenditure to the legislature, has become the preferred framework through which CBAs attempt to influence the provision and distribution of goods and services to society. The routine power of the CBA is expressed through these formal and informal relationships, but it is often qualified and iterative rather than overbearing and dictatorial.

These points are now reasonably well recognised in the literature. In some countries, like Britain, Canada, Australia and New Zealand, the budget-forming department was historically regarded, and accepted by students of public finance or public administration, as an all-powerful central agency able to exert policy influence through the power of the purse (Roseveare 1969; Beer 1956; Diamond 1975; Bridges 1964; Chapman 1997; Weller and Cutt 1976; Savoie 1999, chapter 6). Treasury was regarded as 'god at the cabinet table', swaying decisions this way or that through its monopoly over advice, intellectual power and bureaucratic ruthlessness. The British Treasury was seen as intimidating, standing at the 'the centre of government' as a 'monolithic, mysterious and sometimes a little menacing' institution (Roseveare 1969, p. 10). But there is now a growing reassessment and more balanced appraisal of their roles and influence. Hence, Thain and Wright (1995, p. 500) question the current applicability of an illuminating quote from the first permanent secretary of the British Treasury who boasted his department was the 'department of departments' and at 'the heart of our whole administrative system'. For these authors, Her Majesty's Treasury still remains at the centre of government and 'is the most important institution of British government' (1995, p. 3), yet the remainder of their study is devoted to a detailed demonstration of the limitations of this Treasury control. Similarly, Deakin and Parry (2000, p. 1) suggest that there certainly was an 'overmighty Treasury', and that still now 'those who exercise financial power within the core executive of any modern government possess a special form of authority'. But, they add, that after a major exercise in 'reinventing itself' (in the 1990s), Treasury attempted to abandon its adversarial positioning and surrendered much of its *unilateral* power in exchange for promoting more mutually beneficial, customer-oriented relations with departments.

For Canada, Savoie (1990, p. 323) concluded that despite the structural 'pre-eminence and influence' of the two guardian agencies, spending agencies were often able to enjoy 'the upper hand in shaping the expenditure budget except when special spending restraint measures were introduced'. In *Governing from the Centre*, he subsequently argued that the Department of Finance held a 'position of pre-eminence in Ottawa' but had experienced 'changing fortunes' particularly at the hands of politicians (1999, pp. 156–92). In Australia, Wanna, Kelly and Forster (2000, p. 42) argued that guardian agencies, such as the Department of Finance and Administration, operated from a comparatively strong but continually reinvigorated position of influence, and so were mostly 'able to impose their preferences and procedures' over budgetary outcomes in a parliamentary system. However, their detailed study demonstrated that 'the balance of power in guardian-spender relations does vacillate and shift over time; a win in one year may lead to other types of compromises or defeats in subsequent years'. They reiterated a particular contradiction in modern budgeting recognised since Wildavsky's earliest work (1964) on the politics of the American budgetary process: 'budgets *make* governments powerful, yet budgets exert enormous power *over* governments' (2000, p. 3). Boston (1992, pp. 194, 213) has argued for the New Zealand Treasury that 'no government department has exerted more influence on public policy in recent years', but that Treasury's power rested on its level of support in cabinet and on the degree to which its advice was contestable.

Similar points have been made by researchers studying budget institutions in presidential systems. Tomkin in her detailed study of the Office of Management and Budget (OMB) in the United States found that the office stood 'at a critical point within the nerve centre of the federal government' able to 'exert a significant impact on public policy outcomes' (1998, p. xi). It played the role of 'budgeteer-in-chief' for the president and was involved in budget formulation, negotiation and support, apportioning funds, advising, evaluation, management, information and communication (1998, p. 4). But Congress has also assumed a greater and more formal role in budgeting, and special legislative constraints on spending and tax limits have significantly shaped the budget process – and at the same time reduced the discretionary capacity of OMB. More generally, Schick (1990) attributed the principal power of US budget guardians to their 'rationing function', but argued this power was mediated through both the budget environment and extant budgetary procedures. Over time in this context, Schick found that the rationing controls on expenditure became weakened at the expense of the 'claiming function', resulting in sustained spending growth and a budgetary 'crisis' – a situation in which central budget agencies responded by reconsidering and reshaping their roles (Schick 1997).

In the People's Republic of China, under the Central Committee of the Communist Party, the Ministry of Finance is regarded as exercising an almost dictatorial authority over the annual budget round. Few other agencies are involved in the process and very few of the people's representatives ever have the chance to see the brief summary of budget proposals, often as little as eight pages of tables. Secrecy and exclusivity are imposed as political techniques. But the regions of China notoriously play games and attempt to disguise incomes, while maximising their claims on the central budget. The Finance ministry does not necessarily have its way, and regions can achieve 'wins' despite the centralised rules and procedures.

In continental Europe and Scandinavia the historical perception was often the reverse. Central finance ministries were considered to have a narrow functional or technical bookkeeping role. They did not typically invade the policy prerogatives of other departments and individual line ministers often had a large measure of autonomy. Indeed, traditions of ministerial autonomy were important structural devices constraining the responsibilites and powers of the budget agency. The process of resourcing public policies generally consisted only of identifying revenue streams, estimating the magnitude of legal entitlements and ensuring compliance to due process or accountabilities.[2] More recently, some writers in these countries have argued, in contrast to the experiences of the American and Westminster systems cited above, that these particular ministries have increasingly attempted to expand their traditional role – especially in Germany, Denmark, the Netherlands and to a lesser extent Sweden. After decades of serving as functionary departments, these CBAs have attempted to intervene in wider policy areas, perhaps to impose their preferences over the views of the line ministries. They have attempted to coordinate selected policy areas, they have increased their control over information and increased the monitoring of spending in other ministries. Although these CBAs in most cases do not possess the constitutional power to impose their preferences, they have challenged the previous conventions by exercising their primacy in the control of expenditure. To many European commentators steeped in traditions of ministerial autonomy, this development represents an abuse of power and the improper usurpation of financial power over substantive policy responsibility. But again, most realise it is not a one-way phenomenon and line agencies still have at their disposal many ways to redress the balance of power.

Thus, the influence of central budget agencies is both highly problematical and contextual. CBAs continue to reside within the core executive but this may be because of the fact that better alternatives may be difficult to conceive or implement (for instance, in 1999 the Australian Department of Finance actively discussed the possibility of a merchant bank or accounting firm putting together the government's annual budget as an exercise in comparative costing and contestability of advice – but the government was not interested). However, the environment within which CBAs operate today has changed. Spending demands on government have grown, and the nature and forms of expenditure have changed more toward mandatory payments, legal entitlement obligations or tax expenditures. The *scope* of expenditure control consigned to the CBA is also now far greater than previously, and some would argue their influence has been potentially weakened in the wider process (Schick 2001c). In this climate, some CBAs have sought to invade the policy prerogatives of operational departments to enable them to exert more influence over priorities; others have withdrawn to a stronger monitoring and information-gathering role. Key relationships with other budgetary actors have changed both through a combination of strategic intent and force of circumstance. Certainly, some CBAs have recently and overtly attempted to reassess their role and basic purpose (in the UK, US, Australia, Canada, Denmark and the Netherlands). Some have gone through a process of explicitly asking themselves what essential functions they ought to retain, what specialist services they could deliver, what value they could add to government, and what comparative advantage they still possess. The CBA of today is arguably a more reflexive entity, locked in a more complex and complicated network of relations and facing many more rival or competitive sources of influence. But there is also a sense that the CBA is less sure of its identity, less secure in its roles, and less certain of its contribution to governance (see Schick 1997).

THE NATURE AND FUNCTIONS OF CENTRAL BUDGET AGENCIES

Historically, national treasuries and budget agencies were charged with relatively limited functions. They developed as the original bookkeepers and accountants of government – often in Europe managing the royal treasury and crown finances. Their role was to account for the payments received, reconcile the royal books and inform the monarch or court of the amounts available for expenditure. Later, these accounting bodies gradually came to report to an elected executive while still performing the same basic housekeeping accounting functions. As the desire grew for greater accountability over the use of public funds, these CBAs began to report periodically to the popular legislature – allowing their financial statements to be scrutinised by the elected representatives. During the second half of the nineteenth century through to World War II, CBAs gradually emerged as controllers of the public purse concerned with the *ex ante* regulation of expenditure and financial administrative procedures. They were charged with specified and discrete tasks that were often entrenched either in constitutions or fundamental statutes that stipulated patterns of accountability and provided them with authoritative powers. However, they were not necessarily regarded as politically significant or high status agencies, and well into the twentieth century a British Prime Minister considered excluding the Chancellor of the Exchequer (and thereby Treasury as the ministry) from cabinet (Jenkins 1998, p. 135).

In the latter half of the twentieth century, the roles and responsibilities of CBAs were expanded from their traditional superintendence role over public finance to include macroeconomic policy advice, central banking policy, employment and demand management. Such expansion could be seen either as a logical evolutionary development, or as evidence of opportunism by the sole existing adviser on resource issues interested in monopolising economic advice. Many CBAs simply added these new functions to their existing financial duties – consolidating the broader policy approaches within the executive. These countries have persisted with a *single* agency to perform both macroeconomic policy and budget/resource allocation roles (including the UK, Germany, China, Denmark, New Zealand and the Netherlands). In a few other countries, separate *economic policy* agencies were established within the executive branch – and these were often able to impose some influence on overall resource decisions concerning budgets and expenditure levels. Those nations that chose to divide economic and budgetary responsibilities between separate institutions in effect created a dualistic or bifurcated CBA – with complementary and sometimes competing responsibilities shared between the two institutions (for example, Australia, Canada and to some extent the US). Sweden although it has retained a single Ministry of Finance (with a budget department within it) operates with multiple budget and resource-related central agencies. Occasionally, where more than one CBA exists, a particular role or budgetary function (such as setting expenditure targets or parameters) may be performed or shared by more than one agency, which can create tensions between budgetary agencies at the centre as well as between central and line agencies. The US is the only nation in this comparative study that has established a bifurcated budgetary process between the executive and the legislature at the national level – with both institutions possessing their own discrete budgetary agency. Budgeting at the state or sub-national level in the US, however, tends to have more similarities with the national patterns found in the non-US countries included in this comparative study.

Internationally, there is also no common terminology used in naming CBAs. The names given to CBAs differ substantially, and often even similar labels (such as 'Ministries of Finance' or 'Treasury Departments') obscure very different roles and functions performed by these organisations in different settings. Indeed, sometimes the same departmental names in different countries connote precisely the opposite in terms of the associated roles and responsibilities, leading to degrees of confusion in undertaking comparative assessments. For instance, the Canadian Department of Finance is primarily responsible for economic and fiscal policy, tax policy, debt management, intergovernmental financial relations and establishing aggregate levels of expenditure, but the department 'differs from most of its G-7 counterparts in that it does not review departmental spending in detail' (Savoie 1999, p. 157). By contrast, the Australian Department of Finance and Administration is the agency principally responsible for the expenditure budget, program spending reviews and financial control. The Canadian Treasury Board and its Secretariat are charged with administering government expenditure and producing the expenditure budget, while the Australian Department of Treasury is the main source of advice on economic policy. In addition, the US Treasury has a far more restricted role and policy scope than say the Treasury in either the UK or New Zealand.

Most nations have retained the generic name of the Ministry of Finance (or occasionally the Department of Finance) – and include macroeconomic responsibilities with some or all of the budgetary formulation functions. Others such as the UK, Australia and New Zealand have retained, for historical reasons, the customary label 'Treasury' – departmental nomenclature inherited from monarchical regimes but preserved to evoke tradition, status and authority. The US alone has rejected both conventional labels for its CBAs, establishing discrete elements with management and budgetary responsibilities (the president's Office of Management and Budget and the Congressional Budget Office).

So, as the role and institutional form of the CBA has evolved, comparison across countries became increasingly difficult. There is no common institutional composition of the CBA across countries, and the range of functions of CBAs can differ in practice if not essence over time and from nation to nation. CBAs perform a number of discrete and broad functions which can sometimes be contradictory. Some functions exist but are paid little attention, while some are emphasised greatly, and others change in importance over time. A possible list of the main functions undertaken by CBAs is indicated below.

Clearly, given the range of institutions found internationally, not all CBAs will perform this entire list of functions. Nevertheless, in most polities these functions will be performed to some degree and will involve in part the CBA, either acting individually or in conjunction with another agency or agencies. There will also be some specific functions performed in particular countries that do not appear on this list (like property management and ownership, administering parliamentarian travel allowances, operating vehicle fleets or ministerial car pools as in the case of the Australian Department of Finance and Adminstration). There is also no necessary system of coordination integrating these various functions, or linking these functions to government intentions, or consequences governments hope to achieve from their resource decisions (cf. Wildavsky 1964; 1988). From their vantage point, governments will often regard these functions as *available* policy instruments of economic and social engineering or as accountability imperatives. Governments often exaggerate their pretence of control over the range of these functions, often for public consumption. However, experience suggests they will be faced with many inconsistencies, incongruities and unintended consequences in the budget process and governments will be constantly forced to revise the forms and operations of these functions over time.

Table 0.1   Possible functions of Central Budget Agencies

Key Budget Functions	Instruments	Main Aims/Concerns
Economic function: macroeconomic forecasting and advice	Fiscal and economic plans/outlooks; fiscal balance; medium-term fiscal strategies; whether to maintain or how to employ surpluses	Fiscal discipline and stability; reception of economic statements aimed at financial markets. Arguably the annual expenditure budget is becoming of less importance in macroeconomic policy
Political and presentational function	'Budget Speech' and associated budgetary documentation; ministerial statements, press releases and media engagements; parliamentary debates	Reception and spin – selling a message – writing the headlines for the media; highlighting the government's record, strategies and plans
Revenue/Income function	Taxation authority and types of tax instruments, tax expenditures; some user-charging and sale of services	Provision of resources for collective needs; notions of tax efficiency, non-arbitrariness, simplicity; fairness, compliance
Informational and communication function	Regular exchange of information and costings with line agencies; routinised and *ad hoc* requests for information (submissions or bids); communication of parameters, savings, limits and decisions	Provision of accurate information; the coordination and consolidation of information; advice to to government on projected estimates, costings or purchases
Allocative function	Strategic review; current priorities; policy review; new bids or program augmentation; dividing expenditure shares across functions or agencies	Priority need; redistribution; fitting program to government; services or targeted assistance; service providers; agencies; the range and type of public/merit goods to the community
Financial outlay function	Agency resourcing (revenues and expenses); annual budget measures; and intended outcomes	Public provision and administrative capacity; performance and financial management; in-year expenditure control; compliance
Investment function	Capital works statements; specific policy statements/commitments	Capital works; economic and social infrastructure; asset base; equity injections
Technical efficiency	Resource management, purchaser–provider models; price reviews, efficiency audits, best practice guides	Productivity improvement; evaluation of efficiency; offsets/savings; cost effectiveness; value for money assessments
Evaluative function	Program evaluation and review, appropriateness evaluations	Assessments of program effectiveness; policy assessment and policy management studies
Management/ Performance function	Setting standards or guidelines for performance information, performance management or other management improvement functions	Whole of government influence on improving the outputs and service delivery across the public sector; promoting better management techniques techniques and performance monitoring
Exchequer function	Issuing of warrants certifying the availability of funds, receipts to consolidated revenue	Central funds management; guaranteeing the availability of money; vouching payments can be honoured; ensuring consistency
Accountability function	The presentation of the appropriation bills and associated documents, public scrutiny; legislative budgetary debates	Electoral accountability; scrutiny of the estimates; links between budget projections and actuals presented in the financial statements or public account; scope for media and community review
Territorial-jurisdictional function	Specific funding arrangements for subsidiary jurisdictions; various formulas or negotiated arrangements determine the types and amounts of funding	Various dimensions of fiscal federalism or sub-national financial devolution; financial assistance grants and specific purpose payments; can include aspects of purchaser–provider relationships

Hence, this study investigates the significance of the different institutional structures and compositions of the CBA. It asks how the roles of the CBA have or have not changed, and seeks to understand how CBAs have responded to their changing environments. The various contributors to the study were keen to discover to what extent CBAs have extended their policy interests and imposed their preferences on other agencies. It was important to gauge whether CBAs have been the major initiators of changes and driven reform agendas, or whether they have largely been bystanders. The comparative study was also interested to ask how far (either singly or in conjunction with other agencies) the CBAs are able to maintain control over expenditure and to what degree the CBA is an active player in framing resource decisions and shaping budgetary politics. These are the essential theoretical and empirical questions addressed in this comparative book.

THE NEED FOR COMPARATIVE RESEARCH ON THE CHANGING NATURE OF CENTRAL BUDGET AGENCIES

One of the main aims of this comparative study is to investigate the changing nature of Ministries of Finance and Treasuries principally in major OECD nations. Nine liberal democratic nations were selected ranging from a large and complex superpower to small and self-contained polities. Four larger OECD nations are members of the G-7 with relatively large total GDP levels (the US, UK, Germany and Canada), while a number of the other smaller OECD nations have high GDP per capita (for example, Sweden, Denmark, the Netherlands, Australia and New Zealand). The countries included in the survey were chosen because they reflected a spectrum of different institutional and constitutional configurations. The countries selected either possessed unitary or federal political systems, were parliamentary or presidential systems, majoritarian or proportional representation democracies. In 2001 five countries were led by coalition governments, while the other four had majority governments. Some nations had attracted reputations for budgetary innovation and the adoption of New Public Management (for example, New Zealand, Australia, perhaps Canada, the Netherlands and the UK), whereas others had steadfastly ignored these trends (particularly Germany). Five nations were principally English speaking (although each had followed different historical and political trajectories), while the other nations often had a strong command of English and produced English versions of their budget documentation. The Scandinavian nations of Sweden and Denmark were included because of their very different institutional norms and budgetary arrangements. In particular, Sweden with its multiple budgetary and financial-related agencies was the most institutionally fragmented case – with its CBA functions spread across many agencies and dividing expenditure into 27 separate expenditure areas. Besides the Ministry of Finance there are separate agencies for debt management, financial management, economic management, social security payments. Sweden stands in stark contrast to the unified CBAs of the UK and New Zealand. Additionally, because of the size and significance of the US, separate analyses of the CBA's role at both the federal level and state level (in six mid-western states) were included in this study.

The only non-OECD nation, China, the tenth nation in this study, was included to both highlight a number of fundamental similarities between countries with very dissimilar cultures, as well as pointing to major differences in the ways budgets are framed. China is the sole non-liberal democratic nation, with a political system based on a single party command regime (nominally presidential). Nevertheless, as a command regime the concentration of power at the centre is problematic and it arguably has a weak central administration. But as a developing nation China combined political authoritarianism with marketisation and entrepreneurship; it has produced consistently high rates of economic growth (averaging around 10 per cent per annum over the past 15 years). While state budgets serve many of the same purposes as in the West, there are major differences in the framing of central budgets, the management of funds once they have been allocated, and very different notions of accountability. A brief comparison of the major characteristics of each of the countries included in the study is provided in Table 0.2 at the end of this Introduction.

In each of these countries, the focus of this study is explicitly on the changing role of CBAs – it is not the intention of the research project to focus on macro-economic policy or central bank issues. The purpose of the study is to bring together in a single volume the insights of internationally renowned scholars and specialist researchers in this field, to describe their country's experiences and compare analysis. The research involved investigating CBAs in a country-specific context and addressing an agreed set of common questions/issues. The evidence presented for each country-specific chapter is intended to reflect a blend of practical experience and academic evaluation. Generally, the research was undertaken by an academic observer with relevant knowledge and experience in the field working in conjunction with a specialist practitioner (in most cases someone who was working or had recently worked within the CBA or in areas of close proximity to the agency under investigation). They collaborated to contribute different perspectives to the analysis of the case, which were then combined into a single chapter. In some cases contributing authors had worked both in the CBA and subsequently as an independent scholar (for instance, Gwenda Jensen, Susan Tanaka and Gert Paulsson). In the case of China, Canada and Denmark senior budgetary officials assisted the research and gave feedback on the written drafts but did not wish to be named. Importantly, the analysis contributed in the research partnerships was not intended as a promotional exercise detailing the current preoccupations of CBAs, rather it was intended as an informed evaluation of their capacities and performance – including honest and frank assessments of their weaknesses and limitations.

When Heclo and Wildavsky (1974) conducted their socio-anthropological research on the British Treasury and the Whitehall budgetary 'village' they found a micro-community replete with its own codes of behaviour, languages, conventions and implicit understandings. Shared understandings rather than formal rules provided the basis on which the system operated. First, the village operated on the shared and implicit (and therefore not overt) cultural attitudes and the technical and practical knowledges of its members. Second, the village's currency was measured in reputation and trust (credibility and competency of actors). Practice dictated that the budgetary villagers were *perceived* to be honest just as much as they were honest and reliable. And third, these elements that can be identified as a budgetary-based village society are not official, but shadow and complement the official processes. The power of the guardian budget agency was imposed through its control over the processes, both formal and informal, which it both operated and monitored and through which other players had to proceed as they participated in the budget games. This analysis tended to confirm Wildavsky's earlier framework for analysing the *politics* of budgeting in which four elements were pronounced: dichotomous guardian and spender relations; a lack of formal procedures of financial control; 'routines' to politics emerged from actor strategies over time; and budgetary reforms tended to have limited impact on budget politics.

Given that the rules of the game were set largely by guardian actors, CBAs became the keepers of the faith. They operated almost as ecclesiastical citadels dominated by the high priests of financial control. They were often invasive, punitive and disciplinary when it came to their relations with departments and clients, and generally highly secretive over their information base and assumptions. They were not known as reflexive organisations or as flexible superintendents. Occasionally, in some countries, CBAs believed themselves virtually above the elected government, refusing to share information or provide advice that had been requested. Partly by their important financial role and partly by their own cultural elitism, these CBAs came to regard the appropriate role for themselves as 'command posts' at the centre of executive government (Schick 1997). Such a role was not necessarily incongruous with traditional bureaucratic administration, which was often controlled only by *ex ante* financial controls and the provision of strict line input budget allocations.

Yet, such Kafkaesque agencies may now only exist in the studies of public budgeting of the past. Schick has argued (1997) that the central budget agency within the nation state is now confronted by significant pressures to *change the way they behave and operate as budget related agencies.* He suggested that they have evolved, or are in the process of evolving, from 'combative, centralised, command posts' into more 'hands-off, flexible and strategic investor type agencies'. Often this has been in line with government reforms in other areas of public administration, such as competitive tendering and contracting, or the changes visited to human resources and industrial relations. Increasingly, the 'reinvented' CBAs operate through new negotiated arrangements (and even partnerships) with various spending elements (some inside the public sector such as line departments or executive agencies, and others outside like private contractors or voluntary sector associations). Some operate through contractual-based relationships and purchaser-provider resource frameworks.

This is not to imply necessarily that CBAs are *losing* power or control over the budget process (or becoming less important in the process of change). Indeed, the reverse may be true. But such developments do suggest that the *forms of control, monitoring and intervention* are changing, perhaps becoming less based on Weberian styles of bureaucratic authority and moving toward more integrated post-bureaucratic or business-like frameworks. Some CBAs are now using the concepts and language of business: ownership, stakeholder, investor, strategic behaviour, value-adding, purchaser-provider, agency theory, pricing, comparative advantage and accrual accounting. New frameworks and nomenclature are increasingly being used to differentiate new forms of service delivery mechanisms: focus on key results, outcome and output budgeting, price-based budgeting, financial devolution, de-concentration, special operating or delivery agencies, cost centres, resource agreement frameworks and multi-year budgeting.

The following sections canvass in greater detail the four main questions and themes informing this comparative investigation. The individual country-based chapters that follow have each attempted to analyse these questions and where applicable to their particular CBA explore the themes in greater detail. Specific questions and issues listed under each theme were provided to each author as guides to their chapter and to assist their interpretation of the extent to which the roles of the CBA in their country have been changing or are likely to change.

1. Changing Roles and Responsibilities

This first theme concerns the degree to which CBAs have undergone changes in their roles and responsibilities. This includes tracing the trajectory of the

CBA as a relational player in budget making (formulation, implementation, evaluation and reporting) over the past 10-15 years. Contributors were asked to provide a brief overview of their CBA (single or multiple), how it had evolved, its size and internal structure, internal divisions or specialisations, whether it had expanded or contracted in responsibilities, and whether its formal and informal roles had changed. They also have reported on the range of responsibilities the ministry has and what types of advice it gives to the core executive and outward to other departments or players. The aim of this theme is to establish what budgetary management roles are performed by the CBA, and how the roles actually performed relate to the basic functions required or expected of a CBA. All the researchers felt it was important to provide an account of the evolving/emerging governance environment within which the CBA operated – and this environment included the economy, social changes, political developments, major institutional changes and policy re-orientations.

2. Re-negotiating the Politics of the Budget Process

The second theme recurring throughout the study is the evaluation of the power and influence of the CBA including its agenda-setting roles. Contributors were asked to assess whether the CBA had become more or less powerful or influential over time. To what extent had the influence or power of the CBA changed and adapted (and according to what principles or approaches)? They were asked to identify what may have contributed to institutional and process-oriented power shifts (for instance, changes in procedural systems, public sector reforms, the demise of rivals or rise of challengers, different transparency and accountability regimes, competitive tendering and contracting). Some authors explicitly focused on the opportunities for 'gaming' on the part of both CBAs and line agencies, and how these procedural games have changed or stayed the same in response to different budgetary pressures.

Under this second theme, it was intended to assess the impact of change on the role of the CBA. Has the role of the CBA changed in relation to the budget decision-making process or in terms of other policy processes? How secretive and exclusive has budgeting remained? Does the CBA allocate resources (or advise on allocation) today in different ways than in the past? If major budgetary changes and reforms have been made, are they working and effective or do they need to be rethought/rolled back? What role does the CBA play in this assessment and promulgation? And how active or important is the CBA in broader areas of administrative policy and in the policy areas of other departments or agencies? Is the traditional guardian-spender relationship extant and intact? Has the CBA actually championed administrative reform – if so to what end, to what effect or result? Is the ministry aggressive or passive in areas of policy and administration outside its own immediate purview? Are the underlying rationales shaping budgetary reforms widely shared by all stakeholders, including the CBA, other central agencies and by line agencies?

3. Changing Village Cultures – Inside Central Budget Agencies

The third theme examines the development of administrative versus post-administrative cultures in the CBA – in the way the CBA approaches its roles and how it goes about performing its roles/functions (formally or informally, codified, contractual, policy-based, financial statement based). An aim of the study is to 'get inside' these agencies and provide an account of the perspective of insiders – what was pushed, how and why, and what was resisted, demurred, put off or discredited. How is budgetary decision-making enhanced, facilitated or impeded at the bureaucratic level? Is there a 'village' of dedicated budgeteers with their own language and codes, perhaps jealous of outsiders impinging upon their prerogatives?

How do CBA staff and executives think? How does the agency see itself, its roles and its performance? What sense of identity does the CBA have or display? Does the CBA consistently develop a 'line' on issues or policies it has to encounter? If so, how does it generate a common understanding? Who dominates within the CBA – what types of operators or professionals are in the ascendancy? How do they describe and understand their roles and interactions with others? Capturing these 'in-house' cultures is important as they can form powerful parameters or bounded rationalities in the decision-making process.

4. Future Prospects or Directions for Central Budget Agencies

What does the future hold for CBAs? Have they successfully maintained their relevance and their expertise in regard to contemporary governance? Can they cope with the expectations produced by new or unique pressures? Are CBAs remaining rooted in their old mechanistic and Weberian practices as *ex ante* guardians of the public purse? Or have they evolved into a post-bureaucratic facilitative agency or strategic adviser to government? Are any of the agencies managing to combine elements of both orientations, or are they philosophically and practically incompatible?

How is the CBA trying to re-orient or shape government finances and the procedures of budgeting into the future? What strategies are being advanced and how expansive or limited are they? How successful are they likely to be? What essential elements would be needed to generate success? What future directions are CBA officials expecting? Is the trend toward adopting more private sector-oriented practices, and is this trend likely to continue or be wound back?

What emerging agendas are CBAs having to contend with? Is it likely the institutional structures and design of the CBA will be reshaped or restructured? Is the capacity to govern strongly influenced by the particular nature, forms and roles of the CBA, or can governments largely cope with any institutional arrangement? What if CBAs do suffer from declining capacity, become ineffective or even incompetent? Is the CBA set to become a more important tool of government or will it become eclipsed by other emerging policy, political, and administrative concerns?

These four themes inform the analytical approach of this comparative study. After surveying the 10 country-specific studies we return to these themes in the conclusion.

NOTES

1. A gatekeeping feature recognized from pre-modern times. Exclusive authority over the budget or treasury was a basic form of control and protection. Early mediaeval kings kept the treasury under their beds and personally oversaw its disbursement. As officials gradually took over this task they too took steps to separate themselves from the various 'claimants' (and occasionally from the rulers, chiefly as a means of underlining *their* importance and status). One of the more extreme forms of budgetary segregation was practised in Persia, where the 'treasury officials of the Persian shah have made a secret doctrine of their budgetary art and even use secret script' – the ultimate in maintaining indispensibleness (Weber 1948, p. 233).
2. While in Germany, Hitler's finance minister and president of the Reichsbank, Dr Hjalmar Schact, was regarded as the 'dictator under the dictatorship' (Muhlen 1938, p. 147), the modern Finance Ministry is a more marginal player driven by legal and formalized budgetary rules. It has attempted to increase its power since the 1960s and in recent years has used 'creative budgeting', particularly through the establishment of extra-budgetary funds.

Table 0.2   *A summary of major CBA characteristics of the 10 countries included in this study*

Country & population in millions	System of govt & GDP in $US billion (2001 figures)	Single or dual-multiple CBA	Principal expenditure budget	Year CBA formed	Minister or executive officer responsible	Size of CBA	Other guardians or ration-agencies	Legislative oversight and confidence
United States (275 m)	Federal, presidential, majoritarian, separation of powers ($10,143 bn)	Dual	Office of Management & Budget; Congressional Budget Office	1921 but as OMB 1970; CBO in 1974	President; Presiding officers of Congress	520	US Treasury; President; Congress	Strong but budget vote does not involve confidence
Germany (80 m)	Federal, presidential-parliamentary-coalitional ($1,846 bn)	Single	Ministry of Finance	1945	Chancellor and Minister of Finance	2100	–	Moderate, budget vote does not involve confidence
United Kingdom (60 m)	Unitary, parliamentary majoritarian ($1,424 bn)	Single	HM Treasury	C12th originally as the Exchequer	Chancellor of the Exchequer & Chief Secretary	1500	Prime Minister	Moderate, budget vote involves confidence
China (1,272 m)	Quasi-Federal, single party, nominally presidential ($1,158 bn)	Single	Ministry of Finance	1949	Minister of Finance	610	–	No discernible legislative oversight
Canada (31 m)	Federal, parliamentary, majoritarian ($695 bn)	Dual	Treasury Board Secretariat	1867 and as a separate agency in 1966	Treasury Board President	800	Department of Finance; Prime Minister; PCO	Weak, but budget vote does involve confidence
The Netherlands (16 m)	Unitary, parliamentary, coalitional ($380 bn)	Single	Ministry of Finance	1798 [1848]	Minister of Finance	2000 (250 in Exp. Man.)	Coalition Agreements (post-election)	Moderate, budget vote involves confidence
Australia (19 m)	Federal, parliamentary majoritarian ($366 bn)	Dual	Department of Finance and Administration	1976 but also 1901 as part of Treasury	Minister of Finance	500 (160 in Budget Group)	Treasury; Prime Minister	Moderate, budget vote involves confidence
Sweden (9 m)	Unitary, parliamentary, coalitional ($210 bn)	Multiple	Ministry of Finance	C17th	Minister of Finance	420	Diverse agencies with demarcated functions; party agreements pre-negotiated	Weak, budget vote involves confidence
Denmark (5 m)	Unitary, parliamentary, coalitional ($162 bn)	Single	Ministry of Finance	–	Minister of Finance	850	Coalition agreements binding cabinet	Moderate, budget vote involves confidence
New Zealand (4 m)	Unitary, parliamentary, coalitional ($50 bn)	Single	Treasury	1840	Treasurer	300 (50 in Budget Branch)	Prime Minister	Moderate, budget vote involves confidence

1. 'Good Practice: Does it Work in Theory?' Australia's Quest for Better Outcomes

John Wanna and Stephen Bartos*

The central budget agency in Australia dates from Federation and the establishment of a new nation in 1901. Named the Treasury for historical reasons, it was one of the original five Commonwealth departments and was responsible for all budget-related activities. The Commonwealth Treasury was modelled on the colonial treasuries of the Australian states (which were themselves based on Westminster practice). The Commonwealth Treasury (unlike any other federal department) was given a quasi-constitutional status receiving mention in the Constitution, even if only obliquely.[1] Section 83 of the Constitution stipulates 'no money shall be drawn from the Treasury of the Commonwealth except under appropriation made by law', although it is not clear whether this reference is to the treasury of government meaning the consolidated revenue account, or whether it signifies a department of state *per se*. The word 'treasury' can be interpreted to mean a treasury *function* or Treasury *qua* department. But whichever meaning was implied by the constitutional framers, the Constitution does not stipulate or prescribe any duties or functions to be performed by the institution of the Treasury. However, one of the lasting effects of this mention has been to entrench a position for the Treasury in relation to budgeting, even following the creation of a separate Finance department – most evident in the presentation of the annual Budget to parliament by the Treasurer rather than the Minister for Finance.[2]

A FORTUITOUS BIFURCATION: THE CREATION OF DUAL CENTRAL BUDGET AGENCIES

Treasury was Australia's sole budget agency until the 1970s, when relations between it and the elected government soured – in particular, over the direction of spending and the priorities of government policy. First, the 1972–75 Whitlam (Labor) government and then the conservative Fraser (Liberal–National Coalition

1

1975–83) government expressed clear dissatisfaction with Treasury advice. Their frustration was in reaction to Treasury's intransigence on macroeconomic settings and exchange rate policies, not at that time in relation to budget-related matters. In the traditional Weberian-style bureaucracy of the day, the administration of budgetary functions (or reform) was not afforded much priority by government. In practice, the government only required a basic competence from Treasury in the administration of its cash-based, line-item annual budget. Treasury then with a staff of around 1500 also attached little significance to its budgetary functions other than for fiscal policy calculations, and the various supply divisions tended to operate in relative isolation. Budgetary matters attracted little attention from senior managers in the Treasury.

Treasury was divided into two departments in November 1976 by a conservative prime minister, Malcolm Fraser. This move was something of a surprise, despite the merits of splitting the Treasury having been debated in Australia for around a decade. A separate department was established to administer government expenditure leaving the old Treasury to focus on matters of macroeconomic policy. This institutional restructuring established the preconditions for the development of specialized expertise and innovation in expenditure management and budgetary matters within the new agency. Unlike Canada which institutionally split its budget agencies in 1966, Australia reversed the names of its budget agencies relative to prevailing international conventions. The Treasury was awarded responsibility for macroeconomic policy and retained its name because of tradition, status and its constitutional reference.

The new Department of Finance was given responsibility for expenditure control and resource management across government. It was formed from four so-called 'supply' divisions of the old Treasury gaining slightly over half the staff of the former department (Finance with 840 staff to Treasury's 640). While some officials within Treasury initially felt the two departments would be re-amalgamated (because 'coordination problems' might warrant such a re-merger), there has been no expressed wish from any subsequent government to recombine them. Indeed, talk of re-amalgamation has surfaced only infrequently and sometimes almost accidentally. For example, the National Commission of Audit raised the topic in 1996 but no subsequent action was taken. There remain some 'grey areas' or overlaps of function between the two departments which senior officials have suggested ought to be resolved, for example combining the 'corporate treasury' functions of cash and debt management which are split between the two CBAs. A more substantial merger remains an option and has some advocates within the bureaucracy but there is little evidence that either major political party is attracted to the idea.

Hence, Australia's eventual institutional configuration emerged somewhat serendipitously. The government's main rationale in splitting Treasury was to curb its power; the consequence was to create *two* powerful CBAs more able to specialize and yet perform complementary roles. The emergence of a much stronger expenditure budget agency after 1976 was a fortuitous by-product of a machinery of government change driven by other political motives.

CENTRAL BUDGET ACTORS: SEGREGATED BUT REINFORCING ROLES WITH FLUCTUATING INFLUENCE

Australia has now for over 25 years operated with two functionally discrete budget agencies; both of which remain principal participants in the annual budget process and generally maintain cordial and cooperative working relations. Treasury looks after economic and competition policy, tax policy and revenue forecasts, and international and banking policy. The Department of Finance is responsible for the expenditure budget, government accounting policy and resource management, the government's shareholdings in public enterprises, public assets more generally and at times asset sales (although the latter function was constituted as an autonomous Office of Asset Sales between 1996 and 2001). In 1998 Finance became the Department of Finance and Administration (DoFA) when functions from the former Department of Administrative Services were added to the portfolio. These functions included: the management of the Commonwealth's property portfolio, the administration of ministerial and parliamentary entitlements (salary, allowances and travel), and a variety of residual business functions. In practice, these have little impact on the budgeting functions of the department.

Treasury and Finance operate as a 'tag-team' in the production of the annual budget. They both serve the powerful Expenditure Review Committee (ERC) of cabinet – a decision-making body that funnels and coordinates the budget process and takes responsibility for budget outcomes. As a committee largely of guardian ministers, its principal source of authority is collective political solidarity. With advice from Treasury and Finance, the government declares a set of priorities (following a Senior Ministers' Review in November/December). The ERC then determines which spending and saving options are agreed in the annual budget round (specifying allocative priorities). Together with the Prime Minister's department, Treasury and Finance often mutually reinforce each other's roles and combine in defining parameters, setting aggregate expenditure targets, fiscal discipline and advice on the spending proposals of other agencies ('green briefs'). ERC decisions are taken to a special budget meeting of the whole cabinet for endorsement, but they are rarely overturned or modified.

The two CBAs also have *separate but coordinated* roles and responsibilities, although there is no particular logic to the segregation of functions with respect to budget matters. History, convention and bureaucratic power have determined their relative purchase and functions. There are a number of overlapping functions, and both departments retain a budget division. Within Treasury the primary group charged with overseeing fiscal policy and expenditure aggregates is the General Budget division; while in Finance the Budget Group is responsible for preparing and reviewing the main budget allocations. There is also a grey line between where the functions of one agency ends and the other's begins. As will be argued below, Treasury has been reluctant to relinquish control over budgetary policy advice (especially spending levels) principally because it wishes to maintain some control over expenditure aggregates as part of its fiscal policy. In the Australian budgetary process, it is generally accepted that the benefits of having two economic/financial ministers and dual budget agencies outweighs any additional costs of duplication, competition or occasional breakdowns in coordination.

The discrete responsibilities of Australia's two CBAs align with the broad guardian roles of central budget agencies identified by a number of recent budget commentators (for example, Schick 1997; Schick 2001b; Pradhan and Campos 1996). These roles and the respective departmental responsibilities are contained in Table 1.1.

Within this context, the relative power of Treasury and Finance in their respective roles changes from year to year (and sometimes month to month) as each budget is constructed. The influence of Treasury *vis-à-vis* Finance is not only a consequence of departmental responsibilities, but of the changing relative importance governments have placed on the five broad roles identified above. As Andrews *et al.* (1998) have argued:

> the relative emphasis placed on these broad roles has varied over time and often from budget to budget. The annual parameters of the budget and changing political contingencies have tended to shift emphasis between the roles.

During the 1980s aggregate targets were imposed by governments on themselves but more emphasis was placed on technical efficiency (House of Representatives *Not Dollars Alone* 1990; Forster and Wanna 1990; MAB/MIAC *APS Reformed* 1992). In the 1990s aggregate expenditure targets were initially relaxed by the Labor government (over the years 1991–94), then tightened by the Coalition government (1996–97), then relaxed again (1998–2001) – but over the same time allocative efficiency and new policy re-prioritization became increasingly important to governments. Allocative efficiency is where Finance increasingly focused a considerable amount of its specialist attention. Today, senior budget officials estimate roughly 50 per cent of their time and effort is spent on dealing with issues of allocative efficiency (compared to 20 per cent on technical efficiency and 30 per cent on reporting, consolidation and other transparency tasks).

Table 1.1   The division and coordination of roles of Australia's CBAs

The Guardian Budget Roles Performed	Who Performs the Roles and the Level of Involvement
1. maintain aggregate fiscal discipline to meet the government's economic objectives and maintain fiscal stability	A bifurcated responsibility shared by Treasury and Finance; the Treasurer often sets the main parameters and Treasury has carriage of the fiscal policy stance and taxation policy; both departments advise on aggregate expenditure limits; Finance administers the process of achieving savings and examining cost structures or budgetary pressures
2. impose medium-term expenditure framework — with a three year fiscal plan based on explicit publicly-released targets	A joint responsibility: Treasury and Finance advise on fiscal targets; both collaborate to produce an expenditure framework with a fiscal balance based on hard estimates shown over three years (adjusted also by the jointly produced Mid-Year Economic and Fiscal Outlook, MYEFO); but Finance examines and provides advice on the detailed estimates for the current and out years and on the financial position of the government
3. ensure that the government's resources are allocated efficiently in 'base' budget estimates; to address government priorities by reviewing existing allocations and redirecting spending to the most important areas	A responsibility entirely of Finance; conceived as a budget housekeeping role; reprioritization of commitments; contestability; review of 'prices', value for money, outsourcing and purchaser-provider contracts; usually the process operates in conjunction with input from agencies
4. provide strategic investment advice on new initiatives or spending measures (new bids) or major policy changes	Principally Finance's responsibility: subject to the Senior Ministers' Review and ERC deliberations; investment advice on financing or delivery alternatives; reliance on departmental 'offsets' to partly fund new initiatives
5. enhancing operational/technical efficiency and or productivity improvement through better resource management and incentives	Entirely Finance's responsibility: supported by line department efforts and external accountability agencies (for example, the Auditor-General); has had an 'efficiency dividend' clawback in place for 15 years

Nonetheless, the changing fiscal preferences are not necessarily admitted publicly by governments anxious to impress financial markets with their sound financial management credentials. Governments of both persuasions have been relatively shy of admitting to the strong growth in revenues and in spending levels – often going to some lengths to disguise the trends. Clearly, tighter or more relaxed aggregate expenditure controls imply varying fiscal priorities framed within the economic cycle. But while budget stringency toward aggregate expenditure can vary considerably from year to year, targeting decisions (such as welfare assistance, regional assistance or infrastructure spending) can operate on a separate logic allowing governments to reallocate spending to new priorities. The combination of fiscal discipline and allocative efficiency is now, under the Commonwealth's new outcomes and outputs resource management framework, encompassed in the broad rubric 'sustainable government finances', and measured in terms of maintaining the 'budget in balance over the economic cycle'.

CHANGING ROLES AND RESPONSIBILITIES OF AUSTRALIA'S CBAs

Australia's CBAs have evolved through four distinct historical phases. In each phase key aspects of their roles and responsibilities changed partly in response to the changing role of the state and prevailing attitudes to the role of government, and partly in response to their own normative conceptions of what roles they should perform and how they should perform them (their ability to put forward and institutionalize these roles). In particular, both CBAs have increasingly adopted the view that instead of simply wielding power through their control of the process, they ought to regularly ask how and where they can best add value to the decision-making process and achieve intended government outcomes. These four phases are outlined in Table 1.2.

Government Bookkeeper and Accountant – 1901 to Late 1960s

In the first phase Treasury's routine concerns were with expenditure recording, revenue receipt, debt management, together with bookkeeping and basic audit functions. For the first 40 years after Federation the annual budget was conceived as a financial reconciliation for accountability purposes, not as a tool of fiscal policy. Interest in the fiscal role of public expenditure only developed during and after World War II when Treasury developed an intellectual and policy interest in matters of economic policy. Although the government's postwar reconstruction dominated both political agendas and fiscal policy in the late 1940s and early 1950s, Treasury itself was a relatively minor player in the reconstruction activity, observing from the sidelines and keeping track of expenditure. Throughout the postwar period the Treasury maintained its monopoly over government expenditure matters with little objection from the government of the day. It also gradually emerged to become Australia's most influential agency in dealing with macroeconomic policy gaining more influence than other rival trade or industry departments (Weller and Cutt 1976; Whitwell

Table 1.2   Four historical phases in the development of the CBAs' roles and functions in Australia

Period	Main Roles Performed	Functions Performed	Comments
1901 to the late 1960s	Government Bookkeeper and Accountant	Treasury performed an accounting function over government finances; basic financial administration of limited cash budgets	Relatively small, limited role for the Commonwealth government to WWII; after 1927 repaid state debts and ran a 'national fiscus'; high expenditure growth in the 1960s to mid-1970s
Mid-1970s to early 1980s	Expenditure Controller	Imposed control over annual aggregate expenditure; in-year controls; place ceilings over allocations; cash limits and limits to staff numbers; estimates used for information and planning	Greater rationing by cabinet budget committees; centrally imposed instruments to limit overruns; reduce augmentation; control agencies and ensure they operate within budget; still deficit budgets
Early 1980s to early 1990s	Budget Resource Manager and Policy Analyst	Devolution of flexible resource management within stronger central limits; running costs arrangements; use of forward estimates to limit program and running costs; alternative policy advice/options; use of mini-budgets to 'correct' fiscal balance mid-year	Emphasis on better use of resources; provide medium-term certainty; stress on program evaluation and effectiveness; introduction of an annual efficiency dividend; surplus budgets achieved in late 1980s
Mid-1990s to date	Strategic Adviser (investment and ownership advice; oversight and quality assurance roles; facilitator of price reviews)	Higher level advice on resource prioritization, allocation and investment; appropriation by desired outcome; devolution of many budgetary 'control' instruments to spending agencies; stress on contestable 'price' of outputs; private financing	Commonwealth has withdrawn from many areas of direct service provision; uses other 'suppliers' (other governments, private or voluntary suppliers)

1986). Elementary forward estimates were produced in the mid-1960s, not as a budget measure, but to provide projection data to assist in the formulation of fiscal policy. By the late 1960s and early 1970s the narrow bookkeeping role performed over the expenditure budget by the CBA was becoming patently inadequate and this bookkeeping role was gradually superseded as governments became more policy-driven and their appetite for spending increased.

Expenditure Controller: Mid-1970s to Early 1980s

When Finance began its institutional independence in 1976 it continued performing housekeeping roles still very much in the shadow of Treasury (Wanna *et al.* 2000). With the support of the Prime Minister, Malcolm Fraser, and his cabinet budget committee, Finance gradually increased the centralized budget control. From 1975 to 1982, the new emphasis was explicitly on expenditure control – seeking both to limit year-on-year increases while attempting to ensure agencies remained within their budget allocations in-year. Both the government and the two CBAs monitored their level of success in imposing budget stringency or in containing budget increases to aggregate expenditures. Over this period one of the key characteristics of the Australian system was the Commonwealth's increasing preparedness to impose expenditure restraint upon the States – by directly winding back grants to the States and through its control of annual aggregate borrowing limits in the Loans Council. Indeed, Shand (2001) has argued that this established a 'national fiscus' across the public sector in Australia, whereby the Commonwealth was able to gain fiscal policy leverage in its negotiations with the States and contain excessive public debt. Unlike in other federations, the national government in Australia has been able to influence the overall public sector borrowing requirements across the three levels of jurisdictions – a power exercised mainly by the Treasurer that continues to this day.

While Treasury's involvement in questions of allocative and technical efficiency declined, Finance became more active and established close relations with the Prime Minister. An array of relatively blunt or arbitrary techniques of expenditure control were imposed with direct political involvement, including staff controls to reduce the numbers of public servants, cash ceilings, across-the-board percentage cuts to departmental outlays, the absorption of cost increases by agencies and the introduction of some early user-charging schemes. Capped triennium funding was locked in for selected agencies (such as the universities, scientific and research centres and the national public broadcaster). Toward the end of this period, Finance began to look more closely at the possibility of using program structures and program budgeting and even program-based appropriations as possible ways of containing departmental spending; but although such initiatives were discussed over the period 1981–84 they were never actually introduced.

A further institutional player at the time was the Public Service Board, which maintained the system of staff ceilings and establishment controls on which the government relied to curb public service departmental expenditure. Toward the end of the 1970s it became increasingly clear that these controls did not work in practice. Departments became adept at manipulating the rules (for example, a staff ceiling imposed on the head count at 30 June each year led to a number of agencies employing staff on an annual contract from 1 July to 29 June). Controls on establishment (that is, the number of approved positions in departments, their levels and classification) were routinely ignored. These difficulties were recognized by governments at the time. Some attempts were made to change the system (for example, staff ceilings were replaced with an average staffing level control) but these were largely unsuccessful. With a change of government in late 1983 staffing controls were formally transferred from the Public Service Board to the Department of Finance and quickly subsumed within the overall running costs control system. From that point on, the Public Service Board and its successor the Public Service and Merit Protection Commission ceased to have any role in budgetary controls.

Budget Resource Manager and Policy Analyst: Early 1980s to Early 1990s

In the early 1980s Finance's role gradually shifted from a concentration on expenditure control to one of improved resource frameworks with emphasis on the technical efficiency of government services. In doing so, the department emerged as a powerful central agency concurrently championing a sequence of major budgetary reforms and promoting a wider and more substantial public sector reform agenda. The aim of the reforms was to improve budgetary and resource management across the whole of government. Initially, the creativity of Finance's senior management team was a major driving force behind the reform agenda. Backed by the powerful ERC, Finance used fiscal discipline to impose reallocative measures and a wide range of resource management reforms. Its senior management was able to combine an emergent political will among ministers to contain spending with a desire to enhance productivity and performance within spending departments. Hence, the main institutional benefit of having a separate ministry for government expenditure led to a substantial transformation in the *modus operandi* of the public sector. But the lead role in public sector reform taken by Finance has meant that Australian reforms have tended to take on an overt financial bias and business-like orientation (rather than, say, a policy effectiveness bias or one based on capacity building).[3]

Finance also *increased* rather than relaxed its role as a central command post, becoming the principal conduit through which almost all major resourcing decisions had to pass for approval. Finance dictated the forward estimates of portfolios/programs unilaterally. These 'hard' estimates together formed a rolling four year budget, which in the absence of policy changes would 'roll out' automatically as the budget estimates (an early form of a fiscal plan/expenditure management framework). One of the main hallmarks of the managerialist phase was the better *targeting* of resources within the budget process to achieve desired results in programs (e.g. social justice, means-testing of welfare benefits). Targeting was essentially viewed as a way of redirecting allocations within allocations.

Improvements in technical efficiency occurred through adaptations to budgetary and financial management systems that allowed greater financial flexibilities within tighter overall controls. As a separate budget-expenditure agency, Finance was in a position to impose discipline by insisting on budget 'savings', by continuously looking at cost reductions and the value for money in programs, irrespective of other fiscal considerations proposed by Treasury or the government (e.g. expansionary budgets or taxation policy adjustments). A major distinction was made between the so-called 'program costs' (funds allocated for the community, the objective or the services) and the operational 'running costs' of portfolios/programs (administrative support). Running costs were tightly policed and an annual 'efficiency dividend' was extracted from these allocations before they were disbursed. Program costs were allocated as one-line budgets to portfolio ministers who had discretion to allocate these in whatever way they considered best met their portfolio priorities.

The running costs system, although implemented to act as an effective control over total departmental spending, was nonetheless welcomed by many senior managers in line agencies because it gave them virtually unlimited discretion on spending within their portfolio-wide operational allocation. Previous line-by-line controls on items such as salaries, travel, overtime, consultancies and so on were abolished, leaving managers free to spend on the elements of running costs they considered best achieved their goals. In addition, the running costs rules provided for a carryover or borrowing eventually of up to 10 per cent between years, eliminating the need for an ill-considered 'end of year spend up' which had been the previous practice of managers expecting to underspend their appropriations. The budgetary controls at the macro level, including the efficiency dividend, were in many cases more than offset by the productivity gains which innovative managers were able to find when freed from restrictive central oversight.

The main attributes of managerialist efficiency changed relatively quickly over time. Initially, internal efficiencies were expected from one-line portfolio budgeting, the identification of program structures, the devolution of resource management and financial flexibility. An annual efficiency dividend of 1.25 per cent per annum was imposed over portfolio running costs and maintained for 15 years. Later, program evaluation, reviews of policy effectiveness within existing allocations and various schemes to demonstrate output performance were imposed as routine elements of the annual budget submission round (although with mixed success). A system of departmental 'offsets' for new initiatives became obligatory (requiring agencies to deliver internal savings to be in a position to make new bids). However, productivity improvement was an issue where spenders themselves were able to exert considerable influence. Despite the restrictive frameworks set by the central agencies, technical efficiency remains a domain in which spending agencies have scope to influence resource questions and budget deliberations.

Strategic Adviser: Mid-1990s to Date

In the fourth phase, Finance's focus shifted from improving systems of resource management across the public sector to a higher-level and more detached form of advice on the strategic value of the government's budgetary investments (including purchasing and ownership advice). Essentially this shift was philosophical but coincided with the introduction in 1999–2000 of twin reforms to the nature of the budget and the budgetary processes – first, the adoption of a new budgetary framework based on the identification of specified outcomes and outputs and, second, the simultaneous introduction of full accrual budgeting. These two significant reforms not only changed the way calculations were made to recognize full-cost information in resource allocation, but also changed the principles on which the Commonwealth budgetary processes operated. The assembly of full accrual information was generated both from bottom-up calculations (by making accrual adjustments to the cash-based, 'hard' forward estimates) and from the top-down (identified savings or appropriate levels of expenditure). In place of portfolio budgets allowing ministers greater latitude within the budget year, ministers now were presented with agency-based budgets in which appropriations were made to pre-specified outcomes. Unlike New Zealand, there is no actual 'purchasing' of outputs by ministers to meet their desired outcomes, and indeed Australian ministers explicitly rejected such a formal purchaser model as too simplistic and problematical. Any notion of a purchaser relationship is, therefore, implicit rather than explicit. But agencies became the principal unit of budgeting from which a pre-specified schedule of performance was expected – and which could be presented as a range of goods and services delivered at nominal prices (but variously subject to price reviews, market pricing and contestability). Budget statements were divided into 'departmental' costs (total budgeted operating costs) and 'administered items' (funds administered by an agency but not consumed or controlled by it). Administered items included social welfare payments, payments to the states, program spending, other grants and subsidies, and these expenses may contribute to achieving designated outcomes but do not themselves constitute departmental outputs. Agencies also received funding for their depreciation and liabilities, but were subject to a capital charge.

The essence of Australia's new budgeting framework lies in the funding of agencies according to the outcomes and outputs they are expected to deliver.[4]

The Commonwealth's budgeting framework can be distinguished from those adopted in New Zealand or the Australian states because it is founded on a system of *appropriations by outcome*. Instead of the previous *ad hoc* collection of appropriation by items and programs, outcome appropriations outline the purposes for which the parliament has given the executive authority to spend money (or to be more technically accurate, authority for agencies' expenses). These purposes are expressed in terms of the results expected. The outcomes framework is complemented by outputs (that is, services, administration or products delivered directly by agencies). Revenues for outputs though are appropriated at a whole-of-agency level; so, although amounts are notionally allocated to the respective outcomes, they are controlled in total by each agency. A relatively small proportion of the Commonwealth budget (about 19 per cent) is used to purchase outputs delivered by Commonwealth agencies, the rest of the budget is consumed in transfers, entitlements and administered grants programs.

The main point to bear in mind about the accrual framework is that for the first time the full *price* the government can expect to pay for its outputs is apparent. Information never previously taken into account in the budget – particularly balance sheet information – is now used for both decision-making and reporting. The interrelated elements of better pricing information and balance sheet information produce a much better 'investment' information to the executive and also public benefits in terms of transparency and accountability. There is now a real prospect of comparing the price of government providers with potential competitors (Bartos 2000).

Finance does not determine the government's budget strategy – this is determined by the annual Senior Ministers' Review (consisting of the three guardian ministers, PM, Treasurer and Finance Minister, plus one or two other key ministers). Once these priorities or strategic directions are set, Finance's strategic investor role is to help identify, between various competing alternatives, the best value for money for the government and taxpayers. In this sense Finance's greatest strength is the intellectual capital it is nurturing to become a strategic investor and analyst to its customers. Finance now sees itself in terms of the advice they give to government as equivalent to a combination of the big five accounting firms and merchant banks. Indeed, Finance explicitly searches for the same type of skills mix in its recruitment as its highest performing 'competitors' do in the private sectors.

In moving to higher-level advice on prices and suppliers, a number of Finance's former CBA roles were discontinued or devolved. Finance withdrew from 'the detail' in the budget process, devolving the construction of estimates to line departments through their financial statements and balance sheet information. New budgetary arrangements gave line agencies along with their ministers the responsibility for the determination of outputs and outcomes (and even for costing them). In the first year Commonwealth departments' outcomes ranged from between 1 to 10, while their outputs ranged from between 6 and 66. The costings of these outputs and outcomes are used in the construction of the agency's budget estimates, subject to a quality assurance and strategic review by Finance and the ERC. But given estimates were 'accurate' when they were devolved and are now essentially entered without changes into the computerized accrual spreadsheets, quality assurance is focused on policy changes rather than baseline estimates. New policy bids remain scrutinized in similar ways as previously and a policy decision must be approved by cabinet before an adjustment to base estimates occurs. Spending departments now have control over their own spending and, in theory, can spend as much as they like – running a loss only requires the permission of the Minister for Finance and Administration. Moreover, Finance is no longer involved in the detail of *performance evaluation* (effectiveness measures) but tends to focus its advice on value for money and cost-efficiency issues. The department is also active in advising government on its ownership functions (including asset sales/GBE performance and dividends) and in assessing private financing proposals especially for infrastructural projects.

By 'getting out of the detail' Finance has moved beyond their former practice of 'nit picking' at a set of relatively firm estimates. Instead, in the strategic adviser role, budget advice is increasingly based more on analysing the underlying drivers of public expenditure – such as the ageing of the population, unemployment trends, welfare dependency etc. – and consists of finding innovative ways for government to deal with these problems in ways that may reduce its future exposure. This is roughly congruent with the fact that the annual budget process is becoming increasingly de-emphasized (though retaining importance in terms of the political theatre which accompanies it, but today it is of far less importance in terms of economic and fiscal policy). Following re-election of a Coalition (conservative) government in November 2001 and a change of Finance Minister there is evidence of a return by Finance officials to greater involvement in detailed examination of agency estimates. It is too early to tell whether this means a diminution of the strategic investment advice and analysis; there are some indicators to this effect, including abolition of the dedicated ownership advice unit, and assumption by the Treasury of a lead role in dealing with long-term health and ageing pressures on the budget. To some extent these may simply reflect new ministerial priorities and organizational restructuring (which saw the Finance department's CEO and most of the senior budget officials change in late 2001) or they may represent a pulling back from the extent of devolution originally envisaged in the 1999– 2000 reforms.

RE-NEGOTIATING THE POLITICS OF THE BUDGETARY PROCESS

Although Australia has witnessed a major transformation in the role of its CBAs over time, some elementary political characteristics of the budgetary process remain extant (for example, there are still winners and losers, never enough resources to satisfy the demands, budget rules are initiated or revised by the central agencies). This does not mean, however, that the *politics* of budgetary relations have remained unchanged or that the language, rituals, sites and substance of political engagement have not adapted in response to the changed roles. Three aspects of the budgetary politics are examined here to illustrate the link between the changing role of the CBAs and changing political expressions – they are the politics of the budget process; relations between budget actors; and the political functions of the budget including the impacts of both the economic and political cycle on the power of the CBAs.

The Politics of the Budget Process

Within the budgetary process Finance has attempted to impose formal rules and frameworks over a myriad of relatively informal relationships. At the same it is conscious that budget rules are often characterized by declining utility and if retained too long can become counter-productive to guardian or government interests. Finance is also conscious of the dangers of path dependency either in limiting its ability to provide devil's advocate advice or in enervating its behavioural relations with spender agencies. Yesterday's much heralded reforms can produce less than optimal results, creating rules that lock the CBA increasingly into dysfunctional arrangements. For example, in the managerialist phase the tighter controls over administrative costs (roughly 10 per cent of Commonwealth outlays) was initially effective in containing resource allocations to departments, but gradually spending agencies managed to find ways to evade or circumvent the budgetary controls. Agencies responded to the rules governing the running costs (and the annual clawback of the efficiency dividend) by inventing new policies and re-specifying existing programs to qualify for additional running costs allocations. The running costs rules intended to force greater efficiencies in administrative delivery, but also led to more creative policy-bidding by agencies as a means to augment their base budgets.

Hence, Finance has responded by continually creating and destroying rules and modifying frameworks; changing the terms of engagement not for change's sake but to prevent the disutilities outweighing the benefits and the spenders becoming accustomed to the rule environment. Often rule changes are brought about abruptly due to perceived limitations or dissatisfaction with present arrangements; but in proposing new or replacement rules Finance is often initially unsure exactly what form they will take or less than confident about how they will work. The department also borrowed and adapted ideas from overseas (for example, the British Financial Management Initiative which was adapted to become the Financial Management Improvement Program) and also exported successful reforms to other countries (for example, running costs arrangements that were influential in other OECD nations) (see Wanna *et al.* 2000). Changing rules also introduces new possibilities of game-playing, but Finance has over the past 15 years attempted to reduce the scope for game-playing by various methods to contain budgetary politics. For example, the requirement that ministers find offsetting savings for new policy has proved an effective constraint for many ministers (the exceptions being ministers with sufficient independent political clout to bring forward spending proposals outside the ERC context). Similarly, the requirement that all small proposals (bids for less than $5 million) are first scrutinized by the Finance Minister before going to the ERC, has dramatically reduced the former practice of ministers advancing a multitude of small items in the hope that a proportion would be agreed without scrutiny.

One of the most distinctive frameworks at the centre of the Australian budgetary process over the past 25 years has been the construction of forward estimates and their translation into hard budget estimates. While Treasury has long used estimates to adjust their fiscal policy stance, Finance pioneered a unilateral determination of forward estimates to lock in portfolios. In Australia, forward estimates became amazingly robust – and, as mentioned above, without policy change actually constitute a budget for the forward years. The forward estimates are constructed on the basis of an assumption of no policy change by government, and adjusted three times a year to take account of both economic parameter movements (for example, economic growth, employment) and program specific parameters (for example, trends in client numbers). This framework is quite extraordinary in comparative analysis with budgetary systems of other countries. Forward estimates in Australia ensure a clear ongoing budget foundation, thereby easing the workload for Budget Group, as the only changes they have to make are those that relate to policy decisions (because they know what will happen in the absence of policy decisions). Finance considered it was extremely important to impose a system of expenditure management that provided a firm platform of decision-making for ministers through maintaining the integrity of a set of rolling forward estimates. The department regularly monitors the accuracy of estimates against budget actuals, expecting a variance of no more than 1 per cent (and the Auditor-General undertook and published the results of a similar study in 1999 which it was hoped would be replicated in the future).

In 1999, responsibility for the construction of the forward estimates was transferred (at the request of Finance) to spending agencies. Each agency was given the administrative responsibility for maintaining their estimates and lodging them electronically with Finance. The change was particularly controversial at the time, not least because some argued that agencies had a basic conflict of interest in constructing hard estimates (and would attempt to pad them); that agencies did not have the expertise to perform the task adequately; and that by releasing the estimates Finance would lose one of its principal leverages of power over agencies in the budget process. Finance was also concerned that by devolving estimates it would not be in a position to vouch for the quality of the estimates to ERC, and hence this would undermine its devil's advocacy advice. Since the responsibility for the construction of estimates was devolved the accuracy of the forward estimates to actuals has decreased slightly (to a variance of around 2 per cent) (DoFA 2001). Most of this slippage is attributable to the impact on budget of supply or demand-driven actual expenditure in just two large agencies.

However, the devolution of responsibility for the estimates did not weaken Finance's position. From Finance's perspective the main impact of the change to budgetary processes was a reduction in the level of adversarialism. Instead of Finance determining budget estimates unilaterally and spending agencies often reluctantly having to accept them, a more consensual set of interactions emerged. Line agencies were required to maintain their base estimates and, in the absence of policy or parameter changes approved by cabinet, there should be no changes to their electronically lodged estimate information. This affected the politics of the budgetary process by forcing agencies to take responsibility for the accuracy of their own base estimates with subsequent opportunities for the CBA to check their robustness. Finance now monitors the accuracy of agency budget estimates at the end of the financial year – comparing variations to estimates and seeking explanations from agencies for the variance. In some years departmental item variances may be as little as $50 million across all agencies, but for those without sufficient reason for the discrepancy such end-of-year monitoring can impact on the forward estimates of those agencies.

Professional oversight based on facts replaced the previous system based on subjective assessments. Hard evidence from *ex post* budget actuals rather than *ex ante* arguments about assumptions or parameters characterized the new political context. Estimates were judged according to their subsequent accuracy not on whether Finance 'trusted' the staff of the particular agency concerned. As one Finance official reported:

consensus politics are now needed to achieve our own outcome of Sustainable Gov-ernment Finances. Therefore, Finance has tried to eliminate as far as possible 'game-playing' in the budget process. The margins available for gaming have shrunk sig-nificantly in the outcomes-outputs framework. 'Padded bids' do not really occur in the budget round negotiations because they get found out and they don't really work. The modern CBA is concerned with being results-based rather than focusing on inputs. And the onus has changed because the culture has changed because the framework and philosophy have changed. It is now Finance's role to help agencies achieve an operating surplus. It is no longer just about cash-in, cash-out.

With the introduction of a full accrual budget, Finance had to play a substantial role in bedding down both the new accrual methodology and the outcomes-outputs framework, which was accompanied by a number of problems in its implementation. There were criticisms that agencies did not find the accrual information management system (AIMS) user-friendly, that the outcomes-output descriptions were not sufficiently well defined, and that ministers did not understand the nature of the changes being made. Moreover, given the short timeframe and the novelty of the approach a number of accounting decisions had to be taken as somewhat arbitrarily as they confronted new problems. In July 1999 an independent report into the introduction of the new framework made many criticisms of the implementation while pointing out that that it would take between three to five years to bed the framework down before achieving the full benefits (Vertigan 1999). But such implementation problems did not generate much in the way of confrontational politics between Finance and line agencies.

Legislative requirements also devolved greater financial responsibility on agencies and their CEO/CFOs. These new legislative frameworks have had significant effects on how the politics of the budget process are played out. Increasingly, Commonwealth expenditure management now relies upon the sign-off from CEOs/CFOs and Finance has become much more hands-off in its 'controls'. For instance, the *Financial Management and Accountability Act 1997* (FMA Act) removed a large array of detailed, prescribed rules. The FMA Act is concerned with the regulatory, accounting and accountability framework for dealing with and managing the money and property of the Commonwealth. Agency heads were given greater flexibility and autonomy in financial management but were required to promote the 'efficient, effective and ethical use of Commonwealth resources'. The *Commonwealth Authorities and Companies Act 1997* replaced the diverse accountability, financial and auditing requirements relating to Commonwealth authorities and companies with a single set of core reporting and auditing requirements for directors of these authorities. It also sets standards of conduct for officers. The *Auditor-General Act 1997* and the *Audit and Miscellaneous Act 1977* provided the Auditor-General with enhanced powers and a clearer mandate to focus on audit goals rather than processes. The *Charter of Budget Honesty Act 1998* completed this legislative package by providing that the executive had to publicly declare its fiscal strategy (policy objectives and targets), which had to be based on 'sound financial management'. The charter also required governments to issue a mid-year economic and fiscal outlook and a final budget outcome statement. Together these acts devolved financial responsibility while strengthening accountability over the output and outcomes based budgeting and reporting, as well as disclosing the true cost of government. Finance has also attempted to tighten agency performance requirements by having CEOs sign off on their outcome statements and proposed outputs.

Given the new reporting requirements Finance monitors its own performance and accuracy in predicting the budget surplus by comparing the budget estimates with the updated figures included in the MYEFO paper, and then with the actuals declared in the Final Budget Outcome. So far, in a period of economic growth, a predictable pattern has emerged. The original budget estimates released in May predict a surplus fiscal balance (say $3 billion), the MYEFO paper then predicts a lower figure in November (say $1.5 billion), the estimated budget outcome in the next May budget predicts the surplus at a higher figure (say $3.5 billion), before the final budget outcome document reports the actual figure which then exceeds all other projections (say $4 billion). The same saw-like pattern appears to have held over the past five years, although the specific numbers have varied from year-to-year. Such a pattern initially confounded accountants within Finance who believed the original budget estimate of the surplus *should* be accurate under an accruals framework. To date, however, the estimates have been constructed in a climate of continuous economic growth, with growth in each year proving stronger than predicted at the time of the budget and MYEFO. This phenomenon is an artefact of the methodology Treasury uses for building its budget growth assumptions – it is always a lagging parameter. It is expected that in periods of economic downturn the same pattern will occur but in reverse – namely the projected MYEFO result will exceed the original budget estimate while the final outcome will be worse. An alternative and more positive explanation for the saw tooth pattern within years, could also be that agencies took heed of the warnings sounded in the MYEFO and collectively tightened their spending as a result of this instrument.

Relations between Budget Actors

The introduction of the accrual-based budgetary framework in 1999 also produced something of a short-term turf war between Finance and Treasury over the principal significance of the annual budget and what key information it was meant to convey. Treasury took the view that the budget was the government's fiscal plan and that an *underlying cash balance* (or cash statement) was the principal piece of information for financial markets. Finance took the view that the budget was a financial statement of allocations shown in accrual terms with the *operating result* being the most important measure of well-being. The two departments agreed on a compromise position of publishing both of these, and at the same time they agreed to a fiscal balance measure, the accrual equivalent measure of government net lending. The fiscal balance was the primary budget bottom line target for the first accrual budget.

The rivalry came to a head over the presentation of the first fully accrual budget in 1999 when, in the last stages of preparation, Treasury insisted that its cash-based information be presented up-front as the key fiscal indicators. Against Finance's wishes, Treasury insisted on producing a cash-based budget for public presentation even though at that stage the budget had been entirely produced from the bottom-up using accrual information. This led to some tension between senior Finance and Treasury officials (and their respective ministers) over the nature of the budget documentation and the relative significance of particular information. Treasury won this particular contest over budget presentation but their demand threw the timelines for the preparation of the budget into disarray. In the two subsequent budgets (and in other reporting statements) both types of information have since been presented. Many of the issues at the centre of this dispute were resolved at both the ministerial and departmental level after an independent review (Vertigan 1999). A new protocol signed by the secretaries of Finance and Treasury has since clarified their respective contributions, specified the types of information to be presented and agreed earlier deadlines for the completion of tasks within the budget process.

There are still unresolved issues in the relations between the two CBAs. The Treasurer remains the more senior minister in political terms, and has used this status to continue to coordinate the budget and present the main budget speech. However, the FMA Act of 1997 now specifies that the traditional role of custodian of the 'Treasury of the Commonwealth' is within the responsibilities and powers of the Finance minister not the Treasurer. The ministerial overlap remains a source of some discussion. In 2001 Finance managed to claim for the first time the sole responsibility for certain budget papers (for example, the expenses budget statement No. 4 – *Agency Resourcing*), a statement that was not subject to editing or repackaging by the Treasury.

Routine relations with spending agencies impact largely on one division within the Budget Group of Finance – the Agency Advice Unit (AAU) which is structured according to the main functional areas of expenditure. This unit scrutinizes the agency estimates reconfirming them each quarter for the 45 material agencies and around 200 smaller agencies funded from the public account. The AAU staff are engaged in horizontal liaison with their counterparts in the line agencies (financial officers), ensuring any changes to the estimates are explained, cabinet approvals have been adequately costed, and actual variations to budget estimates are justified. A system of trust and informal communication still persists at this level between guardian and spender counterparts, although this has been eroded somewhat by a high turnover of staff in the respective positions (and within Finance some of these administrative positions are filled with consultant accountants). Beyond the immediate estimates process, relations with spending agencies may variously involve CBA staff charged with advising on long-term budget impacts, financial frameworks, Commonwealth ownership, or in reviewing output prices.

Spending agencies have not played a particularly important role in developing budgetary systems or innovations. Most of these changes are centrally driven and imposed on agencies by Finance. Spending agencies often engage in collaborative implementation of new initiatives, within which they may have opportunity to influence the process or shape the operation and impacts. Instances of this include the collaborative involvement of agencies in the price review exercises commenced in 1999 with eight pilot studies. Agencies were allowed to develop and justify their own pricing methodologies provided they were demonstrably robust. Agencies can still work the system not by contributing innovations to the budget process but by calculating how to behave to suit their interests within the current budgetary infrastructure and processes. For instance, agencies determine whether they will make bids each year, how many they will make, how they will structure their bids, and what level of bid to make (major bids over $5 million are treated differently to minor bids).

The Political Functions of the Budget including the Impacts of the Economic and Political Cycle on the Power of the CBAs

Focusing on internal budget processes and actor relations tends to emphasize the technical aspects of budget formulation – at the expense of some of the other real and important functions of government budgets. Internal assessments may also overestimate the procedural power of the CBAs in the budget process at the expense of the political functions of the budget as the government's plan and a political statement of intent. For instance, the annual 'Budget' is often used to reward or discipline particular ministers and reshape their areas of responsibility. Such decisions are part of the executive power play of the budget village to which CBA mandarins do not usually have much access. The decision to reward or discipline a minister is performed by other ministers usually but not always in the context of the ERC negotiations; it is not part of the CBAs' remit. However, Finance is likely to be required to provide advice on how to impose changes if any reward/discipline options are to be considered.

Electoral considerations and the stage of the political cycle also remain important to the government's strategic considerations and the prioritization through the Senior Ministers' Review. With few Australian direct taxes indexed to inflation, but almost all the indirect taxes indexed, Commonwealth revenues tend to increase even without decisions to increase the tax base. In this context, the prospect of tax cuts (or the promise of cuts) remains an attractive political option toward the end of the electoral cycle. Electoral pressures, by contrast, have meant that many entitlement benefits have been indexed impacting on expenditure projections. For example, aged pensions are indexed and pegged to 25 per cent of average weekly earnings; other programs (for example, grants for health and education) have their own specific indexes. In the case of schools grants the average schools cost index has risen at a rate almost double that of inflation elsewhere in the economy.

Even with legislated requirements for budgets to be based on sound financial management, there is scope for deficit budgets and traditional expenditure injections to meet short-term or expedient political objectives. While the prevailing orthodoxy now assumes that budgets ought to be in surplus (and governments often subscribe to this view rhetorically), there remains scope for manoeuvre and the new orthodoxy still remains to be tested in the context of a severe recession. Australian budgets do not necessarily need to deliver an annual surplus as they are framed over the economic cycle, not according to the public choice doctrines in support of an annual fiscal surplus. In so far as the medium-term fiscal plan indicates that a balanced budget (or surplus) is anticipated in subsequent out-years, then the requirements of sound financial management can be met even within periods of deficit spending.

Despite two decades of economic rationalist discourse in government, the budget is still used as a fiscal instrument to prime the economy at the margins and to support or cross-subsidize areas of market failure (for example, many quasi-commercial activities, the provision of rural infrastructure). Governments have been less motivated to 'save' their surpluses in times of strong economic growth to provide a cushion in periods of lower growth. Rather, governments over the past 25 years have tended to respond to recessions with fiscal injections at the same time as revenues fall and unemployment increases. Australia has not faced a recession without recourse to deficit budgeting, often with the impacts lasting over a number of out-years. Conversely, surpluses have tended to lead to higher levels of expenditure, even with governments preaching restraint. For example, of the six budgets delivered by the Coalition since 1996 only the first two imposed overall expenditure reductions (and only one in 1997–98 actually produced a reduction). Since then the next four budget increased expenditure by between 4–8 per cent per annum.

CHANGING CBA CULTURES: INSIDE THE EXPENDITURE BUDGET AGENCY

Views of Itself

Insider views from the expenditure CBA are important dimensions of how the agency defines its role as a CBA and charts its future directions. The question asked in Finance over the past six or so years has been where does its best influence as a CBA lie? What cultures fit best with its changing roles? Are the cultures inherited from its previous role as a traditional guardian and central command post still relevant to the agency in performing a strategic adviser role? One deputy secretary put this succinctly in 1997, saying once the department operates like an arm's-length merchant bank adviser the 'jackboots will now have to stay in the cupboard' ('at least for the time being', he added).

The main group in Finance performing the majority of expenditure budget functions, Budget Group, does not see itself as an inertia-bound bean counter. Budget Group sees its role as to assist 'its customers' (that is, the Finance Minister and, through him/her, other ministers) make better choices. In the last few years Budget Group has explicitly analysed its own comparative advantage and assessed whether its own internal cultures align with the best performance of its role. It has asked: what is essential about the 'outputs' it delivers, does it perform them best, at what price to the budget, and who else might compete? Such questions go to the heart of the department's own conceptualization of its own performance as a central agency – and to its sustained influence over time. As the department put it: does its fundamental influence (with its own and other ministers and with agencies) come from the traditional *modus operandi* of a budget agency (characterized by micro-management and a devil's advocate stance), or does it come from the clarity and persuasiveness of the analysis it provides. It decided overwhelmingly in favour of the latter conception, and duly attempted to orient the department to this view of itself and way of operating. This decision was not a sudden conversion to a new business model, but represented the continuation of the department's thinking about the directions of reform that dated from the late 1980s.

In this context, Finance's source of comparative advantage (in terms of the whole of government budgetary and investment advice) is the capacity to understand how *all* the budget numbers fit together and, therefore, to be able to display a better grasp of government financial issues. Its central strategic position enables it to add value to government-wide deliberations over and above the individual presentations of agencies (on which any decent accounting firm could provide assurance). It has also developed longitudinal advisory capacities attributable both to its experience in the annual budget process and an increased recognition of the value of long-term research.

Under the new outcomes resource management framework Finance is perhaps more conscious that it has to be a responsive and competitive professional organization – but also able to deliver something others cannot. In Finance's own terms, the department is *only* useful to ministers if ministers think its analysis is sound, robust and helpful. A department that is not responsive to a minister or to the government's concerns is not a useful department. But many in the department would argue that to be responsive does not mean simply being politically malleable. Responsiveness involves other responsibilities. Hence, although Finance fully accepts it has to be responsive to government and its political objectives, this is not interpreted to mean the department is totally submissive to ministers and does not have opinions or favoured approaches on how to conceptualize its work and practice its role. Finance believes it has to be able to put an independent view to government based on its professional integrity. It considers it wrong and misguided for the department simply to adopt a 'yes minister' approach in the name of responsiveness, and still prizes its ability to deliver frank and fearless advice. Hence, high analytical performance rather than the exercise of power are what the department believes sustains its influence and value to government.

Internal Cultures

Finance is in the process of transforming itself from a bureaucratic to a business organization. Its culture has both evolved and been revolutionized through a long process of ongoing change, jolted by the odd injection of transformational reform. This has seen the internal culture change from one of 'nit picking' to strategic analysis; but even now this process is still evolving and has some way to go. The transformation has also resulted in a major downsizing of the budget agency from a staff of around 1000 in the early 1980s to Budget Group with around 160 people in 2001 – a particularly dramatic reduction when compared to the total size of the budget. While there was once a strong internal and insular culture in the 1980s, more recently the culture has become decidedly outward-oriented and based on interaction with clients through technology. Not only are there far fewer to share the culture today, but high turnover and the replacement of staff have meant that very few of those of the former culture remain with the organization today (to some this has had an effect on the collective wisdom of the organization). In 2002 the Budget Group embarked on a concerted recruitment campaign, suggesting its staff reductions are at least in part being reversed.

There is a growing sense the department is 'doing business' not in the sense of competing entrepreneurially in private markets, but in delivering discrete business services to government. But what does being business-like really mean? The department actively promotes innovation within the organization. This means being ahead of the game instead of just reactive to circumstances – to anticipate changes and challenges and to have the flexible organizational structure and work ethic to address them. Finance is now far more a business analyst for government than a public sector spending controller. Inside the department the current language is of agility, responsiveness, adaptability to continually changing circumstances (government objectives, the external business environment, technology, rivals/competitors). It has adopted a 'high performance-oriented culture' with a performance management system considered to be the best across the Commonwealth. Extensive monitoring against internal quality and timeliness targets (for policy work, ministerials, completions, client satisfaction) has focused the department on its core business and become crucial to the department's continued high performance.

Finance now has a variety of long-term strategic partners with whom it regularly consults and collaborates (including Price Waterhouse-Coopers, and IBM Global Services Australia). Both core and non-core activities have been and can be outsourced. There are few things the department does that are off limits to contestability. The department now employs fewer but better people, pays market rates for them with roughly comparable remuneration, superannuation, performance-pay and leave conditions to the private sector. It has adopted a consultant-style approach to its work, based around semi-autonomous work teams and project groups. Group managers have also sought to increase the mobility of project officers to build greater analytical experience.

Finance would argue that some critics operate from a basic misconception when they decry the degree to which some government agencies have embraced business-like practices – seeing business as essentially concerned with rates of return to satisfy private purposes. As a government agency, the purposes of Finance are, and have always remained, public purposes – otherwise government would simply privatize the activity. There are, therefore, some fundamental differences in the reasons for existence and the measurement of performance between private and public organizations. However, this does not mean, in terms of how the department administers itself, that it cannot operate in terms of generally accepted commercial practice. It is important to the performance of the agency that it is now able to operate some basic commercial practices, such as commercial billing, accounting, communication with customers, contractual partnerships and hiring and firing. Concerns about the dangers of a 'government monopoly' increasing the potential for corrupt practices, price-fixing or feather-bedding etc., can be addressed either through a Weberian bureaucratic model with a complex system of administrative rules that prevent this from occurring, or through a modern business-like model that applies commercial discipline and transparent accounting for openness and scrutiny.

Policy Advice

In policy terms Finance no longer considers itself indispensable or assumes it automatically holds a monopoly over budget matters. Departmental perceptions have changed and any former policy significance resting on its exclusive status does not appear of much consequence today. Rather, Finance now considers that the policy functions it performs are contestable and acknowledges the potential of rivals providing competing advice from the private sector. The possibility of private sector competitors performing elements of its functions was not unwelcome to senior departmental managers; indeed, many believed that some injection of competition would assist the department in costing prices for policy advice and in part also demonstrate the value for money provided by the department.

It may be argued that the CBA possesses a *natural* comparative advantage in providing advice on allocative efficiency given the sensitivity of this role and the fact that re-prioritization will often involve assessments of value for money from existing outputs and outcomes. However, simply because the CBA is best placed to advise government on its priorities for allocating expenditure does not mean it performs this role well or that it has the best and most appropriate skill mix 'in house'. This has been an issue for Finance, and there has been some discussion about the types of advisory skills Finance staff should possess – and of what the overall advisory skills profile of the department should consist. To some, the new accrual framework underlined the need to hire financial analysts to operate the accounting technologies and provide financial advice. Certainly the department has considerably increased its accounting and financial specialists, sometimes at the expense of its policy analysts. To others this accounting changeover represented a specific short-term need which was met with the assistance of outside consultants.

In the past, few policy analysts in Finance possessed accounting qualifications or much accounting experience. However, many of the trained accountants hired in recent years, while they may be able to interpret financial statements, do not necessarily have sophisticated policy analysis skills. A series of pertinent questions for the department have arisen: how can the department balance the various types of advice; is financial analysis the same as policy advice; can the department advise on the basis of financial statements alone; and, if not, how does it augment its policy analysis skills; does it have sophisticated policy analysis skills in house or will it have to contract in such skills as required;

should financial analysts be encouraged and trained to develop policy skills (or vice versa) or should teams of analysts with a mixture of skills be used?

FUTURE PROSPECTS AND DIRECTIONS

There are two less acknowledged but important (political) functions of the budget that are not necessarily reliant upon the operations of the CBA or just about 'the numbers'. First, is the budget's role in helping government define the role of the state in society, through both the budget's regularity and its fiscal interventions. Second, is that the debate about what are the 'core functions of government' or the role of the state – a debate that from the CBA's perspective is somewhat pointless. That is, to the CBA there are no core functions of the state only those resolved by the government of the day. The government continually decides through the budget what its 'core functions' consist of at any one time. At the margins of the budget, year-by-year, the budget defines what government is pulling away from or getting further into. It is an organic process and the results aggregate and manifest over time to produce a change in the complexion of the state. As noted above, the trend toward de-emphasizing the Budget as the one salient event and set of documents in the Commonwealth's regime of expenditure management is already well under way. How far it can go partly depends on whether you think government can become even more business-like (in terms of commercial accounting).

The arguments developed by Schick in his 1997 paper are now considered by Finance to have been incorporated into their thinking. Management perceives the department and especially the Budget Group has progressed beyond the new roles identified by Schick. The devolution of expenditure control (subject to tight monitoring) and the provision of high-level strategic investment advice by a small budget agency has shifted the terms of Schick's paradox.

Despite the (often ongoing) perception of the sacrosanct nature of CBAs, they can regularly come under actual challenge (and not just criticism) from authoritative sources. The risk of other sources of budgetary advice being sought rather than that of the CBA has historical antecedents in the Commonwealth. In the 1973–74 budget the Department of Urban and Regional Development – an emerging rival to Treasury on domestic economic planning – supplied the government with key economic and budgetary advice in formulating the budget. It was a disastrous budget, but because ministers had lost faith in Treasury they instead chose to accept advice from another agency (Hawker *et al.* 1979). Realistically, given this climate of competition, it is both conceivable and possible that Finance could be replaced in its tasks by a consortium of one or more of the big five merchant banks and accounting firms. In one sense, it is only the inherent conservatism of government that stops this from occurring.

The main sources of Finance's comparative advantage are its 'brand name' and the specific ways it can perform in terms of responsiveness. With its brand name comes its reputation for analysis, counter-arguments, probity, honesty, confidentiality – indeed, Finance is very hard on security breaches and leaks occur far less frequently than in other departments. In terms of responsiveness, the department is concerned with mechanistic and timely turnarounds (although Finance achieves a response time to 'ministerials' and other briefings of less than half the APS average).[5] This sort of responsiveness is hard to define in a contractual relationship (the variations to contract that would be required to fast-track an urgent issue would be highly fraught). Response times are far faster than would probably be possible if contracted out. But also its responsiveness 'buys' an ongoing independent view to government based on its professional skills. Finance is able to put an argument back to government whether or not government agrees with such advice, asked for such arguments to be presented, or even wishes to hear such counter-arguments. By themselves, these advantages are not insuperable barriers, but it does make the replacement of Finance by a hired consultant trickier and less attractive.

There remain many areas of the management of public resources in need of further strengthening – and some of these have been identified by the department. Perhaps the main problem confronting Finance is the overall measurement and reporting of performance. The adoption of a system of appropriating for *outcomes* (constituting the legal authority for expenditure) and purchasing *outputs* means that Finance has to measure and report on the attainment of outcomes. Yet, considerable difficulties have arisen in actually measuring performance by outcomes even though it is an essential part of the resource management framework. So, despite the difficulties, measuring the achievement of outcomes is an unavoidable and a necessary part of accountability for performance (Bartos 2000). This implies that there is much work to be done in improving performance indicators, especially those most relating to outcomes and effectiveness measures. The CBA needs to develop a greater management and accountability focus on the idea of 'price' and the development of market-based modes of assessment and funding. Departments need to improve the consistency of specifications of outcomes and outputs across Commonwealth agencies. In addition, external accountability bodies need to be educated in 'the benefits and strengths of the framework in enabling them to seek strategically significant data on performance and finances' (Boxall 2000).

A related problem is that agencies have been responsible for setting and revising their own outcomes. Many outcomes are almost meaningless phrases or labels under which enormous activity takes place. This has led to the recognition that the outcome indicators are aimed at too high a level of aggregation, and that as a consequence some important information (in portfolio statements, program estimates or activity measures) has disappeared from the annual budget process. Some agencies may have deliberately avoided providing detailed information or have sought to disguise information under the new system of reporting. Parliament is also anxious to tighten reporting information, finding ways to make it more timely, consistent and with quarterly reports on performance against budget projections (reducing the current 18 months lapse between budget and the annual report).

For Australia's CBAs the future is replete with possibilities but impeded by structural limitations. But many ideas on what might make for better budgeting and improve the use of public resources are on the agenda. For instance, there is debate around whether we should remove the legislative constraints on *annual* budgets allowing multi-year budgeting. There is debate around how to limit the demands for increased expenditure in big ticket items (such as health, defence, education, ageing). To what extent can co-payments and private forms of financing be integrated into public provision? How can governments seek to reduce the 'lock-in' effect of existing outlays and minimize the impact of inheritance? Should we move to divide the budget according to a fixed percentage or ratio of allocations tied to GDP but with flexibility for policy areas? How can accountabilities for performance be tightened in the delivery of public policies? Should we seek to make budget rules more predictable or more changeable once a more business-like and transparent system is in place? These issues are being debated but the practicalities of politics and the imperatives of accountability will also shape any eventual changes.

NOTES

*   We would like to thank Charles Broughton and Alex Gash for their assistance with this project.

1.   The Canadian Treasury Board enjoys a similar quasi-constitutional status, whereby under an original statute (1867) the Board is established as a standing cabinet committee. The secretariat of the Board, however, enjoys no such protection; indeed, a separate departmental secretariat was only established in 1966.

2.   The annual budget in Australia constitutes a consolidated set of projections presented to parliament in a series of substantial budget papers, including revenue and expenditure measures, economic and fiscal strategies, federal–state financial relations, individual portfolio statements, and the Treasurer's budget speech.

3.   Few other Commonwealth agencies were as active in pushing the reform agenda or in leading change. The central personnel agency, the Public Service Board/Commission then the Public Service and Merit Protection Commission, remained relatively weak and its reform pushes faded by comparison. Treasury was uninterested in public service reform, except for competition policy applied to public enterprises. The Department of Prime Minister and Cabinet was preoccupied with the prime minister's immediate agendas and with political issue management (although it led some collaborative federal initiatives in the late-1980s and early-1990s).

4.   Outcomes are the desired changes government is hoping to achieve for the community. Outcomes are broad intentions described by or broken up into key objectives in areas such as social policy (for example, health and welfare), the economy (for example, competition policy) and the national interest (for example, public order and defence). They are specified by ministers in close consultation with the relevant agencies. In most instances, outcome statements perform a specific legal function as the descriptions of the *purposes of appropriations* from consolidated revenue. By contrast, outputs are the products or services delivered by agencies to achieve the outcomes specified by government. They are directly or indirectly (for example, through outsourced services) controlled by the department or agency. All outputs should contribute toward achieving an appropriated outcome. Outputs are not appropriated separately, but are separately identified by agency in the *Portfolio Budget Statements* and *Annual Reports*. Examples include policy advice, administration of payments, and delivery of goods and services.

5.   Ministerials are letters written to the Minister for Finance, where the department prepares a response for his signature with a target turnaround of two days for less complex and five days for more complex matters.

2. Zen and the Art of Budget Management: the New Zealand Treasury

Gwenda Jensen

The task of analysing the Treasury's changing budget agency role over the last 15 years is a daunting one. There is much to write about, because so much has happened. During this period, the Treasury has helped to effect fundamental reforms to the government's financial management system and transformed its own culture and structure in response to the system changes. The government's changing financial position and the introduction of a proportional parliamentary voting system has also affected what the Treasury does. Today, the New Zealand Treasury deals with macroeconomic policy, budget management and resource allocation. The Secretary to the Treasury has recently described its budgetary role as follows:

> We manage the public purse for the Government – and advise on how the Government can get the best quality and value out of public spending (Bollard 1999, p. 2).

To achieve this, the Treasury works as the government's budget facilitator, communicator, coordinator, and analyst. It has managed the budget on behalf of a variety of governments – majority, minority and coalition ones – in good and bad times.

New Zealand's budget process is now almost totally top-down. The government determines the financial parameters and priority investment areas at the start of the process, and departmental budgets must fit within those parameters. There are four distinct phases in the process, as shown in Figure 2.1: the strategic phase; the budget initiatives phase; the legislative phase; and the implementation phase.

The budget management system, operated by Treasury, presently has the following six key characteristics:

- No surprises: aggregate fiscal targets and key budget priorities are determined and publicized at least several months before the budget. Short-

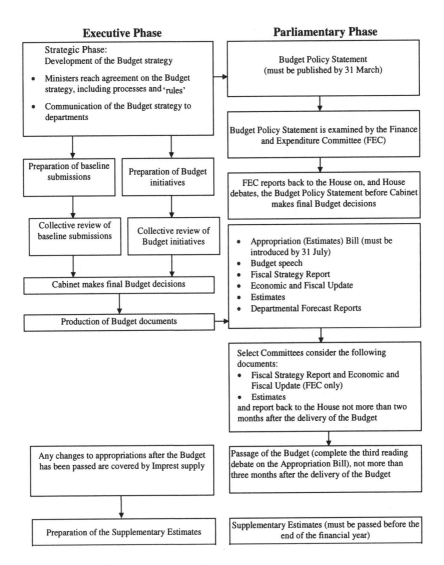

Figure 2.1   Key phases in the budget

term intentions for the budget year and medium and long-term objectives (horizon 10-plus years) are published.

- A fiscal provision: governments set and publish an amount available for new policies and funding cost pressures over their three-year term of office.
- Fixed nominal baselines: departments' baselines are fixed in nominal terms (no inflation adjustment).[1]

- Variable expenses: certain expenses vary in line with demand and inflation rates. For example, the total unemployment benefit expense adjusts automatically to the unemployment rate.
- Outputs and self-management: departments and Crown entities[2] are responsible for managing their own resources to provide the agreed level of services (outputs) within the budgeted amount. Ministers purchase services from departments and other providers.
- Accrual information: budgets and reports are prepared on an accrual basis, in accordance with generally accepted accounting practice (GAAP).

The main building blocks of this budget management system were created and assembled over the last 15 years. The reforms began with state owned enterprises (SOEs), moved on to departments and Crown entities, and then to top-down budget tools and the whole of government strategic budget management. As each set of reforms was implemented, Treasury's budget roles changed. The whole process of reform began with problems controlling expenditure and a perception shared by key bureaucratic players and their political masters that the system was in dire need of an overhaul.

This chapter begins with an analysis of the key stages leading to the present budgeting approach and the implications of reform on the Treasury's role and responsibilities. The structure of the chapter traces the six evolutionary stages of reform undertaken by various governments – in particular, highlighting the importance of major pieces of financial management legislation, namely the *State Owned Enterprises Act 1986*, the *Public Finance Act 1989*, and the *Fiscal Responsibility Act 1994*. The chapter concludes with a discussion of changes to the budget 'village culture' and speculation about what the Treasury's future might include.

PROBLEMS WITH A CENTRALIZED RULE-BASED EXPENDITURE CONTROL SYSTEM

In the early 1980s, the New Zealand public sector was highly centralized. Departments were responsible for both public good type services and profit making businesses. All staff were employed by the State Services Commission. The Treasury and the State Services Commission ran a control system based on an extensive set of detailed, input-focused procedural rules. The rules specified everything from whether department chief executive officers were allowed their own tea sets to how to park a car.

The Treasury ran a cash-based, input-focused budget and control system. The emphasis was on number crunching inputs early in the budget formulation process, using this to affect a semblance of control over line agencies. Usual budget practice was for salary and operating budgets to be regularly adjusted to reflect increases due to wage claim decisions and inflation. The budget focused on a single year, and Treasury was responsible for a central bank account into which all public money was paid. Departments submitted payment vouchers to the Treasury for it to process payments from the central account on their behalf. Treasury had six regional processing offices dedicated to this task alone.

The Treasury prepared cash-based 'public accounts' for the government. Departments were not required to produce balance sheets. Information about departments' asset holdings was not systematically collected and reviewed with the result that departments and the Treasury did not know how much property was publicly owned. A record was kept of public debt, but liabilities for future payments such as deferred employee remuneration were not generally recorded. Information about outputs produced and departments' assets and liabilities was generally unavailable. Such information was not used in budget decision-making or financial reporting.

New Zealand governments from the 1970s onwards declared they would cut back public spending. They tried to contain public sector spending through budget freezes, across the board percentage cuts, cash limits and sinking lids. But evidence suggests these methods did not work. There may have been years where spending appeared to be contained but this was an easy appearance to achieve over the short term with cash accounting. But spending continued to rise as a percentage of GDP, deficits continued and public debt continued to increase, with implications for debt servicing costs.

The Treasury had reviewed the government's expenditure control system in 1967. In response to problems identified in that review, the department introduced some changes. But in 1978, the Auditor-General reported that the government's financial management was poor, and that managers focused on legal compliance rather than the effective and efficient management of resources.[3] In response to the Auditor-General's criticisms the Treasury introduced further improvements, but these have been characterized as 'tinkering' (Norman 1997). In the early 1980s, Treasury's capacity to impose financial management discipline was viewed as relatively weak. Although the Treasury was aware of problems with the government's financial management system, reform was not on the Treasury's list of things to do. But this was about to change.

STAGE 1: REFORMING THE GOVERNMENT'S BUSINESS ACTIVITIES

In 1984, the Lange Labour government was elected, and like previous governments, it wanted to reduce or at least contain public spending. However, unlike previous governments, this one was prepared to undertake fundamental changes rather than tinkering around the edges. In 1986, the government decided that its major trading organizations should be turned into profit-oriented corporations. The government owned a wide range of businesses including three banks, a printer, the railways, telephone, and electricity systems, and a computer business. The changes were aimed at tackling persistent budget deficits and improving economic performance in areas under the government's direct control.

The government asked the Treasury to provide advice on a new business structure for these trading activities – many of which operated within government departments. The Treasury led the development of a new legislative framework contained in the State Owned Enterprises Bill, which was enacted into legislation in 1986. The *State Owned Enterprises Act 1986* transformed these trading activities into company structures with boards of directors drawn from the private sector. They became 'state owned enterprises' or 'SOEs'.

The importance of the SOE reforms is that they simplified the Treasury's budget role by removing a large section of the government from Treasury's traditional input-oriented and rule-driven oversight. The *State Owned Enterprises Act 1986* placed SOEs at arm's length from the government. Their objective was to make a profit. Their boards of directors, not the Treasury, were responsible for ensuring that they operated efficiently and effectively. At the same time, the Treasury acquired two new roles. First, the Treasury began providing 'ownership' advice to the Minister of Finance and Minister for SOEs. This ownership advice was similar in concept to the information company shareholders would need about the company they owned. Ownership advice included information about an SOE's rate of return on assets, strategic investment decisions and business restructuring decisions. Second, the government asked the Treasury to act as its business sales adviser and help to implement the government's privatization program.

Working as the government's strategic divestor, the Treasury's role was to evaluate the arguments for and against sale, present them to cabinet and then, if the government decided to sell, implement that decision.[4] In most cases, businesses were sold to individual purchasers on a competitive tender basis, although during 1999 there were three public share floats. From 1988 to 1999, the Treasury sold, on behalf of the government, 46 substantial government investments including 38 government-owned businesses.[5]

The asset sales program begun by the Labour government continued under the Bolger National government elected in 1990, and re-elected in 1993, and under the National-New Zealand First coalition government formed in 1996. Indeed, asset sales have been a major factor contributing to the NZ$18 billion drop in net public debt over the same period.[6] The present Labour–Alliance coalition government elected in 1999, and led by Helen Clark, halted the privatization program. The Treasury's provision of advice on 'asset divestment' substantially ended in September 1999. The government's purchasing of asset divestment outputs from the Treasury reduced accordingly from NZ$54.3 million in 1998–99 to NZ$0.4 million in 1999–2000, and no purchases of asset divestment advice appeared for 2000–2001.[7]

STAGE 2: REFORMING GOVERNMENT DEPARTMENTS

The government considered that the SOE structural reforms showed clear objectives, better accountability arrangements and better financial information could significantly improve performance. In 1988, the government announced its intention to reform government departments. The Treasury was asked to develop and implement new financial management legislation for departments. The *State Sector Act 1988* and the *Public Finance Act 1989* together delivered the fundamental management and accountability changes that the Labour government desired. These acts devolved management responsibilities to department chief executive officers (CEOs).

The *State Sector Act* gave departmental managers the freedom to manage effectively and made them responsible to the government for their performance. CEOs gained the power to employ staff directly. Prior to this, public sector employment decisions had been the responsibility of a single central agency – the State Services Commission (SSC). The CEOs' performance was now assessed on how well they managed the government's purchase performance and ownership interests on behalf of the government, and their contribution to the government's strategic objectives. CEOs were given incentives to perform, including both rewards (including 'hard' items such as individual performance salary bonuses, but also 'softer' things such as getting a good performance appraisal or scope for upwards promotion) and sanctions (for example, the non-renewal of their five-year fixed term employment contracts).

The *Public Finance Act* shifted responsibility for departments' financial management and financial transaction processing from the Treasury to the departments themselves. The Act made CEOs responsible for their departments' financial performance, financial systems, and preparation of department budgets and financial reports. CEOs gained the freedom to manage inputs (such as salaries and use of fixed assets) to produce the outputs purchased by the minister. The *Public Finance Act* also shifted budgeting and reporting in departments from a cash basis to an accrual basis. From then on, Parliament would approve appropriations within votes in terms of the outputs that they purchased from departments. Departments' budgets and reports had to include an operating statement, balance sheet and cash flow statement. They also showed the outputs produced by the department for the minister and the price of the outputs purchased, which covered depreciation, a capital charge on net assets and goods and services tax (GST).

For the Treasury, the generic legislative reforms meant substantial reductions in some activities and the acquisition of new responsibilities. The Treasury stopped setting and administering detailed rules for departmental activities, their use of funds and accounting. The Treasury began to relate to departments as separate businesses, responsible for managing themselves and running their own financial systems. The Treasury stopped writing departmental cheques and tracking all department cash payments. Instead, the Treasury became responsible for collating aggregated cash and accrual information and monitoring departments' monthly financial performance using the monthly financial statements provided by departments.

The Treasury acquired new responsibilities, including:

- providing quality assurance over departments' financial data;
- implementing the reforms (marketing the reforms, consulting with departments to check progress towards full implementation, help for departments with specifying outputs); and
- monitoring departments' performance (Boston *et al.* 1991, p. 186).

The monitoring of departments became more sophisticated. Monthly accrual-based financial and service performance reports allowed Treasury analysts to monitor the financial performance, service performance and financial position of departments. Analysts would then use this information to inform the next budget round, identify fiscal risks early, and ensure that departments are staying within appropriations; managing cash well; maintaining the Crown's investment in the department at an appropriate level; and making progress on the government's key priorities.

Today, departments have far more responsibility for operational efficiency and allocation decision-making than previously. Departments have better incentives to use their fixed assets and working capital (including cash) efficiently. Since 1992 departmental baselines have been fixed and the cabinet has been generally reluctant to approve any increases other than for new policy initiatives. Departments are charged a capital charge on their net assets (introduced in 1991). This charge is like an interest cost for departments. If departments reduce their net assets then the capital charge expense and asset depreciation expenses both decline – any savings gained by departments can be spent elsewhere, for example on salaries. This arrangement means that departments have incentives to identify any surplus departmental assets and dispose of them.

In some areas there are market pressures that encourage government-owned enterprises to operate efficiently and effectively. Even within central government, where these pressures are least evident, they still operate. In theory, ministers can choose to purchase policy advice from another organization, if they are unhappy with the quality or the cost. Because departments are free to manage their own inputs, they can choose to sub-contract operations and achieve efficiencies through competition between private providers.

Responsibility for budget tasks is now widely spread. As well as preparing their own budgets, many departments also perform a budget advice role for their ministers with respect to groups of Crown entities. A department may produce financial forecasts for a group of Crown entities, negotiate budgets on behalf of their minister and the government, and monitor the Crown entities' financial and service performance. For example, the health ministry advises the minister on the budgets, financial performance and financial capability of district health boards. Hence, budget responsibilities cascade down from the Treasury (responsible for preparing the government's whole budget) to departments (responsible for their own budgets and coordination of other government entities' budgets), to Crown entities and state owned enterprises (responsible for their own budgets). This devolution of budget responsibility means that many different people within government have budget management experience. The Treasury is not the only organization with the unenviable task of explaining that a great new investment idea is not high enough on the government's priorities to warrant extra money! The guardian role now extends to line ministers and their departmental managers.

But back in 1989, only part of this picture was in place. In particular, the whole of government perspective was relatively weak, as was the strategic budget management phase. The next section describes changes to budget decision-making, whole of government information and strategic planning from 1990.

STAGE 3: WHOLE OF GOVERNMENT FINANCIAL MANAGEMENT AND REPORTING

The Labour government did not get a chance to use the financial management system introduced by the *Public Finance Act 1989* due to the election of a

National Party government in October 1990. The new government's first budget – the 1991–92 Budget – was to be the first budget using the new accrual based output financial information. Treasury's fiscal policy advice to the incoming government in 1990 argued: 'Things are bad. The government needs to spend less or things are going to get much worse'. The Treasury projected that without a change of existing policies, the deficit would rise to NZ$5.2 billion (6.3 per cent of GDP) by 1993–94 (Treasury NZ 1990, p. 64). Net debt was projected to rise to NZ$43.9 billion (53 per cent of GDP) by the same year. The Treasury's advice concluded with the statement that: 'a strategic approach to decision making coupled with a total Government commitment to that strategy is essential to this process'.[8]

The Treasury faced the task of managing a new budget system for a new government facing some serious financial difficulties. How well would the new system work? The 1989 reforms envisaged a strategic phase where the government would determine outcomes to which outputs purchased would contribute. Would the new government want to develop a strategic budget phase?

Work on the government's 1991–92 budget began immediately after the election. The budget process illustrated a number of the characteristics seen as important in the Treasury's advice to the incoming government. The process included a strategic phase (culminating on 19 December when the 'Economic and Social Initiative' package was publicly launched in the House of Representatives); tactics to gain strong commitment; and filtering committees of ministers (first used by the previous government). The steps taken in formulating the 1991–92 Budget began to shift the budget from a bottom-up process towards a top-down process. This change was consistent with the ideas envisaged by architects of the *Public Finance Act 1989* that ministers would, at the start of the budget process, determine the broad outcomes they wished to achieve. Ministers would then determine the outputs they needed to purchase to achieve their desired outcomes.

In the 1991–92 Budget, departments provided information about 'the projected resource costs and revenues associated with their outputs or programs; the projected level of Government investment or dis-investment in the department; the projected level of receipts to be collected on behalf of the Crown; and the projected level of payments to be made on behalf of the Crown' (Treasury NZ 1991–92, p. 30). The Treasury also produced three-year projections of the government's total cash requirements and its projected 'fiscal position' in a fiscal outlook paper that gave advice on fiscal strategy options. The production of these two distinct sets of information, detailed accrual information for decision-making about departments' budgets and projected cash flows information for the government as a whole, was 'a major break with the past' (Treasury NZ 1991–92, p. 30).

The government was happy with the improved information. The Minister of Finance, Ruth Richardson, identified the outputs-focused information as an important factor in her identification of savings in the 1991–92 Budget:

> The new focus on outputs brought about by the Act meant ministers had genuinely meaningful information about the services produced by their departments and were in a position to make informed trade-offs between competing priorities. Our exercise was the first genuine yield from the Public Finance Act. Progress would have proved far more difficult to make under the old public accounting system (Richardson 1995, p. 103).

While key ministers welcomed the result, the budget process had been something of a nightmare for officials. The budget timetable was shortened because of the election in October. There were transition problems and departments were still:

> in the throes of moving to the new accounting systems and reforms. They were still getting used to the new language of outcomes, outputs and inputs; their accounting systems were generally in that state of chaos that so often characterizes a changeover of systems (Warren 2000).

The Treasury had to reconcile two different sets of figures – accrual figures for departments and cash figures for the whole of government. 'From the point of view of aggregate fiscal control it was difficult to track the impact of individual decisions onto the overall numbers and know at any point whether sufficient savings had been made to reach the fiscal targets' (Warren 2000). Treasury officials faced many late nights and impossibly long working weeks. Deadlines were missed and the Budget was finally tabled in Parliament on 30 July, just one day ahead of the statutory deadline.[9] In addition to these transitional problems, the 'bid and review' budget system then in use made containing or reducing spending difficult. In this system each budget round started with departments forecasting the costs of existing policies for future years. The onus was on the Minister of Finance (and his associate Ministers of Finance) and the Treasury to justify reductions to departmental forecasts. Departments could introduce new spending proposals at each stage of the budget and re-litigate previously agreed allocations – this biased the system in favour of increased spending. Lengthy negotiations were needed to hold spending at existing levels.

Some of these problems were transitional ones that would not recur. But the lack of consistency between department accrual information and the whole of government financial (fiscal) targets and the use of a 'bid and review' process both warranted further changes to the system. In late 1991, the findings of the new government's review of the public sector reforms, the Logan Review, indicated that more work would be needed on the strategic phase of the budget process. The government wanted to keep the budget process moving towards a top-down process within a clear strategic framework.[10] But to achieve this, further improvements to the budget process were needed.

Two innovations were introduced into the process leading up to the 1992–93 Budget. First, the previous 'bid and review' system was replaced with a centrally controlled system of rolling forward estimates or 'baselines' for departments (following the Australian and Irish experiences). A department's previous year's budget was 'rolled out' to become its budget for the next two years, unless the department could justify an increase. The burden of proof had shifted. Instead of the Finance Ministers and the Treasury having to justify why departmental budgets should not increase, departments had to produce arguments, with supporting financial information, to explain why their budgets should increase.

Second, the budget rules were revised to include a default rule that price rises were not a sufficient reason for a budget increase. Departments were expected to find efficiencies in order to cope with increasing prices. This rule fixed departmental baselines at nominal levels. These two changes reduced the power of spending departments within the budget process, simplified the budget process for the government and the Treasury, and gave the government stronger top-down control over spending. More time had been freed up for strategic decision-making at the top. At the same time, work was progressing on better information about the big picture – the whole of government financial position.

While the Treasury's Budget Management Branch was formulating the 1991–92 Budget, Treasury officials in the Financial Management Branch were building the infrastructure necessary to produce the whole of government financial statements on an accrual basis. Officials needed to establish appropriate accounting policies, develop an information system for collecting and consolidating information from departments and other Crown organizations, establish procedures to gain assurance over the quality of the information, develop a format for the financial statements including the accompanying commentary and analysis, and determine a communication plan to explain the information to local and international audiences (Norman 1997, p. 17). On 30 September 1992, the New Zealand government's annual financial statements for the year ended 30 June 1992 were published on an accrual basis. Earlier that year, the government's half-year financial statements had also been produced on an accrual basis. These were the first whole of government financial statements produced on an accrual basis since a brief experiment with accrual accounting over fifty years earlier. For the first time in over fifty years, the New Zealand government had published a balance sheet showing its total assets and total liabilities.

The next step was to move whole of government *budgeting* further onto an accrual basis. Appropriations and departmental budgets were already on an accrual basis. But there was no forecasting of the government's balance sheet information and the fiscal projections were still cash-based. In her 1992–93 Budget Speech the Minister of Finance announced that all fiscal reporting, including the forecasts included in the Budget, would move onto an accrual basis. In 1994, big picture information concerning 'fiscal reporting' and the government's financial plans was first prepared on an accrual basis encompassing the whole of government. This change anticipated the requirements of the *Fiscal Responsibility Act 1994* by a year.

Whole of government accrual reporting and budgeting required the government to clearly determine its boundaries. The question of whether state owned enterprises and Crown agencies should be included in the government's financial statements proved difficult. This technical accounting issue had implications for budget management and the potential for significant political fall-out. Some organizations, for example universities, had operated under their own independent governing bodies since their creation. They did not accept that they were owned by the government or should be included in the government's reporting entity.[11] SOE boards were opposed to including their financial results in the government's reports, because they believed that this would pull them back into stronger central government budget control and political interference. The Treasury was concerned about the practical and political difficulties of combining detailed information gathered from thousands of different entities into one set of accounts.

A simple application of accrual accounting rules said that most of these entities were owned 'in substance' by the Crown and therefore their financial information should be fully consolidated 'line-by-line' into the Crown's financial statements. But taking this 'pure' approach placed the whole change to accrual accounting at risk. For the first time, different parts of this coherent integrated financial management reform package appeared to conflict. Divisions appeared within the Treasury itself. What was needed was a pragmatic compromise. The solution developed by Treasury officials and approved by the government and Parliament was that the financial results of SOEs and Crown entities should be included in the government's financial statements using an 'equity' combination approach. Using 'equity accounting' the financial results of the entities were included but their effect on the government's financial performance was muted. When governments set future budgets and financial targets they did not need to consider the likely results of these entities in any detail – all the government needed to know was what the total net result would be for the whole group. The Treasury's job of pulling together the government's first set of accrual accounts became manageable.

This decision worked in the short term. But neither the accounting issue nor the control and influence issues sitting behind the accounting issue went away.

There is a Treasury project currently under way to change the basis for combining non-departmental government organizations from the present equity accounting approach to a full line-by-line consolidation approach. Full consolidation is scheduled for implementation in the 2002–2003 Budget. In combination with this 'consolidation project', the Treasury is looking at whether the key financial indicators emphasized in the commentary and analysis that accompanies the government's financial statements are still appropriate.

At the whole of government level, the accrual information produced since 1992 has challenged Treasury officials to provide advice to the government about its 'balance sheet management'. What does a good combination of assets and liabilities look like from a whole of government perspective? Accrual-based financial information brings important financial issues forward into the present. Accrual information has given timely visibility to issues that have a significant impact on future cash flows but would otherwise not be visible. Treasury advice on balance sheet management has included advice on the Crown's exposure to the timber market (forestry assets); liability and risk management issues associated with earthquake insurance coverage and government employee superannuation, and Treasury working papers on a sovereign net worth analytical framework, portfolio theory applied to the public sector, and the Crown's financial risk management. This evolution in the Treasury's previous debt management responsibility was reflected in a structural change. In 1997–98, different groups within the Treasury with balance sheet management responsibilities were pulled together into a new branch, called the Asset and Liability Management branch.

The New Zealand government is the only government in the world that has ceded its right to set its own accounting rules, with the consequence that Treasury does not have a role in determining accounting standards (although the Australian government comes close). The fact that independent GAAP rules are used as the basis for reporting, Treasury feels, adds to the credibility of the statements that are produced. However, the implications of complying with GAAP rules has had quite a big impact on Treasury's responsibilities and on-going work, and recently has become a relatively active policy issue. The present Minister of Finance and his predecessor have both expressed concern about some awkward developments in GAAP and their impact on the reported numbers. Also, there has been conflict between the present minister's ideas about how financial information should be presented and GAAP rules. For example, because of his concerns about the GAAP financial performance indicator, the present minister asked Treasury to develop a new 'bottom line' financial indicator derived from the GAAP numbers. The new number, called 'OBERAC' (operating balance before revaluations and accounting policy changes), has been emphasized in recent media releases (Cullen 2001a).[12] GAAP rules can have significant consequences for the budgeted and reported numbers (for example, an additional NZ$10 billion or so of liabilities was added when the ACC liability was first reported).

STAGE 4: STRATEGIC ISSUES AND PRIORITY-SETTING IN BUDGETS

The Logan Review reported in late 1991 that more work was needed on the strategic phase of the budget process. It found that there was:

> a widespread view among public servants that the structure of performance management had not been completed by the development of an integrated view of ultimate policy goals by Cabinet ... In practice there tended to be a 'bottom-up' process whereby outcomes were defined to explain the purpose of outputs rather than outputs being driven from a set of previously determined outcomes (Logan 1991).

The report of the review suggested that, contrary to public servants' perceptions, ministers did engage in strategic processes; the budget process itself was a comprehensive look at the government's priorities and a central expression of the cabinet's collective responsibility. However, the review found that too much government strategizing was done in conditions of secrecy and haste, with sometimes only a small number of people involved and that this was not conducive to good decision-making.

In response, the government looked for ways to communicate its broad objectives to departments. This was expected to have positive spin-offs for budget preparation, because departments would be better able to adjust their budget proposals to bring them into line with the government's strategic plans. The Department of Prime Minister and Cabinet led the project, with support from the Treasury and the SSC. In 1994, the government published its 'strategic result areas' (SRAs) and identified 'key result areas' (KRAs) for departments. Alongside this project, budget documentation increasingly dealt with strategic issues. The Minister of Finance was determined that decision-making be placed in a strategic framework:

> Among the [Budget] documentation was an important paper describing for the first time the government's entire economic strategy. I had long thought it important that my colleagues see the government's policies in a strategic framework, and that they appreciate where initiatives in their own portfolio areas fitted into the government's wider strategy ... With this in mind, earlier in the year I had presented a strategy document to the Cabinet Strategy Committee. It turned out to be a less than successful

occasion. Colleagues saw my initiative as Treasury-driven, which caused them to become defensive. Having been repulsed in this quarter, my next logical step was to use the budget as a vehicle for articulating economic strategy (Richardson 1995, p. 113).

The 1992–93 Budget saw a further strengthening of the initial strategic phase of the budget so that both aggregate financial targets and the government's desired outcomes were determined at the beginning of the budget process. The 1992–93 Budget included a fiscal strategy annex, which gave more information about the strategic story first provided with the 1991–92 Budget (Treasury NZ 1991–92, p. 70). The following Budget (1993–94) included an 'Economic and Fiscal Outlook' that described the government's overall strategic fiscal policy decisions.

STAGE 5: THE *FISCAL RESPONSIBILITY ACT 1994*

During the period 1992–94, the Treasury began assembling the key components of 'fiscal responsibility' culminating in the *Fiscal Responsibility Act* enacted in 1994. This legislation institutionalized the developments that had been taking place with respect to reporting forecasting and budget strategy. The Act codified and expanded the reporting and fiscal transparency developments that had occurred from 1990 to 1994, and formally introduced a key strategic document – the Budget Policy Statement – into the budget process. The *Fiscal Responsibility Act* required governments to be transparent about both their intentions and the short and long-term impact of their spending and taxation decisions. The hope was that such transparency would make future governments give more weight to the longer-term consequences of their decisions and adopt sustainable fiscal policies. Predictable and stable fiscal policies would help to promote economic growth and social well-being.

Specifically, the *Fiscal Responsibility Act* required the government to:

- follow principles of responsible fiscal management, and publicly assess their fiscal policies against these principles;
- publish a 'Budget Policy Statement' well before the annual Budget containing their strategic priorities for the upcoming Budget, their short-term fiscal intentions, and long-term fiscal objectives;
- publish on Budget day a 'Fiscal Strategy Report' that compares Budget intentions and objectives with those published in the most recent Budget Policy Statement;
- disclose the impact of their fiscal decisions over a three-year forecasting period in regular 'Economic and Fiscal Updates';

- present all financial information (reports, budgets and forecasts) using 'generally accepted accounting practice';
- refer all reports required under the Act to a parliamentary select committee.

The Act required the Treasury to prepare forecasts based on its best professional judgment about the impact of policy. The Treasurer must communicate all of the government's policy decisions to the Treasury so that the Treasury's forecasts are fully informed about the government's intentions.

The *Fiscal Responsibility Act* increased the number and quality of reports that the Treasury must prepare and eased some of the pressures accompanying the Treasury's role as the government's primary fiscal adviser. The Treasury is responsible for preparing the extensive set of financial and economic reports that the legislation requires. But in reality, the Act added little to the Treasury's workload because it was already preparing and, on behalf of the government, publishing much of the information required. But the Act's requirements established that the increased reporting developed in the early 1990s would continue under future governments, regardless of what future governments might prefer. The Act's intention was explicitly to bind future governments.

The more important impact of the *Fiscal Responsibility Act* for the Treasury was the easing of the pressures accompanying the Treasury's role as the government's primary fiscal and economic adviser. The legislation made this role easier because it:

- established a framework of guiding principles for fiscal decision-making which improved the basis for discussions between Treasury officials and government ministers on fiscal issues;
- reduced tensions previously experienced between concerns for longer-term fiscal objectives and present fiscal issues and budget decisions;
- clarified and firmly anchored in legislation the Treasury's responsibility to honestly report the likely consequences of the government's decisions;
- allowed others, outside the Treasury, to comment in an informed way on the government's financial decisions so that the Treasury's burden as expert adviser was lightened.

Furthermore, because the Act laid down principles of responsible fiscal management rather than mandatory targets, the Treasury now has an ongoing role advising governments on appropriate financial objectives in light of developments in public financial management and changes in the economic environment.

STAGE 6: NEW POLITICS – THE ADOPTION OF A MIXED MEMBER VOTING SYSTEM FROM 1993

A referendum held in 1993 determined that the electoral system would change to a mixed member proportional (MMP) electoral system. The effect of this change was felt in the three years leading up to the first MMP election in 1996. Prior to this, single-party majority governments were the norm under New Zealand's simple plurality electoral system. Invariably, one of the two main political parties (the National Party and the Labour Party) would have the majority in Parliament without any need to rely on support from smaller parties. After the 1993 election, some members of Parliament formed new parties. The incumbent National Party government became a minority government and had to rely on support from other parties to retain power. Since late 1994, no party has held an outright majority in Parliament. Governments have constructed majorities through coalition arrangements or been minority governments with support on supply and votes of confidence from other parties. The prospect of the new voting system was an important factor in the government's 1994 decision to develop the fiscal responsibility legislation. Evidence from overseas suggested that a proportional representation system might lead to looser fiscal discipline. The *Fiscal Responsibility Act* was designed to reduce that likelihood. But no one knew what the change to a proportional system would mean for the Treasury's budget agency role. There was at least one surprise in store.

The change to an MMP electoral system led, somewhat unexpectedly, to an improvement in the way government managed its budget. The first government elected under MMP (the National-New Zealand coalition government formed in 1996) developed a detailed coalition agreement during coalition negotiations. The coalition agreement set out the coalition government's three-year policy agenda and contained agreed fiscal parameters. No more than NZ$5 billion of additional expenses and NZ$900 million of additional capital spending would be incurred over the three-year parliamentary term. The concept of three-year fiscal limits was born. The Labour-Alliance coalition government, formed in 1999, continued with this approach.

These 'fiscal limits' have evolved since 1996 into a budget management tool now known as the 'fiscal provisions framework'. The 'fiscal provisions framework' consists of:

- a 'fiscal provision': a spending limit that covers the parliamentary cycle (three years, generally from November to November); and
- a 'counting framework': a set of principles and rules that implement the fiscal provision. The counting framework includes ways to determine when spending should be counted against the fiscal provision.

The 'fiscal provision' is a cumulative three-year total. Fiscal provision amounts are in accrual terms. Separate provisions are set for expenses and for new capital investment. Therefore, the counting framework needs to determine both how much a decision impacts on a provision and on which provision (capital and/or expense) the decision impacts. The effects of policy decisions that reduce expenses or increase revenue are also counted against the provisions, making room to incur new expenses. Expected expense levels within each of the three years are also published. The levels relate to new policy expenses (that is, expenses on top of those projected for existing government programs). For example, an increase in social welfare expenses due to higher unemployment does not count as new policy and does not count against the fiscal provision. If the government decides to create a new social welfare benefit or increase benefits for the unemployed then the resulting expense will count against the fiscal provision.

The fiscal provisions framework focuses on decision-making and on discrete policy decisions. This builds on and extends the past practice of having fixed nominal baselines for most departmental spending, while allowing forecasting changes to fluctuate with the state of the economy. These provisions require principles that determine which items will be treated as forecast changes, and which will be treated as specific policy decisions that 'count'. They are not a direct mechanism to control the operating result in the short term. For example, the provisions do not include some liability valuation changes that impact on the operating result, because these are expected to reverse in the longer term. The effects of the economic cycle are also beyond the immediate control of the government. Generally, as forecasts change through time, the fiscal provision limit is unaltered. This allows other fiscal variables to change as the automatic fiscal stabilizers operate through the cycle. Unemployment is the major cyclical expense.

Since the fiscal provision framework was first introduced in 1996, the Treasury has been responsible for making it work in practice. Initially, to give effect to the coalition agreement, the Treasury had to develop and clearly express the counting rules, communicate those rules to departments, and ensure that departments' budget information correctly applied the rules. Each budget decision paper had to describe how much a decision would 'count' against the fiscal provision. Today, the Treasury's ongoing role with respect to the provisions framework is to:

- provide advice that will help the government to determine its total three-year provision amount;
- advise the government on allocating the provision within the three-year period;

- maintain and further develop the 'counting' rules (used to determine when something impacts on the provision); and
- implement the agreed provisions framework (communication to departments, cabinet paper requirements, Treasury tracking and reports to cabinet and Parliament on provision balances etc.).

The fiscal provisions framework has now become an important financial management tool. Governments can demonstrate that their short-term fiscal policy is consistent with achievement of longer-term objectives through establishing fiscal provisions. The fiscal provisions framework gives a more strategic three-year focus to the budget rather than solely an annual focus. The use of provisions helps ministers to focus on what is within their control, a more definable and manageable target (staying within the provision limits) than the operating balance. The fiscal provisions framework was also a budget tool well suited to managing the spending demands that emerged as the government's finances improved.

By 1994, the government appeared to be moving out of fiscal crisis. The government had achieved an operating surplus in 1993–94 and more surpluses were forecast. Government spending began to increase more rapidly, but still at a rate less than revenue growth; hence, surpluses continued. Budget management processes now needed to adapt to the challenges of a surplus environment. A key issue that emerged was the relationship between fixed nominal baselines and the fiscal forecasts. The Treasury's three-year budget forecasts between 1994 and 1996 assumed that government spending would only increase in those areas that had automatic indexation. All other spending was assumed to remain constant over time. That assumption turned out to be incorrect. Because the fiscal forecasts did not allow for increased spending in future budgets, they understated the government's likely spending profile. This resulted in optimistic projections of progress toward long-term fiscal objectives and reduced the discipline on the annual budget process.

But the fiscal provisions framework helped with this problem. The framework provided a more realistic picture of a government's plans and associated financial implications, and the provisions better informed the Treasury's forecasting and the budget process. Experience so far with the fiscal provisions framework has indicated there is a better match between the Treasury's forecasts and actuals since the introduction of the framework. The fiscal provision limits have also supported sound day-to-day fiscal management in a surplus environment. By first defining an overall limit, the framework has focused decision-making on trade-offs between policy options. All decisions impacting on the operating balance, whether spending, revenue or SOE surplus, are considered in a common clearly defined framework.

In terms of budget management, ministers and chief executives have clear signals on which to base expectations of new resources in each budget round. Provided that the limit is sufficiently tight, ministers and chief executives will be encouraged to reprioritize within their budgets. This should also help the government to deliver value for money. Increasingly, the government is judged by influential stakeholders according to its setting and achievement of fiscal provision targets. In short, the government is attaching its legitimacy to the accomplishment of a set of budget-derived targets.

FURTHER IMPLICATIONS FOR THE CBA

The changes that have taken place over the last 15 years have impacted on the CBA's role and responsibilities. The changes have had further implications for the skills required of Treasury analysts, the Treasury's internal structure and the information system that the Treasury uses to prepare the government's budgets and annual reports. For example, the changes introduced by the *Public Finance Act 1989* changed the job requirements and skills of Treasury analysts. The new relationship between the Treasury and departments and new information available meant that Treasury analysts needed to further develop their business analysis and relationship management skills. After the Act was passed in 1989, the Treasury introduced an extensive training program for their analysts to ensure that their skills matched their new responsibilities. The Treasury's recruitment strategy focused on improving financial and business skills.

Good analysis requires a range of skills and training – economics, finance, business analysis and relationship management skills. Today, the Treasury encourages a team approach to analysis work to ensure that all these perspectives can be brought to bear on budget issues. Analyst training continues to be a high priority. Many Treasury analysts hold a degree in economics, finance or accounting. While there is a predominance of the economic perspective inside the Treasury, this disciplinary orientation is not essential. The main qualities looked for by the Treasury are intelligence (usually evidenced by excellent university grades in whatever subject) and the ability to debate ideas and take responsibility.

The public sector reforms have also meant significant structural change for the Treasury itself. The advent of the *Public Finance Act 1989* prompted a review of the Treasury's internal structure. The then Secretary to the Treasury, Dr Graham Scott, considered that the Treasury needed to be better aligned to the government's key concerns. The devolution of financial management and transaction processing to departments meant some sections of the Treasury were redundant. The Treasury's new structure was announced in August 1989; it gave far more prominence to the Treasury's financial, debt and budget management roles. These were three of the government's big concerns. Three new branches were created: the Budget Management Branch, the Financial Management Branch and the New Zealand Debt Management Office. The Central Finance Branch, which had been responsible for the Treasury's centralized financial transaction processing activities, was dissolved. Most of the Central Finance Branch's remaining activities were taken over by the new Financial Management Branch. The Treasury's six large regional Treasury offices closed and the number of staff doing routine accounting work as reduced from over 100 to just six persons.

The Financial Management Branch drove the reforms until the mid-1990s. It was responsible for:

- financial management reform (implementation, support, oversight, policy development);
- preparation of the Crown's financial reports;
- management of the Crown account (controller function); financial assurance; and
- development and maintenance of the Crown's financial information system.

This branch was the Treasury's powerhouse for the government's financial management reforms. However, the branch no longer exists today. In the overview presented in the Treasury's 1994–95 annual report, the Secretary to the Treasury explained that:

> While the Industries and Financial Management branches have been at the forefront of world-leading public sector reforms, the financial management reforms and large scale corporatisations are now largely complete. It was considered timely to restructure the branches to reflect the refocusing of these activities. The new branch will focus on the opportunities that the State sector and financial management reforms have created, allowing us to give greater attention to Crown balance sheet and ownership issues, including Crown entity governance (Treasury NZ 1994–95, p. 1).

The Budget Management Branch (BMB) was created in October 1989 from a combination of former budget-related branches in the department. The branch advises the government on budget and macroeconomic issues. This includes advice on the strategic approach to fiscal policy, budget process design and budget management.[13] It is not just responsible for budget management but is also responsible for tax forecasting and modelling and macroeconomic policy. Since its creation, BMB has generally only added to its original set of responsibilities (although it lost responsibility for policy coordination and development some years ago).

In order to be confident that good quality whole of government budgets and financial reports could be delivered on time, the Treasury has needed good information systems. The Treasury's Crown financial information systems have developed rapidly over the last decade. When departments took over responsibility for their own financial reporting, the Treasury needed to develop a financial information system that would collect together the information provided by departments to produce whole of government budgets and reports. First, the Treasury developed a budget management system. Completed in 1990, the new management information system was 'a central electronic data base for forecasting and monitoring budgeted and actual Government revenues and expenses and the related cash-flows' (Treasury NZ 1989–90). Because of problems with the reliability of data in the budget management system, the financial management branch used a separate collection system, in 1991, to collect information from departments and consolidate it into the government's accrual-based financial report. Departments completed hard copy schedules, which they provided to the Treasury. The Treasury consolidated the information from departments into a general ledger. But the Treasury experienced major quality control problems with the schedules provided by departments.

Over the past decade, Treasury has carried out a series of information system upgrades. The ledger used to produce the first set of accrual financial statements was replaced with a 'commercial collection and consolidation software package', which 'streamlined the data collection process by allowing the information to be collected electronically and consolidated automatically' (Warren 2000). Treasury staff were particularly appreciative of the automatic 'balancing' checks built into the new system which quickly identified errors in input data from departments. For some years now, the Treasury has been able to produce monthly whole of government financial statements within 25 working days of the end of each month as a matter of routine. The government's annual financial statements take longer, largely because of the extra time needed to audit the final statements. The government's annual financial statements are usually published in September, slightly over two months from the end of the financial year.

The most recent systems development was the implementation of 'CFISnet' in 1999. The CFISnet is a web-based central database for Crown financial information. The system allows departmental users and Treasury analysts to collaborate online in a secure environment. The Treasury budget management team posts Treasury circulars for departments, contact details, deadline information and other sensitive Treasury news directly onto this secure internet site. During the annual budget round, the CFISnet system holds a department's budget proposal, the Treasury's assessment of the proposal, and the cabinet's final decision and makes all three equally accessible to the department and the

Treasury. This has meant a further increase in the openness of the budget process. Before this system was installed departments usually received Treasury feedback on their proposals, but this was not automatic. Departments did not necessarily see the full Treasury assessment of their proposal. Now, Treasury analysts can easily allow their assessments to be made automatically available to departments, which helps to ensure that the assessments are well reasoned and robust. Departments get better information about the basis for budget decisions.

COMING TO A NEW 'VILLAGE CULTURE': NEW LANGUAGE, NEW RELATIONSHIPS

The changes over the last 15 years have fundamentally changed the budget-setting culture within the central government of New Zealand. Language and the basis on which relationships are maintained have altered radically. A whole new set of terminology was introduced during the 1980s and 1990s. Today, officials use the new budget language unself-consciously (Norman 1997). The new jargon (such as outputs, outcomes, inputs, ownership and purchase interests, depreciation, cost of capital and baselines) is part of this new landscape. But the changes are not solely discourse-related. Departments also appreciate being allowed to get on with the job. Recent research found that public sector managers view the public sector reforms very positively:

> The benefits of the reforms are seen as enormous compared with what respondents perceive to be 'bureaucratic and unresponsive systems still commonplace in other governments'. Trust was seen as a 'central ingredient' with managers strongly endorsing the statement that: 'the extent to which you are given trust and advised that you are going to be held accountable acts as a very strong incentive' (Norman 2000).

Scott (1995) has also encouraged Treasury staff to build a good relationship with departments:

> Building a good relationship with a department is necessary to really understand its business ... You need to have built up good personal contact with people who will be open to discussing quite sensitive information with you in the knowledge that both sides will profit from the experience. Establishing such relationships can be very difficult, but I want you to make the effort.

In his advice Scott emphasized professionalism, technical excellence, open-mindedness and constructive relationships. He contrasted the Treasury culture with that of traditional bureaucracies saying that bureaucracies 'tend to be hierarchical, ingrown, unimaginative and isolated ... The Treasury has done better than most ... but we must do more'. Scott's emphasis on professionalism has been continued by his successors and necessarily so, because the financial management reforms introduced in the 1980s threatened to weaken the Treasury's positional power within the government. The basis for budget decisions was changed from secrecy and rules determined by the Treasury to openness and business standards of good management. Such a change had the potential to reduce Treasury's position of privilege and power. Under the new village culture, Treasury analysts know that much of their legitimate power comes from their analytical strength and ability to develop preferred solutions for ministers.

Arguably, a deeper cultural change to the budget 'game' has occurred: like practitioners of an eastern martial art, Treasury analysts aim to excel rather than win. The Zen of budget decision-making is about fashioning a strong, robust solution to shared problems. The best Treasury analysts want to work cooperatively with departments to achieve principled solutions negotiated from a basis of mutual respect within a framework of shared public service objectives. Spending departments that can put together strong analytical cases for change are respected by the Treasury and valued by ministers.

FUTURE CHANGES TO THE ROLE OF THE TREASURY AS A BUDGET AGENCY

Are the next few years likely to be quiet ones for the Treasury? While the Treasury is pleased with the results of the financial management reforms, the Minister for State Services has only given the present public sector management system a 'B minus' (Mallard 2001). Both the minister and the Treasury agree that there is always room for improvement. So more changes are likely in the near future. This section looks at some current developments and speculates on what those future changes might be.

In August 2001, the government announced a 'Review of the Centre', which will 'make an assessment of areas of managerial strength and weakness in the current public sector systems and processes, and identify proposals for change' (Mallard 2001). The review's terms of reference include:

- whether vote structures and vote management processes could be altered to improve fiscal decision-making and financial management across government;
- whether the focus on contracts for accountability has led to a legalistic focus with excessive compliance costs, or a loss of collegiality; and

- whether a focus on narrow performance goals has led to insufficient attention to outcomes, a lack of connection between outputs and outcomes, and a reduced focus on the importance of maintaining long-term capacity.

The concerns evident in the review's terms of reference ('loss of collegiality', 'insufficient attention to outcomes', etc.) indicate a concern that the present system does not support the government's strategic aims. This concern has existed for a while. In 1996, the Schick Report found that the New Zealand system:

> still is geared more to the short-term production of outputs than planning for the long haul, and to account for what has been produced than to evaluate progress in achieving major policy objectives (Schick 1996, p. 53).

More recently, 'fragmentation' in the public sector has been raised as an issue. As a result the Treasury might be asked to develop new ways to facilitate budgeting across organizational boundaries. The government might look at the merits of budgeting by outcomes, rather than outputs. Management by outcomes is already happening in some areas, for example in the areas of road safety.

Concerns have been expressed that the ongoing ability and capability of departments to provide services has been weakened. Both the State Services Commission and the Treasury do some monitoring of the capabilities of departments and Crown entities. The review may make recommendations on better ways to coordinate this type of monitoring.

But the problem may have more to do with the limits of financial information rather than coordination between different organizations. The main capability issue concerns the question of whether the human resources of departments have been run down. Financial reports do not take account of human resource assets. The State Services Commission has been working on ways to measure human resource capability. A question for future budgets might be whether information about human resource capability can be better incorporated into the budget process.

The review might also recommend structural changes for the Treasury, but this seems unlikely. While in opposition Labour and Alliance parliamentarians were able to make much of incidents of public sector inefficiency. Now in government, they want to show the public that they do not tolerate poor management. This would seem to argue for the retention of a strong central budget agency, and the avoidance of any mooted structural change that could result in the weakening of the Treasury as a management agency. On the other hand, the review might find that the Treasury needs to focus more on its central budget agency role. There might be an argument for dividing the Treasury into two organizations – one responsible for budget issues, and the other responsible for economic policy advice (arguments the House of Commons sub-committee on Treasury considered – though rejected – in its review of the British Treasury in 2000).

Changes may emerge over Treasury's role in relation to Crown entities. The State Services Commission is leading a project looking at Crown entity governance issues. New legislation for Crown entities is likely to result from this project. Either the Treasury or the state services commission will be responsible for administering the legislation eventually developed. The change to full consolidation of Crown entities and state owned enterprises will give greater visibility to the financial results of these entities in the budget process. Because of this change, the Treasury has already done development work on key fiscal indicators. This new visibility for non-core Crown finances, combined with ongoing government concerns about governance and financial performance in the Crown entity sector, could lead to an increased role for the Treasury with respect to budget issues arising from Crown entities.

NOTES

1. Inflation was high in the 1970s and 1980s but has stayed between 0 and 3 per cent over the last decade. Since 1989, the Reserve Bank has been responsible for keeping (CPI) inflation low – the present target is 0 to 3 per cent. Treasury working papers 01/24 and 01/25 provide further information about the use of nominal fixed baselines for budget setting.
2. 'Crown entity' is a collective term for bodies owned by the Crown that are not departments, and are not Offices of Parliament or state owned enterprises. Crown entities range from schools and Crown research institutes to regulatory bodies, such as the Securities Commission.
3. Audit Office (1978), *Report of the Controller and Auditor-General on Financial Management and Control in Administrative Government Departments* (Shailes Report), Wellington: Government Printer.
4. Prior to this the Treasury provided economic policy advice on the regulatory regime. The whole process integrated economic and financial advice and had a dual objective of improving economic efficiency and ameliorating fiscal problems.
5. Treasury (1999c), *New Zealand Government Asset Sales as at 30 September 1999*.
6. Net Crown debt at 30 June 2001 was $20 billion.
7. Treasury, annual reports 1998–99, 1999–2000, 2000–2001. The 1989–99 amount is unusually large because of the large Contact Energy sale process in progress that year.
8. Treasury (1990), *Advice to the Incoming Government*.
9. While this date was later than officials had planned, it represented a big improvement in timeliness compared to previous budgets, which had been presented far further into the new financial year.
10. Senior ministers appeared to have had a fairly strong commitment to a clear strategy, both from their own accounts of this period and from their actions (see Lange 1999). Some would argue it was also a case of the Treasury convincing the government that it should follow a neo-liberal strategy (with some ministers stating there was 'no choice'). Certainly, the Treasury advised the government on strategic issues and provided advice on how to achieve its strategy.

11. The issue was what should be included in *the government's reporting entity*, not whether or not a publicly-funded organization was a reporting entity. Each department is 'controlled' by the government and therefore their financial results should be part of the government reporting entity and included in the government's financial results. However, they are also reporting entities in their own right (according to legislation and accounting definitions of a reporting entity).

12. The impact of the new OBERAC figure can be seen in the revised bottom line figure for the year ended 30 June 2001. According to GAAP figures a surplus of NZ$1.4 billion was reported while under OBERAC the surplus was NZ$2.1 billion.

13. The branch's name changed in 2000 to the 'Budget and Macroeconomic Branch', but there were no changes to its functions. The new name better reflected what the branch was doing.

3. 'Above the Fray': the Role of the US Office of Management and Budget

Susan Tanaka, June O'Neill and Arlene Holen

The Office of Management and Budget serves the President by preparing the annual *United States Budget* and carrying out the other statutory requirements, developing integrated fiscal, budget, program and management policies, leading government-wide coordination in policy making, and ensuring, through management oversight, government-wide effectiveness and consistency in policy implementation in accordance with Presidential priorities (OMB's Mission Statement, Strategic Plan FY 2001–2005).

The role of the Office of Management and Budget (OMB) is to support the President of the United States. As the central budget agency of the United States, OMB's core responsibility is the annual preparation of the President's budget request. OMB's role, however, has been stretched beyond the tasks of budget formulation and execution to encompass the development of new initiatives, the coordination of policies proposed by the various executive agencies and White House offices and the oversight of federal programs. OMB's influence derives from the President and reflects his conduct of fiscal policy. Thus, its role changes when a new president assumes office and evolves throughout each administration.

OMB's institutional characteristics reflect the constitutional and political structure of the government of the United States. OMB works for the President, providing him with analytic expertise, a government-wide perspective and a non-bureaucratic structure to help support his policy agenda. OMB has approximately 520 staff. About 30 hold political appointments. The rest are career civil servants who serve successive presidents with equal commitment.

The President's 1967 Commission on Budget Concepts described the budget as follows: 'the budget is the key instrument in national policymaking. It is through the budget that the Nation chooses what areas it wishes to leave to private choice and what services it wants to provide through government'.[1] Since 1967, the budget process has become increasingly centralized, and the Congress has assumed a much stronger role. Annual deliberations make clear that the election of a president or a congress does not always resolve major budgetary choices.

The budget remains at the top of the nation's policy agenda in good times as well as bad. From 1998 to 2001, the policy-makers remained at odds over the budget even though the fiscal outlook was very positive for the short and medium term. Although the events of 11 September 2001 and their aftermath unified policy-makers around the need to provide the resources necessary to respond to a national emergency, it is not possible to predict how long that spirit of bipartisan cooperation will last or what impact it will have for the budget over the short and medium terms. Over the longer term, the ageing of the population will create growing pressure on the budget. To be effective in getting their agendas adopted, future presidents will require a centralized capability to coordinate, monitor and manage the policies and operations of the executive branch and to enforce their decisions. That is the role that OMB plays.

THE HISTORICAL SIZE AND BALANCE OF THE US BUDGET

The size and scope of the US federal government have changed substantially over the years. So too has its budget process. No centralized budget office existed before 1921, but federal expenditures were small (only around 3 per cent of GDP throughout the 1920s) and largely made up of defence spending. The depression of the 1930s, World War II and the post-war expansion of social welfare programs raised the level of federal spending and changed its composition. By 1970, the year the Bureau of the Budget (BOB) was reorganized as the OMB, total federal outlays had risen to more than 19 per cent of GDP, while spending on entitlements[2] and other non-defense programs had risen to 55 per cent of the total budget, far eclipsing defense spending. Since then, spending for annually appropriated programs has continued downward to its current level of approximately 35 per cent of the budget (see Figure 3.1).

After 1970, rising deficits altered the budget picture. During the 1970s and early 1980s, total outlays increased as a percentage of GDP, boosted throughout by rapidly rising spending for entitlement programs and rising interest payments on a growing national debt. Overall discretionary spending maintained a roughly constant share of GDP although defence outlays fell and domestic spending rose in the 1970s. In the early 1980s, the reverse occurred as defence spending grew. Because revenue growth did not match outlay growth, the deficit rose to an average of about 3 per cent of GDP by the late 1970s. A spurt in revenues at the end of the 1970s (resulting from the automatic effect of a sharp inflation on income tax rates) temporarily kept the deficit in check. However, the 1981 reduction in tax rates and a severe recession in 1982 further dampened revenue growth while also putting more pressure on spending. As a result, the deficit grew to unprecedented levels (see Figure 3.2). By 1983, federal outlays reached 23.5 per cent of GDP, and the deficit peaked at 6 per cent of GDP. Although the deficit subsequently declined with economic expansion, it remained a source of concern and preoccupied policy-makers through to the mid-1990s.

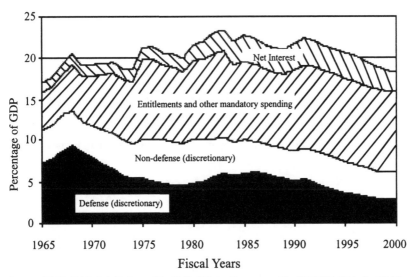

Source: OMB, Table 8.4, Budget of the United States Government for FY 2001: Historical Tables, April 2001.

Figure 3.1   Expenditures of the US Government

The budget picture changed once again in the 1990s, but this time from large deficits to large surpluses. The relatively mild recession in the early years gave way to a period of rapid economic growth, averaging 3.6 per cent a year over the decade. The strong economy fueled a rapid growth in revenues that averaged 8 per cent a year, far outstripping the growth in both GDP and spending. The overall deficit faded as the economic boom helped push revenues to 20.6 per cent of GDP in 2000, the highest percentage ever attained in peacetime, and outlays fell to 18.2 per cent of GDP, their lowest level since 1966. A surplus first emerged in 1998 and grew to 2.4 per cent of GDP in 2000. Policy-makers responded quickly to the rosy outlook by increasing spending and cutting taxes, thereby circumventing the established limits that had previously imposed budgetary restraint. By August 2001, policy actions combined with the economic slowdown pushed the projected surplus for 2001 to 1.5 per cent of GDP, lower

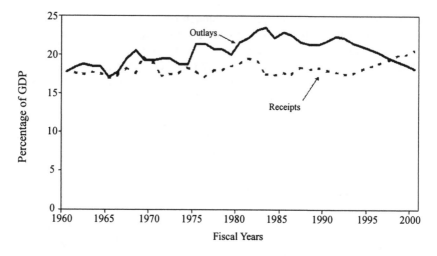

Source: OMB, Table 1.3, Budget of the United States Government for FY 2001: Historical Tables, April 2001.

Figure 3.2   Receipts and outlays of the US Government

than the 2.7 per cent projected only three months earlier but still quite high by historical standards.

By the time surpluses emerged in 1998, nearly three decades of budget deficits had helped to centralize the executive budget process in the US, making it more top-down in its orientation than it was during BOB's days. In 1974, the Congress had assumed a stronger role in the budget process, which reinforced the movement away from bottom-up budgets and toward aggregate targets. The new congressional budget process, led by congressional budget committees and supported by an independent agency – the Congressional Budget Office (CBO) – enabled the Congress to compete more effectively with the President in shaping overall budget and fiscal policy.

THE POLITICAL FRAMEWORK

The US system of government differs from many of its developed country counterparts. Most importantly, it has a presidential system characterized by equally significant but often conflicting roles for the executive and legislative branches. This division of power reflects a historical distrust of strong central government. Not surprisingly, the federal role in the US is proportionally smaller than that of the central governments of most other countries with developed economies.

The US Constitution establishes separate executive, legislative and judicial branches of government and assigns distinct roles to each. The executive and legislative branches are most involved in the budget.[3] By design, political power is diffused and shared – neither the President nor the Congress alone can exert exclusive control over the government. It takes a fairly strong consensus among policy-makers to make major changes. Although the President is the chief executive, he must first be an advocate and a negotiator if he wants his agenda to be enacted into law. While only the Congress can write a law, the law cannot take effect unless the President signs it (and administers it). By contrast, in a parliamentary system, the head of government is confident that government's policies will be enacted by the legislature. In the US, differences in institutional priorities can create as much disagreement between the legislative and executive branches as partisan disputes. Each branch jealously guards its constitutional powers – even when one political party controls both the executive and legislative branches. It is inevitable that the priorities of the legislative and executive branches will differ and that conflict will occur – particularly in an area as fundamental to government as the budget.

Under this system of checks and balances, there is substantial opportunity for conflict. If the political majorities are narrow, as is currently the case in both the House and the Senate, a few 'swing' members can exercise great influence over individual pieces of legislation. In the Senate, any member can stage a filibuster (refuse to yield the floor) and block the chamber's business. The filibuster can only be halted by a vote of three-fifths (60) of the members. When the government is divided (that is, when one party controls the executive branch and the other controls one or both houses of the Congress) the legislative process becomes even more difficult.

A popular aversion to taxes and general skepticism about Washington policy-makers impose political restraint on the US budget, contribute to its top-down orientation and indirectly help strengthen OMB's hand. Spending for all levels of government in the US in 2000 was 28 per cent of GDP (see Figure 3.3). The federal government's share is significant ($1.8 trillion, or one-fifth of GDP in 2000) but is relatively small compared with the spending of most other members of the Organization for Economic Cooperation and Development (OECD). Furthermore, the nature of federal activities differs from those of other nations. For example, health care, which is publicly funded in other countries, is largely financed by private sources in the US.[4] Federal expenditures consist largely of transfer payments to individuals, grants to state and local governments and net interest payments. Together with defence spending, those activities account for almost 84 per cent of total spending. The federal government shares the financial responsibility for many public programs with state and local governments and the private sector, which then deliver the services to the public.[5] Those activities are not exclusively federal responsibilities, however, and are frequently subject to debates about how much the federal government should contribute to them.

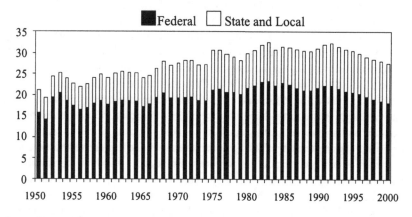

Source: OMB, Table 15.3, Budget of the United States Government for FY 2001: Historical Tables, April 2001.

Figure 3.3   Federal, state and local government expenditures in the US

OMB'S ROLE IN THE BUDGET PROCESS

The US budget has become highly prominent in the national political discourse. During the 1980s, deficits fed popular insecurity about the future of the national economy. But deficits and the prospect of rising national debt also spurred a call for action. Although they differed in their preferred remedies, elected officials first agreed on the goal of reducing the deficit and eventually embraced a target year for balancing the budget (O'Neill 2000). Recently, the annual budget process became more complicated as lawmakers considered alternative uses for projected budget surpluses. While most agreed to use part of the surpluses to pay down the national debt, some would take the opportunity to reduce tax burdens, and some would use surpluses to expand defence and domestic activities.

   In fact, the President and the Congress do not enact a single, consolidated budget into law. There are separate executive and legislative budgets. The entire process from the beginning of executive budget formulation through the close of the operating year associated with that budget takes 32 months.

US law requires the President to submit his budget proposals to the Congress no later that the first Monday in February for the upcoming fiscal year that begins 1 October. In specific, line item detail, the budget request covers over 1,000 accounts and 3,000 program activities. OMB prepares the President's budget request and directs the formulation process for the executive branch. That process begins nearly a year before the President is due to send his budget to the Congress. Typically, departments and agencies begin their internal budget processes in the spring, using the 'out-year' planning levels contained in the current budget request or other guidance provided by OMB. In September, they submit their requests to OMB. If all goes according to schedule (and it frequently does not), OMB reviews the requests and passes back revised levels in mid- to late-November. The agencies may appeal. Ultimately they can take disputes to the President. Before the budget is printed, OMB analysts review all of the numbers and finalize them in January. When the President's budget proposals are sent to the Congress, they are also released to the public. The printed budget and supporting documents for 2002 formed a 20 cm high stack of 12 volumes.[6] After the budget is printed, OMB prepares thick briefing books for White House policy officials, reviews testimony and detailed budget justifications that the agencies provide to the Congress, works with the agencies to draft legislation to implement budget proposals, and tracks the progress of the budget within the Congress. Once the President signs the various budget bills, OMB apportions the funds to departments and agencies for expenditure. Long after the budget year is under way, differences may arise within the executive branch and between the White House and the Congress over revisions to funding levels and the conditions under which appropriated funds can be spent (apportionments).

The congressional budget process begins in earnest once the Congress receives the President's budget request. The congressional budget committees have jurisdiction over the process. The Congress works from baseline projections developed by CBO which assume that current laws and policies continue unchanged and incorporate CBO's own set of economic and technical assumptions. CBO also re-estimates the President's request. Thus, CBO provides independent analyses that the Congress can use to evaluate the impact of proposals to change policies – its own as well as the President's. The budget committees hold hearings, consult with other congressional committees, draft the budget resolution and shepherd the resolution through legislative debate and votes. The resolution establishes the Congress's targets for revenues and spending and reflects its priorities. Once the House and the Senate adopt a budget resolution, it serves as a blueprint for subsequent legislation. Although the budget resolution is not submitted to the President for signature and does not become law, it exerts significant influence over legislative activity. Legislation affecting the budget must comply with the budget resolution or be subject to procedural impediments to its passage.

The congressional budget process was layered on top of the pre-existing process for enacting appropriation, authorization and tax laws. It complicated what was already a complex legislative calendar. The executive and congressional budgets compete through an intricate legislative process (see Figure 3.4) that rarely runs on schedule. At no point in the process do the President and the Congress have to agree on aggregate revenues, spending or the allocation of resources to broad categories of government activity (for example, defence, education, and transportation). The Congress has never voted to accept the President's budget as submitted as its budget resolution. While it works to the President's political advantage if the policy assumptions underlying the congressional budget resolution are consistent with his proposals, he has more leverage over separate appropriation, authorizations and tax bills. Those bills actually determine the amount of government revenue and spending and require his signature to become law. He can veto bills that he finds unacceptable.[7]

The two branches must eventually compromise – even if it means agreeing only to the bare minimum to keep government operating for another year. Otherwise government's 'non-essential' activities that depend on annual appropriations will cease operations. There are 13 appropriations laws that must be enacted to pay operating expenses and fund many programs. There may be a reconciliation bill that bundles together tax and entitlement provisions that are required to meet the targets contained in the budget resolution for revenue and spending, but entitlement programs and the tax system continue to operate in the absence of such legislation. Also, there may be other, separate bills to create or modify programs or revenue provisions.

Throughout the entire process, OMB serves only one client – the President. The OMB director serves as the President's lead negotiator and works closely with political allies in the Congress and in the agencies to advance the President's policies. OMB political officials rely heavily on the analytic work and intelligence gathered by the career staff. Within the executive branch, OMB plays the critical role of managing all aspects of the President's budget, monitoring legislative action and overseeing budget execution. It provides policy guidance to executive agencies throughout the process, coordinates the development and implementation of policy and monitors and reviews agency testimony, legislation and other materials that agencies submit to the Congress in support of their budgets. When necessary, OMB serves as the 'enforcer' to help keep agencies from straying from the President's agenda or from budget laws.

Like central budget agencies in other countries, OMB seeks to promote overall fiscal discipline, good public policy, allocation of resources in accordance with

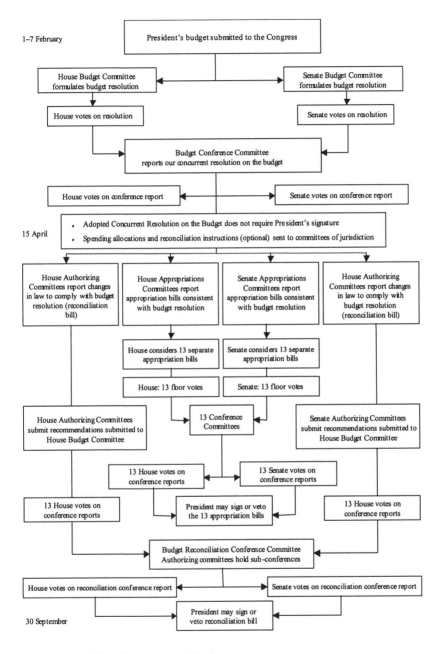

Figure 3.4   The Congressional budget process

the President's policy priorities and enacted laws, and sound financial stewardship. However, other US agencies are responsible for various economic and public finance-related activities. The Treasury is responsible for domestic financing operations, government accounts, revenue collection and payment transactions. The General Accounting Office (GAO), a congressional agency, is responsible for audit activities. A variety of organizations, including the Treasury, the Council of Economic Advisers and White House economic policy councils, provide macroeconomic advice to the President. Other than through apportionments (without which agencies cannot spend funds) and various management authorities provided by statute (which are discussed later in this chapter), OMB exerts little formal control over agencies. It is OMB's proximity to the President that establishes its political clout within the executive branch. According to Roy Ash, Director of OMB from 1973 to 1975, 'it is a fact of law and also a fact of life that the director of OMB has virtually no power and no authority except that which is assigned to him by the President to be performed as an agent of the president'.[8] Unless they are willing to take their differences to the President, agency officials will eventually acquiesce to OMB's directives, although their staffs may work informally with congressional supporters to achieve proposals that were rejected by OMB.

HISTORICAL PHASES IN US GOVERNMENT BUDGETING

The budget has assumed increasing importance as a political issue. For the first half of OMB's 30-year history (and stretching as far back as the 1930s), budget deficits or surpluses were a residual, resulting from individual decisions affecting programs and revenues. Appropriated programs made up the majority of the budget. The President's budget and congressional appropriations committees focused on allocating resources and largely ignored the impact on the government's deficit or surplus position. The consensus goal for fiscal policy was to balance the budget over the business cycle, allowing the automatic stabilizers built into the budget (such as unemployment insurance and the tax system) to cushion economic fluctuations. Even if policy-makers had wanted to set specific deficit or surplus targets, there was no mechanism to achieve them.

By the mid-1980s deficits were projected to grow to unprecedented levels for peacetime. Since then, the popular debate has reduced budget policy to a simple measure of success – the budget's bottom line. Today's lawmakers focus first on surplus or deficit amounts, and then try to make their tax and spending proposals fit. Although that approach has helped bring the budget into surplus, many budget experts believe that it has harmed the policy process by reducing the focus on the merits of specific proposals and placing undue weight on inflexible budget totals. In 1998, the goal moved from overall budget balance to balance excluding surpluses attributed to Social Security (Old-Age and Survivors Insurance and Disability Insurance) – commonly referred to as 'saving' Social Security surpluses. By fall 2001, diminishing projections of surpluses and the prospect of renewed deficits looked likely to move the goal back to the less ambitious objective of balancing the overall budget.

Paradoxically, at the same time that the budget process has become more complicated and the higher political stakes have generated greater gimmickry, it has also become more transparent and stronger. The congressional budget process, the House and Senate Budget Committees and CBO have developed into effective counterweights to the President's executive process and OMB. In addition, non-governmental watchdogs and interest groups and the national media have increased the amount of public scrutiny directed at the budget and at budget decisions.

The Centralized Executive Budget, the OMB and the Emergence of the Congressional Budget Process 1970–80

OMB and the congressional budget process were established at around the same time, but OMB's roots can be traced to the enactment of the *Budget and Accounting Act of 1921*.[9] That act marked the beginning of the movement toward a centralized budget process for the executive branch and established the Bureau of the Budget (BOB). The Congress has always controlled federal appropriations and other budget-related legislation through its power of the purse granted by the Constitution. However, the formal congressional budget process dates only to the *Congressional Budget and Impoundment Control Act of 1974* (CBICA).[10]

More than 50 years earlier, the *Budget and Accounting Act* required the President to submit a consolidated budget, thereby creating an executive budget process.[11] Until then the President had relatively little input into or control over agency requests and did not reshape agency proposals into a coordinated budget proposal. Instead the Treasury compiled agency estimates into a 'Book of Estimates' and forwarded them to the Congress. The agencies worked directly with their appropriations committees to get their budget enacted.

From 1921 to 1970, BOB became an increasingly strong instrument of the presidency. It prepared the President's budget materials and assumed progressively broader authority to review and clear legislative proposals and agency testimony. BOB was initially located in the Treasury Department. In 1939, to strengthen his control over the agencies, President Franklin D. Roosevelt established the Executive Office of the President (EXOP) and made BOB its first occupant – thereby separating budgeting from treasury functions. From the beginning, BOB did more than prepare the President's budget. It helped manage the war effort during World War II, engaged in active efforts to improve government management during the 1950s, and supported the program development activities of President Johnson's 'Great Society'. The BOB staff provided advice to the President and White House staff on the organization of the government, served as troubleshooters on management issues, organized projects to improve government-wide management and assisted agencies with various management issues. BOB was also actively involved in the following: clearing legislation drafted by executive departments for transmission to the Congress; approving information collection requirements imposed by federal agencies on the public; overseeing federal statistical programs; formulating, evaluating and reviewing of federal programs; and coordinating relations between federal and other levels of government.

In 1970, President Nixon signed an executive order that reorganized BOB into OMB. The reorganization attempted to address two of the Nixon Administration's concerns about the powerful agency it had inherited from the Johnson era: the need to reassert White House control over policy formulation; and correction of a perceived erosion in the BOB's attention to management issues in favor of its budget activities. The reorganization also provided a clear separation between the staff that assisted the President with his institutional responsibilities for government management from his personal (White House) staff that were chiefly occupied by political concerns.

The executive order transferred the statutory authority vested in BOB to the presidency, thus providing the President with direct control over agency budgets. Nixon then delegated those authorities back to OMB. The executive order also created the Domestic Council, which was composed of members of the President's Cabinet. The Council was designed to serve as the domestic counterpart to the National Security Council and to coordinate policy formulation. The Domestic Council was assigned the responsibility of formulating the President's policies: OMB was to be concerned with how to implement them. OMB was to be 'the President's principal arm for the exercise of his managerial functions'.[12]

However, responsibilities did not divide between the Domestic Council and OMB as neatly as Nixon's executive order intended. OMB could not separate policy development, program design, implementation and evaluation from its budgeting responsibilities. Nor was it able to shift its attention to management from the policies that drove the budget, especially when the budget emerged as so prominent an issue in each year's political debate.

In 1973, in an effort to increase the President's ability to manage the government, the Nixon Administration reorganized OMB again by appointing four program associate directors (PADs) – who were partisan, non-career civil servants – to oversee broad areas of programs and agencies: national security, health and human services, natural resources and general government.[13] PADs were expected to carry more political clout with agency appointees and be freer in their communications with the Congress than the OMB career staff. In those respects, the PADs improved OMB's effectiveness. There was, however, a downside. The PADs imposed a new layer between the career staff and the director, which has impeded the flow of information. Although many PADs have had substantive expertise, most did not understand budget concepts and were unfamiliar with the budget process. Moreover, the average tenure of a PAD has turned out to be about two years, leaving them with little time to learn the details of their programs, budget accounting and process, and how to make best use of their career staff.

The 1973 reorganization marks the beginning of what some observers have called the 'politicization' of OMB. The career staff of the BOB had developed a reputation for 'neutral competence', or 'a continuous, uncommitted facility at the disposal of, and for the support of, political leadership' (Heclo 1975, p. 81). Neutral competence meant that the career staff was able to maintain enough distance from the policies of any single administration to be positioned to provide their best, impartial judgment to a succession of political leaders. Neutral competence facilitated communication, promoted continuity between administrations, and kept the agency from being perceived as endorsing specific policy positions.

The changing budget environment demanded somewhat different institutional behavior. Prior to 1970 BOB spent little time negotiating with the Congress or tracking legislative action. BOB policy officials would assist the President with overall budget issues, but there were no formal budget negotiations with the Congress on the overall budget because there was no congressional budget process. Most of the budget revolved around appropriation bills, and although BOB staff worked with the agencies or congressional staff on individual issues, most of the negotiations over appropriation and authorization bills were left to the agencies. The agencies handled most of the congressional contacts – BOB did not even have a congressional liaison office until 1970.

From the beginning, however, OMB operated in a very different environment. The Congress was becoming increasingly concerned that one of its principal constitutional powers – control over the federal purse – was in serious jeopardy. Frustrated by President Nixon's increasingly frequent impoundment of funds (refusal to release them for expenditure), the Congress passed the CBICA. The CBICA significantly altered the budget process. Before 1974, the Congress dealt piecemeal with budget matters through separate appropriation, authorization, and revenue measures. Although the Congress, not the President, wrote each bill and controlled the legislative calendar, it had no formal way to manage the overall process and to coordinate fiscal policy. The CBICA created a centralized process led by budget committees in both houses, which allowed the Congress to draft its own budget plan, define its priorities and enforce its own budget as it considered legislation affecting spending and revenues.

In addition, the CBICA created CBO to provide the Congress with analytical and technical expertise that would be non-partisan and independent from executive incursions. CBO's primary responsibility is to provide the Congress with information related to the budget and the economy. CBO issues three major reports each year: its budget and economic outlook is issued in January and provides a preliminary baseline – a policy-neutral set of budget projections that extends 10 years into the future; its analysis the President's budget (issued each spring) re-estimates the budgetary impact of the President's policies using CBO's economic and technical assumptions; and its updated outlook for the budget and the economy (usually released in August) provides a revised baseline that reflects changes in economic conditions and legislation enacted since the beginning of the congressional session.[14] CBO provides the Congress with estimates of the potential impact of legislative proposals (known as bill 'scoring') on the CBO baseline. It also issues a detailed volume of budget options to illustrate the impact of various policy choices.

During the 1970s, the restructured OMB, the new congressional budget process, the congressional budget committees and CBO helped to transform the budget process from one largely directed by the executive branch into one characterized by two separate and often competing fiscal policy agendas. The budget process became more political, economic conditions deteriorated and the size of entitlement programs grew. As a result, budgeting became more difficult and contentious. Between 1970 and 1980, total spending grew from 19.3 per cent of GDP to 21.3 per cent. The share of spending for entitlements and other mandatory programs (not including interest) grew from just under 36 per cent of the budget to nearly 48 per cent and squeezed annually appropriated – or discretionary – spending down from over 61 per cent of the budget to under 47 per cent. Finally, both divided government and budget deficits emerged as the norm rather than the exception.

The Budget Enforcement Years 1980–98

As recently as 1995, deficits of 3 per cent of GDP were projected 'as far as the eye could see'. Annual deficits had averaged almost 4 per cent of GDP between 1975 and 1994. During the 1980s and much of the 1990s, policy-makers passed laws designed to help achieve the consensus goals of reducing the deficit and balancing the budget. That preoccupation with deficits or surpluses essentially has transformed the federal budget from 'means' – a way to frame and support the policy process – to 'ends' – a goal that inhibits constructive debate about policy objectives.

Beginning in the mid-1980s, the Congress and the President recognized how difficult it would be to reach agreement on the individual policy changes required to balance the budget. They instead focused on the budget process and enacted a series of measures to enforce budget discipline. They established aggregate deficit targets, spending controls and the threat of sequestration – uniform, across-the-board reductions – to meet fiscal goals (except in the case of war or economic recession). The *Balanced Budget and Emergency Deficit Control Act of 1985*[15] (also known as Gramm-Rudman-Hollings I, after its chief sponsors in the Senate) set fixed, declining deficit targets to reach budget balance in 1991. When it became obvious that the targets were unrealistic, they were revised and extended in 1987[16] (Gramm-Rudman II), then effectively abandoned with the enactment of the *Budget Enforcement Act of 1990* (BEA).[17]

The BEA proved more effective than previous efforts to enforce budget discipline. It established caps on discretionary spending and pay-as-you-go (PAYGO) rules. The PAYGO provision required offsets for changes in revenues or entitlement spending so that they would not worsen projected deficits. The spending caps and PAYGO rules were subsequently revised and extended in 1993 and 1997 and currently apply to legislation enacted through fiscal year 2002. The law provides lawmakers with flexibility: they can adjust the caps and PAYGO requirements to add funding for emergencies; and they can suspend sequestration during periods of war or recession.

OMB acquired important responsibilities under the budget enforcement laws that strengthened its influence over the budget. The laws require OMB to estimate spending levels and deficits; determine whether various enforcement targets have been breached and, if so, by how much; and to calculate how much spending needs to be sequestered to comply with the enforcement laws. More importantly, OMB is required to estimate (score) the costs of legislation throughout the process, which raises a high barrier to legislative proposals that could cause a breach in specified limits.

Because the Congress was concerned about OMB's objectivity, it also assigned parallel reporting requirements to CBO under the budget enforcement provisions. CBO's reports help improve OMB's accountability because OMB has to explain why its estimates differ from CBO's. The GAO also issues reports related to budget enforcement provisions, but they too are advisory. Because the President's sequestration order reflects OMB's estimates, in the end only OMB's estimates are binding.[18] CBO's reports, however, serve the important purpose of providing the Congress with an independent assessment of the impact of enforcement provisions. Furthermore, the Congress uses CBO's cost estimates to determine whether proposed legislation complies with the budget resolution, making CBO's numbers most relevant to the legislative process.

During the budget enforcement period, control of the White House shifted from Republican Presidents Reagan (1981–89) and Bush (senior 1989–93) to President Clinton (1993–2001) a Democrat. Those administrations represented vastly different views on the role and nature of government. Presidents Reagan and Bush favored limited government and fiscal restraint; whereas Clinton envisioned a more activist government but had promised during his campaign to cut the deficit in half within his first term.

Throughout the Reagan-Bush years OMB lived up to its reputation as the 'Abominable No Men'. The White House policy was to reduce the deficit, mostly through constraining domestic spending. Defence spending initially increased under President Reagan, but fell after the end of the Cold War. Budgeting became very intense. The shift to top-down budgeting and fast-paced negotiations between OMB, on behalf of the President, and the Congress occurred in the early Reagan years. When David Stockman, a former congressman, became OMB Director in 1981, he discovered that the agency was not organized to provide the type of support he needed to influence budget legislation. He wanted OMB to track budget numbers on a real time basis – that is, as bills were moving through the Congress. Under Stockman's leadership, OMB began developing the budget data systems needed to support a more active role in the legislative process. It began continuous tracking and analysis of appropriation bills. Personal computers and better information management systems replaced adding machines and typewriters and vastly expanded OMB's capacity to crunch numbers.

As OMB acquired the technology to respond quickly to the demands from its director for timely information, it drew upon its knowledge and 'can do' attitude to function in the new budgeting environment. Such changes, however, came at the cost of a heavier, and for many analysts a less satisfying workload. For some staff, busy days, nights and weekends were no longer confined to the traditional fall budget season. Budget program staff had less time for program analyses and spent more time crunching numbers and sending requested data to the director to support budget negotiations.

Within the executive branch, the President's budget decisions were often unpopular. Prior to 1970, executive agencies performed the job of defending and explaining the President's budget. But as deficits grew deeper and budgets became tighter, many agencies, concerned with serving their narrow constituencies, could not provide effective support for the President's policies. OMB operated from a government-wide perspective. It was able to articulate overall goals and frame arguments supportive of the President's priorities. After 1970, OMB prepared advocacy materials that the agency's policy officials used to promote the President's budget, not only within the Congress but also with the public. The number of career staff contacts with congressional staff grew in response to the demands of OMB's policy officials for information about the progress of administration proposals. Those activities provoked further criticism about the politicization of OMB from within as well as outside of the agency.

The early Clinton years were difficult for OMB. President Clinton entered the White House with a very different attitude toward government. Although he wanted to increase federal spending partially to stimulate a sluggish economy and partially to expand programs, his options were constrained by discretionary spending caps, PAYGO rules and his promise to reduce the deficit. The new administration was reluctant at first to trust OMB career staff. Many in the administration had spent years opposing OMB's budget initiatives. Clinton vowed to use the CBO baseline for his first budget, calling CBO's numbers more honest than OMB's.[19] Clinton created a new White House policy organization, the National Economic Council (NEC), composed of cabinet officials to coordinate economic decisions. He also set in motion the National Performance Review (NPR) to identify ways in which government could 'make government work better and cost less'. In its recommendations on how to 'reinvent' government, the NPR sought to decrease the amount of control central agencies, including OMB, exercised over agencies. Both the NEC and the NPR represented attempts by the Clinton Administration to strengthen cabinet participation in policy-making and reflected a desire by some to reduce OMB's influence, much like the intended role of the Domestic Council under the Nixon Administration.

However, the new OMB Director, Leon Panetta, who had been the Democratic Chairman of the House Budget Committee, and the Deputy Director, Alice Rivlin, who had been the first CBO Director, expected OMB to play an influential role in the new administration.[20] They were familiar with the role of the OMB career staff, respected their professionalism and became confident of their loyalty. However, many staff in the Clinton White House, like White House staff before them, did not appreciate OMB's responsibility for presenting objective, but often unwelcome, analyses of potential policies.

Budgeting in An Era of Surpluses 1998–2001

By the mid-1990s, a strong economy together with fiscal restraint shrank budget deficits. Surpluses, which were first achieved in 1998, grew to 2.4 per cent of GDP in 2000. Despite a softening in the economy, the CBO's updated outlook for the budget (issued in August 2001) projected that surpluses would hover around 1.5 per cent for 2001–2003, before rising gradually to 3.4 per cent in 2011 (assuming no changes to tax and spending policies and the economy continued to perform as anticipated). During fall 2001, further evidence of the slowdown in growth accumulated, and the economy absorbed a serious shock following the terrorist events of 11 September. Economists and budget experts expected that OMB and CBO would present gloomier budget outlooks in their next (January 2002) reports, but in fall 2001, remained uncertain about the depth and duration of the downturn.

In 1997, the Congress and the President enacted the *Balanced Budget Act* (BBA) and agreed to balance the budget in 2002, largely by extending the caps on discretionary spending and the PAYGO requirements. However, once the budget reached balance, those requirements largely became a formality that the Congress and President adjusted to accommodate their decisions, and there was less pressure to update or strengthen them. Informally, however, policy-makers sought to extend fiscal restraint. Even though the unified budget totals more accurately represent the government's impact on the economy, policy-makers from both parties focused on separating Social Security surpluses from the rest of the budget and successfully established balancing the non-Social Security budget as a politically significant objective.

Although the 1990 BEA had already put Social Security revenues and outlays 'off budget' – or excluded them from determinations of whether budget enforcement provisions had been met – 'saving' the Social Security surplus (or paying down the publicly-held debt by the amount of the Social Security surplus) did not become a realistic goal until the late 1990s. In 1999, the budget produced its first non-Social Security surplus since 1960. By spring 2001, the budget picture had improved so much that budget analysts projected over $3 trillion in non-Social Security surpluses for 2002–11 (and $2.6 trillion in Social Security surpluses). That prompted congressional Democrats and many Republicans to argue in favor of devoting another $400 billion over the next 10 years to retire debt. The additional amount represented the cash surpluses projected for the Medicare program that covers hospital expenses for the elderly and disabled. In August 2001, following the enactment of a $1.35 trillion tax cut and lower projections for near-term economic growth, CBO's 10-year projections of the non-Social Security surpluses had dwindled to about $850 billion, only 6 per cent of which would accrue over the next five years. Thus, even before the events of September 2001, virtually no resources were projected to remain outside of the Social Security surpluses for additional spending or revenue reductions for the next several years.

Predictably, the tone of the budget debate reflects wider economic and political conditions. Deficits imposed restraint. Surpluses released pent up demand for new spending and benefits across the budget. They also allowed President Bush (junior) and a Republican-controlled Congress to enact a major cut in income taxes. That battle was waged largely along partisan lines, demonstrating that the allocation of surpluses is as contentious as balancing the budget ever was. In fall 2001, facing decisions about the level of spending for defense, education, health insurance, the environment, and many other issues, lawmakers were struggling to meet the self-imposed restraint of saving Social Security surpluses. But following the terrorist attacks of September 2001, that goal was displaced (at least temporarily) by bipartisan efforts to address the national emergency and to mitigate the deterioration in economic conditions.

After eight years of Democratic control of the White House, the Republican Bush Administration took office in January 2001. The new President's agenda concentrates on a narrower role for government – lower taxes; stronger defense; and greater reliance on charitable, private and other non-federal organizations for services. Although it is too early to determine OMB's role in the Bush Administration, there are signs that the agency is assuming a key position. The new director, Mitchell E. Daniels, Jr., was on the White House staff in the Reagan Administration. Many of OMB's new political appointees have worked on the budget for the Congress and are familiar with OMB's capabilities.

TRANSPARENCY OF THE US BUDGET PROCESS

The budget and budget process of the US, while complex, is transparent relative to that of many other countries. US budget documents have long been available to the public. The President's budget and its appendices provide an extremely detailed accounting of federal expenditures. CBO provides independent budget analyses, including a cost estimate for every bill voted out of a congressional committee. Those estimates are freely available to the public. The combination of difficult policy choices, divided government, a formal budget process and a media eager to capitalize on the potential drama of the situation resulted in increasingly open budgeting. However, the amount of information available can be overwhelming, making it virtually impossible for most members of the Congress, the media and the general public to absorb anything but the most basic facts about the budget.

Many powerful actors inhabit the budget process. Within government, the congressional budget committees play important and highly visible roles in the legislative process. CBO serves as a counterweight to OMB's estimates and projections. GAO's Budget Issues Group provides additional support to the Congress. During the 1980s and early 1990s, non-governmental watchdog groups joined the debate.[21] Although the coverage of budget issues by national media often tends to focus on the political conflicts, the quality of reporting on some of the debate's economic and technical components has improved. The coverage focuses public attention on the subject and provides a steady stream of information. Daily 24-hour television coverage of House and Senate activities by the C-Span network provides an unvarnished view of the Congress in action for all interested citizens to see.

The US budget community remains relatively small but fluid. It is composed of individuals who, despite differences in institutional roles and political perspectives, tend to share the basic pragmatism demanded by budgeting. It is not unusual for professional staff to move between OMB and CBO, from OMB to the agencies and the budget committees, from the budget committees to OMB (typically as political appointees), and from government to non-governmental organizations and back (mostly to join congressional staffs). The budget and the budget process are complex and involve their own language and rules of behavior. Lawmakers continue to rely on gimmicks when necessary to make the numbers add up to desired totals, but a sufficient cadre of budget cognoscenti exists within and outside of the government to point out the tricks and to help keep the process reasonably open to public scrutiny.

A friendly rivalry has developed between OMB and CBO that keeps both organizations alert. The two agencies are in frequent communication and often use each other as sounding boards to work through the conceptual issues as they estimate the budgetary implications of legislation. Generally, the agencies prefer to resolve technical differences, or at least to identify them clearly. Those efforts are designed to promote accuracy and transparency, making it easier for policy-makers and the public to focus on the substantive issues instead of pricing differences. By law, CBO is prohibited from making policy recommendations and although the Congress can fire CBO's director, cut its budget and staffing and ignore its analyses, the Congress cannot mandate different findings or overrule the content of its reports. As a result, CBO is better able to articulate objective analyses. OMB career staff are often grateful for that.[22] CBO's reports help OMB career staff fend off efforts to tinker with the numbers. OMB staff know that they will have to explain major discrepancies and thus can argue that their materials will be more credible if their views and estimates are reasonably close to CBOs.

FUTURE CHALLENGES FACING OMB

OMB occupies a unique position within the US government. A quote by Constance Horner, Program Associate Director of OMB (1983–85) encapsulates how OMBers see themselves: 'To exaggerate, but not by much, they [OMB career staff] would kill for the President. Any president'.[23] OMB staff are keenly aware that the President determines the amount of influence the agency wields in any given administration. But whether OMB's power is waxing or waning, within the agency, it is considered to be 'a cardinal sin ... not to be ready when the President needs to act' (O'Neill 1988, p. 3).[24]

OMB faces many challenges, but among the most serious are finding ways to strengthen its ability to improve the government management and protecting its analytic integrity from an increasingly bitter political environment while still serving the needs of the President. OMB has faced complaints in those areas throughout its short history. The criticisms seem to reflect nostalgia for the BOB of the 1940s, to the early 1960s, when the agency was small and informal and fulfilled a wide range of management responsibilities that reflected presidential concerns. With no centralized congressional force to contend with, BOB was the 'only game in town'. OMB's budget includes 520 positions, down from its peak of 675 in the 1970s but considerably larger than BOB's 50 staff in 1939. OMB not only continues to perform many of BOB's responsibilities, but also has acquired many more duties and faces increasingly complex issues.

Strengthening OMB's Management Role

OMB's management responsibilities have always been a fundamental part of the organization. 'Old hands' of BOB and OMB like to quote Charles Dawes, the first BOB director, who described the role of the agency as follows:

> the Budget Bureau must keep humble. If it ever becomes obsessed with the idea that it has any work except to save money and improve efficiency in routine business, it will cease to be useful … we have nothing to do with policy. Much as we love the President, if Congress, in its omnipotence over appropriations, and in accordance with its authority over policy, passed a law that garbage should be put on the White House steps, it would be our regrettable duty, as a bureau, in an impartial, nonpolitical, and nonpartisan way, to advise the Executive and Congress on how the largest amount of garbage could be spread in the most inexpensive and economical manner (Timmons 1953).

Three statutory offices within OMB oversee specific governmental operations: regulations and information collection; financial management; and procurement. The statutory offices focus on improving the integrity and efficiency of federal operations. The Office of Federal Procurement Policy (OFPP) was established in 1974 to direct procurement policy. The Office of Information and Regulatory Affairs (OIRA) was authorized in the *Paperwork Reduction Act* of 1980 to monitor the burdens imposed on the public by federal regulations and information collection activities. The Office of Federal Financial Management (OFFM) was established in 1982 to coordinate efforts to improve the integrity of financial systems.

OMB defines management broadly enough to encompass everything from administrative operations to program design and performance. Budget program and management divisions have been alternately separated and combined to emphasize or to integrate those general management activities into the agency's core work. The latest configuration combines staff from separate budget program and general management divisions into resource management offices (RMOs).

OMB has been periodically criticized for devoting insufficient attention to management. Some critics fault OMB for its failure to correct problems with financial and information systems of various agencies and eliminate waste, fraud and abuse. Some accuse OMB of concentrating too much on getting the numbers to add up and making arbitrary budget decisions that purportedly deny agencies the resources they need to improve program delivery and outcomes. A few critics have gone as far as proposing to create a separate central management agency to make up for OMB's perceived neglect of management issues. To date, those proposals have been rejected as potentially creating more problems than they would solve.

Despite criticism about a lack of attention to management, OMB has always paid close attention to management issues. As is clear in the Bush Administration's management agenda for 2002 (released in August 2001), the lines between resource allocation (that is, budget) and management responsibilities are not clearly defined. The administration's new management agenda renews government-wide initiatives like competitive sourcing (identifying activities that can be performed by non-governmental entities and making them available for private bid), improving financial systems and extending electronic government (using online capabilities to enhance government's efficiency and accessibility to the public). The agenda also includes program initiatives that are policy-oriented, such as revising the manner in which states can use federal funds to broaden health insurance coverage for lower income populations and eliminating restrictions against grant awards to religiously affiliated providers of social services.

The US system has little room for managerial flexibility. The design of programs, the regulations that govern their implementation and funding levels often result from lengthy and detailed negotiations among the executive and legislative branches and outside interest groups. Programs often serve multiple objectives, not the least of which are purely political. Neither the executive nor the legislative branch can make major changes unilaterally. Program managers must follow strict procedures and detailed operating handbooks. Few political leaders, including those appointed to run the agencies, want to leave any significant matters to the discretion of program managers. OMB and the Congress both engage in micro-management to achieve their objectives. OMB has used the apportionment process to restrict when and how agencies spend resources and to force agencies to adhere to the President's policies. The Congress has inserted language in congressional reports accompanying the appropriation bills that specifies in detail how funds should be used (describing where field offices are to be located and how many staff they should employ).

OMB has only limited resources devoted exclusively to management and few control levers available with which to encourage agencies to improve their performance. Just as is the case with budgetary matters, it is OMB's proximity to the President that provides it with influence in the management arena. Given limited staff, immediate budget issues tend to take precedence over management issues because the former are always the most visible. Individual management problems, however, can become big enough to have serious implications for the budget. When they do, they receive a full measure of OMB's attention.

Protecting OMB's Institutional Integrity

Has OMB become politicized as some critics have charged? Or, has it always behaved in a political manner as BOB did before it? Given the nature of budgeting in the US, it is hard to imagine that OMB could serve the needs of the President if it stayed clear of budget politics. Today's OMB director expects to be involved in negotiations with the Congress on a wide variety of issues. To support their policy officials, the career staff in OMB have to stay informed about legislative developments and be ready to prepare the materials that argue the administration's case. But just because the agency serves a political function does not mean that its career staff members are politicized. Observers outside of OMB, who rarely have access to the agency's internal deliberations, have mistakenly associated the career staff with an administration's policy positions. And new presidents and their immediate advisors have initially mistrusted the agency and held its staff at a distance. Typically, however, relationships tend to improve within a year.

A better question is whether OMB has maintained its institutional integrity during an increasingly conflict-ridden budget process. OMB staff members have traditionally provided their best judgment to their policy officials unfiltered by political considerations. Political appointees (not career staff) are expected to make political calls. OMB directors rely on the career staff to produce neutral analyses. If OMB staff started to exercise their own political judgments, they would reduce the usefulness of the agency to the President. Politicization would also make it more difficult for OMB staff to collect the information from the agencies and from the Congress that they need to work effectively. Finally, politicization of career staff would affect the agency's ability to recruit and preserve high-quality staff. Staff would be less likely to weather transitions when the presidency changed parties if they became more invested in the policies of particular administrations. Large staff turnover between administrations would erode OMB's ability to serve as institutional memory and permanent staff to the presidency.

Within the budget community, OMB career staff members appear to have maintained their reputation for neutral competence and are respected for the quality of their analyses.[25] OMB remains an attractive employer. But those knowledgeable about the agency fear that the endless number crunching associated with top-down budgeting has displaced OMB's performance of rigorous program analyses. Observers also question whether the political pressure placed on the organization by the White House to make policies look more favorable will eventually damage the staff's neutral competence and erode its analytical capacity.

Integrating Budgeting and Management: Prospects for Performance-based Budgeting

Performance-based budgeting – aligning resources in accordance with desired outcomes for government – is not new to OMB. It is what the budget program divisions have attempted to do all along. In 1993, the Congress and the President enacted GPRA – the *Government Performance and Results Act*. Unlike earlier laws enacted to improve the management of government, GPRA attempts to tie budgeting to management. It requires agencies to set performance goals and provide quantitative measures of the results of their spending and activities. In their 2003 budget submissions, agencies are expected to link their resource requests to their objectives. Ideally agencies will provide information about the impact of their programs – that is, outcomes, not merely outputs.

GPRA assigns OMB with the responsibility for preparing a government-wide performance plan each year. In order to fulfill that requirement, OMB provides guidance to the agencies and reviews their submissions. The executive agencies, however, are responsible for identifying goals, monitoring their performance and measuring outcomes.

Although it was enacted eight years ago, GPRA has yet to change the way budget decisions are reached. The President's management agenda for 2002 calls progress toward using performance information to improve management 'discouraging' (OMB 2001, p. 27). Formulating measurable outcomes is difficult. Integrating performance goals with budget requests can be technically complicated and could require agencies to combine, aggregate or disaggregate activities within and across budget accounts. And staff responsible for drafting performance plans may have little to do with the formulation of the agency's budget. While GPRA provided a fresh opportunity to encourage the agencies to evaluate their programs, critics believe it has spawned little more than a burdensome paperwork exercise. Program sponsors and advocates, including many policy-makers, do not want information that would potentially weaken support for funding. Agencies are beginning to realize that GPRA may not lead to additional funding and, particularly in a Republican administration, may justify reductions in funding and the elimination of ineffective or under-performing programs.

Nevertheless, OMB has announced that the President's budget for 2003 will 'present the American people with the objectives the Administration seeks to achieve in the coming year and provide better information on the linkage between objectives and the matching cost' (OMB 2001, p. 30). In promising to shift resources to more effective programs from less effective ones dedicated to similar goals, OMB will have to overcome serious technical and political impediments by eliminating inefficient and under-performing activities. As OMB Director David Stockman observed almost two decades ago, it is more difficult to eliminate weak claims than weak claimants from the budget.

CONCLUSION

Although other countries reportedly are decentralizing and transferring responsibilities of their central budget office to other ministries, in the US budgetary functions remain highly centralized. OMB continues in its oversight of the budgetary, regulatory, legislative and management activities of the rest of the executive branch. Of course OMB's specific responsibilities adjust to reflect changes in the President's requirements and preferences for managing his administration, as well as developments in the budget process and budget environment. But because OMB performs functions critical to the formulation and enactment of the President's policy proposals, OMB is likely to be a key player.

The budget debate adjusts rapidly to the nation's economic and political circumstances. Budget overseers are able to exercise greater leverage within the Congress as well as in the executive branch when resources are constrained than when they appear plentiful. It was during a long period of deficits that the political consensus to balance the budget strengthened the congressional budget process, augmented the influence of congressional budget committees, and expanded OMB's ability to enforce budget limits. For the interval of January 1999 to August 2001, when projections of large budget surpluses dominated the horizon, lawmakers began to pay less attention to fiscal restraint and question the rationale for budget enforcement rules which had been designed to reduce deficits. But before new budget rules could be drafted, deteriorating economic conditions, policy changes and a dramatic shift in the government's priorities threatened to absorb near-term surpluses entirely and return the budget to deficits. It is inevitable that in the short run the budget debate will again have to face tough decisions about priorities.

Over the next few years, lawmakers likely will search for a new consensus on budget limits. With greater demands for spending for domestic security and defense, policy-makers now more than ever face the difficult task of balancing immediate priorities with longer-term requirements. Should caps on discretionary spending be extended and, if so, at what levels? Should PAYGO requirements continue? Can 'emergency needs' be defined in a way that permits necessary flexibility in fiscal discipline without creating a loophole for every demand that fails to fit under whatever normal framework is eventually created for the budget? Should new measures be adopted to keep the budget balanced at least over the business cycle? Does it make sense to promote the goal of 'saving' Social Security surpluses?

Policy-makers eventually will have to consider proposals to reform retirement and health insurance programs for older individuals. Such changes will have a significant impact on the budget and will present difficult political challenges. Proposed reforms could create technical budgeting and accounting issues that also need to be resolved. Otherwise, the consideration of complex reform proposals could be unduly influenced by how they are presented in budget documents instead of on the basis of their policy merits. On behalf of the President, OMB will be prepared to participate in all those discussions. In addition, the agency will continue to prepare the President's budget requests, monitor the performance of federal programs, coordinate the development and implementation of policies, and otherwise help support the President's policy agenda.

NOTES

1. *Report of the President's Commission on Budget Concepts*, October 1967, p. 11.
2. Federal expenditures in the United States are divided into three categories: discretionary programs include most activities related to national defense and operations of the federal government and require the enactment of annual appropriation laws; entitlement programs provide income support and health benefits to eligible individuals and are funded through permanent spending authority; and interest payments, which are also funded through permanent spending authority.
3. The judiciary becomes involved when there are questions about the constitutionality of budget procedures (for example, the Supreme Court disallowed a law that would have provided the president with a 'line item' veto).
4. In 1994, the public sector provided approximately 46 per cent of health expenditures in the United States, compared with an average of 76 per cent for other established market economies (Schieber and Maeda, 1999).
5. Federal funds represented less than 9 per cent of total spending for education below the university level in 2000 (National Centre for Education Statistics, US Department of Education, http://www.nces.ed.gov/pubs2000/2000068.pdf) and about 32 per cent of national health spending in 1999 (US Centre for Medicare and Medicaid Services, http://www.hcfa.gov/stats/nhe-oact/tables/t1.htm.).
6. The budget documents can be accessed over the Internet (www.whitehouse.gov/omb).
7. The Congress can only enact a bill without the President's signature if two-thirds of each house votes to override the veto).

8. 'Special Report: Congress and OMB', *Congressional Quarterly*, 14 September 1985, pp. 1809–18.

9. Chapter 11, Title 31 of the United States Code, originally enacted 10 June 1921.

10. *Public Law*, 12 July 1974, pp. 93–344.

11. The *Budget and Accounting Act* also established the General Accounting Office (GAO) as the official auditor and investigatory arm of the Congress. The GAO Budget Issues Group has existed in some form since 1974. It responds to requests from individual members of the Congress.

12. 'Message of the President' to the Congress of the United States accompanying Reorganization Plan No. 2 of 1970, 12 March 1970. The authors are indebted to PR Dame and B Martin's unpublished history of OMB (last updated in 1996) for its documentation of the events that shaped the organization.

13. There were five PAD areas during the Clinton Administration – the human resources, veterans and labor area was split between two PADs, one for health, veterans and personnel and one for education, income maintenance and labor. Those areas were recombined in 2001, with veterans' affairs assigned to the national security and international affairs area.

14. CBO also provides the Congress with impartial analytic work on a wide range of topics relevant to its budgetary deliberations. CBO's homepage (www.cbo.gov) provides access to studies, reports, cost estimates of proposed legislation, and other materials.

15. *Public Law,* 12 December 1985, pp. 99–177.

16. *Public Law*, 29 September 1987, pp. 100–119.

17. *Public Law*, 5 November 1990, pp. 101–508.

18. As originally enacted in December 1985, Gramm-Rudman-Hollings I required the directors of OMB and CBO to estimate independently the level of the deficit for the upcoming (budget) year and, if the deficit was projected to exceed the maximum amount allowed, to calculate how much each program would have to be reduced to eliminate any excess amount. OMB and CBO were to submit their reports to the Comptroller General of the United States, who would review the reports, then provide to the President his report on the amount that each program would need to be reduced to meet the deficit target. The President's sequestration order would reflect the Comptroller General's calculations. In its 1986 decision *Bowsher v. Synar,* the US Supreme Court found that procedure to be unconstitutional because it required the President to act on the basis of the views of an officer of the legislative branch, thereby providing the Congress with control over an executive responsibility and violating the principle of the separation of powers. The act was subsequently amended to make the roles of the CBO and Comptroller General advisory and to vest OMB with the authority for making the necessary calculations.

19. According to Director Leon Panetta, that was a political gesture to a Congress controlled by Democrats rather than an intentional slight to OMB.

20. Perspective on the Clinton years was gained from interviews with Directors Panetta and Rivlin conducted in August 2001.

21. The non-governmental groups have helped increase the understanding of budget issues by members of Congress, the media, and the public. Two non-governmental budget watchdog groups – the Centre for Budget and Policy Priorities (www.cbpp.org) and the Committee for a Responsible Federal Budget – were founded in 1981. Both are Washington D.C.-based analytic organizations committed to fiscal responsibility. The Centre is more liberal in its outlook and has expertise in federal, state and local income support programs and tax policies. The Committee specializes in budget process issues and tends to concentrate on larger issues. The Concord Coalition (www.concordcoalition.org) was founded in 1992 as a grassroots organization designed to rally voters to fiscal responsibility (deficit reduction/ surplus preservation). Other organizations focus on tax policy, including Citizens for Tax

Justice (www.ctj.org), founded in 1979, and Citizens Against Government Waste (www.cagw.org), founded in 1984.

22. For example, in 1994, CBO decided that the health alliances proposed in the Clinton legislation to reform the health care financing system were governmental entities and that the mandates imposed on employers to provide insurance coverage to their workers constituted governmental receipts. The Clinton Administration was furious, but privately many OMB career staff agreed with CBO and were happy that the technical issue, in their minds, was resolved correctly.

23. 'Budget Process Is Just Fine, Thank You', *The Wall Street Journal*, 3 September 1984.

24. Paul H. O'Neill was a career employee in BOB and OMB and became Secretary of the Treasury in 2001.

25. Based upon responses to a small, informal survey of former OMB employees and congressional staff and interviews with budget experts conducted in summer 2001.

4. Metamorphosis in Kafka's Castle: the Changing Balance of Power among the Central Budget Agencies of Canada

Joanne Kelly and Evert Lindquist[1]

The late-1990s was a period of budgetary improvisation and opportunism in Canada that both left the expenditure management system redesigned and substantially shifted the balance of power between central budget agencies. Prompted by the spectre of fiscal crisis, the Chretien Liberal government adopted a policy of expenditure restraint that moved the budget from a $42 billion deficit in 1993–94 to a $17 billion surplus in 2000–2001 (DoF 2001, p. 11). Actors responsible for imposing aggregate discipline assumed control over the instruments of budget decision-making and adapted them to best suit their objectives of expenditure restraint. Cuts to both the direct and the statutory components of government spending were achieved by undertaking concentrated expenditure cutting exercises known respectively as program and policy reviews (Aucoin and Savoie 1998; Paquet and Shepherd 1997; Swimmer 1996). In examining the legacy of this era of deficit reduction, this chapter analyses the basis of budgetary politics in Canada and in the role and capacity of different central budget agencies.

We analyse changes that have occurred in the roles and responsibilities of the central budget agencies in Canada, in budgetary politics, and in the village culture. We also discuss the future direction and prospects of the major actors within the central budget agency network both individually and as a whole. In terms of the separate budget agencies themselves, and in common with the chapters on the US and Australia, we examine the extent to which the agencies share 'bifurcated but complementary responsibilities' or behave as competitors. We analyse how the range of central budget agency functions are shared between agencies; how the agencies became active players in budgetary politics and in framing resource decisions; how the balance of power and the tools of budget management have changed over time; and how this impacts on the role of central budget agencies more broadly.

But a story of change requires a context and a point of departure; consequently, we begin with a brief history of the central budget agencies in Canada, and then discuss recent changes to the expenditure management system. Next we turn to the main argument presented in this chapter: that recent changes in the expenditure management system have accelerated a shift in the balance of power within the central budget agencies. This shift in power has impacted on the roles performed by actors within the central budget agency network and budgetary relationships between actors at the centre and within the system more broadly.

Briefly, we argue that recent changes in the broad budgetary environment and system have centralized authority in the hands of the Department of Finance (Finance) and effectively locked the Treasury Board Secretariat (TBS) and to a lesser extent the Privy Council Office (PCO) out of the budget decision-making process. As a result, TBS plays only a peripheral role in two of Schick's three core tasks of budgetary management – maintaining aggregate discipline and allocating resources. Yet ambiguity surrounds any interpretation of this shift and it remains unclear whether the budget office function inside TBS is in the throws of decline or rejuvenation. Some see the organization playing a new role in government; one that emphasizes program integrity and managerial excellence rather than financial probity and restraint. Others argue that TBS has abdicated its guardianship function and joined the ranks of claimants, thereby undermining capacity within the core executive more broadly. But this latter argument assumes that TBS once performed a guardianship role focused on the imposition of aggregate discipline.

Our research suggests this view is unsustainable. If we view TBS as one player in a complex structure of budget agencies, the shift in the focus of TBS suggests realignment within the structures and not necessarily a reduction of capacity as a whole. Further, the budgetary system in Canada is still in a state of flux: the sustainability of the current system is likely to come under increasing pressure as the budgetary environment changes, as organizations adapt to recent changes, and as some of the current budgetary instruments become unsustainable. Within this context, the roles of central budget agencies in Canada are likely to continue evolving.

THE EVOLUTION OF COMPLEXITY AMONG CANADA'S CBAs

Central budget agency arrangements in Canada are the result of a continual, but by no means linear, institutional evolution. Within this history, Finance has been a constant with primary responsibility for fiscal policy and formulating the budget

(Sterns 1965; AGC 1975; Bryce 1986; Savoie 1990). Until 1966, Finance performed all of the activities associated with the central budget office role: it produced the budget, estimates and supply legislation, performed the accountant to government roles, and developed and managed fiscal and economic policy. Finance had responsibility for advising the Minister of Finance as the individual minister responsible for economic policy and as the chair of the Treasury Board – a statutory cabinet committee established at Federation in 1867 with unquestioned responsibility for and authority over detailed expenditure management and allocation. Budgetary responsibility and power was concentrated in the single Finance department answering to a single minister. As new budget institutions were established, responsibility for performing these central budget office roles was dispersed and the unitary authority of Finance came under threat.

The creation of the TBS in 1966 as a separate department reporting to its own cabinet minister was the first, and arguably the most significant, institutional change. Based on recommendations made by the Glassco Commission (1960–63), the establishment of TBS explicitly split responsibility for the budgetary functions of economic policy and of resource management between two departments and two ministers (Benson 1966, pp. 6011–18; Glassco 1963). Finance retained responsibility for economic, fiscal, and taxation policy; TBS assumed responsibility for the expenditure side of the budget (Siegal 1982). While the Treasury Board continued to hold cabinet authority over expenditure allocation, individual ministerial responsibility for both the Board and resource allocation shifted to the President of the Treasury Board.[2]

By end of the 1970s, TBS was clearly an equal partner in the central budget network. The Secretariat had increased in size and budget and had developed a position of considerable power and influence. TBS analysts assumed responsibility for negotiating annual changes to existing programs, allocating new policy money to departments, developing and controlling government spending plans, and producing the legislation required for parliamentary appropriation and supply (Sharp 1966; White and Strick 1970). Anecdotal evidence suggests that individual program analysts held sway over departments, often dealing directly with departmental heads as supplicants, and holding the power to confer or withhold significant amounts of incremental funding through their role in formulating recommendations to the Treasury Board. An early Secretary of the Treasury Board likened his department to Kafka's Castle, with public servants performing their daily tasks in its shadow – 'obeying its rules without reason or recourse, abiding by its decision with resignation, and above all accepting its authority without question' (Johnson 1971, p. 246).

Despite sharing a focus on budget and expenditure management, Finance and TBS worked toward quite distinct mandates and gradually developed individual cultures and conventions. From its inception TBS was intended to be 'more than just a budget bureau'. When announcing the split to parliament, Prime Minister Lester Pearson repeatedly emphasized that the government intended to redefine the Treasury Board as a management board of cabinet (Pearson 1966, pp. 4874–5). This mandate was intended to extend beyond issues of economic policy and expenditure restraint, and reduce the importance of financial considerations on questions of expenditure allocation. Program analysts within TBS examined the expenditure proposals of spending departments in respect to questions of the broader policy agenda, program design and planning, and internal public sector management, not just affordability. As a result, TBS played a rationing function but its commitment to questions of expenditure discipline was always tenuous. In contrast, Finance intensified its emphasis on aggregate expenditure management and fiscal guardianship. The department focused on broad economic management, on taxation policy and on the budget bottom line with very little interest in management practices or expenditure allocation within departments.

The distinct cultures in these two organizations shaped the character of budgetary politics in Canada and the evolution of the expenditure management system more broadly. In many respects, the two departments worked toward the common goal of expenditure control. However their relationship with each other was often fractious, with PCO and the Prime Minister's Office (PMO) it was competitive, and their relationships with spending departments displayed contrasting styles and interest. While TBS negotiated directly with spending agencies, Finance negotiated with TBS. TBS was charged with issues of personnel management, program quality and service delivery. Finance was more interested in setting and then achieving economic and fiscal policy objectives.

The complexity at the core of budgetary politics was compounded by the emergence of several other central budget actors with interests in specific areas of expenditure management. Central agency responsibility for resource management within departments was complicated in 1978 by creation of the Office of the Comptroller General (OCG) with an explicit mandate to 'develop and implement sound management practices in the federal government' (Osbaldeston 1990, p. 440; OCG 1988, p. 11). Time and again, TBS and the OCG found themselves operating in a shared domain as they assumed joint responsibility for implementing management reform initiatives especially in the areas of financial management, program evaluation and parliamentary reporting. In an attempt to unify responsibility for management reform and thereby reduce overlap and potential conflict, the OCG was eventually merged with TBS in June 1993 and the Secretary of TBS assumed the additional duty of Comptroller General. Yet integration has proven difficult and many argue that the Comptrollership Branch operates as a discrete and separate identity within the TBS organization.

Power to allocate the contents of the public purse to individual departments is the most highly contested area of budget decision-making, so it is not surprising that multiple actors in both the bureaucracy and cabinet have vied for authority in this area. During the 1960s and 1970s, Pearson and Pierre Trudeau created central agencies to focus exclusively on policy coordination and resource allocation and developed an extensive cabinet committee structure to support this objective (Government of Canada 1966; 1973; Kelly 2000, pp. 65–77). Initially, the challenge to the established central budget agencies came from the creation of the Board of Economic Development (a cabinet committee) and its secretariat. Subsequently, these arrangements were replaced by two ministries of state: one for Economic Development and the other for Social Development. These ministries were incorporated into the Policy and Expenditure Management System (PEMS) until 1984, when they were both abolished (Schmitz 1989). After this time the PCO and Finance became more involved in deliberations over detailed expenditure allocation rather than broad policy decisions. To this end, each created policy divisions dedicated to policy analysis and development. Decision-making power over a wide range of expenditure management issues was formally centralized with the Prime Minister and Minister of Finance after Jean Chretien assumed leadership in 1993 (Eggleton 1995; Savoie 1999). Together the organizational and systemic changes introduced since 1968 have diminished the role and influence of TBS in resource allocation.

In contrast, the position of Finance in the sphere of aggregate expenditure management has remained largely unchallenged. Only the creation of the obscurely titled Liaison Secretariat for Macroeconomic Policy in the mid-1990s can be seen as an attempt by PCO to countervail the drift of power toward Finance. This unit originally consisted of a single, senior official hired by PCO (from Finance) who reported directly to the Clerk. The primary objective of this position is to provide advice to the Prime Minister on budget matters, independent of Finance, and as part of the PCO it now plays a key liaison role with Finance and TBS in budget formulation.

In sum, there is no single central budget agency in Canada and habitual infighting and territorial contests seem to shatter any illusions of a budgetary village. Responsibility for budgetary and public expenditure management functions is situated within a diverse group of units that cut across institutional boundaries. Together these units form a central budget agency constellation. They share a common language and spheres of interest and to that extent could be described as a budget village. Yet the units themselves are situated within individual institutions that have distinct cultures, operate toward diverse mandates and often have very different understandings of the role a central budget agency should play. Two departments – TBS and Finance – form the core of this structure but at various times as many as five other actors have been included. Sometimes actors in different agencies play complementary roles and work toward a common goal or purpose. At other times the agencies appear to be working at cross-purposes or to be in competition with one another. Institutional relations also fluctuate and there is fluidity in the composition and relative power of actors according to the arena of budgeting being observed. The interrelationship between these contending central budget agencies – Finance and in particular TBS – forms the primary focus of the remaining sections of this chapter.

THE BUDGET SYSTEM AND ROLES OF THE CBAs IN CANADA

Allen Schick characterized the traditional central budget agency as seeking to control budget decision-making by imposing highly detailed controls over line items (Schick 1997). During budget formulation, central budget actors were concerned with limiting increments to the inputs that needed to be purchased by departments to deliver their programs. Once totals were agreed, officers in the central budget agency would keep running accounts to ensure totals were not exceeded. The archetypal budget officer would studiously count beans while ignoring the effectiveness of spending on public health, the economy or defence capability. The decision-making process was bottom up rather than top down and aggregate expenditures equated to total outlays. Outlay totals were seen as tools for ensuring parliamentary accountability and probity, not instruments of fiscal or economic policy. In other words, the traditional central budget agency used detailed line item controls as mechanisms of control over both the aggregate expenditure levels and the basis of resource allocation.

Canada made a marked shift away from these traditional input based instruments in the late 1960s. Under the auspices of program budgeting the basis of parliamentary appropriations moved to outputs (programs) (Doern *et al.* 1988); the government experimented with zero-based budgeting (Gould *et al.* 1979); and in 1979 it introduced a five-year medium-term expenditure management framework (Crosbie 1979; Borins 1982). PEMS also introduced the use of formal policy reserves as a primary tool of expenditure management in Canada (DoF 1979; Doern 1979). Designed to reconcile tensions between budgeting as a tool of fiscal and economic policy and one of policy and resource management, policy reserves were intended to combine top down expenditure control with bottom up policy planning (PCO 1980). To this extent, policy reserves became a means of balancing the respective emphases of TBS and Finance, providing them with separate yet complementary roles.

Understanding the notion of reserves and the way they have evolved in Canada is crucial to explaining expenditure management and the relationship between the various central budget actors. The fundamental principles are to:

- establish an aggregate planned spending limit;
- deliberately under-allocate that total to departments;
- maintain the discipline that departments manage within their allocated totals in the absence of further policy decisions or severe and unavoidable workload increases;
- hold the difference between the total of allocated spending and total planned spending in a number of reserves; and
- use these reserves as a tool to allow policy development throughout the year and to manage the incremental spending pressures that arise.[3]

TBS and Finance operated as something of a tag-team within this system ('good cop, bad cop') sharing responsibility for controlling and allocating spending. Finance established the overall fiscal framework that set out aggregate spending levels and allocated that money across broad policy areas. Finance determined the total amount of new money available for allocation – the policy reserves – as part of this fiscal framework. The Treasury Board, supported by the program branch of TBS, was then responsible for allocating the new money to specific program areas within individual departments. Sometimes implementation of new policy decisions resulted in a new program; however, the money was more typically distributed between existing programs. Once approved by Treasury Board, these allocative decisions were reflected in the expenditure budget set out in the Main and Supplementary Estimates and accompanying documents. The fact that the Budget set out policy decisions without specifying the details of program allocation gave TBS a significant amount of discretion in recommending how and when money would be allocated. In addition, TBS had responsibility for recommending allocations from operational reserves established to deal with pressures from existing programs. This meant that program analysts within TBS assumed a new allocative significance in their negotiations with spending departments. Within this system, TBS and Finance worked cooperatively.

This created two distinctive and enduring features of the budgetary system in Canada. First, an operational distinction was made between policy and program decisions. While this distinction may seem somewhat arbitrary, it should be remembered that a system of program budgeting was introduced into Canada during the late 1960s. Within this context, the concept of a program was given a specific meaning as the basis of parliamentary appropriations or 'votes' to departments. Second, it created a deliberate difference between the intended expenditure figures included in the budget document tabled by the Minister of Finance, and the lower amounts shown in appropriation documents (or the Estimates) tabled by the President of the Treasury Board.[4] The difference in these two totals equated to the amount of unallocated money in the fiscal framework – effectively the total amount of 'reserves'.

While TBS and Finance initially dominated the processes of resource allocation, repeated attempts were made to shift power away from these two central agencies and TBS in particular. The introduction of PEMS shifted authority for deciding how to distribute policy reserves to policy committees (Kelly 2000). PEMS was intended to enable policy committees of cabinet to allocate the resources available in the policy reserves and continue developing policy throughout the year. This gave the Ministries of State for Economic Development and for Social Development (which supported the policy committees) the authority to shape the policy agenda and influence the decisions that were made. Treasury Board and its Secretariat became increasingly sidelined during this period, particularly as the policy committees made their decisions at an increasing level of program detail, removing the degree of allocative discretion that TBS had previously enjoyed (McCready 1984). As a result, TBS became relegated to a scorekeeping role intended to ensure that decisions made elsewhere were reflected in the appropriation legislation and that the relatively more technical Treasury Board requirements were satisfied (Vielleux and Savoie 1988). It also administered an operating reserve to cover workload.

In practice, the use of policy reserves under PEMS proved unsuccessful as disciplinary instruments for a number of reasons (van Loon 1981, 1983a, 1983b). There was little or no political incentive for the policy committees to rob one minister to pay for the new spending proposals of another minister. And partly as a result of the inability of policy committees to make any reallocative decisions, the size of the reserves was often too small to manage political pressures during the budget year. Special pleading to the Prime Minister or Minister of Finance for new policy funding over and above that provided by the reserves – know as 'end runs' – became common. The aggregate expenditure figure included in the budget came to be seen as a flexible estimate rather than an immutable limit.

The practice of allocating formal policy reserves was gradually abandoned as pressure mounted to rein in escalating annual deficits throughout the late 1980s. The size of the individual policy reserves was reduced, then multiple policy reserves were combined into a single reserve and removed from the ambit of the policy committees. Finally, the practice of articulating an explicit policy reserve in the budget was abandoned altogether. But the broader political-administrative culture that assumed 'in-year' incremental spending did not change and new spending pressures continued to mount. With no other distributive mechanism in place, expenditure restraint proved difficult. Some centrally directed expenditure reduction exercises were undertaken to provide funds for new policy rather reducing the deficit (TBS 1989; Mazankowski 1992). Officials in both TBS and Finance attempted to construct more rational and selective expenditure reduction options, but these generally defaulted into across the board cuts to departmental budgets (Clark 1995).

Nevertheless, the concept of under-allocation and reserves remained a central feature of Canada's approach to expenditure management. The Treasury Board managed an explicit operating reserve throughout this period (and still does) and at one stage also controlled an explicit program reserve. Though short lived, this latter reserve was intended to manage minor policy issues that would have fallen in a gap between policy decision-making and requests for operating reserve allocations. Even when the program reserve was abolished, TBS continued to negotiate with Finance for similar allocations that were made as part of the process of budget formulation – what came to be referred to as the 'irritants' process. For its part, Finance continued to establish an informal or hidden reserve within the fiscal framework, meaning that the planned spending declared in the budget was greater than the total actual allocations. This was designed to facilitate some degree of aggregate discipline in the absence of any other effective mechanism to neutralize pressure for new spending between budgets. In doing so, Finance sowed the seeds of what has now evolved into 'prudent budgeting'.

'PRUDENT BUDGETING' COMES TO OTTAWA

In a climate of intense public concern over deficit budgets and government spending, the election of the Liberal government in November 1993 under Prime Minister Jean Chretien heralded a cultural change toward sound financial management (Greenspon and Wilson-Smith 1996; Martin 1994). The new Minister of Finance, Paul Martin, tied his own political legitimacy to deficit reduction. One attendee at Martin's first meeting with senior officials in Finance recalls the following statement being made:

> ... he said 'I am not going to go out five years. You guys (Finance) can't even predict next year, why do I want to hang my hat on what you are going to say five years from now? Because it is my butt that is in the wringer on this, not yours. It's my public credibility. I don't want to be known as the Finance Minister who always overshot his targets like the other ones'.

The five-year expenditure plans were replaced by two-year rolling deficit targets, which later became a commitment to balanced budgets. Officials in

Finance knew these deficit targets were to be achieved 'come hell or high water'. In response, Finance with the varying degrees of support from the other central agencies established three mechanisms to achieve these targets.

First, 'prudent budgeting' changed the process of calculating aggregate expenditure and revenue figures in the budget. Instead of using economic assumptions developed internally, Finance turned to leading private sector economists for their predictions of economic growth, unemployment levels, inflation rates and so forth. It adopted the average of these figures, built in a prudence factor, and then used this as the basis for its budgetary forecasts. A contingency reserve of $3 billion was then added to aggregate expenditure. Initially, this prudence factor was not explicitly disclosed whereas the contingency reserve was.[5] The latter reserve has been consistently used to guard against the impact of adverse changes in the economic climate and, if not required, is committed to debt reduction and not available for additional spending or tax reduction.[6] Finance continues to build less explicit prudence factors into forecasts of aggregate program expenditure, although the impact of these calculations is difficult to identify. The effect of 'prudent budgeting' was to inflate spending figures (assuming a worst case scenario for both statutory spending levels and public debt interest repayments) and reduce expected revenues. The amount of prudence built into economic forecasts was essentially an informal policy reserve.

Second, the Program Review exercise undertaken in 1994 was designed to eliminate the annual budget deficit by allowing the government to achieve targeted and permanent expenditure cuts to the spending base of departments (Aucoin and Savoie 1998; Lindquist 1996). This exercise required a substantial shift in the budgetary role of central and line agencies. Central agencies played two important roles in this process: they set the fiscal targets with an eye to aggregate discipline and then played a challenge role during negotiations over the allocation of cuts. Finance calculated the total expenditure reduction needed to achieve its deficit targets and then set individual savings targets for each department. Line agencies were made responsible for achieving these savings targets by reviewing their program base in accordance with a set of 'getting government right' policy guidelines. Both Finance and TBS undertook concurrent program reviews from a government-wide perspective. Program sector analysts in TBS developed 'TBS Perspectives' (with an eye to performing a challenge function throughout the process) and these documents were shared with officials in relevant spending departments.[7] Policy branch officers of Finance also reviewed various departmental programs but kept their findings and recommendations much closer to their chests. Spending departments were unlikely to find out the content of these Finance papers and there was little (if any) negotiation between departmental program officers and Finance. Once the initial reviews were completed, the responsible line minister presented a report on how the department would achieve its cuts to the program review of cabinet. The committee based its final decisions on both the ministerial presentations and recommendations in the reports by TBS and Finance.[8]

Third, the aggregate savings targets that underpinned Program Review were explicitly higher than required to achieve the deficit reduction targets. These additional savings were used to provide incremental funding for new spending priorities during the next two budget rounds. This ability to deal with policy pressures during budget formulation and throughout the budget year was in itself a key factor in maintaining aggregate discipline. It allowed Finance to achieve its deficit targets without having to restrict the spending impulses of most cabinet ministers.

Together these three mechanisms provided the basis for successful deficit reduction to occur because they addressed questions of policy and politics. The moral imperative created by fiscal crisis enabled Finance to introduce these tools but, as we argue below, introducing these tools provided a more permanent shift in budgetary politics that further empowered Finance.

THE IMPACT OF 'PRUDENT BUDGETING' ON THE ROLES OF FINANCE AND TBS

The advent of 'prudent budgeting' and subsequent adaptations to the expenditure management system has shifted the relative roles and influence of the three central budget agencies. On the one hand, Finance has consolidated its control over aggregate expenditures and expanded its influence over allocating resources during budget formulation and throughout the budget year. In stark contrast, the extent to which TBS and PCO influence decisions on resource allocation has shown a marked decline. Today, however, there is arguably a broader shared understanding of the strategic direction of the government at the ministerial and deputy ministerial levels (Lindquist 2001). Changes to the expenditure management system introduced under Chretien have reinforced the accretion of power in Finance and PMO, gradually weakening the formal budget decision-making system. As a result, the central budget agencies have become increasingly competitive with one another: PCO and TBS have proposed strategies designed to increase their role in budget decision-making; while Finance has sought to retain its authority by blocking these new strategies. In particular, TBS is engaged in a process of internal redefinition that has the potential to change fundamentally the roles it performs in resource management and budget decision-making. How this redefinition process will affect its budgetary functions remains a point of contention that will be discussed later in the chapter.

Finance has used two primary levers to consolidate its power and authority: its ability to move unilaterally in many areas related to its responsibilities; and its power to control the timing and extent to which fiscal framework information is made available. Using its capacity to move unilaterally, Finance has consolidated its control over aggregate spending and expanded into resource allocation. Finance was able to change the basis upon which budget figures were calculated and reduce the extent to which overly optimistic economic assumptions meant budget objectives were not achieved. Similarly, Finance was under no obligation to consult other agencies when moving from five-year fiscal plans to two-year deficit targets or when setting expenditure targets and limits that enabled the minister to achieve these stated policy objectives. Nor did Finance consult when, under Program Review, it moved from a bottom up to top down process for determining aggregate program spending levels, despite initially usurping the authority of TBS. Traditionally, Finance received figures on total departmental spending from TBS and incorporated them as a given into the economic plans. Under Program Review, Finance set out desired departmental spending levels that accorded with the fiscal plan and then charged the rest of the system with achieving those targets. However, this latter change was short-lived and Finance quickly returned the responsibility for calculating departmental spending levels to TBS.

The decision by Finance not to bring down a Budget as expected in February 2001 provides a vivid illustration of the capacity of Finance to act unilaterally to expand its influence in resource allocation. One major consequence is that the usual deadlines for budget development were absent, relieving Finance of any requirement to disclose information on the amount of additional funding available for allocation. In the absence of a formal Budget, any semblance of an inclusive or coordinated resource allocation system disappeared. This has been replaced by an *ad seriatim* string of individual expenditure decisions ('in-year') that are typically negotiated between Finance and line agencies.

Finance exercises its ability to control fiscal information in two quite different time frames: during budget formulation, and in between budgets. Budget formulation is generally preceded by a consolidated priority-setting process in which full cabinet meets to debate overall priorities and the two policy committees then use the result as a framework for making recommendations on specific policy proposals. In recent years, however, it appears that the influence of both cabinet and the policy committees has waned. While full cabinet retreats still take place, their significance in establishing an effective policy framework appears to be diminishing. Recent changes to the formal expenditure management system articulate that cabinet and committee recommendations constitute advice to the Prime Minister and Minister of Finance who retain final authority over budget decisions (PCO 1998).

Consequently, the policy committees have no deliberative authority in resource allocation.

In addition, no information on the amount of money available to fund new policy is given to policy committees, and therefore policy deliberations occur without either pressures for restraint or pressure to arrive at compromises between policy options. New policy proposals can now be presented to policy committee without identifying a source of funding – so-called 'unfunded Memorandum to Cabinet'. This reform was initially introduced to stop Finance blocking policy initiatives being presented to policy committees by refusing to identify a source of funds. In practice, however, the reform compounded the lack of discipline within the formal expenditure management system. Policy committees have no incentive to reject any policy proposal or to consider the resource implications of their decisions. Policy deliberations are unencumbered by expenditure constraint or any knowledge of the amount of fiscal flexibility that may (or may not) exist. Ministers know under 'prudent budgeting' and an expanding economy, there will always be a significant amount of fiscal flexibility available (the prudence factor) for Finance to release as it develops a new fiscal framework for the coming year.[9] The net result is a stream of 'approvals in principle' which may or may not receive funding. These do not necessarily undermine aggregate discipline, but nor do they constitute an effective instrument of policy prioritization or resource allocation.

Within this context, the 1999 Speech from the Throne can be seen as a deliberate move to pre-empt allocation decisions by Finance in the budget. This speech was unusually 'budget-like' in its degree of expenditure detail. The speech came before the budget and therefore proved an effective means for PCO and PMO to overcome the timing advantage that Finance otherwise enjoys in controlling the budget formulation process by making a pre-emptive claim on fiscal flexibility that the Minister of Finance has no choice but to fund.

Between budgets, Finance has the additional advantage that there is no budget-tabling deadline to force a decision-making timetable. During the budget year, a number of factors will indicate to Finance whether additional money is available. These include: if it becomes clear that the full amount of the prudence factor is no longer necessary; if actual revenues within the current year exceed forecasts; and if forecasts for statutory spending within the current year prove too high. These resources are allocated via an informal process of bilateral negotiations between the Minister of Finance and either the Prime Minister or a spending minister.

Here again, the timing is almost totally under the control of Finance and there is rarely an official statement that additional funds are available in the system. The ability of Finance to control these 'in-year' allocative decisions is increased by the fact that the funds available are predominantly time limited rather than ongoing and must be spent within the current budget year. This renders the money useless to most departments who have little capacity to usefully spend significant amounts of money if it is received late in the fiscal year. The result has been a rash of 'foundations' – non-government entities created to receive and invest large blocks of funds, and to manage disbursements over a number of years. More recently and perhaps in light of criticism from the Auditor-General over the accounting practice by which funds paid to foundations are charged to a single budget year, such flexibility has been used predominantly to pay down the debt.

As a consequence, the role of TBS in approving the *status quo* expenditure levels has been reduced to a technical exercise involving little more than mere addition. The mechanism for determining baseline expenditures for ongoing departmental spending is referred to as the Annual Reference Level Update (ARLU) exercise. This is used to calculate the level of departmental spending in individual departments and forms the basis for the aggregate expenditure totals from which Finance constructs the fiscal framework. There is, by explicit design, no attempt to use ARLU to review or alter existing spending allocations or to impose any discipline on known or emerging pressures on existing programs.

EFFECTING A METAMORPHOSIS IN TBS

Within this context, it is hardly surprising that TBS finds itself in a state of transition. The capacity of TBS to play its traditional role in resource allocation has been weakened by a number of factors apart from the expansion of Finance. First, policy decisions have tended to become narrower (more specific and detailed) leaving significantly less scope for the Treasury Board to make any material program decisions in allocating the related funds to departments. The current result is that most policy decisions are rubber stamped by the Treasury Board with its role relegated to providing technical approvals such as those for terms and conditions that apply to contribution programs, or setting future requirements for evaluation reports. Second, policy decisions have increasingly come to be seen as the allocation of a block of funds to a department for which the department then becomes responsible for deploying in the most effective way to achieve the policy objectives that underpin the approval. As a result, there are few requirements for policy proposals to be costed in detail either as they are being developed or when considered by policy committees. This has significantly lowered the demand for costing analysis and challenged the natural role for TBS. Third, the increasing power of Finance described above has the incidental effect that its analysts tend to deal more directly with departmental detail than in the past, even if on a selective basis. And, as a direct consequence, these analysts develop views on program detail that better positions them to influence their inclusion in the final allocation decision.

As a result, TBS is seeking to redefine its role as a central agency based on the 'management board' concept (TBS 2000). Throughout the 1980s and 1990s, departments became increasingly critical of TBS, considering it too control-oriented and therefore impeding rather than facilitating management improvement (Clark 1995). And while Canada led the field in moving away from input based budgeting, it has been much slower to pick up on other aspects of the new public management (NPM) movement. When coupled with the appointment of successive secretaries with an interest in managerial reform, it is not surprising that the department is seeking to breathe life into the 'management board' concept.

The notion of TBS as a management board for government is not new. It was used by the Glassco Commission that was instrumental in the creation of TBS in 1966 and repeated in the report of the Lambert Commission in 1979 (Glassco 1963; Mallory 1979). While often referred to within TBS, the mantle was not adopted in any meaningful or tangible way until recently. In 1997, the Prime Minister announced in a press release that the Treasury Board was to become the management board of government. Since that time, there have been repeated efforts within the organization to clarify what it means to be a management board (Potter 2000). Without this more operational definition, the concept cannot be used to provide a unified vision or to concentrate the management reform agenda within TBS.

Despite continued debate over the meaning of a 'management board', the increased emphasis on managerial issues within TBS has been reflected in the changing organizational structure and the allocation of financial and human resources (Clark 1995; Lindquist 1996). Most recently, the unity within the organizational units that made up the core budget office within TBS was diminished when the program branch was disbanded in August 1996. Instead of a single branch headed by a deputy secretary, there are now four individual program sectors reporting directly to the secretary as independent organizations. The expenditure management sector, which acted as the guardian within the program branch, was radically reduced in size and scope, and given the added responsibility for integrating the management board concept throughout the department. At the same time the comptrollership branch assumed some of the expenditure management functions performed by the expenditure management sector, adding to the diffusion of the central budget agency functions. On the other hand, the service delivery components within TBS have grown rapidly. The human resource management branch – effectively the personnel officer to government – constitutes almost one third of the TBS operating budget. Two other service-based sectors have also grown in recent years – the chief information officer branch was created in 1997 to address the Y2K problem but was then retained to take a lead in developing and managing the implementation of the government's on-line initiative; and the service and innovation sector grew from a three-person group within the old expenditure management sector into a sector with eight units. Together these sectors constitute almost 40 per cent of TBS's operating budget.

TBS has also attempted to move away from using control instruments designed to ensure compliance and probity to allow more managerial flexibility – to let managers manage. Throughout the 1990s, it gradually relaxed detailed controls over departmental operating budgets allowing carry-over provisions and greater freedom to allocate funding according to operational requirements. Government-wide (or horizontal) mechanisms have been developed and promoted by TBS in an effort to enhance the efficiency of resource usage within departments. These include the comptrollership modernization initiative, pilot studies for single window service delivery, government on-line, and redevelopment of the financial information systems (FIS). The latter initiative consolidated innumerable different financial systems into seven clusters and facilitated the introduction of accrual accounting. More recently, TBS became involved in the 'modernizing human resources initiative' aimed both at developing non-legislative proposals and examining the government's human resources legislative platform.

New tools of accountability are being developed so that TBS can become aware of management issues in departments and to help departments manage their programs and resources more effectively. This is primarily the responsibility of the comptrollership branch under its policy responsibilities for internal audit, program evaluation and results based management. The responsibility for implementing the active monitoring policy, an initiative signalled in *Results for Canadians* in direct reaction to the crisis that enveloped the Department of Human Resources Development, has been given to the expenditure and management strategies sector.[10]

But significant issues underlie many of the initiatives that TBS is pursuing on the management board front. At present TBS is attempting to convince departments to adopt numerous management improvement initiatives largely reflective of the NPM agenda. Typically, TBS has relied on exhortation and persuasion as its primary tools in bringing about management change. Yet, it is unclear how effective these tools will be if the plethora of extant Treasury Board policy directives remains unchecked. In some instances (for example, the comptrollership modernization and the government on-line initiatives), TBS has offered financial inducements to encourage management change. Specific sectors within TBS took control over a special purpose fund that was then allocated to departments in support of the initiative. While a successful mechanism for bringing departments to the table on these initiatives, this practice is likely to create a situation where TBS is required to claim additional funding on behalf of its target departments. Further, TBS continues to wrestle with balancing its 'kinder, gentler' approach with the need to take unpopular corrective action when there are clear indications of significant management deficiencies in certain departmental programs (Clark 1995, p. 246). TBS will require more than exhortation and persuasion to achieve its objectives: it is likely to be unpopular with line departments and will require significant policy support from the Prime Minister as well as members of the Treasury Board.

TBS is also attempting to use the management board concept to reconstruct its role as a central player in the budget decision-making process. While TBS may appear to be a shadow of its former expenditure management self, it would be premature to perform the last rites. Senior TBS staff advise the President of the Treasury Board on issues to be discussed in policy committees and attend those committee meetings. They provide information that enables Treasury Board ministers to discuss whether existing programs are adequately funded and if not, the implications of inaction. In addition, TBS is working with PCO and Finance in an effort to develop new processes that facilitate reallocation within departments. Perversely, the President has become a lone voice of expenditure restraint at the policy committee table as the Minister of Finance rarely, if ever, attends. The President has a thankless task in delivering a repetitive message of restraint as the Board discusses MC after MC in a process unbounded by any expenditure constraint. A conflict of interest is also beginning to arise due to the fact that the current responsibilities of TBS include those of a policy proponent (thus both claimant and spender) for three major policy initiatives with potentially large bills attached (namely, government on-line, human resource modernization and official languages).

More recently, TBS attempted to broaden budgetary debates to include consideration of whether additional funding should be allocated to support ongoing programs, not just to new initiatives. 'Program Integrity', as the initiative was called, had the objective of increasing the relevance of TBS in an area where there were real issues to be addressed – the management of political and program risks in areas where departmental capacity to deliver expected program results was in doubt. Program Integrity was intended to be an enduring and long-term initiative that would focus on the alignment of existing programs with current government priorities and the need for reallocation, more than on the need for incremental program funding. But the deliberate focus of the initiative in its first year was on the need for incremental funding as the government moved from the legacy of Program Review and deficit reduction into surplus budgeting. In response, Finance began to depict TBS as a claimant on the budget and used its power of the purse to portray the recommendations by TBS as unaffordable. In doing so, Finance undermined the objectives of the initiative and eventually killed it. Whether this response by Finance was an effort to retain its new-found dominance of the budget process or due to a lack of understanding is debatable. Either way, Finance has effectively blocked reform in this area.

In sum, the position of TBS as a CBA continues to evolve and many questions still need to be addressed. The rise to predominance of Finance has limited the ability of TBS to influence matters of resource allocation. The management board mantra has become widespread within Treasury Board, yet each grouping interprets the concept differently and adopts a distinct approach to promoting management improvement. This has led to a new round of criticism from departments that TBS has no coordinated management agenda and is overburdening departments with its initiatives. More recently, TBS issued *Results for Canadians*, a publication that sets out a broad management framework within which TBS will operate (TBS 2000). But more work is needed before this framework can be said to be operational, and more fundamental questions need to be addressed about the nature of the organization that TBS wants to become. In particular, one critical dimension along which tensions need to be addressed is the current uncomfortable juxtaposition of central budget agency functions and the more operational, service delivery and policy-oriented roles that underpin the direction other parts of TBS are undertaking. Should TBS attempt to regain some part of its previous role in aggregate expenditure control and resource allocation? Did it, in fact, ever play the former role? Are these more traditional expenditure management roles, which require tough and contentious decisions to be made about resource allocation and reallocation, compatible with a management improvement agenda rooted in facilitation, persuasion and policy leadership? Is a material operational role in service and policy delivery compatible with the notion of a central agency, even one focused on management improvement? More fundamentally, does TBS have sufficient capacity to carry out any of the functions in a sustained and convincing manner?

CONCLUSIONS AND FUTURE DIRECTIONS

Much of the experience in Canada lends support to Schick's argument that 'the central budget agency within the nation state is now confronted by significant pressures to change the way they behave and operate as budget related agencies'. This is perhaps not surprising given that Canada operates within an international environment shared by other countries in this study and therefore many of the broad trends observed globally are evident (Wanna and Kelly 1998). For example, the management reform agenda has been picked up by TBS, detailed line item controls have been discontinued, and medium-term expenditure frameworks have been used since 1979.

Yet once the changes are explored in greater detail the experience of Canada does not always fit with the broader trend. First, the factors usually seen as a primary impetus for reform are absent. The relative proportions of statutory and departmental expenditures have remained fairly stable since 1976. While some of the elements that make up the NPM agenda are evident in Canada (purchaser-provider split, accrual accounting), they are nowhere near as pervasive as in other Westminster countries. Second, the direction of change in expenditure management and its implication for budgetary politics and the CBA functions appear to differ from those suggested in recent writings. On the one hand, many of the tools that Schick associates with a new budget agency had been introduced in Canada from the late-1970s. On the other, budget decision-making remains highly centralized and there is little evidence of a shift toward more strategic mechanisms for expenditure allocation (Schick 1997; Pradhan and Campos 1996).

Time and again, the evidence suggests that the split in budgetary responsibilities has shaped, and continues to shape, both the willingness and capacity to redefine the CBA role. The initial balance of roles and responsibilities of actors between central budget actors has been undermined by recent changes in the broad budgetary environment and system. This has centralized power in the hands of Finance and effectively locked TBS out of decision-making process. As a result, TBS plays only a peripheral role in maintaining aggregate discipline and allocating resources.

The resultant vacuum within TBS has seen the organization focus on its management agenda, assuming a role of claimant in contrast to Finance's guardian role. This suggests an institutional 'identity crisis' somewhat different to that conceived by Schick. The shift toward managerial issues within TBS has produced internal tensions within the department that weaken – some argue undermine – the capacity of TBS to operate as a central player in the budget decision-making process. At another level, the relationship between TBS and Finance has shielded the latter from dealing with the programmatic implications of the tools used to impose expenditure restraint, and therefore from the most intense pressures to change. As Finance controls most areas of budget decision-making, this situation reduces the extent to which control of the public purse can be used to lever management reform.

Yet, when we look at all of these changes in the relative power of Canada's CBAs, it is apparent that the Canadian budgetary system remains highly traditional in many respects. There is little evidence that responsibility for detailed resource allocation has been devolved from central to line agencies, or that the more powerful CBA (Finance) is adopting a more hands off approach. Indeed, the opposite appears to be true. Budgeting today is continual, linear and highly centralized. The expenditure management system is in a state of continual adaptation and hence there are few opportunities to develop the culture of trust and certainty upon which most modern budgetary systems are based. Further, there are few opportunities where funding options can be compared with one another, or where the trade-offs inherent in all public resourcing decisions can be debated or recognized. The systems that once made Canada a world innovator in the area of public expenditure management, have all but been abandoned in the pursuit of deficit reduction.

The future direction of CBAs in Canada is difficult to predict. Certainly the current situation remains in a state of flux. The existing expenditure management system is largely a creature of the current political and economic environment. Despite some indications that ministers in cabinet are frustrated by their apparent lack of influence, any attempt to change the system is unlikely to succeed without a change in leadership or an economic crisis. More practically, there appear to be increasing demands for an expenditure management system that reduces incremental pressures on program spending and extends the purview of budget decision-making to include expenditure for ongoing programs. The events of 11 September 2001 and the resultant economic and security crises heightened these demands. The degree to which any subsequent changes will affect the relationship between the CBAs or merely consolidate the existing arrangements is contentious. Finance still dominates the current expenditure management system; it is unlikely to release this power without a fight. TBS has come to a fork in the road of its development as a CBA; it could either work to re-emphasize its role as a CBA, abandon this responsibility in favour of becoming a management service delivery agency, or continue in its attempt to balance the two roles. The dispersion of roles across Canada's CBAs places definite limits on the ability of TBS to redefine its role unilaterally and any substantial change in the expenditure management system will require prime ministerial attention to cut the Gordian knot (Lindquist 1996). Nevertheless, the impetus for change appears to be mounting as economic and security policy pressures increase the need for expenditure re-allocation within a disciplined fiscal framework. Taken together, these factors suggest that we are likely to witness further metamorphosis in the roles of CBAs in Canada.

NOTES

1.   The authors wish to recognize and thank Mike Joyce, Assistant Secretary, Treasury Board Secretariat for his significant contribution to this chapter. However, the opinions expressed and conclusions drawn are those of the authors unless otherwise stated.

2. The Minister of Finance remained an ex officio member of the Treasury Board but, at least in recent times, incumbents have established a practice of rarely, if ever, attending.
3. Generally speaking, the reserves used fall into either of two broad categories: policy reserves that enable the government to initiate a limited amount of new policy spending between budgets; and operating reserves that enable additional funds to be allocated to deal with unavoidable workload pressures that emerge in existing programs. Reserves established within each of these categories have varied both in number and objective. Not all reserves are either explicit or visible outside the central agency network and neither are some visible outside Finance.
4. The distinction between 'the budget' and 'the estimates' is a fundamental feature of the Canadian system. Put simply, additional spending for new policy is described (in words) in the annual Budget Speech as in most countries. The President of the Treasury Board tables the Main Estimates (including the appropriation bills) a few days later, but these do not incorporate all new expenditure announced in the budget. For a new policy to be included in the estimates legislative provisions it must be approved by Parliament. Once this occurs the process of updating the Estimates (via supplementary appropriations) is a largely technical exercise carried on between the Treasury Board Secretariat and individual departments. Consequently, there is no debate about whether the budget estimates are 'accurate' in Canada. By definition the estimates are always accurate – the most recent budget estimates indicate precisely how much money parliament has been asked to provide.
5. There have been changes in the way prudent budgeting operates. In the first two-year fiscal plan, the contingency reserve was set at $2.5 billion for 1994–95 and $3.0 billion for 1995–96. In subsequent plans it was set at $3.0 billion for each year. In 1999, the 'prudence factor' was established as a separate figure in the budget documents rather than being built into the economic assumptions fed into the econometric models of Finance.
6. As stated in the Budget Plan 2000–2001, the $3 billion contingency reserve 'is used primarily to cover risks arising from unavoidable inaccuracies in the models used to translate economic assumptions into detailed fiscal forecasts and unpredictable events. It also provides an extra measure of backup against adverse errors in the economic forecasts. It is not a source of funding for new policy initiatives. If not needed, it will be used to pay down the public debt' (Department of Finance 2000).
7. These documents identified opportunities for savings; alternative delivery opportunities; the public interest component of programs; the legitimacy of the federal role; scope for partnership with the private sector; and opportunities for cost recovery/user fees (Lane 1995, p. 5).
8. Discussions in this ministerial committee and the 'shadow' committee of deputy ministers focuses on identifying the program changes needed to implement the savings targets assigned by Finance rather than on the targets themselves. While some departments did attempt to have their targets reduced, few changes were successful. One reason this discipline held was the widespread acceptance that the aggregate expenditure reduction targets established by Finance were legitimate and this meant that a reduction in the target of one ministry would simply add to that of others.
9. Finance's prudence factors are effectively an expression of economic risk and thus the amount of the prudence factor increases in each successive year of its forecasts, representing the increased uncertainty the further out in time those forecasts are made. For example, in its October 2000 Fiscal Update, the prudence factors were set at $1 billion for the current fiscal year 2000–2001 and $2 billion for 2001–2002.
10. The Expenditure and Management Strategies Sector is the successor to the old expenditure management sector referred to at the beginning of this section. Making this sector directly responsible for strategic planning and the implementation of major management focused initiatives is a further indication of the current desire to blend expenditure management with broader management functions.

5. Control through Negotiated Agreements: the Changing Role of the Treasury in Controlling Public Expenditure in Britain

Richard Parry and Nicholas Deakin

For decade after decade, the United Kingdom Treasury (Her Majesty's Treasury, headed by the Chancellor of the Exchequer) has remained an object of fascination for political observers and academic commentators. It is a central budget agency but also much more – an elite corps, a keeper of secrets, a repository of techniques, a way of thinking about the purpose of public policy. Its central place in the British core executive has resisted all challenges, and its mystique has given it an international influence not accorded to most central budget agencies.

We have been fortunate to be able to observe recent developments in the Treasury's organization and strategy.[1] Our own interview access to the Treasury ran from 1995 to 1998. Since our book was published (Deakin and Parry 2000), the main lines of Treasury policy and organization have not changed: Gordon Brown remains Chancellor of the Exchequer and Sir Andrew Turnbull Permanent Secretary, and expenditure is determined by a mixture of one-year and three-year allocations. Devolution within the UK (the revival of the Scottish Parliament and creation of the National Assembly for Wales) has not much affected the scope of the Treasury's responsibilities as a previous system of formula-based block funding to Scotland and Wales has been carried forward.

Recent research on the Treasury has been much aided by the extensive evidence assembled by the House of Commons Treasury Select Committee for its report on HM Treasury, published in February 2001. Most academic commentators on the Treasury submitted evidence to the Committee, and part of our own is reproduced at the end of this chapter as an appendix. This sets out the view we have been promoting during the course of our research that the Treasury's dominance is inevitable and that the best strategy would be to educate it and reinforce it rather than create institutional counterweights to it. This remains a minority view, and the debate continues to be cast in its traditional form of the Treasury's defending itself and nearly everyone else wishing to constrain it. The first memoir of a Labour Treasury minister (Geoffrey Robinson's *An Unconventional Minister* 2000) has now been published, and there is a fascination in journalistic and semi-academic writing with the presumed jealous conflict between Gordon Brown and Prime Minister Tony Blair. A best-selling account by a journalist with good access to Blair's thinking (Rawnsley 2000) was republished in 2001 with additional information suggesting that Blair had come near to moving Brown from the Treasury after the 2001 election. A prominent political broadcaster then wrote an entire book on the rivalry drawing on many unattributable sources but not on the two protagonists (Naughtie 2001). All this political noise calls for a longer perspective, which this chapter seeks to provide within the four themes of the book: changing roles and responsibilities over the past 10–15 years (in the Treasury's case relatively unchanging); re-negotiating the politics of the budget process (in which there have been major changes); changing village cultures (in which the Treasury has tried to re-invent itself culturally); and future prospects and directions (in which we conclude that the political relations between Prime Minister and Chancellor is the key variable).

CHANGING ROLES AND RESPONSIBILITIES OF THE BRITISH TREASURY

The British Treasury is the prototypical combined or unified central budget agency, because of its concentration of responsibility for economic policy, fiscal strategy and public service delivery. It is also a monopolist of information, with no parliamentary rival playing a role equivalent to that of the US Congressional Budget Office. The Treasury has not seen any major attack on its functions since the Department of Economic Affairs (1964–69). One fringe responsibility acquired was that of civil service pay gained in 1981 but lost in 1995. However, the decision in 1997 to transfer power to set interest rates from a joint decision of the Treasury and the Bank of England to an independent Monetary Policy Committee of the Bank of England (operating with an inflation target set by the government) changed the internal orientation of the Treasury towards the underlying drivers of economic and social development. If Britain were to enter the Euro, even more levers of policy would be lost, and the process would be likely to go even further.

Other economic departments have implicitly been established by prime ministers as rivals or at least counterweights to the Treasury. The Department of Trade and Industry (formed in 1970 but split into its two components from 1974 to 1983) has often seen itself as a pro-business counterweight to the financial orientation of the Treasury. The Department for Education and Employment (1995–2001) was another potential economic competitor but was always close to the Treasury in its policy themes. The Department of Health and Social Security (1968–88) did not work as an integrated department and the Treasury picked off its components after it was divided, with Social Security becoming, under Gordon Brown, a colony of the Treasury. A reorganization after the 2001 election into Departments for Work and Pensions and for Education and Skills reinforced Treasury priorities.

Traditionally, the Treasury was organized into directorates under second permanent secretaries: Economic Advice, International Finance, Public Expenditure and Domestic Economy (the 'Treasury knights'). In 1994–95 there was a *Fundamental Review of Running Costs* that became an opportunity for a major organizational reappraisal. It was done as part of a wider government exercise into program expenditure (the 'Portillo reviews'). As the Treasury had very little program expenditure of its own, the choice was between exempting itself from the exercise or using it as an opportunity for, in Patrick Dunleavy's term, 'bureau-shaping' to obtain the optimal mixture of rewarding and achievable work. The latter course was chosen by Sir Terry Burns (Permanent Secretary 1991–98), an academic who had been recruited by the Thatcher government as Chief Economic Adviser. Burns saw himself as a modern manager, aware of modern business practices, who felt that the context of the Treasury's business was changing. He launched a 'change program' in 1991 and used the Fundamental Expenditure Review (FER) to sweep up a number of other activities to improve communication and morale.

The review was done on the same lines as a 'scrutiny', a form of efficiency exercise and program review developed by the Thatcher administration, with a middle-ranking high-flying official (Jeremy Heywood, now Tony Blair's Principal Private Secretary) and a senior industrialist (Sir Colin Southgate of EMI Music). Heywood was sent to the Harvard Business School for three months and absorbed theories of delayering, building long-term relationships, stripping out non-core businesses, pleasing the customer and empowerment.

The review was based on interviews within the Treasury and generally written comments from its customers. Geoffrey Robinson, a wealthy industrialist and MP who was a junior Treasury minister in 1997–98, sums it up neatly as 'a report that, despite excessive management jargon and buzzwords, did reduce costs and delegate responsibility' (2000, p. 49). The important themes were:

- delayering of the hierarchy, with losses of posts at senior levels and more power to team leaders;

- the separation of spending and budget functions (partly reversed in late 1998 as a Public Services Directorate including General Expenditure Policy was created);
- the proactive role of spending divisions (advocating spending in some cases);
- written documentation – contracts ('concordats'), strategy papers; and
- cross-cutting issues (like social exclusion, the coordination of housing policy and housing benefit, and the links between social security and employment) (HM Treasury 2001a).

The new Treasury organization launched in 1995 is flatter and looser, with six directorates headed (in 2001) by managing directors (formerly directors) and directors (formerly deputy directors). The key operational level of the department now consists of 60 or so teams whose leaders relate non-hierarchically with their directors and relate to ministers directly. Treasury staffing, cut by about a quarter at senior level after the FER, has started to rise: total staff numbers rose from 1,460 to 1,534 in Labour's first term, an indication of how tiny the Treasury is (HM Treasury 2001b, table 10). It remains a source of wonder just how few people there are in many of the teams in relation to the influence they wield.

The Treasury's relations with other parts of the core executive are bound up with the political relationship of the Prime Minister and the Chancellor of the Exchequer. The image of the 'Iron Chancellor' (Tony Blair's term for Gordon Brown) is historically misleading. Chancellors have often been weak figures, and Prime Ministers have not always sided with them in spending arguments. But in recent years an orthodoxy has developed that neither can flourish without the other, and that the political risks of a breakdown in the relationship are great. Margaret Thatcher tried the patience of her long-time Chancellor Nigel Lawson once too often in 1989, and he resigned to write a superb exposition of his record (Lawson 1992); she survived his resignation by only one further year. John Major dismissed Norman Lamont in 1993, the latter sourly refusing to accept responsibility for Britain's departure from the European exchange rate mechanism the previous year; Major's political fortunes stayed at rock-bottom until his record defeat by Tony Blair in 1997. Although Blair and Gordon Brown often appear to be tense rivals, it is universally believed that they would find it hard to survive apart.

Under Brown, internal barriers have grown up in the Treasury between officials who are or are not admitted to the thinking of Brown and his entourage of advisers who came together in opposition. The key figure is Ed Balls, a former financial journalist who became Brown's main adviser in opposition and then his principal aide in government. Balls became a conduit for civil service briefing to Brown and, with his evident ability, was later appointed Chief Economic Adviser (a senior, but not permanent, civil service position). Geoffrey Robinson well describes the 'bloke-ish' aspect of Brown's entourage when he says:

> Gordon often remarked that it was a love of football that first brought us all together. It certainly played its part; and we all had our roles. Gordon was chairman of the club. Its coach and captain and main striker. Ed Balls was deputy in all roles, and in charge of policy and tactics in his own right (Robinson 2000, p. 32).

Terry Burns, the Permanent Secretary inherited by the Brown team, was never admitted to this inner circle and took early retirement in 1998, to be succeeded by Andrew Turnbull, the first in the office to emerge from a public expenditure background in the Treasury but who has retained a low public profile.

The Chancellor's policy interest is advertised by setting up a team on 'Work Incentives and Policy Analysis' under his former Principal Private Secretary Nicholas Macpherson (later a Director in the Budget and Public Finance Directorate). The team was later renamed 'Work Incentive, Poverty and Distributional Analysis', further sharpening its purpose as the Chancellor's commitment to reduce child poverty implied a greater interest in the distribution of income and wealth. There are also new teams on Welfare to Work and Public Services Productivity. The balance inside the Treasury has shifted, with Macroeconomic Policy and International Finance concentrated in one directorate, while the 'spending side' has two (Budget and Public Finance, and Public Services). This is not so much a change of role as a continuation of a long-term process in which the Treasury reinforces its capability in important areas.

RE-NEGOTIATING THE POLITICS OF THE BUDGETARY PROCESS

Since 1960 the process of public expenditure control in Britain has passed through several phases, ultimately revolving around the Treasury's conception of whether its interests are best served by tight control of detail or by a self-regulating hands-off system. The Treasury's instincts for control could be captured in the image of the panopticon, surveying activities in every part of government and assembling and absorbing information. But there is another part of their mentality that seeks to devise and install business systems that can guarantee the delivery of the Treasury's desired outcomes. Hence, we have a mixture of short-term control regimes (1976–79, 1984–87, 1997–99) and an attempt to set up systematic procedures.

We can identify six eras of spending control in Britain. Until the 1960s there was a straightforward incrementalist pattern of *fragmented bargaining*, in which items of expenditure were determined individually within departmental 'estimates' and the aggregate total emerged only after the event. Spending was detached from taxation and economic policy and was vulnerable to an upward creep of expenditure. The Treasury was continually worried that the main themes of the 1940s welfare state (house-building, educational expansion, and a free, universal health service) would provide an irresistible force.

Second, the 1960s and early 1970s saw the new PESC process (Public Expenditure Survey Committee) introduced after the Plowden Report (1961) (Cmnd 1432). The process took its name from a committee of departmental finance officials chaired by the Treasury that prepared options for ministers. The first PESC report was published in 1961 and a system of comprehensive five-year 'forward looks' took shape in the mid-1960s. Plans were by program (not department) and expressed in 'funny money' (so-called *survey prices* prevailing in the autumn before the year of the survey and in *volume terms* which stripped out both general and relative inflation; at the time it was thought that the prices of public sector services would rise faster than private because there was less room for productivity improvement – the *relative price effect*). Plans were related to forecasts (usually optimistic) of the capacity of the economy to absorb government expenditure, but not to the tax-raising process. The committee met to prepare options for ministers and the outcome was expressed, from 1969, in an annual White Paper 'The Government's Expenditure Plans'. There was also consolidation of most grants to local authorities into a block grant (the Rate Support Grant from 1966). Originally, the PESC system sought to assert the primacy of economic objectives over the collective purpose of the welfare state. Later, it allowed rapid and sometimes uncontrollable increases in the both the cost and volume of welfare services as the Treasury had feared.

The third era began under the impact of an economic crisis in 1976 that required an IMF credit. *Cash limits* were imposed on over half of public spending alongside the volume plans. The main exceptions for social policy were social security benefits and primary health care (including drugs) which were 'entitlement', 'demand-led' programs where services could not be denied to those eligible for them. In 1980, a 'medium-term financial strategy' sought to relate taxation and spending for the first time and target the Public Sector Borrowing Requirement (the budget deficit of the entire public sector). From 1979, there was direct control on civil service, and later National Health Service, staff numbers.

Fourth, from 1982 the entire plans were expressed in cash terms (cash planning) which included (implicitly) an element for growth and an element for inflation. Entitlement programs remained non-cash limited. The PESC no longer met; disputes were resolved by bilateral discussions between Chief Secretary to the Treasury and spending ministers, arbitrated if necessary by a so-called Star Chamber (a cabinet committee) of the less involved senior ministers. The annual White Paper was arranged by departments not programs from 1986, and issued in departmental annual reports from 1991. From 1990, local authority self-financed expenditure (then the poll tax) was excluded from the planning total in an ill-fated attempt to have total local accountability for poll tax levels.

In 1992, a fifth stage of expenditure planning changed the framework in a way that proved to be very favourable to the Treasury through a cabinet commitment to topdown planning. This involved agreement on an aggregate total and then negotiation to achieve it through a cabinet Public Expenditure committee (EDX) chaired by the Chancellor and run at official level by the Treasury. From 1993–94 a 'control total' (formerly New Control Total) reinstated local authority expenditure. In November 1993, a 'unified budget' covering both taxation and spending (like the US or Australian federal budgets) was presented for the first time, late in the year rather than the traditional spring. From 1993, all departments had 'fundamental expenditure reviews' coupled to reviews of senior management structures; as we have seen, the Treasury's own review produced major organizational changes.

The sixth era is that of New Labour. The last Conservative Budget was in November 1996. The Blair government, elected in May 1997, decided to respect the Conservative spending plans in aggregate and by department, for both 1997–98 and 1998–99, while it conducted Comprehensive Spending Reviews (CSRs) – in the event, some changes were made between years and departmental headings. Chancellor Gordon Brown presented his first Budget in July 1997 and his second, after abandoning the autumn unified budget, in March 1998 (there have also been 'Pre-Budget Statements', with economic forecasts, a few spending announcements, and previews of new policies, in the autumn of each year). It was decided in 1998 to set plans for three years (1999–2002) for most departments (departmental spending limits or DSL) but to retain some (especially social security) as annually managed expenditure (AME); these were announced in July 1998. A second CSR exercise, published in July 2000, rolled forward the plans to 2001–2004. Following the implementation of a policy set under the Conservatives, a system of resource budgeting and resource accounting is from 2001–2002 providing an accruals basis to government accounts that is more neutral in its economic treatment of the various categories of expenditure. Accompanying these limits have been Public Service Agreements (PSAs), a set of performance targets for each department. Under Labour, cabinet's Public Expenditure committee (EDX) became PX and later Public Expenditure and Public Services (PSX) with a joint secretariat from the Treasury and the Cabinet Office. In theory, this should become the centre of government decision-making on spending matters, but it does not seem to have met with the frequency necessary to do this, a result of personal power-plays within the cabinet.

The report on the CSR, entitled *Modern Public Services for Britain: Investing in Reform* (July 1998) was headlined as an annual real terms increase over the three-year period in education of 5.1 per cent and in health of 4.1 per cent, compared with an increase of only 1.8 per cent in other services. The 2000 CSR report, *Prudent for a Purpose: Building Opportunity and Security for All* (Cmnd 4807, July 2000) presented new headline figures of 5.4 per cent a year for education and 6.1 per cent for health. Many of the data in the CSR reports are not directly comparable with previous plans, or with each other, especially in social security. 'Total managed expenditure' is very close to general government expenditure and is broader than the control total; the implication is that no expenditure is to be left unmanaged, whether on an annual or triennial basis.

The successive CSRs have introduced *cross-cutting budgets* based on *cross-departmental reviews*. In 1998, there were four: local government finance, the criminal justice system, illegal drugs, and provision for young children ('Sure Start'). By 2000, there were 15 (see Cmnd 4807, chapters 21–37), including many which give a clue to Treasury preoccupations: government intervention in deprived areas; Sure Start and Services for the under-5s; young people at risk; welfare-to-work and 'ONE' (the new single gateway for working-age benefit and employment service, since re-named 'Job Centre Plus'); criminal justice; crime reduction; illegal drugs; the 'active community' (volunteering etc.); and care and support for older people. Generally, budgets for these cross-cutting programs are held by departments, but there are some 'pooled budgets' controlled by committees of ministers. What the documents are very coy about is the role of the Treasury in choosing the topics for these reviews and chairing them. Important officials on the spending side in the Treasury were influential, such as Gill Noble on criminal justice and Norman Glass on Sure Start.

The CSRs have offered a progressively tighter link between spending allocations and performance agreements. The first batch of Public Service Agreements was not published until December 1998 (Cmnd 4181), five months after the spending allocations, and some, including social security, not until March 1999 (Cmnd 4315), when the more detailed Output and Performance Analyses were also published. In contrast, the 2000 PSAs (Cmnd 4808) were published alongside the CSRs, and supported in November 2000 by more detailed *Service Delivery Agreements*.

The tables below contrast the CSRs of 1998 and 2000, concentrating on the social policy areas that are Labour's priorities (note that the 'Education and Employment' figure is for spending by the central government department; the education total is a comprehensive figure including local authorities). Note the flat trajectory of spending in the 'Conservative overhang' years and then the jump in expenditure as Labour's own plans superseded the Conservatives. Plans in the first CSR took the five-year real terms increases in education and health to around 18 to 19 per cent, and in the second CSR to 30 per cent. Social security has risen more slowly with economic growth and the hiding of Working Families Tax Credit as a tax expenditure. The Chancellor has also repeatedly found that net expenditure room could be declared in the form of higher revenues and lower expenditure than previously estimated. Low actual spending growth

Table 5.1   Labour's expenditure plans and selected components 1998 CSR (in real terms)

	Conservative Overhang		Labour's Own Plans			
£ bn 1997–98 prices	1997–98	1998–99	1999–2000	2000–2001	2001–2002	Overall Change
Education & Employment	14.7	13.8	14.7	16.0	16.8	+14.2
Health	35.3	36.1	38.1	39.9	41.5	+17.6
Social Security	94.4	95.6	98.4	98.4	101.2	+5.9
Education (UK Total)	36.2	37.1	39.0	41.3	43.1	+19.1
Total Departmental Expenditure Limits	162.7	164.0	169.7	175.6	180.5	+10.9
Total Annually Managed Expenditure	157.1	160.2	163.3	166.3	170.8	+8.7
Total Managed Expenditure	319.8	324.2	333.0	341.9	351.3	+0.8
as % GDP	40.1	40.0	40.3	40.5	40.7	
Outturn	39.6	38.6	37.9			

Note: Social security (benefits) not published in real terms, estimated from deflator for total managed expenditure.

Source: *New Public Spending Plans* (Cmnd 4011, 1998), tables 2 and A3; outturn from *Public Expenditure Statistical Analyses 2001–02* (Cmnd 5101, 2001), table 3.1.

in 1998–99 and 1999–2000 and the use of End Year Flexibility (a new freedom given to departments to carry over under-spent funds between financial years) has caused a backing-up of expenditure that boosted resources in 2000–01 (see Table 5.1 below). Social security has been the main contributor, offering in November 1998 a £1.5 billion underspend in 1998–99 (only four months after that in the CSR) and then £1.6 billion, £2.4 billion and £3.0 billion in the succeeding three years.

The result is that, as a proportion of GDP, Labour's actual spending performance has fallen short of the 40 per cent level that their plans imply. Ironically, this 40 per cent level was a target for the size of the public sector set by the Major administration that at the time seemed hard to achieve. Between 1997–98 and 1999–2000 the outcome fell progressively further behind the plans (Table 5.1), reflecting better-than-expected economic growth and lower-than-expected expenditure. The 2000 plans then sought to push the ratio of spending to GDP back up to over 40 per cent (Table 5.2).

Table 5.2   Labour's expenditure plans and selected components 2000 CSR (in real terms)

	1998 CSR Period		2000 CSR Period			
£ bn 1999–2000 prices	**1999– 2000**	**2000– 2001**	**2001– 2002**	**2002– 2003**	**2003– 2004**	**Overall Change**
Education & Employment	15.4	18.5	20.3	21.9	23.3	+51.3
Health	40.9	44.3	47.2	50.7	53.6	+31.1
Social Security	100.3	100.5	103.3	103.9	105.4	+5.1
Education (UK Total)	40.6	44.8	47.2	49.7	52.4	+29.0
Total Departmental Expenditure Limits	176.8	190.9	202.4	213.1	223.1	+26.2
Total Annually Managed Expenditure	163.9	172.5	172.5	173.4	176.1	+7.4
Total Managed Expenditure	340.7	363.4	374.9	386.5	399.2	+17.2
as % GDP	37.7	39.3	39.7	40.1	40.5	

Note: Social security (benefits), annually managed expenditure and UK education expenditure estimated from deflator for total managed expenditure.

Source: 2000 Spending Review (Cmnd 4807), tables A1–A4 and A9.

Table 5.3 A comparison of the 1998 and 2000 CSR (annual increases in real terms)

1998 CSR/ 2000 CSR	1999– 2000	2000– 2001	2001– 2002	2002– 2003	2003– 2004
Education &	+6.5	+8.8	+5.0		
Employment		+20.0	+9.7	+7.9	+6.4
Health	+5.5	+4.7	+4.0		
		+8.3	+6.5	+7.4	+5.7
Social Security	+2.9	0	+2.8		
		+0.2	+2.8	+0.6	+1.4
Education (UK Total)	+5.1	+5.9	+4.4		
		+10.3	+5.4	+5.3	+5.4

A comparison of the 1998 and 2000 plans (Table 5.3) makes clear the increasingly ambitious scale of spending increases on education and health. As the figures for the crossover year 2000–2001 indicate, the government had to inject more money to correct its previous underspend against plans in the run-up to the general election. Even this did not solve the problem, with the provisional outturn of total managed expenditure for 2001–2002 coming in at £363.7 billion (in cash terms), £7.9 billion less than the plans set the previous year (HM Treasury 2001b, tables 1 and 2). This emphasizes how complete has been the reversal of the context of the budgetary process under New Labour. Far from dealing with overspends and economic or fiscal slowdowns, the Treasury's problem (at least until the events of September 2001) has been to find ways of spending effectively and on time the money that the government has been prepared to commit.

The next spending review is set for 2002, which highlights the curious issue of why a process setting three-year targets is taking place every two years. The effect of this is that the final year of the cycle is superseded by new plans, and so it is never possible to appraise whether spending targets and associated performance measures have been achieved. This is highly convenient for a government keen on 'quick wins' and headline election pledges. It also allows unspent money from previous years to be rolled up into eye-catching real terms increases in the new plans. The reason it has happened is related to the electoral cycle. Governments in reasonable shape will seek to hold elections every four years rather than run until the end of a five-year term, a successful strategy of Margaret Thatcher in 1983 and 1987 and Tony Blair in 2001. It is not practicable to conduct a spending review in an election year. Therefore, the reviews are timed for the end of the first year and third year of a term of office and instead of an annual expenditure cycle we have a biennial one – a more relaxed timescale but still a highly structured one that never leaves the spending departments out of control and fits in comfortably with the historical strategy of the Treasury.

CHANGING VILLAGE CULTURES

The long-running basic model of behaviour between the Treasury and spending departments, one of *bargaining* based on *information*, persists in spending negotiations. Within the Whitehall 'village' the Treasury and spending departments need each other and have a partly adversarial, partly collegial working relationship. Thain and Wright (1995), in their major 1990s study, speak of 'negotiated discretion' with a 'slight edge' – 'simultaneously, the Finance Division [of the department] can be conducting its relationship with the Expenditure division [in the Treasury] in the "business-mode" in one issue, negotiating adversarially on another, briefing its Minister for a confrontation in a bilateral on a third, and having a "flaming row" on a fourth' (Thain and Wright 1995, p. 200). This was our perception also. The protocol of communication is understood: it will frequently be hard and unreasonable in correspondence but softer on the telephone (the key medium). Meetings tend to be rather formal and less frequent than might be expected given the physical proximity of the actors.

At the ministerial level, all routine spending negotiations are managed not by the Chancellor but by the Chief Secretary to the Treasury, who is also a cabinet minister and for the past 15 years has tended to be an up-and-coming politician on the track to be a departmental Secretary of State (Blair got through four in his first term, which is not untypical). These negotiations are usually through correspondence and can put the departmental minister on the defensive and asking for favours. Wherever possible, ministers try to draw upon other political resources, especially the favour and interest of the Prime Minister but also election pledges or parliamentary concern. In emergencies like the outbreak of foot-and-mouth disease in early 2001, negotiations can become heated as the Treasury tries to disentangle necessary expenditure from departmental 'try-ons'.

Our own research found that the personality of officials was a key variable. What is very difficult for a spending department is a combination of an uncongenial personality with the weight of Treasury power and the ability to use legal or procedural requirements to get their way. These behavioural traits worry senior management: as Turnbull told the Treasury Select Committee: 'it is a hard driving place and it ought to become a more human, more people orientated place' (HM Treasury Committee 2001, p. 135). Some of the findings from the FER drove the Treasury to a 'charm offensive', in which they ran annual surveys of what spending departments thought of them and took pride in their improving ratings.

The Treasury has taken its pick of the ablest recruits to the civil service and has acted as a staff college for Whitehall. Traditionally, Treasury knights were sent off to low-profile departments like Trade or Transport to crown their civil service career with a permanent secretary job. More recently, there has been a reversal of direction, with more officials coming from outside after external advertisements of posts: one of the spending directors, Lucy de Groot, is a former local authority chief executive. This reflects in part the tendency of promising Treasury officials to depart, either permanently or on secondment, in the face of the restricted pay and promotion opportunities in the post-FER Treasury. Our own research identified the value of previous service in a spending department as a contributor to a more balanced approach to the job (Deakin and Parry 2000, p. 90), Gender and academic background are also important, and a self-assured male Treasury official with a degree in economics cannot be a very comfortable negotiating partner for a spending department.

What can be galling for the spending departments is to see traditional expressions of Gladstonian rectitude, sometimes irksome but predictable as reflections of a public service ethos, replaced by derivative and shallow characterizations of public sector behaviour. This kind of mentality is evident in the FER and follow-up work, and was well expressed by Sir Steve Robson, widely regarded as among the ablest Treasury officials in recent years, shortly after his retirement:

> Improvement in anything requires change and the public sector is very bad at change. Risk aversion is deeply ingrained among public servants. There is no reward for successful risk-taking and severe, often public, criticism if risk-taking is unsuccessful. The result is a predisposition against risk. Yet change involves risk. The absence of competition in the public services means that there is nothing to shake this cosy state of affairs. Improvement requires that activity should be taken out of this risk-averse environment into one that has a more balanced approach to risk-taking. This means into the private sector (Robson 2001).

In the face of these sentiments, it is not surprising that many officials in other departments adopt an anti-Treasury line even when they concede that a strong Treasury is necessary. Sir Alan Bailey (a retired official with a mix of Treasury and other experience) put this well in written evidence to the Treasury Committee:

> The problem is that the Treasury has increasingly carried over into a very wide range of policy debates the special rights and privileges which it needs to have for the purpose of controlling public expenditure ... in practice a Prime Minister is nearly

always inclined to support his Chancellor. Knowing this, Treasury officials have become increasingly confident in enforcing their views on a wide range of topics, as against officials and ministers in other departments. This can ... demoralize departmental officials if their continuing responsibility and knowledge can be casually set aside by some clever but unaccountable official from the Treasury (HM Treasury Committee 2001, p. 95).

A related approach for which we have some sympathy is to redefine the 'strong Treasury' – in the words of former spending chief official Sir Nick Monck – as 'useful shorthand for many attitudes, arrangements and approaches at ministerial and official level' (Monck 1997, p. 279). If the political system as a whole has a coherent understanding of the macro-economy and the public sector's place in it, there is less of a need to embody this understanding in the Treasury and its officials. The approach of these officials can come to be disliked deeply by those whose whole career has had a spending orientation. One former permanent secretary of the Department of Social Security, Sir Michael Partridge, put it this way to the Treasury Committee:

> The sort of people they ought to have are people who are skilled in running financial management and controlling public expenditure. That is a sceptical frame of mind. Making policy is a rather different frame of mind. You have to be imaginative, constructive, think the unthinkable and then think what is practical and what is political. That is a whole new set of skills and they are quite different from financial management and public expenditure skills and you need both (HM Treasury Committee 2001, p. 122).

In the event, the Treasury Committee's report reflected this line of thinking in its condemnation of undue Treasury influence in welfare and industrial policy-making, and rejected the predominant expert line (as propounded, for instance, by David Lipsey in his recent book that praises the Treasury for 'providing a serious, considered and now even successful core to the country's governance' (2000, p. 263)). Despite all that the Treasury had done to change its behaviour and set medium-term expenditure frameworks, it still had to face the conventional criticism that it was too powerful and ought to be checked.

FUTURE PROSPECTS AND DIRECTIONS

The 2001 general election delivered a second overwhelming Labour majority, barely reducing the 'landslide' of 1997. Tony Blair is in very little danger of difficulties from other parties or from backbenchers within his own party. The House of Lords, sometimes a source of problems even for governments with

Table 5.4   The Treasury's Public Service Agreement targets 2001–2004

---

1. By 2004, to raise the trend rate of growth from the current estimate of 2.5%;
2. RPI inflation to be kept at 2.5% as specified in the Bank of England's remit;
3. Over the economic cycle to maintain a) public sector net debt below 40% of GDP, b) the current budget in balance or surplus;
4. Achieve an improvement in value for money in public services year by year;
5. Improve UK competitiveness by narrowing the productivity gap with US, France, Germany and Japan over the economic cycle [joint target with Department of Trade and Industry];
6. Increase employment over the economic cycle [target contributes to Welfare to Work PSA];
7. Make substantial progress towards eradicating child poverty by at least a quarter by 2004 [joint target with Department Social Security (now Department for Work and Pensions)];
8. Increase the number of countries participating in the global economy on the basis of internationally agreed and monitored codes and standards;
9. Relief of unsustainable debt by 2004 for all heavily-indebted poor countries (HIPC) committed to poverty reduction, building on the internationally agreed target that three quarters of eligible HIPCs reach decision point by end-2000 [joint target with Department for International Development];
10. By 2002–2003, deliver £1 billion of savings in Government procurement through the Office of Government Commerce.

Source: HM Treasury 2001a, table 1b.

large Commons majorities, is in baulk awaiting the completion of its reform process. However, the Prime Minister faces two interrelated problems. On economic policy, there is the timing of the referendum on entry to the Euro (on which the Chancellor's position will be crucial) linked with the general question of future relations between Blair and Brown over the course of the next term. These issues dominate the political landscape and tend to obscure more reflective discussion of the Treasury as an institution and the ways in which its activities have developed and extended over the course of Labour's first term.

The best indication of how the Treasury views itself, at this stage in its history, is in the Public Service Agreement targets it has adopted for the period 2001–2004. A selection of these is shown below in Table 5.4.

Three things stand out about these targets: they range ambitiously wide into policy matters that go beyond Treasury organization; they implicate other departments in the personal priorities of the Chancellor; and they are drafted in relative terms that allow a win to be declared in time for the next election. As with all departments, the Treasury has sought to focus its targets more precisely compared with the rather indiscriminate ones of 1998 (when the Treasury had 33). The earlier detailed targets on social policy have been subsumed into a single target on child poverty.

Brown as Chancellor has sought to enforce the proprietorship of the Treasury over fiscal and economic policy, and particular over the five tests for Euro entry set in 1997 when the government made a political commitment in principle to join the system. These tests (focusing on the extent of economic convergence and any possible adverse impacts) are widely regarded as vague and subjective and a tactic for delaying the decision to call the promised referendum on Euro entry until a politically opportune time. The technical assessment of these tests – and even when the exercise is to begin – has been reserved to Treasury responsibility rather than opened up to collective government decision.

Similarly, tax policy is reserved for the Chancellor's year-by-year budget, except for manifesto pledges in 1997 and 2001 not to raise the basic or higher rates of income tax nor extend VAT to food, children's clothes, books, newspapers and public transport fares. Striking evidence of the tight control Brown has exercised could be observed in the 2001 election campaign. At press conferences, Tony Blair sometimes seemed to need the Chancellor's personal permission before making any comments on economic policy: when asked about fiscal matters his response was 'I can't make a budget'.

In this context, changes in the structure and personnel of the government machine receive eager scrutiny. In the post-election restructuring of government, the Treasury won one victory, when the Department of Trade and Industry was put in the hands of Blair loyalists, with former Treasury minister, Australian-born Patricia Hewitt, as Secretary of State. Pre-election leaks that the DTI would be built up as a counterweight to the Treasury were not borne out as the former Secretary of State, Stephen Byers, was moved to a lesser job at Transport and Local Government.

Against this, Brown faces a more systematic bureaucracy working directly for the Prime Minister. The Number 10 Downing Street Policy Unit is being integrated with the Private Office under Chief of Staff Jonathan Powell, and the Prime Minister has taken on personal responsibility for service delivery, especially in health. On 22 June it was announced that Michael Barber, an academic who had been in charge of promoting school standards, was to be in charge of a new Policy Delivery Unit at Number 10, with a 'Whitehall official' telling the press in Blair-speak 'this post is about delivering relentless progress. It involves chasing across departments and making sure that Downing Street is aware of problems coming down the track' (*Financial Times* 22 June 2001). There is also to be an Office of Public Services Reform and Forward Strategy Unit. Number 10 retains two creations of the first Blair term, the Performance and Innovation Unit (PIU) and the Social Exclusion Unit, whose reports have promoted joined-up government. The PIU's report *Wiring It Up* (2000) is the fullest statement of how the Treasury, Number 10 and the Cabinet Office might collaborate in pursuit of better policy-making.

The picture has been complicated by the appointment of Deputy Prime Minister John Prescott to the Cabinet Office, the other administrative arm of the Prime Minister and the Cabinet Secretary. This post (known as the 'enforcer') has previously served as an exit route for a marginalized minister, and this applies to Prescott as well. But Blair has also brought into the Cabinet Office Lord (Gus) Macdonald, a Glasgow trade unionist, turned journalist, turned media executive, who is much favoured for his business drive and persuasive personality. The bureaucratic apparatus of the Cabinet Office is concerned with civil service personnel management, but also the general brief of modernizing public services and promoting electronic government. It produces upbeat documents (like the much-derided annual reports of the government, now abandoned) but cannot match the Treasury's role as enforcer and deliverer of policy outcomes. All the evidence is of Treasury's reluctance to relinquish control of the PSAs as the legitimate basis of its intervention in departmental policies in a multi-year spending regime.

A variety of roles are now available to the Treasury. Politically, it can be a resource for the government and its collective purpose, or more of a resource for the objectives of the Chancellor personally. In policy terms, it can range from being a strictly constructed ministry of economics and finance, distinct from the functional departments, to a manager of policy development and service delivery. The general trajectory of the Treasury is towards a policy-manager role for a strong Chancellor. Starting out in the nineteenth century as a low-level calculating machine usually headed by nondescript personalities, the Treasury was transformed by some influential Chancellors (especially Gladstone and Lloyd George) into a bureaucratic power – a recognized elite with a distinctive mentality. In a civil service valuing intellectuality, the Treasury deployed the greatest brain-power of all. Able ministers have always liked being at the Treasury, and the department has always revelled in having a strong minister at its head. But the system seldom produces Chancellors with an optimal combination of expertise in economics and experience on the spending side of government.

Not all Chancellors have been power-grabbers. Some were politically weak and failed to flourish, such as James Callaghan (1964–67), Anthony Barber (1970–74) and Norman Lamont (1990–93), while others were easy-going and collegiate (notably Kenneth Clarke (1993–97) whose approach was formed during many years in spending departments). Two notable Labour Chancellors, Roy Jenkins (1967–70) and Denis Healey (1974–79) were major political figures generally adjudged a success in the job but who failed to impose an independent economic perspective. The recent Conservative chancellors serving long enough to make a systematic impact fit the pattern of growing assertiveness in the job: Geoffrey Howe (1979–83) set the macroeconomic objectives of Thatcherism and left spending departments to cope with the consequences; Nigel Lawson (1983–89) was an egocentric economic virtuoso with ambitions to use the Treasury to engage with certain social policy areas, notably education, but on a personal rather than institutional basis. He was much less of a policy and delivery person than Gordon Brown, a Chancellor of calculating ambition and economic literacy who has attracted the Treasury's power to himself.

There has not been a complete aggrandizement under Labour, because Brown, and hence the Treasury, have been selective in their engagement with policy areas. Health has been left to Blair, and the details of education, crime and defense policy do not seem to be of great preoccupation. But Brown has built up the policy capability of Treasury in the interrelated issues of pathways into the labour market, family incomes and child-care provision, and the interface between tax and benefits system. Here Brown's policy preference, reflecting a long-standing Treasury position, is to adopt income guarantees set according to household status and ultimately means-tested, rather than to maintain a universal rights-based benefits system. Brown's transfers to families with children have been much more generous than anything before, but the basic Treasury framework remains.

In recent times, the Treasury's interest in policy outcomes has partly been an opportunistic reaction to the hollowing-out of its influence on economic policy. One of Terry Burns' permanent secretary colleagues quotes him as saying: 'of course, macroeconomic policy is very boring at the moment because everybody agrees on it, there is nothing really to do, and microeconomic policy we have handed over to other people, so we are getting very interested in social policy' (HM Treasury Committee 2001, p. 114). But this can only happen if the Prime Minister is prepared to allow it. Despite protests from his ministers, backbenchers, the media and relevant experts, Blair has licensed Brown to engage with social policy.

As we say in our Select Committee evidence in the Appendix, we do have a real 'new Treasury' characterized by greater delegation to spending departments, a more open personnel policy and an awareness of the risks of dysfunctional behaviour. In Whitehall terms, it is notably non-hierarchical and fearless in argument. It has built up its analytical capacity in the interface between social and economic policy and it remains a world model of an integrated, prestigious central budget agency. The ground gained by the Treasury in the last four years is unlikely to be wholly relinquished under Brown's successors, from whatever party or personality type they might be drawn. But ironically at the present time, when its position is so secure, the Treasury's reputation is suffering from unstable political relations between an assertive and rather secretive Chancellor and a Prime Minister who, lacking the capacity to act upon his official title of 'First Lord of the Treasury', is building up other parts of the core executive on his own behalf.

NOTE

1. This chapter draws on our project on 'The Treasury and Social Policy' done as part of the Economic and Social Research Council's Whitehall Program (Deakin and Parry 2000). For a compendium of the program as a whole, see Rhodes (ed.) (2000).

APPENDIX: EXTRACT FROM MEMORANDUM SUBMITTED TO TREASURY SELECT COMMITTEE, APRIL 2000 (SEE HM TREASURY COMMITTEE 2001)

Discussion of 'Treasury power' tends to confuse formal rights, relative weight in government, and assertiveness in behaviour. We are inclined to think that after the FER and the CSRs we do have something of a 'new Treasury' which recognizes the risks of having a reputation for indiscriminate negativity. It is looking for an intellectual rather than an organizational victory over social spending departments. It is happier than it has ever been to award discretion to public spenders judged to be on-board (as most strikingly in the delegation of approval of virtually all Health Service capital spending and in the reversal of its initial strong suspicion of the concept of the Next Steps Executive Agency within the civil service); but it is no less confident than ever to hammer away disputatiously when a department is judged to be concealing possible savings.

This amounts to a partial detachment of the *Treasury as an organization* from the *Treasury function.* By the latter we mean, not so much the repression of expenditure, which has always been partially contracted-out to the Finance Divisions of departments, as the imaginative consideration of the relation of specific policies to overall economic objectives. If other departments could be made to think 'correctly' in the Treasury's eyes, much of the traditional thinking about the need for a strong Treasury might become obsolete. The Treasury could remain assertive, but it would not need all the formal controls and interventions on which it has relied. The fact that estimation of expenditure has become more robust as the economy has improved since the mid-1990s has been an important factor. Under Labour, a systematic under-estimation of revenue and over-estimation of expenditure year by year has facilitated an improvement in relationships.

Our conclusion from our research was the paradoxical one that those most concerned about Treasury power might prefer to reinforce its analytical capability about public service delivery in preference to keeping it weak, overstretched and uninformed. We found that while the Treasury does not have a first-order free-standing social policy it has developed a need to consider the social policy implications of its central role in promoting the government's economic policies. We were struck by how the Treasury had been playing a co-ordinating and policy development role before 1997 on the 16-18 age group; how it has promoted the internal market in the National Health Service and the purity of the customer–contractor relationship; and how it has made the running on a number of social security matters that appeared liable to escape control or be open to abuse. After 1997 it has immersed itself in work and welfare issues (an area of strong personal interest to the Chancellor), adopted a wholesale strategy of using tax expenditures and means-testing, and brought social security under control (with its former colleagues installed in key positions there).

An alternative approach would be to build up the Cabinet Office still further as a third force between the Treasury and the spending departments; but its institutional weight is of a wholly lesser order and in practice it has become more of a partner of the Treasury in a fused 'core executive' setting and monitoring policy objectives. Various mixtures of roles are possible, and a stronger Treasury capability and presence as government policy is formulated should not necessarily be seen as undesirable. Our research suggested that the best approach may be to reinforce the policy analysis capability of the Treasury, in terms of staffing strength and the importation of staff and expertise from the rest of Whitehall and beyond. If the Treasury continues its transition from a permanent bureaucratic elite corps to a repository of ideas and staff drawn from a variety of backgrounds it would be better equipped to bring a full range of considerations to the many expenditure decisions to which it will always be central.

6. No Revolution in Sight: the Evolving Roles of the Central Budget Agency in Sweden

Gert Paulsson

According to Wildavsky (1988) the budgetary process is a very important component and routine of government politics. His original arguments were derived, of course, from America in the post-war period of expansionary public expenditure. By contrast, Mattsson (1998) has argued that the budgetary process has become even more important in Sweden during the last years of the twentieth century. He presents two reasons for this increased importance: the severity of the financial crises facing the Swedish government during the early years of the 1990s; and the reforms that were carried out in the budget procedure in the mid-1990s. As this chapter will explain, with increased importance being attached to the State Budget procedure, the institutions that are responsible for overseeing that procedure – Sweden's central budget agency – has emerged as one of the most powerful actors in the government organization.

The notion of a central budget agency (CBA) is not a well-defined or all-embracing term. First, the function itself may encompass different tasks (see, for example, the Introduction to the present volume). Second, the CBA is organized in quite different ways in different countries. Some such as New Zealand or the United Kingdom have a unified agency with wide ranging responsibilities. In the Swedish government, the same set of CBA functions are *shared* among *several ministries* in the government and *several government agencies*. Nevertheless, we can still consider the Budget Department (BD) in the Ministry of Finance (MoF) as Sweden's main budgetary/expenditure CBA. The reason for this is that the BD plays a very central role in the State Budget procedure.

In carrying out the CBA functions, the BD and the associated government departments and agencies are influenced by context and changing circumstances. During the last decades this context has changed rather dramatically. The general economic situation for the government sector has changed, the political situation has been less than stable due to coalition and minority governments and new

126

parties in the parliament, and massive public management reforms have been implemented. One consequence of the New Public Management (NPM) reforms is that there is now a growing tendency to question some of the roles performed by the CBA and especially the ways in which the CBA functions are carried out. This issue has been identified more generally by Schick (1997, 2001b), who argued that the main reform trends of NPM during the past decade were increasingly incompatible with the traditional CBA role. The aim of this present study, therefore, is to identify the tasks and roles of the Swedish CBA, and examine how it is performing its functions under these changing circumstances.

The study is based upon a *contingency approach*. Thus, the roles and tasks of the CBA are considered to be closely linked to developments in the context in which the function is carried out, including the iterative interrelationships between the CBA and its context. However, the relationship between the CBA and its context is by no means assumed to be causal. Rather, a more holistic and multi-faceted view is applied, close to the type of contingency approach that Van de Ven and Drazin (1985) call the systems approach to contingency studies. That approach is holistic in the sense that it is accepted that there are multiple contextual variables, multiple design variables and multiple performance variables, and that these variables may affect each other in a mutual way. According to Van de Ven and Drazin such an approach is a reaction towards the reductionist contingency approaches that are sometimes employed. In using the systems approach, one must address 'in simultaneous manner the many contingencies, structural alternatives, and performance criteria inherent to organizational life' (1985, p. 347).

The chapter is based upon a selective literature study, the author's own experiences[1] and discussions with former and present employees in the government. References are also made to the results of internal projects within the BD concerning, for example, its organizational culture.

THE INSTITUTIONAL CONTEXT OF THE BUDGET DEPARTMENT

This section of the chapter presents the main characteristics of the institutional context in which the Budget Department is located, and a brief presentation of the department and its development.

The Public Sector in Sweden

The public sector in Sweden is large by international comparison, with taxation comprising 52.8 per cent of GDP in 2000 (Ministry of Finance 2001a). It employs around 30 per cent of the total workforce. The public sector is organized across three levels; national/state, regional and local. The national/state level consists of the Riksdag (parliament), the government (*regeringen*) and government agencies. At the regional level, the county administrative boards (*länsstyrelserna*) are a part of the state administration, while the 22 county councils (*landstingen*) are more like regional municipalities. Finally, the local level consists of about 250 municipalities (*primärkommuner*).

The county councils and the municipalities are by tradition relatively independent from the national/state administration. They are able to levy their own taxes. In spite of their formal independence, it is nevertheless important to be aware of the fact that they receive lump sum transfers from the central government, and that a large proportion of their work actually has to do with implementation of policies that are decided upon by the Riksdag and the government.

Executive Government

At present, the national executive government consists of 20 ministers, while the central administration (or government offices – *regeringskansliet*) is organized into 10 ministries, plus the Prime Minister's Office and the Office for Administrative Affairs. The Swedish government is different from the governments in most other countries in at least three respects. First, government departments (ministerial offices) are relatively small. In 2000, they collectively employed just 4,472 persons (Regeringskansliet 2001), including persons working abroad in the foreign administration.

Second, Sweden has a long tradition of relatively large and semi-autonomous government agencies. The number of agencies is about 250 and the total number of employees in these agencies is about 200 000 (Statskontoret 2000). The autonomy of the government agencies is enshrined in *The Instrument of Government Act* (*Regeringsformen*), where it states that 'neither any public agency, nor the Riksdag, nor the decision making body of a local government commune may determine how an administrative agency shall make its decisions in a particular case concerning the exercise of public agency against a private subject or against a commune, or concerning the application of law' (chapter 11, §7). In addition, several ordinances, for example, the Ordinance on the Executive Management of the Agencies (*Verksförordningen*), state the rights and duties of the agencies and the Directors General. This autonomy includes all government agencies. However, Larsson (2001) argues that some agencies are more closely linked to the government than others. Examples of such agencies are the National Financial Management Authority (*Ekonomistyrningsverket*), the Expert Group of Public Finance (*ESO*), the National Audit Office (*Riksrevisionsverket*), the Swedish Agency of Government Employers (*Arbetsgivarverket*) and the Swedish Agency for Public Management

(*Statskontoret*). Their tasks are, among other things, to support the government with evaluations and the modernizing of public management.

Third, decision-making in the government is explicitly collective. Individual ministers only make decisions concerning the internal organization and administration of his/her ministry. This also means that an individual minister is not responsible to the parliament for the activities within his/her ministry, and definitely not for the activities of any of the agencies operating within their policy area.

The Ministry of Finance

The Ministry of Finance (MoF) is one of the largest ministries in the core executive. In 2000 the MoF employed 419 persons. Only the Foreign Ministry and the Office of Administrative Affairs had more employees (Regeringskansliet 2001). Two ministers head the MoF – the Finance Minister and deputy Finance Minister. In addition to the two ministers, four state secretaries, a chief political advisor and a small group of political advisors and press secretaries constitute the political leadership of the ministry.

Internally, MoF is organized into six small departments – the Budget Department (*Budgetavdelningen*), the Fiscal Affairs Department (*Skatteavdelningen*), the Economic Affairs Department (*Ekonomiska avdelningen*), the Financial Markets and Institutions Department (*Finansmarknadsavdelningen*), the International Department (*Internationella avdelningen*) and the Administrative Department (*Administrativa avdelningen*). In addition, MoF also contains a number of divisions – such as the local government division (*Enheten för kommunal ekonomi*), the county administrative division (*Länsstyrelseenheten*), the housing division (*Bostadsenheten*), a division for state companies and property (*Bolags-och fastighetsenheten*), a division for information (*Informationsavdelningen*) and a legal secretariat (*Rättssekretariatet*).

The Budget Department

The Budget Department (BD) forms one of the largest departments in the MoF. It is organized into seven line divisions with the following responsibilities. Four of the BD divisions are 'contact divisions', meaning they are responsible for the budget negotiations and other contacts with the spending ministries (supply divisions). Another division is responsible for budget compilations, aggregating the various estimates and expenditure actuals across government and then following up and forecasting at the overall level. One division provides advice on financial management and performance management, and is responsible for, among other things, the developmental activities in the area and control of the National Financial Management Authority (*Ekonomistyrningsverket*), the National Audit Office (*Riksrevisionsverket*) and the Swedish Agency for Government Employers (*Arbetsgivarverket*). Another division looks after European Union (EU) matters and oversees the Swedish charge to the EU budget. Finally, there is a small staff division, which is responsible for coordination of the budget procedure in the central administration of government (the government offices).

The number of staff attached to BD is small by international standards, but as Table 6.1 shows the number has risen considerably in recent years.

While the total number of staff has grown in the 1990s, the number of managers has remained relatively static. There is also a trend in recruitment to broaden the professional training and experiences of BD staff, particularly to include PhDs. On the other hand, Table 6.1 does not show what kind of activities the employees are engaged in, and it has not been possible to discover such precise data. However, it is a general opinion among officials at the MoF, that the number of budgeters employed in the contact divisions has remained relatively unchanged. Thus, it is the other functions of the BD that have expanded during the period. This is partly due to Swedish membership of the EU and the

Table 6.1　Employees and educational background of staff in the Budget Department[2]

Employee Background	1985	1989	2001
Total number of employees			
(incl. managers)	29	27	68
Number of managers	7	7	8
Average age of employees	37	35	36
Average number of years spent in BD	3	3	4
Educational Background			
(percentage of staff)			
− Bachelor of Science	73	84	76
− Master of Political Science	15	4	5
− Architect	4	4	−
− Master of Law	4	−	6
− Civil Engineer	4	−	−
− Land Surveyor	−	4	−
− Doctor of Philosophy	−	4	6
− Master of Philsophy	−	−	3
− Licentiate of Philosophy	−	−	3
TOTAL	100	100	100

subsequent growth of the EU division, but there has been a rise in the number of employees at the division for total compilations and the division for financial management and performance management as well.

According to official publications (Ministry of Finance 2001a), the BD has four *main responsibilities*: budget policy and implementation; budgetary, organizational and structural issues in the public sector; financial control and auditing; and the municipal financial principle. The tasks and responsibilities of the BD are further elaborated in the *Internal Activity Plan 2001* for the MoF. In that plan, the BD is assigned the following areas of responsibility: budget policy; budgetary control and accounting of government finances; budgetary, organizational and structural issues concerning the public sector; follow-up of public sector finances; financial management and performance management of the government sector; government auditing; local government (especially where formal responsibility does not lie with some other agency); and prioritization within the public sector and between different expenditure areas. This is probably the most comprehensive articulation of the many and potential responsibilities of BD.

The *main objectives* of the BD are further elaborated in its *Internal Activity Plan 2001*. It lists its main objectives as being to achieve:

- high budgetary discipline;
- continuous examination of the public commitment;
- efficient use of resources within the public sector;
- high economic efficiency in the wider society through, among other things, improved competition, a strict budget policy, improved budget discipline and improved resource utilization within the EU; and
- reliable forecasts, analysis and estimates as a basis for government decision-making.

In addition to the above-mentioned responsibilities and objectives, the ministry's 2001 plan contains a list of especially *prioritized activities and projects* for the BD. Examples of such activities and projects are to:

- prepare and examine all material for the two-yearly government budget meetings;
- prepare proposals and participate in cross-ministerial working groups concerning proposals in the areas of social security, public welfare production, employment policy, growth and justice;
- work on cross-sectoral projects and in-depth analysis within the following areas: defense, the judicial system, information technology, environmental issues, retirement issues, educational issues and regional issues;

- carry on institutional reforms through the further development of the budget process and financial and performance management;
- begin the work on principal and long range strategies for each expenditure area[3] and other important activity areas; and
- investigate the current state of government auditing, a new audit office under the Riksdag, and the government's need for auditing and investigation capacities.

In carrying out its CBA functions, the BD works closely with other related MoF departments – for example, the Economic Affairs Department (*Ekonomiska avdelningen*) and the Fiscal Affairs Department (*Skatteavdelningen*), as well as with bodies attached to other ministries, such as the Division for Public Management (*Enheten för förvaltningsutveckling*) in the Ministry of Justice, the National Debt Office (*Riksgäldskontoret*), the National Financial Management Authority and the Swedish Agency for Public Management (*Statskontoret*).

A CHALLENGING CONTEXT

The ability of the CBA to perform its roles and achieve its objectives is strongly affected by the challenging context within which the CBA must operate. This section of the chapter contains a brief overview of some of the more important changes from the point of view of the BD and the work it is charged with undertaking.

Economic and Fiscal Context

The Swedish public sector expanded rapidly during the 1960s and 1970s. In 1998 the tax quota was about 53 per cent while public expenditure was about 63 per cent of GDP. This trend helped generate a growing consensus among the political parties over the past decade that there was no room for higher taxation and no scope for further expansion of the public sector. Instead, most parties began to question which public activities could be sustained and whether taxpayers were getting value for money in services.

As a consequence of this change of orientation, the central government finances have undergone a rather dramatic change especially during the late-1990s. At the aggregate level, the balance of the state budget recorded a large deficit of Skr 250 billion in 1993 whereas by the year 2000 the budget was in surplus to the tune of Skr 102 billion. The use of expenditure ceilings has been the focus of the public debate since they was introduced in the 1997 budget round. To date, the government has succeeded in remaining below the stipulated ceiling every year since then. However, the government has taken specific measures during several of these years in order to make that happen. So, altogether, the state finances look brighter today than they did one decade ago. However, the ageing population in Sweden is no doubt a threat in the future. Some commentators also argue that the relatively large public sector may still pose a problem for Sweden in the future.

Political Context

Until the early-1970s, the Social Democrats had occupied office for several decades. During some terms the Leftwing party in the Riksdag supported them, but they were most often able to act almost as a majority government. In the elections of 1976, 1979 and 1991, however, the bourgeois-liberal parties formed coalition governments. During the rest of the 1980s and the 1990s the Social Democratic party was only able to form minority governments, which have been supported by either the Leftwing party, the Agricultural party (traditionally a bourgeois party), or a combination of the Leftwing party together with the Green party. Altogether, the governments of the last decades have been a succession of either minority governments or coalition governments.

In contrast to the former strong majoritarian governments, these more recent minority or coalition governments require adaptations or other arrangements to be made to the State Budget procedure. In practice, minority governments require two parallel or subsequent coordination processes in the budget preparation phase. The first coordination requirement involves ministers in the government and their respective budget bids/proposals, while the second coordination process takes place between the major party in the minority government and the supporting parties. From experience, coalition governments usually require more extensive inter-ministerial coordination than do governments of one party with a majority in the Riksdag or minority governments relying on support from minor parties. Greater political uncertainty and the changing political situation have both strongly affected the work and approach of the BD in preparing the State Budget.

Public Management Reform

Sweden has a long tradition of public management reforms, the historical development of which has been presented in several reports (see Gustavsson 1985; National Audit Office 1998; Finansdepartementet 2000). However, several of the more recent reforms have had an effect on the roles and tasks of the BD.

As previously mentioned, the relative autonomy of public agencies is a deeply rooted tradition within Swedish government. In the late-1980s several changes in financial management were made that enhanced agency autonomy. First, specified appropriations were replaced by so-called 'frame appropriations' (*ramanslag*). That change meant the Directors General of the agencies had more freedom to choose among possible production factors, and had the ability to carry over surpluses or deficits between budget years. Second, an 'internal bank' was established in the National Debt Office, making it possible for the agencies to borrow for investment in fixed assets. Both these changes led to a further delegation of authority and responsibility to the directors general.

A performance management system was introduced, both in the relationship between the government and the autonomous agencies, and the relationship between the Riksdag and the government. The implementation of the system in the former relationship began in the late-1980s. It has led to the inclusion of non-financial objectives in the annual approval documents (*regleringsbrev*) that the government issues for each government agency, and performance information in the annual reports from the agencies to the government. The exchange of non-financial objectives and performance information between the Riksdag and the government has increased in connection with the issuing of the *Budget Act* in 1997. The *Budget Act* stipulated the government's obligation to report the objectives for the coming budget year, and the result of the previous budget year (2§). To date, this reporting has been contained in the government's Budget Bill. However, this may change in the near future, since the Riksdag has asked for more in-depth information from the government about the results of its activities. This information will be delivered in special documents (*resultatskrivelser*) during the spring.

In 1993, a new accounting model was introduced in the entire government sector.[4] The model was based upon accrual principles, and it led to an entire change in the reporting of financial information in the annual reports from the agencies to the government. A few years later the use of accrual principles was extended to the relationship between the Riksdag and the government. Since then accrual accounting has formed the basis for the Consolidated Annual Report for the Government (*årsredovisning för staten*) that is presented to the Riksdag.

The financial crisis in the Swedish government in the early-1990s triggered an intense discussion about the State Budget procedure. One reason for that was that several studies reported a strong relationship between the institutional arrangements surrounding the budget procedure and the financial problems facing successive governments. It was also stated that Sweden had one of the sloppiest institutional arrangements in Western Europe through which to formulate budgets.[5] In particular, the bottom-up procedure in the budget preparation phase was criticized. This critique prompted the adoption of several reform measures. First, a three-year expenditure ceiling was introduced for the first time in the preparation of the State Budget for 1997. Second, the procedure for budget decision-making in the Riksdag was changed, leading to an almost completely top-down decision-making process occurring over two stages. In practice, this then meant that a similar top-down process occurred in the internal budget preparation phase for the central administration (government offices). Third, the allocation of authority and responsibility between the Riksdag and the government was laid down in the *Budget Act* issued in January 1997.

Finally, during its last two terms of office, the government has focused increasingly on the development and implementation of a public administration policy *(förvaltningspolitiskt handlingsprogram)*. In that policy three basic values are stressed: democracy; security of life and property; and efficiency. General public policy programs now have to aim to express the following values: enhanced internationalization; openness; service quality; and better human resource management. The adoption of a formal public administration policy may well be seen as a reaction towards the previous strong focus on efficiency and 'managerialism' in the reforms that were carried out in the 1980s and the early-1990s.

HOW THE RECENT CONTEXT HAS IMPACTED ON THE GENERIC ROLES OF THE SWEDISH CBA

In this section an attempt is made to analyse how the generic roles of the CBA have been adapted to meet the changing context. I wish to discuss these roles in relation to how the CBA performs the basic tasks of the budgetary system; when it performs such tasks over the three phases of the State Budget procedure; and how it has reoriented its behaviour to maintain an overall 'control approach'.

According to Schick (1997, 2001b) all budgetary systems have three basic tasks. The first is to maintain *aggregate fiscal discipline*. Though that task is traditionally considered to be very important, the way it is carried out may differ between different countries and from time to time. The second task is to allocate resources in accordance with the political priorities (that is, promote *allocative efficiency*). An important precondition for this task is to find ways to make it possible to reallocate resources based on information about the effectiveness of various programs. The third task of the budget system is to foster *operational efficiency*. That task aims at motivating decision-makers at all levels of the government organization to pay attention to the relationship between input and output of their activities.

To perform these tasks, the roles of the CBA are different in the different phases of the State Budget process. Three distinct phases can be identified. The first phase involves *preparatory budget work* and takes place prior to the budget year, focusing on forecasts, calculations, negotiations and decision-making concerning the budget. The second phase is *budget implementation*, which takes place during the budget year. For the CBA this phase is focused on follow-up, forecasts, reporting and, if needed, decisions about changes in the existing budget. The third phase involves *follow-up and evaluation,* and it takes place after the end of the budget year. During this last phase, final reporting is complemented with more in-depth evaluations of actual results. Lessons are also learned for future budget years. These three phases of the State Budget procedure are of course overlapping. Hence, a thorough understanding of the interplay between the different phases may be an important aspect of the analysis of the role of the BD.

Finally, the CBA may employ different behavioural or interactive approaches in carrying out its tasks. One way to articulate this is to distinguish direct approaches from indirect approaches. A *direct approach* implies the CBA is directly involved in the setting of specific appropriations or objectives, while a more *indirect approach* implies that it would concentrate more on the development of the institutional arrangements surrounding the State Budget procedure. To sum up, the roles of the CBA can be discussed in connection with the basic tasks of the budget system, the various phases of the State Budget procedure, and the control approaches chosen.

Securing Aggregate Fiscal Discipline: the Most Important Role of the CBA

It is a widely held opinion among those involved in Swedish government and politics that the primary role of the BD is to act as a central guardian against the demands of spending agencies with the intention of preventing higher expenditures leading to budget deficits. As can be seen from the *Internal Activity Plan 2001*, high budgetary discipline and aggregate fiscal discipline are among the main objectives of the department. In carrying out that task, the BD is involved in all phases of the State Budget procedure. However, prior to the 1990s the BD expended almost all its effort on the *preparatory phase*, while the follow-up and evaluation of the actual revenues and expenditures was less emphasized in government. There are several indications that this has changed during the last years, due to the introduction of the expenditure ceiling in 1997. As a consequence of the strong focus on this institutional arrangement in public debate, the government has been determined not to break the announced ceilings. Thus, continuous monitoring and forecasting of expenditures during the budget *implementation phase* has been introduced. Although most government agencies, spending ministries and the National Financial Management Authority are involved in in-year monitoring, it is, nevertheless, the prime responsibility of the BD.

Traditionally, the contribution of the BD to the attainment of aggregate fiscal discipline was relatively *direct*. However, it can be argued that the development of the institutional arrangements in the budget area in the mid-1990s has meant the department has had to focus on *indirect* methods as well. In conjunction with the strong political commitment to budget reform instruments and the introduction of the *Budget Act* in 1997, it is obvious that the BD has had a strong influence on the budget reforms adopted during this period. For example, it was the head of the division for financial management and performance management in the BD who wrote the white paper triggering the entire development process (Finansdepartementet 1995). On the other hand, there are indications from BD that it has higher ambitions in relation to the more *direct* and relatively detailed controls of expenditure. One such indication is the introduction in 1999 of the so-called three-percentage rule. That rule deals with instances where government agencies have appropriation savings (*anslagssparande*) exceeding 3 per cent of their appropriation amount. When this occurs negotiations are held between the spending ministry and the BD concerning whether the agency will be permitted to carry forward its underspent amount to the next budget year (with the implication being that the carry forward is not automatic). This rule has led to rather detailed end-of-the-year discussions between the BD and the spending ministries concerning individual appropriations. However, internal research indicates that the rule is used with discretion, and appropriation savings in excess of 3 per cent have not been automatically withdrawn.

The CBA and Allocative Efficiency: a Strive for Influence in General Policy Issues

There are several indications that the BD today engages in broader policy issues concerning allocative efficiency in the government sector than was once the case. The *Internal Activity Plan* requires BD, as one of its main objectives, to maintain a continuous examination of public commitments and of the efficient use of resources within the public sector. Among the prioritized activities mentioned in the same plan are, for example, preparation and examination of all material for the two-yearly government budget meetings, and preparation of proposals and participation in cross-ministerial working groups concerning the areas of social security, public welfare production, employment policy, growth and justice, work on cross-sectoral projects, and in-depth analysis within the following areas: defense, the judicial system, information technology, environmental issues, retirement issues, educational issues and regional issues. It is apparent from the *Internal Activity Plan* that the BD is supposed to be *proactive* in these processes and not simply *react* to proposals that are presented by the spending ministries.

It is true that issues concerning allocative efficiency are almost entirely concentrated in the *preparation phase* of the State Budget procedure. In the implementation and follow-up phases, little effort is made to find out whether the resources are allocated in an efficient way. In these phases, the focus of both the government and the BD is almost entirely on expenditure control.

A more proactive role in the preparation phase of budget deliberations now involves the BD in more active, policy-oriented participation in the allocation of scarce resources across the Swedish government sector. Whether or not this is a new role for the BD or an extension of a previously emergent role is difficult to assess. However, there are several indications that the involvement of the BD in these issues has increased and broadened. First, in recent years, overall priority setting has been determined at a one or two-day government budget meeting usually held in February or March. This strategic meeting has become an important part of the State Budget procedure. During that meeting the ministers are supposed to reach agreements on fiscal policy and the overall allocation of expenditures among the expenditure areas. Deliberations during these meetings are based upon a proposal from the Finance Minister. The BD and the Economic Affairs Department in MoF are heavily involved in the preparation of the proposal document during January and February. While the spending ministries and the Economic Affairs Department are involved in the preparation of consequence assessments and forecasts, the BD maintains the strongest influence over the proposal. In this way the BD is able to influence the agenda of the most important meeting for priority setting in the early part of the budget *preparation phase*.

Second, during the Social Democratic minority government's last term of office (1998–2002), it was supported in the Riksdag by the Leftwing party (*Vänsterpartiet*) and the Green party (*Miljöpartiet*). As a consequence, the internal arrangements of the budget *preparation phase* have been altered to make it possible for negotiations to take place between the three parties prior to the delivery of the spring budget bill and the budget bill to the Riksdag. These party negotiations occur after the internal negotiations between the MoF and the spending ministries have taken place. Thus, the negotiations between the Social Democratic government and the two supporting parties are based on the proposal resulting from the internal negotiations in the government. In order to coordinate the negotiations with the Leftwing and Green parties, and make sure that the changes that follow from these negotiations are within the limits of the expenditure ceiling that the Riksdag has already approved, the Finance Minister is given responsibility for overseeing the negotiations. This means that the MoF, and especially the BD, is closely involved in the negotiations, and thus in the discussion about possible changes in the prioritization between different policy areas in the budget *preparation phase*.

Third, a few years ago, the BD initiated an internal project aimed at listing possible policy areas where savings could be found. The project was internally named 'the vacuum cleaning project', and was an example of a more *proactive* and *direct* approach from the BD in the area of allocative efficiency. The end results of the project were discussed with the political leadership in the MoF, but as yet it is difficult to assess the effect the project has had on reallocation.

Fourth, another component of the 1997 reforms to the State Budget procedure was the requirement to include in the yearly budget documentation all the issues that have consequences for government finances. Prior to that, several issues with possible financial consequences were dealt with in separate bills. Since the BD coordinates the State Budget procedure (but may have had a weaker role in the preparation of some of the separate bills), this has led to an increased *direct* influence of BD in the area of allocative efficiency.

Finally, the introduction of performance management in the central government sector in the late-1980s meant that measures of output and outcome were included in the State Budget procedure. This also increased the influence of the BD on policy-oriented issues. However, it is doubtful whether the inclusion of this information in the yearly budget procedure has had any major effect on priority setting in practice. There is still a widely held view in many government offices that the BD remains rather number-oriented in the *preparation phase* of the State Budget procedure, and that the focus on outputs and outcomes has not increased its role in the implementation and *follow-up phases*. On the other hand, the BD and its staff agencies have certainly been actively engaged in the development and implementation of the performance management system by pursuing development projects and promulgating circulars. Thus, it is possible that the department has had a more *indirect* influence on the overall development of performance management through the development of institutional arrangements.

Hence, there is considerable evidence that the BD is engaged in the task of attaining allocative efficiency in the government sector, but that this task is to a large extent carried out in the budget *preparation phase* of the State Budget procedure.

Development of Instruments for Improving Operational Efficiency: Public Management or Public Administration?

The task of improving operational efficiency is focused on the relationship between the central agencies and line agencies. It includes both the yearly planning and control of the agencies in connection with the State Budget procedure, and development and implementation of an institutional framework for that planning and control. According to the *Internal Activity Plan* for the BD, the department should be involved in both these issues. The former has to do with the implementation of the budget in the government sector, and remains one of the main responsibilities of the BD. Concerning the institutional framework, the *Internal Activity Plan* states that the department has a responsibility for financial management and performance management in the government sector. One of the tasks particularly prioritized in the activity plan is to initiate further institutional reforms to the budgetary and planning processes and to the process of financial and performance management.

The more *direct* planning and control of agencies is generally undertaken by the ministry responsible for the individual agency. The BD is responsible for three such agencies.[6] In addition to that, the contact divisions in the BD are involved in discussions with the spending ministries concerning the Approval Letters (*Regleringsbrev*) that are given to each agency in the *budget preparation phase*. These letters include both appropriations and other financial restrictions, and objectives and non-financial performance measures. However, experience of these discussions suggests they are almost entirely focused on appropriations.

The present institutional planning and control framework was largely developed during the late-1980s and 1990s as a consequence of the introduction of performance management, a new accounting model and the public administration policy. The framework now consists of several components. Authority over and responsibility for the directors general of agencies is stipulated in the Ordinance on the Executive Management of the Agencies (*Verksförordningen*). This ordinance is the main responsibility of the Division for Public Management in the Ministry of Justice. In addition to that ordinance, the framework includes ordinances that specify the information agencies are obliged to provide the government in various phases of the State Budget procedure. One example is the ordinance concerning the Annual Reports and Budget Documentation. This ordinance is the main responsibility of the BD.

Each ordinance is supported by more detailed directions (*föreskrifter och allmänna råd*) and action plans (*handlingsprogram*) for the agencies, and circulars for the government. The detailed directions are the responsibility of the staff agencies, such as the National Financial Management Authority, while the responsibility for action plans and circulars rests with the government. One of the more important action plans in this area is the Public Administration Policy (*Förvaltningspolitiska handlingsprogrammet*), which is the responsibility of the Division for Public Management in the Ministry of Justice. Among the circulars, the Circular for Approval Letters (*Regleringsbrevshandledningen*) is also one of the more important since it specifies the information to be exchanged between the government and its agencies. Again responsibility for this circular rests with the BD.

Since the BD is responsible for most of the ordinances and circulars included in the institutional framework for the planning and control of agencies, it is fair to say that the department has a substantial *indirect* influence on the operational efficiency of the government sector. However, the main responsibility for development and implementation of instruments for improving operational efficiency is divided between the BD and the Division for Public Management in the Ministry of Justice. Furthermore, these two actors do not always agree on a proposed direction of reform. Generally, the B̆D has been the main proponent of the New Public Management reform agenda, while the Ministry of Justice's Division for Public Management has tended to emphasize values other than efficiency – as indicated in action plans such as the Public Administration Policy. This disjunction may be seen as a struggle between the norms of traditional *public administration* and the more recent adoption of business norms associated with *public management.*

CONCLUSION: THE SWEDISH CBA – A PLAYER WITH MANY STRINGS TO ITS BOW

The above analysis shows the BD in the Swedish Ministry of Finance is heavily engaged in all three basic tasks of the budgetary system outlined by Schick. Furthermore, the BD is variously active in all phases of the budget and uses both direct and indirect approaches. The main discussion in this chapter has focused on the current roles and tasks of the BD. There are several indications that the department has adapted to the changed circumstances affecting the public sector. One example of this is the increased emphasis on follow-up and forecasts and the increased engagement in developing tools for improving operational efficiency. Whether these and other changes represent a more general change in the role of the BD is not immediately obvious. There are certainly many indications that the BD has been involved in a broad range of tasks for many years, such as the imposition of aggregate fiscal discipline and advice on operational efficiency. Concerning the more policy-oriented issues in connection with allocative efficiency, it is less clear whether substantive change has occurred. On the one hand, there are indications that the BD has been involved in these issues for a long time. For example, the commissions that have preceded most major reforms in the public sector have often included representatives from the BD. Furthermore, Larsson (1986) argues that the BD and the Prime Minister's Office have long formed some kind of 'inner cabinet' responsible for coordinating government policy. However, it seems that the BD has been engaged in a broader range of issues during the last years, and that this engagement has been more proactive. One example of the latter is the so-called 'vacuum-cleaning project'. Concerning operational efficiency, there appears to have been an increase in both the direct planning and control of agencies and in developmental activities. However, it must be acknowledged that many of the more financially oriented tools for planning and control of agencies have long been the responsibility of the BD.

To conclude, the tasks and roles of the BD are changing continuously. It is difficult to clearly identify changes in the overall roles of the department. Nevertheless, during the last decades the BD has been somewhat more engaged in the later phases of the State Budget procedure, more proactive in policy issues in connection with allocative efficiency, and more involved in the non-financial aspects of the planning and control of government agencies. So, what then are the possible drivers of change in the tasks and roles of the BD? It is reasonable to assume that changes in the context of the BD have propelled the changes to its tasks and roles. Thus, the reorientation of the BD to focus on the later stages of the budget process occurred in conjunction with the introduction of expenditure ceilings after 1997. Another example is the increased focus on aggregate fiscal discipline that occurred in connection with the financial crisis affecting the Swedish government in the early-1990s.

Finally, what are the future prospects of the Swedish CBA in relation to expenditure control and budgetary management? Overall we must conclude that there is no revolution in sight. The BD will continue to be an important actor engaged in various ways in all the important tasks of the Swedish budget system. The emphasis of the work performed by the BD will certainly continue to evolve over time, responding in particular to the political situation of Swedish politics, the economic circumstances faced by Sweden, and the further impact of public management in the government sector. But, as in the past, the roles of the Swedish CBA will continue to be widely conceived as we move into the future.

NOTES

1.   The author's own experiences are rather extensive. First, in the early 1990s he worked as a political advisor in the coordination function (*samordningskansliet*) at the Prime Minister's Office (*Statsrådsberedningen*). In that position he was involved in the negotiations between the four coalition parties in the government. In these negotiations, representatives from the BD were often invited to present the point of view of the BD on various issues that were on the political agenda. Second, in the mid-1990s, he was a senior advisor in the National Audit Office (*Riksrevisionsverket*) and The National Financial Management Authority (*Ekonomistyrningsverket*), working with developmental projects concerning financial management and performance management. In that position he witnessed first-hand many of the functions of the BD relating to developmental activities in that area. Finally, from the late-1990s until recently, he was employed at the BD, working on the development of better financial management and performance management practices. In that position he became familiar with the inner life of the BD. Altogether, these personal experiences are an important input in this research project.
2.   The data is received from the Department of Administration in the Ministry of Finance.
3.   The Swedish state budget is structured into 27 separate expenditure areas.
4.   The accounting model is presented in English in Ekonomistyrningsverket (2001).

5.   See, for example, Finansdepartementet (1995), for a more in-depth discussion of the topic.
6.   The National Audit Office, the National Financial Management Authority and the Swedish Agency for Government Employers (partly).

7. A 'Super-Ministry' or a Void of Politics? The Transformation of the Dutch Central Budget Agency: the Ministry of Finance[1]

Jouke de Vries and Kutsal Yesilkagit

This chapter examines the changing role and orientations of the Minister and Ministry of Finance in the budgetary process in the Netherlands. The traditional view (roughly pre-1980) was that Finance played a pivotal role in the budgetary process. However, since the beginning of the 1980s some major political and economic developments have occurred which have had important impacts on the Dutch political system. Among these developments are the transition from Keynesian economics to monetarism, supply-side economics and public choice; the adoption of EMU norms; and the prosperous international economic tide that has led to budget surpluses in many OECD countries. The main overall question in this chapter is how have such external developments affected the position of the Minister and Ministry of Finance? Has Finance become a 'super-ministry'; has Finance's position declined; or is it the continuation of the usual politics under different guises?

The structure of this chapter is as follows. There are two main parts. The first part introduces the role, position, and actual performance of the Minister of Finance and the Finance department. It examines the legal-institutional framework of the budgetary process and the laws and regulations that stipulate the formal tasks and duties of the Minister of Finance. Here it is suggested that the Minister of Finance occupies a relatively weak legal-institutional position. Beyond the formal laws are a series of important budgetary norms that have been politically agreed and form the framework rules pertaining to the handling of expenditures and revenues in the budget round. Finance ministers are able, if they demonstrate the political will, to exploit these norms to particular ends. The next section argues that the personal style of Ministers of Finance can be seen as an important variable shaping the budgetary process, influencing outcomes and determining the functions performed by the Dutch CBA. It is necessary to analyse the personal style of successive Finance Ministers against the prevailing political and macro-economic context. Although it may be considered that these features are relatively autonomous of each other, we argue that the interrelationship between ministerial style and the politico-economic context illustrates much about the steering capacity of both the minister and the CBA. The penultimate section of the chapter focuses on the role Finance played with regard to the uptake of New Public Management ideas, particularly with regard to public sector reforms and financial management reforms. Finally, this chapter ends with a general assessment of the changing role and position of Finance.

THE LEGAL-INSTITUTIONAL FRAMEWORK OF THE DUTCH BUDGETARY PROCESS

Before we examine the particular transformations of the Ministry of Finance, it is essential to know something about the organization of the ministry and the institutional framework of the budget process in the Netherlands. The Ministry of Finance is politically headed by both a minister and a junior minister. The merit-bureaucracy is headed by a permanent secretary (who is often party-aligned but not necessarily of the same party as the minister). The Ministry consists of four directorates-general: the Chief Treasury, the Budget, Fiscal Policy and Taxes. Besides these directorates-general there are several central staff organizations. In essence, almost all budgetary, financial, revenue and fiscal functions are concentrated within the single organization. Around 1700 staff work at the core-ministry located in The Hague, while in the regionalized tax authorities another 32,000 people are employed.

Together with other continental systems, the Dutch budget system differs to a significant extent from the majority of Anglo-Saxon budget systems. The most salient feature of the Dutch budget system is that the budget process is anchored in the Constitution (Articles 65 and 105 of the 1983 Constitution). A further basic statute derived from the Constitution, the *Law on Accountability (Comptabiliteitswet)*, stipulates the rules and procedures for parliamentary debate and consent and the issue of ministerial accountability for the budget. In practice, the budget process is subject to changes and revisions, but the main point is that budgetary politics in the Netherlands is founded upon law backed by the written constitution.

The *Law on Accountability* regulates in detail the process of budget-making. Some sections of the law have changed as a consequence of regular revisions, but the main aspects prescribed by law are as follows.[2] First, the *Law on Accountability* defines the main components of the budget, the budgetary calendar year, a time schedule, the presentation of the budget, and the procedures for changing budget. Another section ascribes specific responsibilities for (parts of) the budget to members of the executive.[3] The same section further prescribes exactly how different items should be registered and presented within the budget. Third, the *Law on Accountability* defines the formal position of the Minister of Finance in the budget-making process. A fourth section of the law is devoted to the position and discretions of the General Accounting Office. Individual articles of this law give detailed prescriptions for interactions and relationships between cabinet and parliament and between the members of cabinet and the Minister of Finance. Hence, budgetary politics in the Netherlands occurs within a rigid institutional framework.

This formal legal institutional framework for budget-making ascribes a number of specific tasks and functions to the office of the Minister of Finance. The formal role of the Minister of Finance is founded on three sets of rules and regulations. The Regulations of the Council of Ministers (RCM – *Reglement van orde voor de ministerraad*), a number of Council of Ministers agreements concerning the process of budgetary decision-making, and, most importantly, the *Law on Accountability* (*Comptabiliteitswet*) shape the formal role and position of the Minister of Finance as well as constrain his behaviour. Formal rules do not reflect actual behaviour; rather they stipulate the boundaries of possible alternatives for behaviour of the person who occupies the position of minister. Formal rules also affect the behaviours of other actors (civil servants, cabinet members, non-central governmental actors, and interest groups) because formal rules make others anticipate the behaviour of the person operating under the formal regime.

So, to what extent have the formal rules guiding the position of the Minister of Finance changed in the last 20 years? The RCM considers the Minister of Finance equal to other ministers.[4] He, thus, has no formal powers to influence the budget-making process. The only minister who has such powers is the Prime Minister, who presides over the council and other sub-councils, sets the cabinet agenda and remains *primus inter pares*. The power of a Minister of Finance does not transcend that of a minister of any other department. Hence, to exercise influence over the politics of the budgetary process, the Finance Minister is dependent upon informal strategies and resources available to him as the minister responsible for public finance and upon his relationship with the Prime Minister.

A Council of Ministers' decision dating from 1919 is more specific about the discretion of the Minister of Finance (Toirkens 1988, p. 169). This decision stated that it was the Finance Minister's duty to inform new ministers that:

- all draft bills, as well as other proposals to be presented to the Members of the Council, should be submitted first to the Minister of Finance;

- during debates with the Second and First Chambers, ministers are not allowed to make any promises that would imply a rise in spending without the prior consent of the Minister of Finance or the Council of Ministers;
- changes or amendments within draft bills that are proposed by parliament and granted by the minister in question leading to a rise in spending will not be made without the prior approval of the Minister of Finance;
- measures or regulation with substantial financial consequences will not be taken without the prior approval by the Minister of Finance and the Council of Ministers even when there exists budgetary slack for such measures or regulation.

With reference to the formal position of the Minister of Finance according to the RCM, there are no sanctions attached to this decision other than *ad hoc* informal sanctions.

The *Law on Accountability*, finally, contains the rules and procedures concerning the organization, formulation and submitting of the Central Budget (van der Pot and Donner 1983, pp. 509–11; Kortmann 1990, pp. 211–13). During the last decade, the Law has been continuously revised; the last two times (2000) as part of a range of treasury (*schatkist*) and budget reforms (Tweede Kamer 1999–2000, 26974, nr. 3).[5] The role and scope for discretion of the Minister of Finance are subject to change, too, but we can sum up the following 'constants' in the Minister's formal position based on the latest revision of the *Comptabiliteitswet* (CW 6, Staatsblad 1995, p. 375). First, the Minister of Finance must inform and maintain contacts with the Second and First Chambers and the General Accounting Office (*Algemene Rekenkamer*). Second, he is responsible for coordinating the budgeting process in general, keeping track of the budgeting process in other departments. His ministerial colleagues are obliged to send him the necessary financial and budgetary information and other records, either at his request to perform his control tasks (Articles 35–38) or due to the pre-scheduled budgetary year agenda. Third, but within the frame of the second point, the Minister of Finance is responsible for the production of budgetary documents (Article 9). And fourth, the Minister of Finance is responsible for the Treasury (*'s Rijks schatkist*).

However, the *Law on Accountability* does not mention anything about conflict resolution in cases where disputes between the Minister of Finance and ministers of spending departments arise. Overspending, demands for more budgets, the (low) quality of financial information, and the exceeding of time limits are all possible and plausible causes of such disputes. Disputes have to be resolved within the Council of Ministers (Kortmann 1990, p. 211). This brings the question of the position and influence of a Finance Minister back to the RCM. As far as it concerns the Minister of Finance, the *Law on Accountability* describes his position and prescribes the tasks and responsibilities within the confines of financial management and the budget-making process, but it does not ascribe formal sanctions to deal with conflict situations. In conclusion, the three most important formal regulations that define the role of the Minister of Finance have not substantially changed. The *Law on Accountability*, which is the most important law, has regularly been updated, but the paragraph on the position of the Finance Minister has remained the same on crucial points.

DUTCH BUDGETARY NORMS

The legal-institutional framework of the Dutch budget process described above provides the most important formal parameters for the role and position, and in the end, the functioning of the Minister and the Ministry of Finance within, respectively, the Council of Ministers and interdepartmental network of Dutch central government. However, as argued by one of our respondents, a Minister of Finance who relies solely on his/her formal position would signify an admission of weakness.[6] Paradoxically, then, the legal-institutional framework is only invoked in periods of Finance's weakness. And, indeed, the actual position of Finance (both the minister as well as the civil servants) depends heavily on budget norms.

From World War II until the present day, we can distinguish four main frameworks of budgetary regulation. The first two budgetary norms employed in this period were the conjunctural budget norm (1950–59) and the structural budgeting norm (1959–78). Both were frameworks based on Keynesian economic theories but differed with regard to dealing with anti- and pro-cyclical periods and the use of mid-term planning. These budget norms were succeeded by frameworks based on monetarist theories, first on the real deficit norm (1983–93) and then on an index-related budgetary norm (1994–2002) known as the 'Zalm-norm' that currently prevails and is expected to prevail at least until the general elections in May 2002. These budgetary norms have a structuring effect on the position and political-administrative room for manoeuvre of Finance. The establishment of framework rules is ultimately a political process in which the leaders and financial experts of political parties play a dominant role. Once agreed upon, and when continually supported by a parliamentary majority, these evolving budget norms form the arena within which political parties advocate or oppose their respective program expenditures or cuts, spending departments defend their departmental budgets, and Finance draws the contours of the financial and fiscal policies to be pursued and if necessary proposes cuts.

We shall illustrate this by comparing the structural budget framework (1959–78)[7] with the consequences of the so-called 'Zalm-norm' (1994–2002). Both frameworks are comparable because both prevailed under conditions of economic growth, which was fixed at about 3 to 5 per cent per annum. Budgetary politics under both frameworks were thus aimed at the allocation of spending across different policy sectors. They differed, however, in the modus of budgetary policy-making, which in the earlier period was more political than in the second period.

The following example, told by one of our respondents, illustrates this point. Jelle Zijlstra who was Minister of Finance several times (1958–59, 1959–63 and 1966–67) was (in)famous for his 'red ballpoint'. Under this earlier regime, yearly budgetary allocations between Finance and spending departments took place under bilateral negotiations. Ministers of spending departments each year submitted their departmental budgets. These 'wish lists' were scrutinized by Zijlstra in their presence. This ritual occurred each year, after cabinet had determined the budgetary room. It took place at a high political and administrative level, involving the ministers and director-generals of the respective departments. The Office of the State Budget Inspectors (*Inspectie Rijksfinanciën* – IRF), under the Directorate General of the State Budget of the Finance department, also played a crucial role. Operating as a 'countervailing power' in the budgetary politics, budget inspectors tended to know beforehand the upcoming demands of virtually each departmental unit before they were put before the minister.

Compared to this period, the politics of the budgetary process became depoliticized from 1994 onwards for two reasons. The first and main reason is the adoption of the so-called 'Zalm-norm', named after the Minister of Finance, Gerrit Zalm (1994–2002). The 'Zalm-norm' is based on the following rules: (1) prudence in forecasting of economic growth; (2) dividing income from expenditure; (3) in the event of financial setbacks, coverage is found from within each department's own budget; (4) expenditure on social security and public health is isolated from the rest of the government budget; (5) budget decisions are taken during the formation of the coalition cabinet; after that, discussions are closed.[8] The last condition has been instrumental in the depoliticization of the budgetary process. Budgetary decisions are only taking during the formation of a new cabinet and remain fixed during the entire coalition period. A debate on these norms would mean nothing less than a weakening or questioning of the basic foundation on which the coalition rested. Consequently, since 1994 the yearly budget round has taken place without substantial political struggles, either between political parties or departmental agencies. The yearly expenditure ceilings set by the 'Zalm-norm' bound the political parties; spending departments were forced to account for drawbacks from their own departmental budgets.

Second, the budgetary process under the Purple Coalitions (I and II) has also been depoliticized, according to another respondent, as a consequence of the growing technical complexity of the budget, as well as the growth of the total number of budget items at the level of central government. The neat lists Zijlstra used to scrutinize with his red ballpoint have turned into complex documents. Consequently, the *politics* of the budgetary process have gradually evolved into the *administration* of the budgetary process. The Office of State Budget Inspectors has become a more differentiated unit in Finance, with specialist inspectors for every department/policy sector. Moreover, the educational backgrounds of the inspectors have become more differentiated. Where once only economically-trained inspectors prevailed, there are now increasingly more inspectors with a legal and public administration background. The approach of IRF has become more 'managerial'.

The above cases where budget-making occurred within the context of economic growth contrast sharply with the period between 1979 and 1993. First, the period between 1979 and 1982 was dramatic and politically haphazard as Keynesian economic ideas were abruptly replaced by monetarism. This reflected itself in the subsequent cabinet crises and short-lived coalitions between 1980 and 1982. Added to political crises was the huge rise of the budget deficit and national debt (from 4.6 per cent and 44 per cent respectively in 1979, to 8.3 and 55 per cent in 1982). The period remains known as the 'Dutch Disease'. The first of the three Lubbers' cabinets (1982–86; 1986–89 with the Conservative Liberals – VVD; and 1989–94 with the Labour Party – PvdA) was clearly the harbinger of the 'no-nonsense' era. As discussed below, from the mid-1980s, New Public Management reforms would gain sway and form the foundation for performance-oriented budgets and accrual budgeting. Before this could take place, the first Lubbers cabinet implemented its budgetary framework based on the 'real debt norm'. Under this norm Onno Ruding adopted a 'time-path approach' that targeted a fixed annual percentage of deficit reduction, regardless of the prevailing conjunctural conditions. Unexpectedly high expenditures or low revenue incomes were redressed by new rounds of slimming down. The position of Finance between 1983 and 1993 was not without exaggeration described to the authors as 'fat years for Finance, meagre years for the country'.

PERSONAL MINISTERIAL STYLE AND MACRO-ECONOMIC CONTEXT

We now shift focus to the behavioural or style options available to Finance Ministers. Next to the *Law on Accountability* and budget norms, it is also important to consider the personal style of the Finance Minister. At the same time, we also take the political and macro-economic context into consideration. The actions and tactics employed by Finance Ministers in handling their portfolio responsibilities seem to result from the interplay of financial-political circumstances and their personal styles. Although both parameters could have an independent effect, we thought that we could best illustrate these in conjunction with each other. In relation to the macro-economic context we distinguish and describe the roles of Finance Ministers in two periods. The first period is characterized by economic crises and budgetary shortfall and extends roughly from 1975 to 1994. The second period begins in 1994 with the advent of the first Purple Coalition (1994–98) and is characterized by economic growth and budgetary surpluses – a feature that occurs for the first time since the beginning of the second half of the 20th century. While the pace of economic growth tends to slow down and inflation has risen to be one of the highest in the EU at the time of writing, there is still a budgetary surplus, and 'investment' is the key political word rather than budget cuts. We shall return to this period when we discuss the implementation of financial management reforms later in this chapter.

For the first period, we turn to Toirkens (1988) who has provided an in-depth analysis of the behaviour of subsequent Finance Ministers between 1975 and 1986. Her main argument was that while macro-economic factors (for example, economic growth, the imposition of the tax burden and the size of the financial deficit) were important indicators, 'the actions of the Minister counted heavily ... he does not want a hole in his budget' (Toirkens 1988, p. 169). Together with the (weak) formal position of the minister – he has no special position *vis-à-vis* his colleagues – these interests compel him to choose a conflict-minimalization style of behaviour. The greatest danger for a Dutch Minister of Finance whose sole and most important aim is to reduce the budget deficit is to become isolated and overruled by the ministers of the other spending departments.

Under conditions of rising budget deficit Toirkens found that Finance Ministers often reverted to one of the following behaviours: (1) anticipatory behaviour; (2) lenient behaviour; (3) persuasive behaviour; (4) support-seeking behaviour; and (5) interfering behaviour (Toirkens 1988, p. 172). She found anticipatory tactics most likely to occur when financial economic prognoses predicted a severe backdrop that urged for the adoption of a radical adjustment program or when a number of adjustment programs were geared to each other. Leniency, by contrast, seemed to be the most common behavioural norm for Finance Ministers. Toirkens' study showed that Dutch Finance Ministers almost never managed to impose the adjustments deemed necessary. Although the *Law on Accountability* does give the Finance Minister the means to block specific expenditures of other ministers before he has given his consent, in the practice of adjustment politics this remains a dead letter and the outcome of the struggle depends on the negotiation skills of the ministers involved.

Third, Finance Ministers often reverted to the use of persuasion as tactic. Toirkens distinguished between 'persuasion-with-arguments' and 'persuasion-by-threats' or a combination of both. The ultimate argument or threat was based on the future course of the budget deficit should remedial measures not be taken. However, to use persuasion by threatening was only a viable option under extreme circumstances. Lacking formal authority on budgetary decision-making the Finance Minister needed to be more adaptive to other views. Support-seeking, the fourth possible tactic identified by Toirkens, was such a role. A Finance Minister has to seek support from his civil servants (for example, those in the important interdepartmental economic coordination committee) to support his views in negotiations with other departments. Support-seeking behaviour was often conjoined by the employment of personal networks within cabinet or the exertion of influence within bilateral negotiations.

The fifth and final type of tactical behaviour was interference with departmental budgeting processes. Some Finance Ministers between 1975 and 1986 were renowned for the high level of interference with departmental budgets and the implementation of adjustment programs at the departmental level. Toirkens distinguished two different periods (1988, p. 183). Until 1982, Finance Ministers did not intervene in the details of other departments' budgets. The Finance Minister let other ministers implement the adjustment programs, but monitored afterwards whether the proposed adjustments had met the criteria previously set. The Finance Minister only proposed alternative adjustments in cases where individual adjustment proposals fell below these criteria giving the line minister 'a second chance'. However, the intensity of interference changed drastically after 1982. Fons Van der Stee (Van Agt Cabinet III, 1981–82) made a habit of sending 'a stream of letters' to spending ministers with detailed forecasts of economic and financial decline and countervailing adjustments. He reaped the irritation of his colleagues; all his letters contained the same text except that the figures were different (Toirkens 1988, p. 88). He also posited question marks against planned expenditures agreed upon earlier by the cabinet (Toirkens 1988, p. 183). Onno Ruding, Van der Stee's successor in the Lubbers Cabinet I (1982–86), applied the same tactics but perhaps pushed a bit further. Ruding tried to expand his influence outside the 'narrow' departmental spending budgets, wanting to add the social welfare sector and social welfare contributions to his sphere of influence. He appointed his civil servants and some of the Finance-oriented Economic Affairs department to working groups and interdepartmental committees working on social security issues. This brought him into an increasingly adversarial relationship with the Minister of Social Affairs and Employment (Toirkens 1988, p. 184ff).

The personal styles and tactics employed by Finance Ministers also had an effect on the established norms and rules within the Finance Ministry. The break with the 'non-intervention principle' just described, challenged the prevailing Finance view over negotiation with other departments and political-administrative actors. Wim Duisenberg (Den Uyl Cabinet, 1973–77), for example, used to hold weekly working groups with his staff to determine a ministry position to take to the Council of Ministers meeting. The position then determined remained the first and final position the minister would take in the Council. In the event that he 'lost', Duisenberg was forced to return with a decision formulated at the cabinet meeting overruling the preferred departmental advice. The relationship between Frans Andriessen and his staff was quite different – as a minister he did not feel the need to remain constrained by departmental advice. According to one of Toirkens' respondents, Andriessen told his civil servants that he attached 'great value to your [that is, the civil servants'] judgment, but this is a political process and there lies a sort of canal at the point where you stop and my final position in that political process' (Toirkens 1988, p. 187). However, not only did Andriessen not listen to advice, but he was not much of a negotiator and Finance civil servants never knew beforehand what the likely outcome of the cabinet meeting would be.

The attitude and practice towards negotiations changed radically under Van der Stee. Van der Stee always asked his staff for a bottom line, the final position he could take in the negotiations within cabinet. Van der Stee reasoned as follows:

> Being right and getting right are two entirely different things. It is just completely unimaginable that the Minister of Finance will get things his way for the entire four years. It is also unimaginable that 14 or 15 colleagues will always go home with bleeding heads. They must have success some time (Toirkens 1988, p. 188).

Ruding continued this pattern in the four years under Lubbers I, to the shock of Finance civil servants. As one of them told Toirkens: 'a Minister of Finance asking for a bottom line ... now, that was really unique. Finance always considered itself to be "right" but when the Minister of Finance did not make it his own proposal we knew for sure that things would go wrong' (Toirkens 1988, p. 187). Ruding's behaviour might be explained from the fact that he was an international banker when he took up office. With this financial market background and a monetarist orientation, he entered politics with the idea of 'getting things done'.

From 1990 onwards (the period of the third Lubbers cabinet onwards), Finance has had two Ministers of Finance: the Social Democrat Wim Kok (1990–94) and the Conservative Liberal Gerrit Zalm (1994 to the present). To begin with the former, although being a working class Social Democrat and former president of the largest labour union (FNV), he studied at the Nijenrode Academy for Business Administration, then a private elite institution from which many Dutch 'captains of industry' have graduated.[9] In the second half of the 1980s, the former Prime Minster and party leader Joop Den Uyl brought him to the Labour Party (PvdA) in a period when a Conservative Liberal and Christian Democrat coalition was in power and severe adjustment programs were high on the agenda. He succeeded Den Uyl as party leader but lost his first election as a party leader in 1986, which was a severe drawback for him. When the centre-right cabinet fell in 1989, Kok brought his party into the coalition with the Christian Democratic CDA. In that cabinet, he became the Minister of Finance. However, as one respondent told us, Kok was party leader, Deputy Prime Minister, and Minister of Finance at the same time. The combination of these diverse political roles, the official believed, proved difficult and detrimental from the Finance Ministry's point of view.

Combining the party leadership with the position of Finance Minister in a coalition cabinet is almost guaranteed to create conflicts between the austerity principles of budgetary policy-making and the political demands of his party in government. It also gives rise to potential conflicts in cabinet with party colleagues who head the spending departments administering public policy issues promoted by the party. As Deputy Prime Minister, Kok was responsible for the unity and coherence of cabinet decision-making. While every member of cabinet is collectively responsible for the coherence of policy, the Deputy Prime Minister is the second most senior minister in cabinet and has a special responsibility to coordinate and mediate the process of collective decision-making. Hence, although Kok as head of the Finance Ministry between 1990 and 1994 was a heavyweight Social Democrat (and later Prime Minister), in practice he operated on the edge of intersecting forces and conflicting pressures.

The difficult and complex position of Kok becomes clearer when we discuss Zalm.[10] First, Zalm is an economist and his professional career began in the Ministry of Finance. He left the department and became the director of the Central Planning Bureau, the formal socio-economic advisory body of the Dutch government. Unlike Kok, Zalm was not burdened by having to perform any other position within the cabinet. He was neither party leader nor Deputy Prime Minister. Zalm was simply a specialist Minister of Finance for 100 per cent of his time. He has also survived such that he will shortly become the Netherlands' longest serving Minister of Finance. For the Finance department, Zalm is the ideal minister. He is, as one of our respondents said, 'one of us'. He understands the 'Finance view' and implicitly follows the logic of the 'architecture'[11] of the budget process. As a minister, Zalm is primarily preoccupied with defending and promoting his policy of budgetary discipline, within the principles of the 'Zalm-norm', leaving the management of the budgetary process, which includes budget-related interactions with other departments, to his civil servants. Having this leeway, Finance officials have been able to design more effective budgetary procedures or 'architecture' that supports and improves the position of their minister *vis-à-vis* other ministers and departments. Whereas the rationales and behaviours of a political minister such as Kok did not always accord with the department's rationales, with Zalm they have.

NEW PUBLIC MANAGEMENT REFORMS AND THE ROLE OF THE MINISTRY OF FINANCE

The sections above have discussed the parameters that determine the position and functioning of the Minister of Finance and the Finance Ministry within the budgetary process. Below, we shift perspective and examine the role of Finance within the introduction and dissemination of New Public Management (NPM) ideas in the Netherlands. The adoption and translation of NPM ideas began with organizational reforms to the public sector and then spread to more specific financial management reforms – with the VBTB program being the latest reform initiative.

Public Sector Reforms: Privatization and Agencification (1982–90)

The advent of the Lubbers cabinet in 1982 changed the prevailing balance of power between the Ministry of Finance and the other spending departments in the domain of administrative reform. The financial-economic crisis of the welfare state, and the subsequent replacement of Keynesian economics by monetarist ideas, transferred the prerogative in matters of administrative policies from the hands of the Ministry of Interior Affairs to those of Finance. In contrast to the history of public management reforms in most Anglo-Saxon countries, the NPM reforms to the Dutch central bureaucracy were, to paraphrase Barzelay (2001, p. 72), rather a 'spillover effect' from the economic and financial reform policies. In order to eliminate the budget deficit, Finance initiated a set of organizational reforms within the public sector, and only later, when a substantial part of the public sector had been privatized or 'agencified', did the Ministry of Finance adopt government-wide financial management reforms, such as the introduction of performance-based financial management regimes.

The dominance of Finance began with the installation of the first Lubbers cabinet in 1982, continued under the second Lubbers cabinet established in 1986, and lasted until 1990 (Kickert and Verhaak 1995; de Vries and Yesilkagit 1999). During this entire period, public sector reforms were primarily regarded as an instrument to contain expenditure growth and reduce the financial pressures placed on the central budget by department budgets. An interdepartmental committee working under the aegis of Finance scrutinized the other departments searching for organizational units that could be hived off from the host department and hence from the departmental budget. This interdepartmental committee (namely the Interdepartmental Guidance Committee for Privatization (IGCP or *Interdepartementale Begeleidingscommissie Privatizering*), enjoyed significant political support from an informal coalition of cabinet members, including both the Prime Minister and Finance Minister who shared neo-liberal orientations. The head of the IGCP himself and a number of its members adhered to the same ideological orientation, irrespective of their party membership.

As a result of this level of political support, the IGCP was in a position to act independently with regard to the selection of departmental budget items and able to require the relevant secretaries or directors-general to establish working groups within their departments to produce feasibility reports concerning the units targeted for privatization. Despite these procedures, the process of selection and assessment still endured delays. Several departments, especially those that had no representative within the committee, resisted the prerogative of Finance. Hereupon, the IGCP designed a new procedure for the selection and assessment of targets and proposed this to Ruding. First, the IGCP proposed to replace the bureaucrats within the department's working group with externals. Second, the IGCP proposed to appoint a manager from the private sector to the position of chairman of the departmental working groups. Third, the IGCP hired consultants to provide a secretariat to the groups. This way, the IGCP removed departmental civil servants as much as possible from the privatization process. Moreover, the IGCP imposed the costs of the external experts on the departments. Since privatization was promoted as the main means of priority of slimming down government, the IGCP actually succeeded in having these procedures installed and executed.

After 1990, the role and influence of the Ministry of Finance changed as the politics of agencification were played out under a new coalition government, which again included the Labour Party. Under the third Lubbers cabinet (1990–94), Kok officially dropped the priority his department had attached to the policy of privatization mainly for party political and ideological reasons. Initially, he regarded the agencification program as an anti-public sector orientation reminiscent of the neo-liberal right cabinets of Lubbers I and II. However, now ensconced as Finance Minister, Kok also began to reconsider and adopt some of the neo-liberal economic ideas of his predecessors. Gradually the perspective of the Ministry of Finance became more important to him than the interests of the Labour Party. Yet, Kok did not make clear his somersault to the Labour Party. In a gesture towards the left wing of his party, he stated publicly that privatization was no longer on the agenda and that 'the fire of privatization was not burning' in him. Instead, he announced that he would look at public reforms from a more pragmatic stance. But as the Minister of Finance, he was nevertheless caught up in an ongoing public sector reform program. He merely changed the definition of public sector reforms; the preferred word was no longer privatization or agencification, but now 'autonomization' (*verzelfstandiging*) was considered the primary goal of the public sector reforms.

The Ministry of Finance continued their agendas but working within this redefinition. They were supportive of the change largely because the IGCP had already succeeded with the agencification of a large number of departmental units. By 1990, the projects of 31 departmental units with 113,745 civil servants were already agencificated.[12] The agencification of another 13 departmental units with 8475 personnel was well under way at this time (Hamer and van de Ven 1993, pp. 173–75). Compared with the figures for 1988 (Meer and Roborgh 1993), this meant that almost half of the total number of personnel employed by central departments and state enterprises (113,745 out of 245,000 personnel) were already hived off. From 1990 onwards, the emphasis shifted to the implementation of liberalization policies in a range of social and economic domains such as the public utilities, market liberalization, legal advice, and shopping hours. In this domain, however, the Ministry of Finance was not a key player. Rather, the Ministries of Economic Affairs and of Justice coordinated the operation that supported marketization, improved the quality of (competition) laws, and deregulation. The focus of Finance in this period shifted towards the reform of the budget process and the financial management systems of the central state and other public bodies.

FINANCIAL MANAGEMENT REFORMS: FROM POLICY BUDGETING TO POLICY ACCOUNTING (VBTB)

Currently the most important budget reform program in the Netherlands is the implementation of the so-called 'From Policy Budgeting to Policy Accounting' (*Van Beleidsbegroting tot Beleidsverantwoording* – VBTB). This program was presented as a fundamental reform of the organization of budgeting and accountability. It is an important example of the pre-eminence of NPM ideas in the Netherlands. The essence of the budgetary and financial management reforms transformed the previous system of input-oriented line item budgeting to one based on performance-based principles. Not only have the key incentives and orientations of actors been altered, but also the format and content of budget documents as well as the existing procedures and timing of the budgetary process have changed. The implications of adopting the new accounting policy of VBTB are broad and are likely to have profound institutional consequences in the future. Not only are the present reforms changing the essential parameters of the politics of the budget process, but they are also extending the role of the Minister and Ministry of Finance beyond their conventional preoccupation with the financial-economic domain into more general areas of policy-making and the earlier stages of policy decision-making.

The intellectual roots of the VBTB reforms came from two different sources. The first was that of *administrative learning* generated from experiences associated with the improvement of budgetary policies and the refinement of its instruments. The Ministry of Finance was a key actor in this process. In November 1986, a working group in the department (called Differentiation Administrative Procedures) had issued an 'Operation Accountable Order' (*Operatie Comptabel Bestel*), which was intended to improve the legitimacy and control of government expenditures. This order resulted in the fourth revision to the *Law on Accountability* (including the introduction of double bookkeeping). Subsequently, the working group delivered a report on 'building further on administration'.[13] With this report, the Ministry of Finance took the first step in the development of a results-orientated, or performance-based, system with which to steer government agencies.

The initial structural reform under the rubric of the VBTB occurred in 1994 with the introduction of the 'internal and external agency-model' (Articles 70–73 in *Comptabiliteitswet, staatsblad* 1995/375). According to the new agency-model rules an internal agency ('agentschap') is defined as a departmental unit with executive tasks for which the minister is entirely responsible, except for the unit's internal financial management.[14] The reforms promised that the financial management of the new 'agentschappen' would improve because they would be given clearer objectives, a tighter definition governing their products and services, a more transparent determination of cost prices, and an increase in internal managerial discretion. Under the prevailing cash-obligation system, these units had little or no room at all for output-oriented management and made output-based control difficult for the responsible minister to impose. The administrative relationship between the departments and the new 'agentschappen' has come to be known as 'output-oriented management' (*resultaatgericht management*). In this model, the minister or department managers relate to the internal agency in a purchaser-provider or buyer-producer contractual relationship. The 'contract' contains agreements about output, cost per unit, and the level of quality. Currently there are about 22 'agentschappen' in operation.

The Ministry of Finance has continued this trend towards output or results-oriented management in central government agencies. In March 1997, Minister Zalm sent a note entitled 'From Spending to Costs' to the Second Chamber (Tweede Kamer 1996–97, 25257, nr. 1). In this note, the minister proposed the adoption of a result-orientated steering model (*resultaatgerichte besturingsmodel*) including a system of assets and liabilities (*baten-lastenstelsel*) for governmental agencies, as well as the development of performance indicators and measurement techniques. A follow-up note that was presented within the interdepartmental policy analysis (*interdepartementale beleidsonderzoeken*) framework further specified these proposals under two headings: 'business management executive agencies' and 'financial renewal'.[15] While the report 'Towards Results'[16] (Ministerie van Financiën 1997) provided a conceptual framework for selecting departmental units, a subsequent letter by the Minister of Finance (Tweede Kamer 1996–97, 25509, nr. 1) listed 14 departmental units to be placed under either one of the above-mentioned themes.

Today, the Ministry of Finance is continuing its efforts to reform the administrative behaviour and financial management practices of the central government apparatus. Two recent efforts occurred in the revision of the *Law on Accountability* (that is, the sixth and seventh revisions). The sixth revision concerned the separation of departmental budgetary bills and financial accountability reports. The seventh revision (2000) broadened the applicability of business management processes from 'agencies' to the entire departmental organization.

The second source of inspiration for the VBTB reforms arose from the work of the Second Chamber's Committee on Government Expenditures.[17] On 18 February 1997, the committee sent a report containing an evaluation of the workings of the committee itself to the Chairman of the Second Chamber. One of the problems detected by the committee was the slow pace of financial accountability procedures. The committee stated that the sixth revision of the *Law on Accountability* had achieved improvements. However, the committee added that the period of four months that usually lay between the submitting of financial accounts by individual departments to the Ministry of Finance (on 23 April) and the latter's submission of these reports to the Second Chamber (the second or third week of September) was too long a period for the Chamber to perform its scrutiny task effectively (Tweede Kamer 1996–97, 25396, nr. 2, p. 3). On 23 April 1997, the Committee on Government Expenditures held a conference on this subject to advance their point that the financial accounting process should be expedited.

On 9 June 1997, the Second Chamber passed a motion supporting the committee. It asked the President of the General Accounting Office[18] and the Minister of Finance to establish a working group to explore how the financial accountability procedures could be quickened (Tweede Kamer 1996–97, 25396, nr. 3). In his letter of 1 October 1997, the Minister of Finance agreed with the foundation of such a working group. He also announced a further revision of the *Law on Accountability* (Tweede Kamer 1996–97, 25396, nr. 7). In June 1998, a commission consisting of members of the Committee on Government Expenditures, representatives of the General Accounting Office and a number of departments, presented its report 'Annual Report in the Political Arena'.[19]

The cabinet note VBTB, which was presented to the Second Chamber on 19 May 1999, was largely based on the annual report. It contained chapters on how the new budget and accounting procedures were to be organized, as well as how the budget cycle was to be altered.

The Logic of VBTB

The VBTB reforms aimed to effect a radical change in Dutch budgetary politics. Whereas the former budgetary methods only focused on input budgeting and financial accountability of departmental budget items, VBTB brought in policy accountability. In other words, the budget process now centres around two documents: the departmental budget and the departmental annual reports. For each document, VBTB established two sets of questions. The first set of questions aimed at improved departmental budgeting asks departments to answer: (1) 'what do you want to achieve?'; (2) 'what are you going to do for that?'; and (3) 'how much will that cost?'. The second set of questions relates to the annual reports, and requires departments to account for their performance against the intentions originally shown in their budgetary documents. Departments have to address the questions: (1) 'have you achieved what you intended?'; (2) 'have you done the things you intended to do?'; and (3) 'have you spent the amount of money you thought the program would cost?'. The VBTB reforms went as far as prescribing the format of future departmental budgets and year reports (Ministerie van Financiën 2000) as shown in Table 7.1 below.

The reasoning behind the format is to require departments to produce clear and readable budgets and consistent accounts for the Parliament and the audit

Table 7.1 The format for budget and annual reporting after the introduction of VBTB

Departmental Budget Format	Departmental Annual Report Format
• draft of bill	• accountability survey
– budgetary survey	• reading instructions
• reading instructions	• policy section
– policy agenda	– policy agenda
– policy items	– policy items
• financial management section	• financial management section
• agency section	• agency section
• background appendix	• judgment of auditor/financial controller

'controllers of the state'. The new style or format requires departments to reflect liabilities, expenditures and incomes in one simple overview. The inclusion of reading instructions is intended to make the surveys manageable. The policy sections form the core of the new format – and hence of VBTB. The policy section is new compared to the previous budget documents. The policy agenda contains a brief list of policy priorities a minister intends to address the following budgetary year. The most important trends and aspects towards which policies will be oriented should also accommodate the prioritized issues. The section of policy items contains a list of approximately ten items that correspond with a specific policy area. For each item, the department or the minister should give (1) the goals of government policies in the specific area, (2) which instruments or activities will be employed to achieve the goals, and (3) how much money is needed for that purpose. VBTB lays stress on the measurability of the policy goals, which means that goals should be presented in quantitative terms. The more quantitative this part is, the more easily departments can provide figures about performance and the better Parliament can control the achievements of each individual department. The more technical details of the policy items are not discussed in these subsections but in background appendices, relieving the policy section from an overload of technical and complicated details.

The financial management section should include information on the steering and control of activities within the department. A further sub-set of this is the agency section (agentschappen) that presents the financial overview of agencies forming part of the central department but which enjoy their own discretion on financial management. These agencies deserve a separate discussion. The last section of the departmental year report includes a standard report by the General Accounting Office, which is the formal 'controller of the state'. Finally, next to departmental year reports, the Minister of Finance will present the financial year report of the entire state to the Second Chamber. This document contains the main framework of budgetary policy and the main financial management policies of the state.

Nevertheless, in analysing this new format procedure, we must make a number of caveats. VBTB formally commenced in September 2001. The overall effects of VBTB on the position of the Ministry of Finance will probably not be fully apparent until a decade from now. Moreover, several respondents argued that VBTB represented a radical change in name alone and that its claims have mainly symbolic content. Finance often presents this reform as its own initiative and as a logical-rational follow-up of financial management reforms started at the beginning of the 1990s. In reality, the involvement and role of Parliament is no less important. The basic ideas of VBTB imply nothing less than the strengthening of the position of Parliament as the controller of the executive. The calls for the strengthening of the position of the Second Chamber stemmed from the first Purple Coalition and were uttered by, among others, Labour Party MPs Jan van Zijl and Rick van der Ploeg,[20] and some of these (especially van der Ploeg) had urged the adoption of accrual accounting in the development of VBTB.

At the same time, however, Finance officials, in particular the Inspectors of the State Budget, have vehemently resisted these repeated demands of the Second Chamber. To them, Finance had always considered policy outputs in its advice to the minister. Moreover, they claimed that public statements on policy outputs in the formal departmental budget documents were compromise formulas at best, with experience showing that it was extremely difficult to match the financial interests of Finance and the policy goals of spending departments. The explicit fusion of financial and policy goals in VBTB, thus, went against the practice of budgeting in the past. Furthermore, experience with accrual accounting, which is the basic financial management technique of VBTB, has not been satisfactory to date. Accrual accounting is operational in a large number of municipalities and from the practices there Finance believes it is extremely difficult to translate private sector financial techniques into the public sector. What exactly is an 'investment' in the public sector? In a similar vein, it is not clear what 'outputs' are, and how they can be 'measured'. In general, then, while private sector management and financial techniques have been adopted with great vigour, a process in which Finance played a key role as we saw above, the operationalization of key concepts within the public sector has remained weak and troublesome.

CONCLUDING ANALYSIS: A 'SUPER-MINISTRY' OF FINANCE?

What can we conclude from these analyses? What is the role, scope and position of the Ministry of Finance and how has it changed? First, the position of the Ministry of Finance in the budgeting process has always been of importance because of the eminence of funding as a prerequisite for administration and politics alike. Its influence varies, though. The variations are due to incidental factors such as the state of the government household, the personality and party political importance of the Minister of Finance and his relations with the Prime Minister. It is clear from the above analysis that, in times of budget deficit, the Finance Ministry dominates the budgetary process by imposing targets on spending departments. The Netherlands ran consecutive budget deficits between 1973 and 1994. With a sense of urgency regarding the necessity of budget control, there was a broad political consensus and support for more stringent action by the Finance Minister. Seconded by the Prime Minister, his position became so strong as to allow him solely to determine spending norms. Structural budgeting led to protracted strife between Finance and the spending departments.

In 1994, the Purple Coalition took office and Zalm became the Finance Minister. The 'Zalm-norm' created a period of political stability. Reinforced by strong economic growth and stability in socio-economic relations, Zalm turned a deficit into a surplus. His index-related way of dealing with surpluses and separating them from deficits elsewhere rendered the political deliberations over the budget relatively benign. According to some observers, the budget process has become void of politics. The disappearance of overt party political differences over the budget cannot be accounted for by these incidental factors alone. Rather, it seems to have to do with the advent of a new generation of civil servants within the various departments, leaving their technical, apolitical, result-oriented stamp on the budgetary process. There are countertrends, though. One of these is the renewed ambition of many politicians and the sense that, with budget surpluses, new policies can again be devised and implemented. These countertrends could potentially weaken Finance's stance.

Opinions differ as to the scope and effect of the VBTB reform process. The latest round of reforms appears to be a logical extension or closure of developments that began in the early 1970s. Since 1973, successive Dutch governments have sought to curb government spending and regain control over the budgetary process. VBTB implies a shift from input to output budgets and improved accountability for performance. Because the voters and members of the community are viewed not as citizens but as clients in NPM, many civil servants feel that they should increasingly take into account value for money and the taxpayers' wishes regarding public services. It is, after all, public money that is spent. Being accountable to public clients has taken on the form of trying to express in outputs what it is that is done with public money; backward mapping from services to instrument to objectives to goals. A new moment of public accounting has thus been created (the third Wednesday in May), to account for the way in which last year's budget has been spent. Critics of VBTB point at the way in which Parliament has dealt with budgetary information hitherto; focusing on details, looking to micro-manage inputs, while furthering the interest of specific constituencies, instead of focusing on overall accountability for performance.

Accrual accounting is another area of dissent. The validity of balance-sheet accounting for the public sector is questioned in the Netherlands. Private sector budgeting techniques have always appealed in times of deficit or crisis, but it remains to be seen whether an adequate definition of government investment and the appropriate depreciations and amortizations can be found. In our opinion, VBTB is still in its infancy. Its material results remain limited. It is, however, a sound indicator of the shifting role and position of the Ministry of Finance. Under the current economic conditions, the spending departments possess adequate leeway in appropriating funds. Finance, however, has assumed a new responsibility in that it critically reviews and comments on policies. Increasingly, the Ministry of Finance is a policy-partner to be reckoned with. It no longer employs just accountants, fiscalists and economists, but also enlists the services of students of public and business administration. The tensions with the spending departments have eased partly because the make-up of the departments differs less and less. Civil servants that have worked in and been socialized by Finance find their way all through the central government bureaucracies. The private, closed 'village' life, as described by Heclo and Wildavsky (1974), has given way to a globalizing village, integrating in the outer world, with strangers settling in the village and villagers moving out.

It is too soon to determine which way the balance between Finance and the spending departments will go. Much will depend on the way in which VBTB evolves and is taken up in the spending departments. If, or when, economic recession hits the Netherlands, a return to the old ways of budgetary politics remains a strong possibility. But even then, the budgetary process will not be the same. A new generation of civil servants has been trained, steeped and socialized in the 'Zalm-norm', VBTB and accrual accounting. The Hague 'village' is no more; it has given way to a world populated by young, results-oriented 'policy-managers' who have far less appreciation of the twists and turns of politics.

NOTES

1. The authors are thankful to the respondents who agreed to be interviewed and in particular to L.H. Kok and A. Bestebreur of the Ministry of Finance who facilitated this research project. It goes without saying that the authors alone are fully responsible for the analysis provided in this chapter.
2. For the purpose of illustration, we here use the fifth revision of the *Law on Accountability* (1995).
3. Thus, the law ascribes responsibility for the budget of the Royal House to the Prime Minister; the budget of the *hoge colleges van staat* and that of the Queen's Cabinet to the responsibility of the Minister of Interior Affairs; the national debt to the Minister of Finance; and departmental budgets to each individual minister.
4. We should mention that the Dutch Constitution has recognized the Council of Ministers as a formal organ only since 1983 (Article 45). The same article further only mentions the Prime Minister as chairperson of the Council. The Council of Minister is recognized as a collective decision-making body. The Constitution does not mention any individual ministerial position outside this scope.
5. The first *Comptabiliteitswet* dates back to 21 July 1927 (*Staatsblad* 259). The law was revised in 1976 and accepted by publication in *Staatsblad* no. 671 of 8 December 1976. Since the second revision, the law has been revised five times; the eighth revision is currently under way. We here use the sixth version of 10 July 1995 (*Staatsblad* 1995, p. 375).

6.   The respondents interviewed for this research project included: L. Alting – Ministry of Economic Affairs; M.P. van Gastel – Ministry of General Affairs (PM's Office); A.R.A. van den Ham – Ministry of Public Health, Welfare, and Sports; D.J. Kraan, R.R. ter Kuile and M. van Steenbergen all from the Ministry of Finance; R.I.J.M. Kuipers – Ministry of Social Affairs and Employment; and R. van Zwol – Ministry of Interior Affairs.

7.   The structural budget framework required the cabinet – including Finance – to prioritize the available financial room on expenditures and incomes. Next, this framework also enabled the determination of the middle term budgetary slack. Instead of attempting to stabilize conjunctural cycles on a year-to-year basis, the budgetary foresight was set for several years.

8.   Although not explicitly mentioned as part of the 'Zalm-norm', in this period there emerged the practice in which revenues from the exploitation of natural gas reserves and revenues from the sale of stocks are redirected towards a fund used for financing large infrastructural projects.

9.   In recent years, Nijenrode became the (private) Nijenrode University. It still specialized in business administration, but no longer *the* elite institution for the economic and business elites.

10. The coalition cabinet of which he is part consists of the three parties (Labour Party, Conservative Liberal VVD, and Social Liberal D'66) forming together the Purple I and (currently) Purple II coalition.

11. The term 'architecture' is NPM newspeak for 'structure' or 'organization' in the Netherlands. The term is introduced by public administrationists, academicians as well as consultants, and is affiliated with concepts such as business process re-design or re-engineering.

12. Of this number 10,500 civil servants came from the Postbank and 90,000 from the PTT.

13. Heroverwegingswerkgroep Differentiatie Beheersregels (1991), Verder bouwen aan beheer, Den Haag.

14. In terms of bureaucratic autonomy, the 'agentschap' is a bureaucratic agency with autonomy on internal finance, but that further resides under full ministerial control (as regards to management and policy, that is, structural autonomy and legal autonomy).

15. *Bedrijfsvoering uitvoerende diensten* and *Financiële vernieuwing*.

16. *Aansturen op resultaat*.

17. *Commissie voor de Rijksuitgaven*.

18. *Algemene Rekenkamer*.

19. *Jaarverslag in de Politieke Arena*.

20. Van der Ploeg is an Oxbridge trained professor of economics at the University of Amsterdam and was an MP in the first Purple Coalition. He is currently the junior minister of Culture.

8. Aiming for Centrality: the Politico-administrative Strategies of the Danish Ministry of Finance

Lotte Jensen[1]

Arguably, the significance of the state budget on the Danish politico-administrative scene has decreased over the past decade. Several major expenditure items are not controlled by the budgeting process but by separate legislation; several state owned enterprises (SOEs) are operated off-budget, and the 'net principle' enables public organizations to expand their activities if they can cover it by their own revenue (Beck Jørgensen and Mouritzen 1997, p. 159). At the same time, it is widely held that the influence of the central budget agency (CBA) on the politico-administrative arena has increased considerably.[2] Although the nature and extent of the increase is a source of dispute both in the media and in academia, most observers agree that the Ministry of Finance has developed into the lead ministry over the past decade. This is consistent with the ambitions expressed by the permanent head in 1991 (Eldrup 1988, 1996; Østergaard 1998, p. 351). In the budgetary process, the Danish CBA has been regarded as 'second to God' and a 'modern Richelieu' (Knudsen 2000, pp. 32 and 34). Newspaper headings have regularly labelled the Ministry of Finance as 'the ministry of power', 'King of the Castle Island'[3] or the 'new absolute monarchy' (Børsen 10/3/1998; Information 23/12/1998; *Berlingske Tidende* 28/11/1999).

The budgetary process is but one mechanism by which the Danish CBA has identified, understood and prosecuted its role in central government and beyond to the wider public sector. Consequently, the main object of this chapter is not just to explain the role of the CBA in the budget process, but to examine what role budgeting plays for the CBA in its wider politico-administrative strategies. The questions addressed are: how have the organizational strategies of the Danish CBA developed since 1980, and how successful have those strategies been?

This chapter reviews the role of the Danish CBA up to the election of November 2001 and refrains from speculation about the political and organizational consequences of the Social Democratic coalition government giving way to a Liberal coalition after eight years of office. The underlying argument of the chapter is that the Ministry of Finance has succeeded in bringing itself to the centre of the politico-administrative processes over the past 20 years. It has done so by employing a deliberate strategy of selective and minimalist organizational design and by mastering and acting upon a skilled reading of modern steering conditions. The CBA's quest for politico-administrative centrality, however, is neither unchallenged by other actors nor unproblematic in terms of economic, political and ideological circumstances. The chapter proceeds by unpacking the context, the ambitions, the organizational design and the game playing within the politico-administrative environment, in order to uncover the conditions under which the struggle for centrality continues.

THE CONTEXT

Key Economic and Demographic Features: the Policy Discourse

Denmark differs from most other countries in this book by the level of public spending as a percentage of the GDP, which is just above 50 per cent. Another key characteristic is the high level of taxation equal to 49.5 per cent of GDP when direct and indirect tax are included (Danmarks Statistik 2000, p. 159). According to the annual Budget Review (Finansministeriet 2001a) Denmark has achieved its fifth public sector surplus on the trot. Such good news, however, is immediately tempered by the observation that Denmark has already spent or pre-allocated much of this surplus. The debt issue has its own important political history but is currently evoked as a disciplinary mechanism or brake on spending. This aspect was expressed by the former Finance Minister, Pia Gjellerup, in conjunction with the Budget Report in May 2001. She said:

> I'm please to note the continued solid surpluses on the central government finances. Maintaining surpluses is essential, because it enables continued instalments of debt [to be repaid]. It is crucial for the Danish government that unpaid bills are not left to the next generation. The debt must be settled in order to secure the financing of the welfare services without having to increase taxes – also in 10 to 15 years when the expenditure pressure will be increasing due to the ageing of the population.

Debt is expected to fall to 38 per cent of GDP by the end of 2001 (Finansministeriet 2001e).

Since 1960 Denmark's demographic profile has changed and the forecast for 2040 suggests that fewer people in the workforce will have to provide for an increasing number of – particularly elderly – people outside it (Danmarks

Statistik 2000, p. 27). In economic terms this is seen as a 'demographic bomb' under the welfare state. Moreover, the competition for – especially skilled – staff is likely to compound pressure on wages within the public sector (Finansministeriet 1999g, p. 286). The tax level, the foreign debt and the demographic bomb, are essential components in the CBA's discourse about future economic policy.

The Relationship between State and Local Government

Denmark is a decentralized polity (Page 1991) encompassing 14 regional authorities and 275 municipalities; the status of which is expressed in the Constitution (§82) and best captured in the expression 'monitored autonomy'. For historical reasons (Knudsen 1995, p. 358), the municipalities hold a politically strong position in Denmark and may on some occasions create block voting across parties in Parliament if legislation goes against the interests of the sub-state level. Also counties and municipalities set their own tax rates, currently about 20 per cent points of total taxes (Danmarks Statistik 2000, p. 142). Local government reform in the 1970s devolved substantial responsibilities for welfare provision to the sub-state levels (mainly social, health and education). Hence, in 1999, the Danish counties and municipalities spent 56 per cent of the total public consumption, yet only raised around one-third of this from their own taxation; the rest was reimbursed from the centre (Danmarks Statistik 2000, p. 137). Moreover, 79 per cent of public employees are employed at the sub-state level.

Hence, local governments play an important part in Danish society and the economy. Their national organizations (Local Government Denmark and the Association of County Councils in Denmark) are connected to the Finance Ministry in a system of annual negotiations and agreements over the sub-state economy and tax levels (Blom-Hansen 1996; Christensen 1998). These negotiations run procedurally separate from national budgeting, but the outcome of the negotiations is fed into the annual budget round. The tax-spending agreements are negotiated centrally but individual municipalities can evade these limits (Blom-Hansen 1996, p. 286). From the CBA's viewpoint, the economic management potential of the negotiations has decreased, as the national organizations of local governments have no effective means of enforcing the agreements (Blom-Hansen 1996, p. 299). Negotiations have lost legitimacy in the CBA where they are seen as 'sanding up' or 'singing the last verse', as a senior executive remarked. No solution to the problem has yet been announced, only a 'recognized need for re-orientation' (Østergaard 1998, p. 313). Although this chapter does not deal specifically with the relationship between the central state and local government, it should be remembered that the decentralized Danish system restricts the CBA's control over the total public expenditure.

Parliament, the Appropriation Process and the Formal Conditions of Budgetary Discipline

According to the Constitution (§§45 and 46) a draft appropriation bill must be presented to Parliament no later than four months before the fiscal year and passed through the normal legislative procedures. The Constitution states that no expenditure can occur without the consent of Parliament (§46.2). In practice, and subject to a Finance Minister's circular, appropriations are allocated directly from Parliament to ministries (currently 18). The draft budget bill and bills for supplementary expenditure are presented to the parliamentary finance committee (PFC) composed proportionally of all parties represented in Parliament. Until 1924, ministries were able to apply directly to PFC for additional appropriations. In 1917–18 supplementary appropriations were twice as high as the budget itself (Østergaard 1998, p. 75). The Finance Minister of the day characterized the PFC as a bunch of 'good Samaritans', who only encouraged applicants to 'add an extra naught' to their estimated needs (Østergaard 1998, p. 75). Against this background, he first suggested and later successfully formally imposed the rule that no applications could be sent to the PFC without the prior consent of Finance (Statsministeriet 1924). Danish budget procedure has remained governed by administrative rules, not legislative requirements. Denmark has no organic budget law or financial management legislation, apart from legislation governing accounting and auditing.

The increasing centrality of the CBA has simultaneously weakened parliamentary involvement in the annual budgeting process (Østergaard 1998, p. 376). PFC scrutinizes the Budget in September, prior to its presentation in Parliament. The committee members split the Budget sections between them and traditionally members are obliged to inform each other – across political differences – over points of interest. Members can ask unrestricted questions to the relevant ministers. PFC meetings are closed, confidential and secretive, no minutes are taken and members are not allowed to reveal to the press any other than their personal remarks unless it is collectively agreed. The role of the PFC is under-researched but evidence suggests it serves a formal rather than substantive role. The PFC does not take part in the political negotiations about the Budget and only becomes involved once overall spending limits and the proposed distribution between ministries has been set. In this part of the process the PFC is limited to asking questions with little time to cover a very encompassing document.

The ability of the CBA to impose budgetary discipline on the line ministries is not secured by regulation – and rules are generally regarded as the least important element in the equation. The prowess of the CBA rather depends on the political status of the Finance Minister *vis-à-vis* his or her colleagues in government; on the leadership and internal power relations and loyalties within ministries; and on the ability of spending ministers to create alliances in Parliament that the CBA cannot control or oppose. As one senior official said: 'if you have a good case for a supplementary appropriation which enjoys enough political support, the CBA can do nothing but send it onto the PFC for approval'.

Since 1909, no party has held a majority in the Danish Parliament and election periods are not fixed (Constitution §32.2). The so-called 'earthquake' election in 1973 increased the number of parties in Parliament to ten, and since then there have never been fewer than eight parties in Parliament (Bille 2001). This situation generates minority coalition governments giving small moderate parties a disproportionate influence relative to their electoral base. But rather than bombastic ideological fights, Danish political culture emphasizes the importance of bargaining, negotiation and compromise. For new legislation it is necessary to be able to 'count to 90', as the ministerial jargon goes, there being 179 seats in Parliament. Hence, for the Budget to be passed it must be backed by a sufficient number of members (mandates). In the Danish political culture, it is seen as 'irresponsible' *not* to vote for the Budget and only the radical parties at both ends of the spectrum ever refuse. However, as any member of Parliament is free to propose amendments to the Budget, including new expenditures or tax cuts, the Budget eventually passed by Parliament can look very different from the one proposed by government if the Minister of Finance does not try to control the process. Therefore, producing the annual Budget can be a frustrating and tortuous process as Mogens Lykketoft (1999, p. 3), a former Finance Minister, explained:

> The Ministry of Finance is bound to be the place where many threads are drawn together. That is partly a function of the role we play in budgeting, but also a function of the tendency to lump together issues by the end of the Budget negotiations. It's inherent to the parties' way of thinking that dead issues may come back to life by the end of the process. Therefore, there will be a 'ketchup' tendency in a number of areas towards the end. That may cause some ministers to say: 'why are *we* thrown into the black pot this time?' But often, from the minister's point of view, it presents an opportunity to get something through that had gone dead, and it is also plainly necessary to link issues in order to get the Budget through in the end.

In a narrow sense, the budget round is of decreasing significance. The annual parliamentary dogfight over proposed spending plans for the following year only concerns a small proportion of the total Budget. In a broader sense, however, the Budget round is the arena *par excellence* on which structural reforms in a variety of or across policy areas can be tabled and traded against pet issues of different parties. The process as such, therefore, is of increasing importance for economic and structural policy. Moreover, the Budget round serves as an important symbolic barometer of the political prowess and standing of the government as a whole. Failing to establish a parliamentary majority supporting the Budget is considered a vote of no confidence against the government

The Central Departments and their Autonomy

The Danish central administration encompasses 18 ministries of varying sizes, ages, budgetary weight and political importance. The system is uni-departmental with one department the central unit to each ministry.[4] Departments encompass a varying number of subordinate agencies, quasi-independent institutions and SOEs. Four key features influence the relationship between the CBA and the other ministries.

First, the comparative political standing of the CBA depends on the support and latitude the Finance Minister is given by the Prime Minister to perform core executive functions.[5] Østergaard (1998) exemplifies several occasions where this has not been the case and where individual line ministries circumvented the CBA and secured extra resources or additional attention bordering on a core executive role. Second, the Danish PMO is small and serves only the Prime Minister – it lacks the functions (and organizational ambitions) of a cabinet office. This leaves a gap open on the bureaucratic arena for a competition about becoming the meta-coordinator. Over the past 20 years, Finance has consistently aimed at filling this gap. Third, 'ministerial responsibility' means that once individual ministers are formally appointed as political and administrative heads of their organization, they alone decide how the work is organized and performed. They enjoy sole responsibility for their ministry including its subordinate agencies, and can be legally prosecuted (Constitution §16). This constitutional arrangement has shaped the territorial culture. In terms of coordination across ministries, there is therefore a limit (but no *fixed* limit) to how far the CBA can invade the territory of other ministries, especially when other ministers are held accountable. Finally, in terms of administrative politics, the consequence of ministerial autonomy is that no core ministry can legally impose specific organizational principles onto another ministry. Culturally Finance can (and does) proselytize new steering ideas and management tools, while offering supervision and consultant assistance. Yet, the tools in this area are indirect and primarily economic or cultural. Financially, the CBA may put pressure on organizations through its budget analysis and benchmarking. It may enforce accounting principles,[6] or can promote contracting as a management tool by building it into the payment structure of the permanent secretaries. The CBA can also try to deliberately export its rationality to other ministries through the high internal turnover of senior management (hoping those exported will subscribe to the economic rationality once they represent the spender side) (Jensen 2000b, p. 227).

The 'Integrated Model' of Ministerial Advice

Advice to ministers and the government is based on the 'Danish integrated model' (Finansministeriet 1998). Political-tactical advice is almost exclusively provided by the career bureaucracy. There is no tradition of state secretaries, junior ministers or special political advisors.[7] This creates competition *within* government as to who should perform the role of a crosscutting chief advisor. For individual ministers, their permanent secretary plays that role (Finansministeriet 1998). But for the government as a whole or for cross-portfolio issues, different actors within the core executive can play this role in the absence of an overarching cabinet office. Internal government coordination has no formalized form in Denmark. Each government organizes its own structures and procedures for coordination. In recent years, the government's Economic Committee (EC) has played an increasingly significant role at the centre of the governmental decision structure (Jensen 2000b). The weekly meetings of the EC have been headed up by the Minister of Finance seconded by the Minister of Economic Affairs, representing the other coalition party in government. Four other, primarily economic, ministers have been included. All substantive political decisions have been agreed in this forum over the past ten years. As stated by the former Minister of Economic Affairs, Marianne Jelved: 'In this government, issues of conflict are resolved in the Economic Committee. Relatively few things appear in the Coordination Committee if there is any disagreement' (Knudsen 2000, p. 77).[8] The EC has been aided by a parallel group of permanent secretaries – the 'steering group' – with weekly meetings headed up by the permanent secretary of Finance. Advice to the government has hence, to a significant degree, been produced by or channelled through this group to which the CBA has prime access.

Recent Political History and 'the Abyss'

During the 1970s Social Democratic governments generated considerable public debt. In 1979 the Minister of Finance announced publicly before leaving office, that Denmark was 'heading towards the abyss', referring to the increasing debt. The principal dilemma between higher unemployment or greater public involvement in the economy was resolved in favour of the latter (largely influenced by the unions). The CBA felt expenditure was spinning out of control. The situation led to a feeling of 'deep worry and frustration' as well as a feeling of 'humiliation' within Finance. For example, meetings concerned with Denmark's economic situation were held by the Ministry of Labour, rather than as usual in Finance (Østergaard 1998, pp. 292–93). So intense were the problems, the Social Democratic government collapsed under the pressure in 1982. For the CBA, this period still serves as a historical frame of reference. It was a time neither the organization, nor the minister, would choose to revisit (Østergaard 1998, p. 352). However, as a senior executive remarked, the 'abyss' crisis 'made it an awful lot easier to be Finance Minister' because it was now publicly acknowledged that public finance was a fundamental problem in Danish politics and something had to be done. The Prime Minister mused aloud about the retiring Finance Minister in his diary notes, writing: 'did he really have to put it that bluntly? Why, now that he is leaving the sinking ship?' But he ended up concluding: 'on the other hand, perhaps it good that people realize it is a serious situation' (Østergaard 1998, p. 292).

The Social Democratic government was followed by ten years of Conservative coalition governments. The party political change became an important ideological-political support to the emerging ideas in the CBA. Hence:

> Suddenly it was interesting and legitimate to talk about concepts like outsourcing, de-regulation, marketization and privatization. In the CBA, the frustrations of the past years were followed by a new self-consciousness, bordering on 'Besserwissen'. The Finance Minister was also Deputy Prime Minister and there was a feeling that anything the Ministry of Finance aimed for was now possible (Østergaard 1998, p. 313).

Concerned about the public deficit, the incoming Conservative government initially put the economy on top of its political agenda. However, the intentions were short-lived and as economic conditions improved internationally, according to a CBA executive 'the government turned into self-satisfied mode after year one'. The government's initial enthusiasm for privatization was abandoned in the face of public disquiet.

But the changing political context provided an ideological fillip to the reform attempts brewing in the CBA and a coherent 'modernization program' was launched, suggesting a variety of reforms from the NPM drawer. Slogans like 'choosing welfare – competition with free choice for citizens' entered the discourse (Finansministeriet 1992). Over the years reform attempts became more technocratic than party political or ideological. Numerous of the reform attempts, first launched by the Conservative government, were later implemented by the Social Democrats after 1993 under slightly different labels (Jensen 2000a). Although the initial ideological push helped Finance reassert its influence in the executive core in the mid-1980s, a serious long-term focus on expenditure politics proved more important than the colour of the rhetorical wrapping paper. As a previous permanent secretary of Finance stated in a public lecture in 1999:

> The Ministry of Finance has had two political scoops. The one when the Conservatives wanted to prove that they could steer the economy in 1982 and the second, when the Social Democrats wanted to prove that they could do this even better in 1993.

Drawing the context together we find a picture of a country with a healthy economic situation, where the idea of a latent 'crisis' had to be evoked to generate action. A large welfare-oriented public sector exists, in which a significant proportion of the Budget is tied to mandatory expenditures; the budgetary process functions as a 'garbage can' for a variety of policy initiatives complicated by the perpetual situation of minority governments and the need to maintain support from minor parties. The Constitution stipulates a high degree of ministerial autonomy that necessitates indirect, rather than direct steering; and there is significant scope for political advice to the key coordinating group at the centre of government. There also remains an increasingly unsatisfactory steering relationship with respect to the self-managing municipalities and their expenditure requirements. Political uncertainties over the past 20 years have provided a backdrop to the emerging politico-administrative strategies of the CBA. The CBA must now negotiate the new 'de-ideologized' climate, with an organization wallowing midstream and currently experiencing additional uncertainties caused by changes to both the political and administrative leadership of the organization.[9]

STEERING PARADIGMS OF THE CBA

Finance's official history employs the 'budget chain' metaphor to explain the Danish budgetary process (Østergaard 1998, pp. 376ff), starting with overall political priorities followed by specific strategies, operational budgeting, appropriations (supplementary appropriations), accounting and finally auditing. The argument suggests:

> the Ministry of Finance is concentrated on the earliest links in the chain. This reflects an increasing acknowledgement on the part of the Ministry of Finance that budget politics or expenditure politics are inseparable from policy-making in the areas related to the expenditure. As a consequence, coordination, participation in policy-making and budget analysis of specific policy areas have become focal activities (Østergaard 1998, p. 380).

This, however, is not interpreted as a lack of interest in the later links of the chain. Rather, these latter activities have become institutionalized to a degree where only supervision and advice is necessary, while the very last link – performance measurement – has attracted significant attention, as will be discussed below.

The 1980s: Escaping the 'Death of the Detail'

By the late-1970s the thinking of the CBA toward expenditure management was influenced by the increased prevalence of economists in the ministry's internal staff profile.[10] The concept of expenditure control as a steering object entered the discourse, as well as the perception that greater overall steering of the public sector economy was necessary. As a result, the first review of the total public sector budget was published in 1979 (Finansministeriet 1979). A key budgetary reform emerged extending the old idea of budget ceilings to a 'total ceiling' principle for all line ministries encompassing running costs as well as mandatory expenditure (Olsen 1988). According to this theory, single ministers were made responsible for covering new initiatives or increased mandatory expenditure within the total ceiling, or covering new initiatives *via* changes in the legal regulations of entitlements. Also, line ministries became obliged to report their expenditure status to the CBA four times a year and to report if Budget ceilings were to be exceeded. Ministries were prevented from 'exporting' tasks to the municipal level without also making provision under the ceiling. The ceiling principle implied greater discretion at ministry and agency levels in order to enhance managerial efficiency. An important change was the possibility to carry forward unspent appropriations in order to enhance flexibility and efficiency. At the same time the 'net principle' was introduced, which allowed institutions to increase expenditures additionally by generating extra revenue. However, the technique of combining departmental running costs with demand-driven mandatory spending was soon to prove a significant problem – as ministries faced with increasing mandatory expenditures often found themselves starved of funds for their own purposes and unable to collect parliamentary support for specific cutbacks necessary for re-allocation under the ceiling.

During the 1980s the role and prevailing culture of the CBA was aimed at moving away from detailed control to a broader economic control over the budgets of the line ministries. This was seen as enhancing overall fiscal control. Moreover, the annual state budget was now analysed in terms of the broader impact of the public sector on the economy as a whole (Togsverd 1988). Economic steering was ideologically underpinned by the political concern about the proper role and size of the public sector. The other key change in this period concerned the status of administrative politics. Generally in the shadow of budgeting, organizational concerns were gradually afforded more attention by the Conservatives' Finance Minister. This only fuelled the rivalry between the two parts of the ministry. A symbolic indicator was that the annual Budget Review, which had existed since 1979, was issued in 1988 as a 'Public Sector Review' implying that organizational modernization and economic improvement were simply two sides of the same coin (Østergaard 1998, p. 321). Furthermore, the tight and very time-consuming regulation of employment numbers was supplanted by a more decentralized ceiling model, where only the most senior recruitment were still to be individually confirmed by the CBA (Østergaard 1998, p. 316; Olsen 1988). The score seemed to be 1–0 to 'the softies' (the organizational people) over 'the hardies' (the budget people), but the tables were to turn in the subsequent period. Despite the disputes, ideas about public management had now gained an important footing in the public discourse allowing them to be extended and re-interpreted in the decade to follow.

The 1990s: Going from 'Brake Block' to 'Proactive Initiator'

Finance's orientation toward hands-off 'expenditure control' was challenged by a new permanent secretary after 1991. He already had a longstanding career in the CBA and was familiar with its processes, culture and ambitions. He characterized the 'old' CBA of the 1980s as 'imbued with a defensive and awaiting attitude' (Eldrup 1988). He criticized the fact that it never took any initiatives, but waited for the other ministries to come up with their (normally expensive) initiatives to which it would then say 'no' (Eldrup 1988). The CBA's attitude toward the environment was 'suspicious and critical' (Østergaard 1998, p. 350). By contrast, his vision, which unfolded over the next decade, was proactive and premised on taking the offensive. 'We will no longer wait for the other ministries to come to us with their initiatives. The Finance Minister must – supported by the CBA – be able to predict the problem areas and sometimes take the initiative first, so that the Finance Minister sets the scene' (Eldrup 1988). He summarized the transformation as going 'from a braking block to an initiator' (Østergaard 1998, p. 350).

This indicated a fundamental shift in the way the CBA conceptualized steering. Steering was less about *ex ante* 'control' and more the art of making other actors steer themselves within broad parameters set by the CBA. This required a cooperative negotiating relationship with other ministries, calling for new organizational skills within the CBA (Eldrup 1988).[11] Fritz Sharpf's expression of 'self-coordination in the shadow of hierarchy' most appropriately captured the new steering paradigm (Scharpf 1993, p. 145). This change was not evidence of fading interest in political direction, but an acknowledgment that even though 'the devil is in the detail' death may be there as well. Detailed control of the ministries was considered a suicidal strategy. Consequently, the organizational strategy became akin to Kooiman's 'second' and 'third order governing', where 'first order governing' covers the concrete problem-solving or opportunity creation, 'second order governing' involves the deliberate creation of institutions within which other actors interact to achieve desired goals; and 'third order governing' covers the deliberate attempt to create a normative framework guiding the actors whilst they act their strategies out within the second order institutions (Kooiman 2000, pp. 157–61). The CBA embarked on both second and third order strategies.

A clear example of second order governing was the introduction of contracts, both at the institutional and personal performance level. Contracting was intended as a means of self-steering within agreed parameters (Eldrup 1999, p. 21) and was introduced by the CBA in 1991 as an experiment with 15 agencies. To kick-start the process, the CBA was directly involved in the first contractual negotiations and initially provided a budget-guarantee for the agencies concerned. In the subsequent batch of contracts the CBA withdrew from the negotiations and removed the financial underwriting. Line ministries then had to manage by themselves. It has since become a preferred policy on the part of the CBA to stimulate contracting, but the CBA (particularly its internal management agency) invests significant resources in developing self-steering tools for ministries and offers advice on the ways to measure organizational success. The substantial steering of each contractual institution, however, remains the responsibility of the ministries themselves.[12] Success is reviewed annually as part of the performance evaluation of permanent secretaries, conducted by the Finance Minister along with the permanent secretaries of Finance and the PMO (Jensen 2001b). By 2000, more than 80 agencies and institutions were on contract with their line ministry.

Other evidence of second order governing concerns the design of the governmental decision structure and the position of the Economic Committee. Clearly, the CBA cannot itself decide how the government organizes policy coordination. But once the EC was established as the lead committee, it provided an institutional conduit through which the CBA was able to expand its influence. Any major expenditure initiative from line ministries has to be approved by the EC, and line ministers are summoned to argue their case with, as one senior executive put it, 'the burden of proof on their side'. He argued that 'the EC now institutionalizes the economic solidarity of the government. It is seen as a very strong political anchoring of the expenditure concern'. The EC also brings the CBA to the heart of government coordination. Although the EC serves as a collective guardian and 'makes sure the Finance Minister gets less worn down', according to a senior executive it spends 'ninety-nine per cent of its time on proactive issues' (Jensen 2000b, p. 238). These include larger structural reforms within crosscutting policy areas. And increasingly, the CBA is now setting the agenda, laying out the overarching principles, playing the role of arbiter between ministries who fight against each other over turf. In sum, second order governing takes several forms, but what unites these interventions is that the CBA does not interfere directly in all steps in the process; rather, it seeks to shape the outcome by determining the parameters for other actors to operate within.

Evidence of third order governing is found in the huge increase in CBA publications. As the previous permanent secretary reported: 'analysis and public opinion building has become much more central. Last year we published about 60 books' (Eldrup 1996, p. 3). These publications range from 300-page economic analysis to 'easy listening' pamphlets. Third order governing requires a re-habilitation of administrative politics with changes of emphasis and interpretation. Warfare over this agenda between the budget 'hardies' and the organizational 'softies' was defused in 1994 when the latter were subsumed under the former. Initially observers saw it as the possible 'Endlösung of administrative politics' (Beck Jørgensen 1996, p. 32). But the permanent secretary of the CBA saw the change as 'administrative politics becoming high politics' (Eldrup 1996, p. 7). He warned 'some people see this as the death of administrative politics. That is not true!!! ... Administrative politics is many things – also effective institutions. If, for example, you define enterprise management or enterprise accounting as administrative politics, there is nothing the matter with administrative politics whatsoever' (Eldrup 1996, p. 8). In this way administrative reforms are seen as a necessary tool for economic steering. Moreover, from the point of view of the organization people, economism can serve to 'up the currency' of administrative politics, or as one senior executive suggested: 'today, administrative politics can flex the muscles of expenditure politics' (Jensen 2000b, p. 244). A win-win discourse now drowns out the trench warfare talk of the 1980s. Also administrative politics has become increasingly technocratic and professionalized. In order to play the role of the authoritative measurer, it is no longer enough just to 'have opinions' about public organizations. Mastering the latest measuring techniques and the fashionable 'steering-talk' of the day is a precondition for playing the role of 'third order governor' able to communicate in the language in which organizational quality is assessed. A significant amount of resources has been devoted by the CBA and its agency for governmental management to remain at the forefront of administrative politics.[13]

CURRENT POLITICO-ADMINISTRATIVE GOALS AND TASKS

The official goal of Finance is to 'enable the Finance Minister and the government to make the best possible decisions to sustain a sound economic policy'. Two components are embedded in this goal. First, the CBA aims to be a central advisor to both the Finance Minister and government. 'Advice' in this respect is not just reactive (when asked for), but to a significant degree ought to be 'proactive'. The second component of 'sound economic policy' sets the substantive qualitative standard for the best possible advice. It also serves to enhance the power of the CBA, so that economic criteria become the baseline political criteria, against which other substantial criteria must be argued. At the concrete level, these goals are translated into the following CBA functions: analysis of the socio-economic development; budgeting and budget analysis; negotiating the economic frames with counties and municipalities; and strengthening effectiveness in public organization through administrative politics. Further, the CBA points out that in delivering services to the Finance Minister and the government its staff must combine outstanding formal qualifications with an understanding of the actual political situation at any point in time.

Through the spectacles of organization theory, the explicit focus on 'sound economic policy' could be seen as a basic concern over organizational survival in an ecology where other challenges or perspectives are extant. Although it may be difficult to conceive of a modern state without a CBA, its role and influence now depends on active, rather than adaptive, survival strategies. The mantra of 'sound economic policy' expresses an exclusive discourse in which the CBA plays the central part. Through the theoretical spectacles of governance theory (Klijn 1996) the proactive strategy of the CBA is to perform the functions of 'the governor'. It aims to be the fulcrum on which the complex steering traffic of late modern governance systems depends. Governing will involve three different types of games: control games, coordination games and creativity games. The first game is about controlling public expenditure, the second is about pro-actively coordinating the policies of other actors and the third game is about forming the public sector discourse. The following sections address the organizational capacity of the CBA and examine how able the Danish CBA is to play and combine these games.

Matching the CBA's Organization and Strategies

The Danish CBA has existed for 150 years and is centrally located in the 'red building' on the Parliament square. Over this history one of the marked features has been that the size and responsibilities of the core department have decreased periodically. In the mid-nineteenth century the central department encompassed the national bank, the Ministry of Taxation and Customs, the postal services, the colonies (of which Denmark had very few), the Statistical Office; and at the agency level it also included the State Insurance Company, military pensions, accounting, debts and liabilities. Responsibility for economic policy was reduced once a separate Ministry of Economic Affairs was established in 1947 although some tasks have moved back and forth between the two ministries (for example, pay and personnel policy). A further reduction took place when an independent Ministry of Taxation and Customs was created in 1973. For three decades (1960–

91) government auditing was also the responsibility of Finance until it was transferred to Parliament (Østergaard 1998 pp. 18; 260–61; 365).[14]

Organizationally, the Ministry of Finance has evolved from a convoluted structure of nine internal departments with 46 sections and three sub-agencies in 1965, to one central department with 11 internal sections and three agencies currently. The organizational philosophy, poetically expressed by the former permanent secretary, has been to 'get rid of dead flesh' in order to 'keep close to the hurricane at the political center of government' (Eldrup 1996, p. 6). Prior to 1988, there were three internal departments, Budgeting, Pay/Personnel and Administrative Politics. In 1988 the latter two merged and in 1994 this merged department became a subsection of the Budget department. Responsibility for outstanding debts and liabilities was decentralized to a separate Financial Administrative Agency, and governmental accounting and management likewise to the Agency for Governmental Management. Lately, wage and personnel policy was decentralized to a new State Employers Authority. The core department has been well and truly 'bureau-shaped' (Dunleavy 1991) and 'kept mean and lean' as a former employee puts it.

The present organization has a flat structure with three levels: the permanent secretary, six deputy secretaries and 11 section heads, of whom eight have budgetary functions, one deals with macroeconomic assessment, one with expenditure politics and one with administrative politics. No section is engaged solely in budgeting. The organizational aim is that all staff members do both 'routine' and 'development' work on a 50:50 split. 'Development' covers analyses, report writing, reviews and negotiations. Tasks are circulated regularly between sections to keep the organization fluid and to prevent loyalties towards external parties hampering the budgeting process (Jensen 2000b, p. 234). The organization is reshuffled annually and appears ever-changing (Østergaard 1998, p. 354). This includes the seven deputies who, while individually specialized, are structurally 'floating' and do not head up subordinate units.

Decision-making and Production Processes

Internal processes are a mixture of hierarchical authority, network-like interaction and autonomous competencies. The last major restructure in 1994 was widely perceived as a victory for the 'hard' economists over the 'softer' organizational theorists, but an alternative explanation is that it was a strategic attempt on the part of the permanent secretary to centralize the access and advice to the Minister (Østergaard 1998, p. 355). The fluid structure of 'deputy chiefs' with no 'indians' reduces the opportunities for internal empires and consolidates the definitive influence at the top. The organizational decision processes resemble a normal bureaucratic hierarchy; only they work quickly so the base of the organization receives timely responses needed for action. As a former CBA staff member described it: 'coming from Finance to this ministry was like coming from a six-lane motorway to a winding country road'. The CBA culture is strong and explicit. 'It is amazing how little time in Finance it takes you to learn what to think about things', a younger staff member remembered. Generally, the leadership has been able to steer the organization firmly *via* the culture and flatter structures of the organization rather than *via* pompous power demonstrations. The leadership has also been widely respected internally for its ability to position the organization strategically *vis-à-vis* the environment. To some extent staff members trade a subordinate position in the internal hierarchy for a superior collective gaming position in the environment.

If decision-making is hierarchical, the mode of production is not. It is organized along project networks across sections and levels, and draws together competence from across the organization. The floating structure enables teams to work on flexible, crosscutting projects and respond to the environment faster than if a rigid structure of separate responsibilities existed. Deputies can draw on several sections for their projects. Likewise, sections can choose between deputies for sparring and supervision. This is described as 'an internal market'.

Finally, an element of professional autonomy has become a key ingredient of Finance's activities and its production processes. The framework for the budgetary process is premised on Finance's annual financial reviews, economic forecasts and surveys, and these are supplemented by budget analysis of selected policy areas. The authority and legitimacy of these analyses among the line ministries or in the wider public are derived neither from the internal hierarchy nor the organizational power relations between the CBA and other actors. Authority and legitimacy are derived from acknowledged skills, competencies, techniques and value standards within the economics profession nationwide and internationally. Economic analysis prepared by Finance is scrutinized and compared to analyses conducted by the financial markets, universities and business schools, the Economic Council[15] and international economists. Therefore, analysts in the CBA need to possess a degree of professional autonomy, which is generally granted by the organization (Jensen 2001a, p. 89). Finance is likely to be criticized if there is suspicion that analytical conclusions have been overruled by political expediency or other organizational priorities.

Thus, in its decision-making capacities we find a profession-dependent organization that is hierarchical but flexible. Delayering has meant that the CBA has become an increasingly unitary actor, with internal process allowing strong leadership to develop. Internally, the organization is relatively manoeuvrable, making it possible to approach the environment strategically and proactively. Lastly, it builds its organizational kudos on its ability to shape the economic agenda based on a reputation for quality research.

Culture

Finance sees itself as guardian of the *public interest* usually interpreted to mean the public *economic* interest. This phenomenon was expressed by a middle level manager:

> In a line ministry, I know by experience that it is more difficult to sustain the illusion that you serve the public interest because you pursue special interests, which you full well know you are serving ... Our special interest may be economy, and you might say that this is a special interest too. But it is much easier to identify with what you are serving. It may sound pretentious to say 'the public interest', but it is much easier to feel a sense of rationality in what you are doing. I like to work in the Ministry of Finance, because I feel it easier to accept and explain to myself why I do what I do (Jensen 2001a, p. 98).

The sense of serving the public breeds a collective 'parental' mentality – a belief that departmental staff are able to rise above the insatiable and ever-demanding spending agencies. There is a sense that, like children, the spending departments have to learn to share – and that if everybody got what they wanted, there would be nothing left to the others.[16] There is also a perception of structural elitism and Finance staff generally feel the quality of their work is superior to that of other ministries. Their comparative advantage is proactive policy-making based on the notion that in a democratic polity the legitimacy of policy-producing bureaucrats hinges on their ability to convince other actors – including their own minister. Over nigh on a decade, staff have been confident that the Minister, Mogens Lykketoft, was strong enough to pick and choose policy options and turn ideas down that he found poor. Within the confines of the department, staff members are also conscious of the role of playing 'political sparring partner' to the Finance Minister, helping him/her to position his policy *via* analysis and public dissemination. This has raised some public and parliamentary debate, especially over the EMU campaign, which again fuelled fundamental debates over 'the Danish model' of political advice (Jensen 2001a).

Another element of Finance's culture is that it provides a distinguished learning environment for the best graduates from economics and political science faculties. This relates to the high level of competence among staff members and to the fact that staff 'get to do things here you would never get to try elsewhere, you learn an awful lot here and it won't block any routes to a further career' as a junior staff member explained. Although the CBA recruits staff directly from the universities, at the same time, there is a high turnover at the base of the organization, where the average experience is less than two years.

In Finance's culture ideology matters less than the focus on effectiveness. Effectiveness is no longer seen as a part of any specific ideological program, but as 'rationality itself'. The CBA embodies that rationality, as expressed by a middle level manager: 'I think it is important to understand the self perception in the house – that we are a personnel group who feel we stand for common sense' (Jensen 2001a, p. 98). Effectiveness is embedded in the CBA culture – as one experienced staff member explained: 'If you had a Budget area, you were really busy in November because of the Budget negotiations. Then you were really busy again in May-June because the Budget proposal had to be finished. And you were busy in January making the first outlines. But for example in April-May, it was relatively peaceful ... Now it is busy all year round ... There are no seasons – only deadlines'. The busy work environment is a part of the culture and widely accepted. 'People would not really like a part-time culture and Lego toys in the corners' as a middle level manager puts it. However, it also fuels the high turnover. Younger staff members see it as a training ground and a 'CV investment', and move elsewhere if they want a less stressful job or to start a family. 'The family policy of this place is the policy of the single', said one employee.

PLAYING MULTIPLE GAMES IN MULTIPLE ARENAS

Control Games

The classic control game played is the budgeting game with spending ministries. In the early 1980s, the aim was to decrease public sector growth. Currently, the aim is 'zero growth' – meaning less public growth than the growth of the economy. Although the CBA conducts three-year budget estimates (Hammer 1999, p. 44) and agreements between the CBA and ministries can be reached for more than one year, the control game is mainly played as a repetitive one-year play in two acts. The first act between January and June is internal and concerns ceilings for each ministry and clearing up the political deals with key politicians. The public act occurring in Parliament between September and November is about gaining support for the Budget as a whole including the attached issues, conditions and supplementary legislation, which is either proposed by the government or set as a condition of support from parties outside the government.

Step one in the internal game is the discussion in the Economic Committee about expenditure targets across ministries. When these are agreed, step two involves bilateral negotiations between the CBA and the line ministries over the specific size of the annual ceiling, where new initiatives as well as possible cutback opportunities are explored in the game. The process is structured by guidelines issued by the Ministry of Finance (Finansministeriet 2001b).

Following the 1984 Budget reform, the CBA's only interest here is the level of the ceiling. In order to estimate the appropriate level, the CBA conducts more detailed budget analysis of selected areas on which to base the judgments of ceiling levels. Budget analysis can be carried out on the initiative of the spending ministries themselves (in order to 'get in there first'), or it can be initiated by the CBA, for example prior to a four-year budget agreement for the police (Finansministeriet 1999a) or if 'problematic areas' are identified, as for example urban renewal (Finansministeriet 1999a). Both the CBA and the line ministry participate in the analysis. The analysis creates a platform for a game in itself, since the analytical perspective sets the parameters for organizational success or failure in the end. Each of the parties naturally seeks to get the analysis carried out on their 'home turf', so the line ministry will argue for substantial, qualitative criteria and the CBA will work on financial criteria. The game can be explained as follows according to a spending ministry budget official: 'their job is to say if we were to cut this program, how could that be done? Of course, it starts out by being hypothetical, but at the end of the day, the conclusions end up in the neat summary tables that the negotiators can overview in the budget negotiations'.

The core resources for the CBA are the analytical capability and the organizational stamina in a very busy environment. As explained by the same budget official: 'they are much more used to keeping a high level of conflict for a much longer period of time. They simply just go on forever'. The massive turnover in the CBA adds to the information asymmetry between the CBA and line ministries (Christensen 2000), but as expressed by a middle level manager, information asymmetry is not regarded as a problem, since too much information on line ministries and their programs just 'sucks you in'. Also, the relative power of ministerial organizations, and their executive leadership in particular, plays a role. Weaker permanent secretaries may pursue a conflict avoidance strategy toward Finance executives, who are renowned for their merciless style of negotiation. A possible strategy for the spending ministry is to try to 'kick' the policy issue in question 'upwards' to the political level, so that the line minister may approach the Finance Minister directly, and then hope for a political resolution or re-framing of the issue.

The budget negotiations between line ministries and the CBA are bilateral, although spending ministries do find out information about each other's negotiations with the CBA to some extent. 'Clearly, we have our contacts and we know what's in the pipeline in other ministries, but we don't know the details, of course' one line ministry official explained. Informally, there is a sense of 'fair share' between at least some spending ministries during the negotiations, but the accurate details and the aggregate overview – and hence the informational power – is the preserve of the CBA. This gives the CBA a favourable bargaining position, since no other actors know the bigger picture for certain.

The internal control game is an exhausting battle for which the CBA is organizationally well equipped and seen as a superior player. The CBA can always evoke the constitutional requirement that the Budget must be presented four months before the spending year, and that 'the show must go on' – at high speed. The CBA's centrality in the game has a longstanding institutional history, and the CBA is specialized in the sense that each section deals with the Budget of a specific ministry. The annual battle is well covered in the media where the typified roles of winners and losers are depicted for mutual benefit. Media coverage reinforces the mythology of an undefeatable army of 'budget sharks' and exposes self-pity on the part of the various spenders (Christensen 2000, p. 4). It must be recognized, though, that there are vast differences across ministries in terms of their strength to fight back. This strength can be derived either from a politically strong minister or from ministries that organize themselves strategically to be two steps ahead and overtake CBA strategies.

Control games have also focused on mandatory and discretionary types of expenditure. As mandatory expenditure began to constitute an increasing proportion of the Budget, the CBA attempted to control this through 'total ceilings' after the 1984 Budget reform. The intention was that each ministry must manage both types of expenditures within the ceilings. This implied that single ministers, in order to 'find' money for new initiatives or cover increasing mandatory expenses, had to seek parliamentary approval for specific cutbacks. This proved unfeasible in the parliamentary situation, and so the 'total ceiling' game became dysfunctional or at best a signal of the expenditure target nominated for the individual ministries. Agreements about specific changes in mandatory expenditure would also take place in the second act involving Parliament where budgetary proposals are traded off against other policy issues in order to gain majority support. The CBA's success is heavily dependent on the negotiation skills of the Finance Minister and senior staff, and on the ability to produce documents, proposals and alterations continually through the negotiating process.[17]

In a parliamentary minority situation, the outcome of the game also depends on the ability to persuade other parties about the importance of 'the sound economy' principle, especially in the context of successive budget surpluses. The Social Democratic coalition government was often able to win support for this perspective 'to the right' in Parliament, but such an agreement was bound to draw criticism from the leftist part of the political hinterland. Governments of whatever hue walk an inevitable tightrope. Nonetheless, larger structural reforms that make a difference with regard to mandatory expenditure, as well as cultivating the idea of 'the necessary modesty' cannot be dealt with in the 'heat' of the annual Budget negotiations. Both have longer time perspectives and require other resources than the up-front 'first order governor' skills of clever budgetary personnel and experienced negotiators. This is where the coordination games and the creativity games come into the picture.

Coordination Games

Coordination games concern two key aspects – the CBA's standing within the decisional structure of government, and its role as an agenda-setter and 'the leading think-tank' for concrete policy development across ministries (Østergaard 1998, p. 383).

The current decision structure provides an online opportunity for the CBA to influence government priorities and policy agendas. The most recent example of this was the pension reform in 1999 which altered the criteria for withdrawal from the labour market and hence decreased future liabilities for mandatory expenses. The reform passed with the support of the right in Parliament, indicating the widening influence of the CBA on the policy domains of other ministries. In this case it was possible for the CBA to build on the internal control games where the CBA occupied the institutionalized centre of events and information. But the reform was also an example of long-term rationality accompanied by short-term costs. In effect, the reform undermined an election promise made by the Prime Minister that pensions would not be touched (Pittelkow 2001, p. 107). Subsequently, the credibility of the Finance Minister received a flogging in the media. The Prime Minister had to apologize for the fact that the pension reform was not 'explained well enough' (Information 19/ 12/1998). This, however, was insufficient to prevent opinion polls turning against the government, bringing forth a critique from the Opposition leader that 'it is obvious to everybody, that with the current Finance Minister, so much power is centralized in the Ministry of Finance. I believe it is possible to have a strong Finance Ministry while avoiding the problem of having one line minister after the other politically steered from there' (*Jyllandsposten* 1/11/1998).

To a significant extent, coordination games take place backstage in the bureaucratic machinery. Several aspects of the Budget negotiation games for instance are preceded by lengthy commission work on selected policy areas (for example, policies for adult education which were included as a part of the Budget agreement for the year 2000 (Finansministeriet 1999b). The commission report stated that the commission held 13 meetings between May 1998 and August 1999, and that the work was headed up and mainly carried out by the CBA. The analysis reflected the CBA's interests as the focus was primarily on financial and steering matters whilst other topics were explicitly left out (Finansministeriet 1999c, pp. 12–13). Report writing provides an effective way of setting the basic parameters for the fast and heated discussions during subsequent budget negotiations.

In playing coordination games, the CBA depends on a variety of less formalized and institutionalized resources. Whereas the CBA has a core responsibility for 'making ends meet' in the control game, it has to continually build up and cultivate the base on which it stands as a coordinator. One key resource is political. It is crucial to have a strong Finance Minister with a leading position in government and reliable support from the Prime Minister. In such circumstances the Economic Committee operates as the central coordination forum, allowing the CBA to become focal to governmental policy-making and priorities. Second, organizational resources are important. In order to continually feed policy agendas, high quality reports and policy analysis into the political process an appropriate composition of good quality staff with high motivation, political antennae and analytical skills is required. Third, the CBA cannot neglect bureaucratic politics and it is necessary to be wary of potential competitors hoping to win a slice of the action or shift the coordinating agenda away from Finance's priority of 'the sound economy'.

Political resources are inevitably uncertain. It is hard for a new Finance Minister to match the experience and master the necessary political skills. Also changes in the government's decision structure may increase complexity in the coordination landscape and detract from the automatic centrality of the CBA. Other ministries have also come to realize that 'knowledge is power' and accordingly research units have begun to proliferate in line ministries providing competing interpretations of different policy areas. Some ministries have begun to define themselves as 'natural coordinators' providing the perspective through which overall policy must be seen. Therefore, one of the central concerns of the CBA is to broaden its legitimacy base by insisting on the imperatives of the economic agenda – and this is where the third and last types of games enter the picture.

Creativity Games

Compared to the previous games, creativity games are more fuzzy and open-ended, where the aim is to influence the discourse about the public sector, the relationship between state, market and civil society and even the nature of humankind. The more solid end of the spectrum is the economic analyses interpreting the 'state of affairs' of the Danish economy, analyses that frame the continual policy debates. Ever since 1979, the CBA has issued annual Budget Reviews. Today, this is supplemented with quarterly budget surveys as well as an annual Financial Review dealing with macroeconomic and structural policy issues. These publications used as the basis for the budgetary process are mainly targeted at a professional audience. The success or failure in this area depends on whether the analyses are seen as representing accepted mainstream economic theory by the profession. There are two possible pitfalls. One is substandard analysis and the other is political inflection. Whereas the former is rare, the latter does occur – as in the case of the Danish EMU debate when Finance was accused of playing a propaganda role for the proponents. Its stance was contested by an independent council of economic experts (the Economic Council) and attracted substantial media criticism for alleged arrogance (Jensen 2001a). This is, however, not a commonplace event.

Two other areas are important for the creativity game. The first is the launch of new internal steering paradigms in the public sector. The other is influencing the wider public debate. Concerning the first issue, the permanent secretary of the CBA summarizes the state of affairs in public sector steering paradigms as follows:

> In the 1980s capable steering tools were established with regard to the economic ceilings. The 1990s became the decade where performance management was put on track. The task of the coming decade will be to get performance management to make sense for the individual employee in an ever-increasing part of the public sector (Eldrup 1999, p. 32).

Most internal reforms in the 1990s concentrated on providing better measuring and reporting tools and improving incentive structures. They included: contracts (Finansministeriet 2000c); enterprise accounts (Økonomistyrelsen 1998); benchmarking (Finansministeriet 2000b); effective processes (Finansministeriet 1999d); and finally the new wage system and its implications for performance-based pay (Finansministeriet 1999e, 1999f). Together, these initiatives build institutions to animate rational human beings to perform better and get rewarded accordingly (Nørgård 2001, p. 125). The strategy is to internalize effectiveness as an incentive for the utility-maximizing employee while stressing the moral value since 'we are dealing with taxpayers' money'. But as recognized in the quote above, these institutional reforms cannot stand isolated. First, they need to make sense to public employees as a part of the wider work situation and its value structure. Accordingly, an increasing interest in softer leadership tools has developed (Finansministeriet 1999g). Second, 'hard core' incentive-steering has been accused of neglecting the qualitative sides of public sector performance, which has led to a recent focus on values and ethics (Finansministeriet 2000a). So, although the process of reform has been a long haul, many commentators now agree that the reform process has altered the way public sector employees are invited to look at themselves. The process, however, has not been without friction or downsides such as goal displacement, ethical dilemmas or workaholism – and there is now interest in a new balance being sought in a 'balanced score card' approach to management (Økonomistyrelsen 2000).

The proliferation of 'steering bibles' represents a huge challenge for the CBA to keep up with and master the latest techniques in order to remain the central player. To some extent this can be done by deliberate professionalization, the result of which is a kind of self-reinforcing monopoly: only the super-measurers can tell what real measurement is. On the other hand, measurement techniques need to be disseminated and translated into the logic and meanings of the existing public institutions if they are to offer a real alternative to older forms of control-steering. This leaves the techniques and their normative underpinnings open to re-interpretation, scrutiny and critique.

The third element of the creativity game concerns the wider public debate about the public sector and its future challenges as well as the relationship between citizens and the public sector. Finance has attempted to translate the concerns of macroeconomic policy into an accessible format for the wider public. The 'demographic bomb' has led to concerns about people leaving the labour market too early or an increased reliance on sections of the labour force not quite up to scratch (Finansministeriet 2001c). The debt issue has led to concerns about 'a sustainable future' (Finansministeriet 2001d). For the latter, the 'citizen' as 'customer' and 'taxpayer' has been evoked in order to put pressure on the public sector 'from below'. While the municipal level provides a significant proportion of welfare state service, these municipalities are beyond the direct reach of the CBA. So Finance has adopted a pincer movement strategy of cooperating with the national associations of counties and municipalities about public sector reforms from 'above' while trying to increase citizen's awareness of public sector effectiveness 'from below'.

Hence, a widespread interpretation of the influence of the CBA on the public sector discourse is that it has created a huge hegemony permeating all elements and debates of the public sector. It is here, there and everywhere like a 'mantra' (Information 24/09/1999). In a country with a tradition for substantial central state interference and hierarchical steering, the CBA looks like the monarch in modern disguise – hence, the newspaper headings mentioned at the outset of this chapter. This conclusion must, however, be tempered by consulting the other side of the Danish 'folk spirit' – an egalitarian culture that does not wish to see trees grow into heaven. Scepticism about the 'ruling class' goes all the way back to the absolute monarchy as well, or in the words of John Steinbeck: 'If I were a dictator I wouldn't occupy Denmark for fear of being laughed to death' (Knudsen 1999, p. 153).

CONCLUSION: THE PARADOX OF LESS IS MORE

'Less is more' was the dictum of the functionalist architect Mies van der Rohe, who led the German Bauhaus school of architecture, went to America during the war and returned to Europe to shock and inspire colleagues with his dramatically minimalist style. The dictum captures the essence of the organizational strategy of the Danish CBA over the past 20 years – a strategy typified by 'getting rid of dead flesh', aiming at a smaller, simpler and more strategic organization, while gaining more influence on the continual and interdependent games on the politico-administrative scene. The analysis illustrates how CBA has gone from a steering paradigm built on direct control, detailed regulation and a re-active attitude toward the environment to one focusing on general steering, indirect institution building and proactive policy-making. The current relationship to the environment was seen as three distinctive, but interrelated games with differing actors involved, different resources needed and different strategies employed.

Control games are the most consolidated, building on the constitutional requirements governing the Budget and the longstanding institutionalized centrality in the budgeting process and information streams. In this game, the CBA is the core player, embodying the public interest and profiting from the legitimacy stemming from being the only responsible player, serving no special interests. However, as far as public expenditure is concerned, this game covers a decreasing proportion, because of the increase in mandatory expenditure and the significance of municipal expenditures. Consequently, it becomes imperative to engage in attempts to alter socio-economic structures and coordinate policy programs across ministerial territories. This imperative takes the CBA further into the political realm and, hence, makes it dependent on political resources; namely, a strong Minister of Finance and a decision structure in government that grants the CBA a centrality in the process and enables it to interfere substantially in the policy domains of other ministries. It also necessitates a strong analytical and politically sensitive organization, both of which the CBA leadership has successfully given priority to over the past ten years.

The strategy of 'getting rid of dead flesh' and creating a smaller organization in which encompassing routine work has been traded for a smaller, more manoeuvrable entity, has enabled the CBA to successfully take the lead in internal bureaucratic coordination and inter-ministerial games. But it is a risky gaming position which depends on the political prowess of the Finance Minister, as well as the strategic ability of the CBA leadership. The advantage to coordination, however, is simultaneously a possible disadvantage when it comes to the question of broader public legitimacy. A strong power position inside government is not automatically transferable to the parliamentary arena or the public at large. Therefore, creativity games become unavoidable if the CBA wants to set the broader agenda and ensure 'the sound economy' is continually on the top of the political agenda as the principal criterion of Danish politics. Whereas the CBA has no interest in returning to the hell of the 'real' economic crisis of the 1970s, its strategy and gaming position depends on the public perception of a potential crisis looming around the next corner if nothing is done to avoid it. For the CBA to be effective thus requires the paradoxical need for economic progress and economic crisis to be present at the same time. As the former Finance Minister, Pia Gjellerup, remarked upon her arrival: 'It is much easier to be a Finance Minister when the bottom is about to fall out of the exchequer, than sitting on top of it trying to keep the lid on when it is full'.

NOTES

1. The sources of this chapter include written documentation and interview material collected over four previous research projects. It also builds on experience gained from my two months stay in the CBA in May–June 2000. While many departmental staff agreed to be interviewed, it was a condition that all quotations would remain anonymous. The conclusions drawn and interpretation of the interview material remains my own. I must thank all interviewees involved and in particular Mogens Pedersen from the Danish Ministry of Finance for his help. Also, I would like to thank John Wanna and Torben Andersen for their editorial advice and my research officer, Mikkel Havelund, for his speedy assistance.
2. In a Danish context the CBA is the department of the Ministry of Finance. The organization will be described below.
3. The 'Castle Island' is the Danish equivalent to Whitehall.
4. The uni-departmental idea was recommended in an administrative commission report from 1962 (Administrationsudvalget af 1960, 1962). The idea was a distinction between overall issues and directly policy relevant tasks on the one hand and 'routine administration' on the other. The former should be located in a relatively small department close to the minister, whereas the latter should be more specialized and refer to the minister through the department. By 1994 the CBA became uni-departmental.
5. The core executive refers to Rhodes and Dunleavy (1999).
6. From 1997, enterprise accounts became compulsory for all major public institutions (www.oes.dk). The system has been continually debated and evaluated, for two main reasons: first, that the compilation of – in principle – control information tends to create information overload; and second, that private sector enterprise accounts are unsuitable for public sector organizations (Skærbæk 1999).
7. There is a longstanding normative academic as well as newspaper debate about the Danish model and its exceptions well beyond the scope of this chapter (see Jensen 2001b).
8. The Coordination Committee was the vital coordinating group in the Conservative coalition government of the 1980s and encompassed almost all ministers. During the Social Democratic government, it has played a more passive role.
9. Before the election in November 2001, the longstanding and very forceful Finance Minister, Mogens Lykketoft, moved to the Ministry of Foreign Affairs after eight years of heading up the CBA. The incoming Conservative government appointed another minister in November 2001. There was also a change of permanent secretary in early 2001.

10. The Danish civil service was traditionally dominated by the law profession. By 1980, the proportion of top executives with legal training (pay band 38 upwards) was still more than 50 per cent and even in 1997 lawyers count for more than 40 per cent of all civil servants. Economists started to break the monopoly in the postwar period (Finansministeriet 1998, p. 42). In the CBA, an important change took place when a leading economist was recruited as permanent secretary in 1962. This had a knock-on effect on further recruitment policy. Today 35 out of the 56 academic CBA staff members are professional economists, followed by political scientists who account for a further 21.

11. The current job description available on the web states that 'A lot of the work consists of contacting and negotiating with other ministries and organization. Therefore staff members must be extrovert and authoritative' (http://www.fm.dk/finansministeriet/Finansministeriet).

12. This 'hands off' steering can, however, be selectively modified through budget analysis as explained below.

13. One of the current developing themes is the employment of 'controllers' in line ministries, which was recommended by the CBA in 1996. The total number of controllers has risen significantly both in line departments and agencies (today constituting around 80 persons) and the figures are still increasing (ww.oes.dk).

14. The loss of the National Audit Office was not a voluntary choice by the CBA.

15. The Economic Council is an independent, but corporatively balanced body created in 1962 to conduct independent analysis of the Danish economy and coordinate the various economic interests. The council has 29 members from government ministries and interest organizations. It is headed up by three 'Economic Wise Men', normally university professors (www.oem.dk/ministeriet/).

16. Although officially Finance staff are asked to comment on the 'additional expenditure *needs*' of line ministries, the departmental culture regards these requests as 'additional expenditure *claims*'.

17. The longstanding reputation of the CBA in these processes is that it is a 'well-oiled machine' (Østergaard 1998, p. 352). A former Finance Minister has described the CBA during a budget negotiation process as 'a dream': 'It is a huge machine, where one group figures out economic-political solutions one step ahead of the negotiations, another group is the technicians keeping together the details, so no later than a few hours after the final political agreement there will be a book presenting everything in the right way, and finally a group that takes care of the presentational side and is able to explain everything persuasively' (Østergaard 1998, p. 352).

9. Tempering the Rechtsstaat: Managing Expenditure in Re-unified Germany

Roland Sturm and Markus M. Müller

Budgetary decision-making in Germany relies strongly on legal and formalized procedures. The importance of the legal framework for budget-making is due principally to the central role the idea of the *Rechtsstaat* plays in German public life. The *Rechtsstaat* idea sustains rule-based decision-making. It not only works to prevent arbitrary decision-making, but it also produces a common understanding of what is right or wrong. Government officials regard the *Rechtsstaat* idea as a constitutional framework establishing legal norms; only occasionally are these legal norms seen as restrictions, most of the time they are accepted as standards to be met.

The administration of public finance is governed by the rule of law stipulating principles of accountancy and budget regulations. Since 1970 the regulations for budgetary principles are laid out in the *Haushaltsgrundsätzegesetz* and those for budgetary rules in the *Bundeshaushaltsordnung*. The *formalized* nature of German budgeting reflects an outdated constitutional idea that spending is a neutral or technical exercise for which experts in the Ministry of Finance are responsible. Changes to program spending are seen to be the result of 'high politics' concentrated in parliament and subject to parliamentary procedures. This formal logic appears to guarantee democratic principles in the decision-making process, because parliament is supposed to be the place for an open debate on budgetary priorities to be executed by the government.

In Germany, as in other countries, the neat distinction between executive and parliamentary decision-making no longer describes reality. It is impossible to define *a priori* the boundaries of 'routine' in budgeting – whether budgetary decisions are politicized or non-politicized, routine or non-routine, depends more on the issues decision-makers have to deal with than on the division of powers between parliament and the executive. Moreover, with the advent of political parties as forces that dominate decision-making processes, a certain tension between bureaucrats and political appointees has developed. And even if the latter are not always closely involved in decisions there remains the possibility of political involvement or interpretation of a bureaucratic decision which may have been regarded as non-controversial.

Party politics have generally sidelined parliament, but in Germany this has not completely emasculated parliament in budgetary decision-making. The budget committee of parliament can still exert influence (Sturm 1988). Yet, the major role of parliament, especially when it comes to highly politicized or non-routine decisions, is to legitimize decisions already taken by government. The role of parties in budgetary decision-making is also of importance because parliamentary parties have special committees that deal with different aspects of expenditure policies, as well as with the budget as a whole. Ministers have to mobilize the support of their parliamentary parties for their policies. Before the Minister of Finance introduces the Budget Bill to the Bundestag, his parliamentary party is given the chance to debate and comment on it. This exchange of ideas usually concentrates on the broad budgetary outlines or on some of the more controversial budgetary issues. But party backbenchers can challenge the figures, as Conservative MPs did in 1998 when they considered the Finance Minister Theo Waigel's data was not sufficiently trustworthy (Feldmeyer 1997, p. 7).

Coalition government also has two consequences for budgetary decision-making. The first is that the ground rules for budgeting, especially for expenditure policies, are written down in the coalition treaty between the parties in government. These treaties have now become the rule, and over time they have become longer and more detailed. Whether this is a mere expression of Germany's law-minded political culture or of greater initial distrust between coalition partners is open to debate. The coalition treaty of 1994 mentions, for example, the new government's aim to keep the growth rate of public expenditures below the economic growth rate. In the foreseeable future expenditure levels should be reduced to the pre-unification level of 46 per cent of GDP (Kohl *et al.* 1994, p. 8). Such agreements cannot foresee the political future, which means they are *de facto* unstable political compromises. The second consequence of coalition governments is that they have introduced new levels of decision-making outside the framework set by the constitution; primarily, a small group of party heavyweights in government who are represented whether or not they are members of the Bundestag or of the government of the day. This negotiation circle is flexible in its response to new economic and political developments and can determine policy courses for government even before cabinet formally decides. Such negotiations outside cabinet (or bilaterals between spending ministries and the Ministry of Finance) gain importance when a Chancellor, as with Helmut Kohl, dislikes too much debate on economic issues in cabinet (*Der Spiegel*, 2.10.1995, p. 25). The mechanism of consensus-building in coalitions also produces a parallel structure of task forces formed by the coalition partners. They monitor and influence decision-making between ministries with regard to decisions on expenditures. This means that there is an increased tendency toward the political second-guessing of decisions which were once the preserve of civil servants (Manow 1996, p. 101f). Hence, in addition to the formal arrangements of decision-making these new modes of decision-making have to be taken into account.

Before we examine the way budgetary decisions are made in this political context, it is first necessary to explore the fairly stable formulation process and institutional framework of budgetary decision-making (Sturm 1989, p. 140ff.; Horst 1995, p. 245ff.). The stability of the decision-making process may lead one to the conclusion that the German CBA – the Ministry of Finance – is technical, non-intrusive and removed from party politics. Part of the reason the bureaucratic core of the Ministry of Finance has appeared to remain above politics is that this ministry has not been responsible for defining a new economic paradigm.[1] More importantly, and unlike the civil servants in the UK Treasury (Thain and Wright 1995), the bureaucrats in the German Ministry of Finance have always seen themselves more as administrators than as policy-makers. There has also never been a serious debate in Germany over whether the Ministry of Finance should be restructured or reformed (either inside government or even among students of public administration). In this respect Germany is again different to many other OECD countries.

THE FORMAL BUDGETARY FORMULATION PROCESS AND THE ROLE OF THE FINANCE MINISTRY

The German budgetary cycle begins in the last few months of the calendar year when the Ministry of Finance reviews the experience of previous budget decisions. Between December and January, the Ministry of Finance sends letters to all ministries and those federal agencies that have their own budgets. These letters indicate vague budgetary priorities (especially the need for cut-backs) and provide technical guidelines. The Budget Guidelines (*Bundeshaushalts-ordnung*) establish the major guidelines for the budgetary process inside government departments. Paragraph 9 of the *Bundeshaushaltsordnung* stipulates that every institution which has the right to control its own budget must nominate a person responsible for this budget, and that this person is responsible for coordinating the budget-making process and serving as a link with the Ministry of Finance. The office of a 'commissioner for the budget' in each ministry (*Beauftragter für den Haushalt*) would appear to be little more than an administrator handling routine political matters. However, the commissioner is granted additional powers beyond collecting data produced by his or her ministry.[2] The office of the budget commissioner in each ministry gives the impression of being a smaller version of the Ministry of Finance.

Budget-making is bottom-up and incremental. It is built on a historical base and operates on accepted notions of fair shares. Bureaucrats in spending ministries when asked about their future budgetary needs always come in too high. They generally make ambit claims (with some padding), but shy away from excessive claims in order to maintain their credibility. Heads of sections and divisions within spending ministries perform the role of policy advocates, but they do not determine the budgetary strategy of their ministry. They are controlled by guardians inside the spending ministry itself. The budget division (*Haushaltsabteilung*) of each ministry scrutinizes proposals and asks the policy advocates to cut their demands. A final meeting of the ministry's top bureaucrats, in which the minister is involved, agrees on the ministry's budget proposal which goes to the Ministry of Finance.

The budget division of the Ministry of Finance is divided into four sub-divisions, each responsible for at least four departmental budgets. These sub-divisions organize their work in sections or taskforces (*referate*) focusing on individual departmental budgets. The budget division is one of nine divisions of the Ministry of Finance, and is controlled by one of two permanent secretaries (*Staatssekretäre*) and one of the two junior ministers (*Parlamentarische Staatssekretäre*). After the Ministry of Finance has collected and evaluated the budget proposals of every ministry in the early months of the year, negotiations between the Ministry of Finance and the other ministries begin (usually in April). The greatest number of controversial items (though not the most important ones) are resolved by negotiations between the task forces of the ministry in question defending their expenditure plans, the budget division of their own ministry (budget commissioner), the section of the Ministry of Finance responsible for the budget of the spending ministry, and a representative of the Federal Accounting Office (*Bundesrechnungshof*). If it is impossible to come to a resolution at this level, the conflict will be handed up to the next level in the hierarchy (*Abteilungsleiter-Gespräch*). In this round of negotiations the policy and budget heads of the spending ministry try to defend their spending plans against the arguments of the relevant heads of the budget division in the Ministry of Finance. Compromises reached at this stage usually receive cabinet approval (Korff 1975, p. 11).

Big questions tend to be dealt with at the political level. Ministers may negotiate directly with the Minister of Finance in an attempt to find a solution for the budget problem informally. Where necessary a more formal meeting would include the permanent secretaries of both ministries, the head of the budget division of the Ministry of Finance and the budget commissioner and relevant officials from the ministry in question. Here the government's political priorities would count, as well as the relative political strength of ministers including their proximity to the Federal Chancellor. The outcome of a confrontation between ministers is defined by the expectations of the Chancellor, the logic of coalition government, and the strength of convictions held by a minister. One strategy used to reduce conflict is the determination of an early cabinet decision on expenditure totals and the size of the PSBR which is guided by the estimates of the task force on tax estimates (Kunas 1982, p. 50). These decisions provide a stable frame of reference for the Finance Minister's negotiations with departmental ministers. Another strategy to deal with conflicts on budgetary allocation is to point to external restraints on decision-making. The most important restraint, and incidentally a most powerful argument in budget negotiations, is the set of Maastricht criteria on financial and macroeconomic indicators. This applies not only to Germany (across all levels of government), but also to other member states of the European Union who intend to participate in the European Monetary Union.

In legal terms the Minister of Finance enjoys a privileged position in the German cabinet. Paragraph 28(2) of the Budget Guidelines gives the Finance Minister a suspensive veto for all expenditure decisions of the cabinet, which can become an absolute veto when supported by the Chancellor, even if these two are in a minority position in cabinet. The political decision-making process has so far been effective in keeping most budgetary controversies out of cabinet. The Finance Minister's suspensive veto remains a latent instrument that to date has never yet needed to be invoked. In today's political climate it is more likely a minister would use the media rather than cabinet to attack the Finance Minister, but this breach of cabinet discipline would probably end a minister's career. Ministers who consider that their unfulfilled demands did not receive sufficient attention may try to relaunch their bids when the government's budget proposals are presented to parliament. Both strategies were applied in the 1970s and 1980s. In times of crises Finance Ministers have attempted to secure an all-party consensus on some basic features (disciplines) of the budget. Recently, budget discipline has been reinforced by the imperatives of sound financing of expenditure and the aim of an annual balanced budget.

In July the cabinet makes its final decision on the federal budget. In August the expenditure proposals are simultaneously passed on to the Bundestag and the Bundesrat. The first reading of the budget in the Bundestag takes place in September.

The federal budget consists of three sets of documents: the *budget law* (that defines expenditure totals), the *aggregate budget* with tables on the budget as a whole, and the *departmental budgets* (Kunas 1982, p. 47). The aggregate budget provides the following information: a summary of the budget total of revenues, expenditures and authorizations for future spending, a summary of the means for financing the budget (net balance of financing requirements or surplus, and a borrowing plan showing the revenue from loans and the spending required for repaying debts). In addition, several annexes to the federal budget contain cross-section summaries, such as a breakdown of revenue and expenditure by economic category, a functional breakdown, a summary of the self-balancing items, and a staff list showing all the posts of lifetime staff, wage and salary earners and military personnel.

Departmental budgets provide the details of revenues, expenditures and authorizations for every department. They are subdivided into chapters and titles (items). Chapters represent the budgetary amounts for agencies or specific policy fields. Titles are the smallest units of a budget (roughly 8,000 titles) that identify special items or purposes of expenditure. Most titles are provided with additional explanations. The system of titles and their classification is based on economic category which is standard for all public budgets in Germany.

For technical reasons, and as a way to implement new policy priorities, the budget law is often accompanied by other legal provisions. They present the intention to amend legislation to achieve the budgetary aims or to restructure policy fields where necessary. Sometimes even decisions on taxation accompany the budget. In cases of emergency or unforeseen expenditure needs, supplementary budgets may be used to provide the necessary resources. A further way of meeting financial shortfalls is the provision for additional expenditures due to unforeseen and unavoidable needs. The Minister of Finance may authorize such expenditures (*Notbewilligungsrecht*), but is expected only to approve the additional spending if there are compensatory savings elsewhere in the budget. This power has strict limits (Kunas 1982, p. 52). For instance, it may only be used if additional expenditures cannot be postponed until parliamentary authorization has been secured in the form of a supplementary budget. For practical reasons, the legislature has waived the requirement of its approval when additional expenditures are relatively small or when they are the consequence of an entitlement. Recently, another instrument of the Finance Minister for steering expenditures has gained importance: the freezing of expenditures. In this case ministers have to seek the permission of the Finance Minister to spend their budget if a single expenditure exceeds a certain cost limit. Every major expenditure – though there may have been prior agreement on the policy in principle – now becomes dependent on the short-term availability of public funds. All these emergency decisions are taken outside the government's annual financial planning exercise. Although five-year expenditure plans (*Mittelfristige Finanzplanung*) still survive from the Keynesian decades of the 1960s and 1970s, they are for practical purposes little more than empty shells.

The 1990s have been dominated by expanding expenditures but also by concerns over budgetary reduction measures. One way restraint has been attempted is for the Chancellor and the Finance Minister to identify a specific amount of reduction that is then distributed among all ministries. In effect, the budget cycle operates inversely to produce the announced savings outcomes, and with ministries then fighting over their lists of suggested funding reductions and playing political games by mobilizing their clients. Sometimes, they propose a politically well-backed spending program for abolition, knowing this will cause public pressure on the Finance Ministry and the Chancellor to provide extra funding. The more capable of game-playing a spending minister is, the more likely he or she will survive budget reduction rounds without suffering major cuts.

The use of off-budget funds has recently become more important although their existence is not a new phenomenon (Sturm 1994, p. 140f). They can be set up outside the regular budget to finance expenditures. In 1987 the Federal Statistical Office counted 22 off-budget arrangements with a total volume of DM 8 billion of which only DM 2.8 billion was registered in the regular budget of DM 188.6 billion. By 1996 off-budget funds had grown to DM 442 billion, most of which were tied to *erblastentilgungsfonds*. Decisions on these funds are divorced from the regular budgetary procedures and from the restrictions on credit-financing of expenditures as defined in the German constitution (Article 115). The more relaxed features of off-budget funds may tempt governments to make use of them for their budgetary strategies, though these funds operate from a legal point of view in a grey area, because Article 110 of the constitution stipulates that the annual budget has to cover all taxes and expenditures (Kilian 1993).

German re-unification caused the use of off-budget expenditures to become endemic. Parliament defended this development with the argument that the aim, character and dimensions of the unification process were fundamentally different from traditional budgetary needs (Badura 1995, p. 7). Special purpose funds for the numerous single tasks of reconstructing the East German economy have been created especially for two reasons. The first reason was a politically convenient misperception, namely the assumption that most of the funds would become automatically superfluous after a transition period of four years. It was argued that they would fund specific purposes but create no costs for the federal budget, because the privatization proceeds and the economic recovery of East Germany would cover all costs that might temporarily arise. The second reason also had much to do with political cosmetics. The plethora of new funds hardly known to the general public and excluded from the publicity of the budgetary decision-making process could hide budgetary risks and problematic expenditure decisions, which allowed the federal government to argue at home and abroad that it was still cutting back the role of the state in the economy.

Our research leads us to the conclusion that despite the fact that German unification marked no doubt a very important turning point in German postwar history, the nature of which could not be more different from political routine, traditional instruments of budgeting defined by the constitution still continued to have enormous normative power. Furthermore, where political decisions were made to waive the rules in order to cope with special problems, the new procedures were kept as similar as possible to the rules of the old regime. It is also evident that any deviation from routine budgeting was chosen implicitly under the condition that decision-makers would return to traditional procedures as soon as possible.

THE MINISTRY OF FINANCE AS A POWERFUL, SINGLE CBA

The concept of a *central* budget agency is problematic in countries where budgetary authority is dispersed among several institutions at one level of government. For instance, in the United States, OMB and the Treasury are rivalled to some extent by the CBO, while in other nations such as Canada and Australia dual agencies co-exist. However, at the federal level in Germany, the co-existence of two agencies fundamentally involved in budgetary decision-making is totally foreign to our normative and institutional beliefs (as it is for most other unitary parliamentary systems). In Germany there is a single, powerful budget agency – solely involved in federal budget formulation – the Ministry of Finance.

Today, the federal Ministry of Finance consists of ten departments (or divisions) with a staff of roughly 2,100. The ministry has grown in importance since the 1960s and is now widely seen, not only as the most powerful ministry in government, but also as overloaded with too many fields of activity. Each department consists of a number of sections or taskforces called *referate* (ranging from 11 and 24) covering the policy areas of tax policy, financial and monetary markets, federal property management, European Affairs, the federal budget, intergovernmental financial affairs, and financial and economic policy. Departments are headed by public servants (Ministerial Directors) who report (or are overseen) by three secretaries of state (*Staatssekretäre*).

As the sole budget agency, the federal Finance Ministry has grown in importance and functions over time. Since 1969, it has gained organizational strength and functions which have expanded its administrative and policy ambit. For example, in 1969, the former Federal Treasury (*Bundesschatzministerium*) was abolished and its functions were partly transferred to the Finance Ministry and partly to the Economics Ministry. The Economics Ministry has no real input into the budget process, but focuses on macroeconomic policy and industrial development. The ministries of Economics and Finance were combined in the early-1970s but after an interim period of merger both ministries were again separated. However, in the process of separation the Finance Ministry was granted authority over financial policy more generally, including banking and monetary policy issues. Then in 1998, after the abolition of the Postal Ministry, authority to administer the government's privatization and public ownership issues (especially the publicly held shares of Deutsche Telekom AG) was transferred to the Finance Ministry. After the election of the new Social Democratic-led government in late-1998, important competencies of the Economics Ministry were transferred to Finance. These included both a complete policy division, responsible for Financial and Economic Policy (*Grundsatzfragen der Finanz- und Wirtschaftspolitik*) and responsibility for European policy. Since the transfer of these two crucial departments from the Economics to the Finance Ministry, there has been some suggestion of rivalry or institutional competition in the area of economic policy. The former Finance minister, Oskar Lafontaine, demanded these transfers in 1998, but his successor, Hans Eichel, has appeared less committed to the new arrangements – although it is said that his ministry has sought to prevent him from agreeing to return these departments back to Economics. Certainly, the Economics Ministry believes it has been deprived of crucial competencies.

While these administrative changes reflect a general rise of importance of the Finance Ministry, they have had only indirect implications for budgetary policy-making in the ministry. The Budget Division in the Finance Ministry (*Abteilung II: Bundeshaushalt*), still remains only one among nine divisions. The other accumulated financial and economic functions have merely expanded the influence of the Finance Ministry in other areas. Moreover, the tendency towards using off-budget funds as means to engage in policy areas outside the regular budget process does not imply a decline of institutional strength of the Finance Ministry. The Finance Ministry is, in general, still in charge of the off-budget funds created and allocated outside the regular budget process.

Germany is also a federal nation and as a consequence there exists a vertical fragmentation of budgetary decision-making. Every *Land* possesses a mini-version of the federal Finance Ministry that matches functionally and organizationally the structure of the federal agency. Similar budgetary processes are employed across the various jurisdictions. However, whereas budgeting is an autonomous process in each *Land*, fiscal matters are not. All levels of government are fiscally interlocked and typically depend on broad consent requirements (for example, tax changes). This specifically German version of interlocking federalism creates enormous hurdles for deficit control policies (Sturm with Müller 1999, p. 82).

THE MINISTRY OF FINANCE AND CONFLICTS OVER RE-UNIFICATION

The problems of re-unification highlighted a lack of coordination in the German core executive. The Chancellor's Office promoted German unity for political reasons and dictated the speed with which treaties with the GDR were negotiated, neglecting the financial consequences of important political decisions, such as the introduction of the German Mark in the GDR. A major conflict soon developed between the Chancellor's Office and the Ministry of Finance. In the Chancellor's Office the Reconstruction of East Germany group (*Aufbaugruppe-Ost*) became the driving force even with regard to basic budgetary decisions, whereas the Economics Ministry (led by a Liberal) and the Finance Ministry (led by a Bavarian Conservative) often came up with conflicting ideas about the financing of German unification. The result was a lack of a clear financial and budgetary policy, marked by some creative budgeting, some muddling through and some inertia. Significantly, the re-unification initiative remained with the Chancellor's Office (Czada 1995, p. 76).

The Initial Period of Transition: 1990–94

Initially, German unification provoked a conflict between the old Länder and the federal government over the 'fair share' of the financial burden to be shouldered by the different levels of government. The compromise found was codified in the German Unity Fund (*Fonds Deutsche Einheit*), which limited the contribution of the Länder to 50 per cent of the DM 95 billion loan, while leaving the federal government the responsibility for any additional cost overruns (Sturm 1991, p. 169ff). At the time this seemed unproblematic, because the federal government believed in a second 'economic miracle'. However, shortly after the 1990 election, East Germany experienced a dramatic economic crisis and the federal government's commitment to cover all additional costs provoked a major budgetary upset (Andersen 1992, p. 240ff). It soon became clear that the Unity Fund, consisting of the DM 95 billion in borrowed money and a further DM 20 billion contribution from the federal budget, was not enough to provide sufficient funding for the East German Länder. Inevitably, the Unity Fund had to be increased on several occasions. In the end, the federal government paid DM 49.6 billion and the old Länder in the West contributed an additional DM 16.1 billion. In addition, both the federal government and the western Länder had to cover their share of the costs for the interest and repayment of the DM 95 billion loan.

What was the budgetary logic behind the establishment of the German Unity Fund? From the outset it was clear the new Länder were in need of substantial financial aid in order to guarantee them, not only the budgetary resources to match those available for the Länder in the West, but also an additional surcharge to allow them to catch up with the West. The intention behind this income tax surcharge was to use these funds specifically to improve the East's infrastructure. It was considered appropriate to guarantee the new Länder a level of funding which equalled 120 per cent of the average per capita income of the Länder in the West. However, it was not clear where this figure came from. Experts in the Ministry of Finance agreed among themselves that the 120 per cent decision was the result of an 'iterative process'. Yet, the figure stuck and has since remained the yardstick for determining the financial needs of the East German Länder.

In order to reach the funding target of 120 per cent between 1990 and 1994, a combination of three funding strategies was chosen: funding from the German Unity Fund; additional taxes and duties levied in the new Länder; and third, the East German Länder were asked to incur higher deficits than was the rule among the western Länder. The federal government believed this was not a problem because the new Länder started with zero public debt. The relative importance of these three sources of finance for the East German Länder can be illustrated by a glance at the 1991 budget of Saxony. Its own income base consisted of DM 4 billion in tax revenues, a further DM 8.8 billion provided by the German Unity Fund, and a DM 5 billion loan (Kilian 1991, p. 425). This breakdown demonstrates the overwhelming importance of the German Unity Fund for the financial survival of the eastern Länder. It also indicated a ticking time bomb was likely to explode in 1994 when the government planned to abolish the Unity Fund.

To understand the budgetary reaction to German re-unification it is necessary to analyse the history of federal financial relation in Germany. The western Länder had to negotiate in a budgetary framework in which the allocation of revenue to the different levels of government in Germany was largely inflexible. They feared that the existing system of fiscal equalization between the Länder would be used to solve the crisis. Under this system the West would have had to pay for most of the needs of the East, because it required the financially stronger Länder to subsidize the financially weaker ones. During negotiations on the Unity Treaty, the West German Länder formulated the idea of a new fund to provide the eastern Länder with sufficient financial means. Their main goal was to exclude the new Länder from the fiscal equalization arrangements until they were rich enough to participate in a system that was initially set up only to compensate for variations in peak income.

The federal government had different intentions (Schäuble 1991). It wanted to use 50 per cent of the German Unity Fund to fund its responsibilities in the East (Schwinn 1997, p. 69). Besides its routine tasks, such as road construction or air control, the federal government was confronted with additional responsibilities because of the lack of an efficient public administration in East Germany. This was reflected by the fact that in the very first months of the transition period, federal government expenditures in the East made up 45 per cent of total federal expenditures (Fiedler 1990, p. 1267). Moreover, during the negotiations over the Unity Fund it became clear that the Länder were not willing to allow it to be used to co-finance federal government activities. The federal government even offered to reduce its claim to just 15 per cent of the Fund (Fiedler 1990, p. 1267). But, a coalition of the old and new Länder blocked this demand, and the federal government received nothing. In short, the power of the federal Ministry of Finance over budgetary discretion was severely limited by the combined power of the Länder. The federal government had no choice but to accede if it did not want to slow down or endanger German re-unification. It agreed to exclude itself from the financial benefits of the Fund, because its political priority was to secure the rapid ratification of the Unity Treaty. In the end, the Unity Fund became a substitute for a nationwide system of fiscal equalization, a system that was finally introduced on 1 January 1995.

Both the federal government and the Länder regarded the negotiations on the financing of German unification as a power struggle although there was the symbolic appearance of a joint effort (Patzig 1991, p. 579). For the federal government the Unity Fund represented yet another off-budget item. It was formally established as a 'special federal fund' under the responsibility of the Ministry of Finance. A council of ministerial experts was established at the Ministry of Finance to represent all governments involved in borrowing the fund. Although it was initially intended to have wider responsibilities, the council became simply a group with the task of winding up the fund when the federal government and Länder eventually repaid their borrowings.

In terms of budgetary decision-making, the off-budget solution had a number of advantages. First and foremost, special funds were exempt from the deficit restrictions of Article 115 of the German constitution (Patzig 1991, p. 582). There has been considerable debate on this mode of financing German unification (Eckertz 1993b; Gottfried and Wiegard 1991; Henneke 1991; Kilian 1991; Patzig 1991; Heun 1992; Wieland 1992). The dangers of creating off-budget debts are obvious. However, when asked about their opinion, ministerial experts in the Finance Ministry argued that quick solutions were needed and there was no choice. Thus, assuming constitutional reform was impossible, solutions had to be found which used well-known and politically non-controversial budgetary devices.

Interestingly, the creation of an off-budget fund was defended by the former Minister of Finance and Economics, Karl Schiller (from the then oppositional Social Democratic Party), who said in his testimony during the budget committee hearings of November 1990 that outlays for the maintenance and improvement of human capital in the former GDR must be grouped as investments. If this were done, expenditures for German re-unification would not violate the deficit restrictions of the German constitution which allow deficits only up to a level that matches investments unless the country is in a severe economic crisis. In the legal debate (Patzig 1991, p. 583) it was felt necessary to justify the deficits in the Unity Fund with arguments that avoided making the Fund a foreign body under the constitution. A simple reference to the fact that German re-unification was an extraordinary event did not seem to suffice. The view developed that the best way to meet this unexpected challenge in budgetary terms was simply to do more of the same.

The fact that a prominent politician from an opposition party agreed in general with the off-budget fund solution was no accident. Experts in the Finance Ministry agreed that Bundestag opposition was never a problem with regard to the operation of the Unity Fund. Parliament also did not play a significant role. And even more surprising, the Federal Accounting Office never audited the German Unity Fund, although it no doubt had the right to do so. Ministerial experts only remembered a report of the Federal Accounting Office in 1993 that explained in broad terms the functioning of the German Unity Fund. It would appear that a high level of consensus emerged with regard to the chosen strategy to finance the transition of East Germany.

The budgetary decision-making of the Finance Ministry in the transition period was characterized by the adherence to procedural routines. First, it respected Länder interests and the power balance of federalism. Second, the federal executive's priority of re-unification contributed to consensus-building and to the federal government's highly cooperative behaviour with regard to budgetary conflict. Third, whatever the results of the political bargaining process, it needed some technical points of reference (the 120 per cent yardstick for funding the new Länder). Ministerial experts in Finance said that they had 'calculated something', even though they could not remember how that figure had been achieved. Technical precision was used to produce legitimacy. Fourth, and most importantly, the existing legal regime (namely the fiscal regime and its budgetary rules) continued to exert a normative effect on executive decision-makers as well as on their counterparts in other decision-making bodies. This is not to say that decision-makers shied away from innovation. On the contrary, major departures from the *status quo* were made. What remained intact, however, was the normative framework for proposing and assessing such departures and for analysing the problems to be solved. Efforts were made to justify innovation by recourse to older rules. The tendency to classify innovations within the formal system of budgetary principles and rules may also have prevented more fundamental budgetary reform from occurring.

The New Fiscal Regime: since 1995

Contrary to initial expectations, the German Unity Fund provided only a temporary and partial solution for the problem of financing German re-unification. In 1993 further negotiations between the federal government and the Länder were expected to clarify the terms under which the new Länder could join the fiscal equalization arrangements. The compromise found offered additional financial transfers to the East worth DM 50 billion (OECD 1993, p. 103). But the compromise was also codified in law in 1993 and was supposed to consolidate public finances after 1994. The package was in substance a return to the constitutional routines but it changed the federal–Länder fiscal relationship.

The Ministry of Finance knew that the 120 per cent formula provided over the period 1990–94 to the East German Länder was insufficient to prevent them from going further into debt. It concluded that the new Länder could not keep on going into debt at the same speed as they had since re-unification had occurred. The ministry stressed the importance of financial planning especially with regard to the maintenance of an appropriate revenue base and over possible limits for future deficits. Thus, new ways of creating income had to be discovered, and the German Unity Fund was not acceptable as a long-term solution. It was considered a contingency measure that remained foreign to the Basic Law.

With the help of three strategies the Finance Ministry and the Länder tried to provide a more permanent base for the financing of German re-unification. First, the new Länder were fully and permanently integrated into the fiscal equalization arrangements applying nation-wide. This move raised the amount of funding to be redistributed among the Länder from DM 3 billion to DM 11–12 billion. Second, the way the joint federal-Länder VAT revenues were distributed was changed. Following a proposal made by the Bavarian Ministry of Finance (Eckertz 1993a) the federal government agreed to increase the Länder share of the VAT income from 37 to 44 per cent. The new Länder would receive a 'pre-payment' from this revenue (an amount set aside for the eastern Länder before the VAT was distributed to all Länder according to the size of their population). This added another DM 12–13 billion to the income of the new Länder. Third, the system of federal grants to the Länder was extended to include the new Länder. As a result total grants increased from the DM 3 billion (received by the western Länder up to 1994) to DM 25 billion. These federal grants were block grants with no strings attached, and most of this money (about DM 23 billion) was reserved for the new Länder.

So, although ways of funding the eastern Länder were found, there was no heroic effort to question the *status quo* of the legal budgetary framework. The repair work done was aimed only at keeping the old vehicle of federal-Länder fiscal arrangements on the road. In the post-1994 arrangements, neither the 120 per cent income formula for the new Länder budgets, nor budgeting procedures came under serious review. Even though Article 5 of the Unity Treaty stipulated that federal legislators were asked to consider constitutional changes, including with respect to federal financial relationships, there was no new solution found to the financial arrangements of unification. Despite the occasional rhetoric, decision-makers have done their utmost to avoid radical changes in the fiscal constitution.

Additional Federal Spending in the New Länder

Financing the budgets of the new Länder was the most significant problem of re-unification, but it was by no means the sole commitment from the federal government. Under Article 91a and 91b of the Basic Law, the federal government was obliged to co-fund the so-called 'common tasks' of the federal and Länder governments, as well as investments of special importance to the Länder and to local governments (Articles 104a IV of the Basic Law). Such subsidies were able only to be given for legally defined special purposes. They could not be used freely by the new Länder to improve their budgetary situation.

The federal government also wanted to avoid subsidizing the eastern Länder under the existing *Structural Aid Act 1989*. The reason for this was a reluctance to codify subsidies in law. At the time it appeared impossible to identify which specific needs in the East could justify subsidies. The federal government therefore preferred a flexible policy that was responsive to the demands of the new Länder. But the flexibility and *ad hoc* nature of the programs also brought with it problems. For instance, the status of federal subsidies directly to local governments in the east (for schools, hospitals, nurseries, but by-passing the Länder administration) could be regarded as unconstitutional (Kirste 1995, p. 208) to the extent that the federal government's intervention violated Länder rights or ignored the budgetary competences of their parliaments. For many of these *ad hoc* interventions the traditional rules for specifying subsidies were ignored. This may be explained by the fact that the obstacles to arriving at a bi-lateral consensus on providing or spending funds were much lower. Both partners involved, the federal government and the recipients in the new Länder, collaborated in ignoring some ground rules of budgeting.

But by early 1993, the federal government determined that this kind of flexibility was not to be tolerated. Federal financial assistance was codified in Article 35 of the federal consolidation of public finances law. Under a new *Investments Subsidies Act* a total of DM 6.6 billion was granted annually to the new Länder for the financing of investments of special importance over a period of ten years (Bundesministerium der Finanzen 1997, p. 137). Funding was supposed to help with investments in public transport, environmental protection, the construction of housing, urban development and the like. The main purpose of federal funding was now to create some room for manoeuvre for the new Länder budgets by substituting federal funds for Länder funds to finance current investment programs.

Hence, after a short period of turmoil federal programs to finance German unification were anchored in the traditional framework of budgeting. The Chancellor presided over the initial steps towards re-unification (Lehmbruch 1991, p. 587), but when the Unity Treaty was negotiated, other political actors especially the Länder demanded a greater role. It is hardly surprising that Länder extracted a high price from the federal government because they felt their interests had been ignored for so long. It seems that policy-making within the executive regarding the financing of German re-unification was initially intended to be proactive, but in the end became reactive with financing organized in the framework of the old fiscal regime. Whatever alternatives there may have been, after some rounds of negotiations with the Länder, the federal government compromised in order to secure a fast process of unification. Concerns about the size of the budgetary challenge became of secondary importance, although to be fair the situation did not allow for intense political bargaining. Thousands of East Germans had immigrated to the West and the Chancellor saw no alternative to an immediate decision in favour of an economic and monetary union (Schwinn 1997, p. 39).

THE LIMITS OF CREATIVE BUDGETING IN THE RECHTSSTAAT

Germany managed to fund the re-unification program while retaining its belief in the rechtsstaat and the importance of the budget law. Even under extraordinary circumstances German policy-makers held on to the strong legal culture guiding the country's public administration. Indeed, the *status quo* of traditional budgeting has become more than a welcome routine, it has also become the essential denominator on which a wide range of potentially conflicting interests can be negotiated. Among the core executive in Germany there is a fear that any change affecting this delicate political equilibrium will have unforeseeable and perhaps deleterious consequences. Consequently, there remains a strong preference that incremental, reactive and short-term corrections of budgetary routines are a much better choice than the search for a fresh start.

The really interesting questions we dealt with above was what is the degree of budgetary flexibility beyond these rules and how does the complexity of the institutional actors impact on budgetary decisions? Re-unification both changed the bargaining power of other actors in the budgetary process and provided a major test of the system's ability to cope with adversity. Emerging as an external factor, re-unification has had far more impact on the German state than internal administrative dynamics. And, indeed, Germany has studiously avoided embracing such internal reforms as New Public Management.

Initially, political interest in re-unification was the principal issue and financial issues were less pronounced. The financial challenges of re-unification were severely underestimated by the political executives both at the federal level (the Chancellor and Finance Ministry) and in the Länder. Confronted with unfolding emergencies, which demanded value judgments and provoked conflicts of interests, the federal government was unable to impose its preferred solutions and had to compromise with the Länder. The federal and constitutional nature of Germany guarantees an important role for the Länder. Although the federal government has wide responsibilities, the Länder have insisted that some of that responsibility be shared. Hence, the context of re-unification changed the set of relevant actors in the decision-making process, and brought new players to the table. As budgetary problems gained greater prominence (and reached a certain level of political importance) the actors had to find grounds for consensus and compromise.

An immediate period of turmoil was not followed by a breakthrough of new ideas or creative budgeting, but by a period which was characterized by hectic diplomacy between the Länder and the federal government which had as its major aim the return to well-entrenched traditional budgetary procedures. When it turned out that this was not sufficient to cope with the size and the dimensions of the budgetary problem, the federal government resorted to the use of off-budgetary measures, but only in reaction to new problems and overwhelming political pressures. Instead of shaping the budgetary process to make it fit for the new problems, the government became a victim of never-ending new budgetary needs. The formal budget process was not a means of policy coordination across government or an explicit instrument for coordinating different policies in the spending ministries. Rather the budget process continued to limit spending wishes and impose a restrictive framework over the use of public funds. It remained a purely technical system. Other funding adjustments had to be made initially outside the formal budgetary process.

It was also clear that when politicians tried to cope with the unexpected problems of financing German unification they were not particularly successful and had eventually to rely on expert officials. The expertise of the Finance Ministry eventually enabled government to react adequately to the non-routine problems. From the Finance Ministry's perspective, the emergencies created by unification could not be ignored. Necessity required that some temporary and *ad hoc* strategies were undertaken to protect the process of German re-unification. With input from the Länder, a series of bargains were codified in the German Unity Fund, and emergency funding strategies were treated as extra-budgetary. These were regarded as adequate measures at the time but always as temporary adjustments. But within a matter of a few years these non-routine adjustments were reincorporated within the routines of the formal budgetary process. Routine decision-making remains rule-based, though it allows for some flexibility. One may argue that this flexibility has recently been overstretched, but as the aftermath of re-unification demonstrates every rule needs also some room for interpretation.

NOTES

1. This is in stark contrast to the Ministry of Economics under such ministers as Ludwig Erhard or Karl Schiller.
2. For example, the commissioner has a say in matters of financial planning, in the decision-making on expenditures, contracting-out and in the creation of civil service jobs. The budget commissioner comments both on the desirability and the quantity of new appointments. This means that he has a crucial voice in matters of resourcing and may therefore potentially erect formal hurdles for politicians and bureaucrats seeking new resources. The commissioner also has free access to information and the right of veto in all matters of financial relevance. His veto can only be overridden by the executive in charge, that is the minister in case of a ministry or the president or chairman in case of an independent federal agency. For federal ministries this means that the minister himself or herself must explicitly waive the budget commissioner's veto. Here the commissioner can act as a catalyst, who can transform any (presumably minor) decision into a controversial political question to be resolved by the minister. Hence, budget commissioners have more than a purely technical function. They serve as both a watchdog and a catalyst, and are a potentially important ally for those who intend to protect themselves against budget cuts or who want to increase their share of the pie of budgetary expenditures.

10. Not so Much a Model, More a Way of Life: China's Fragmented Authoritarianism in Budgetary Management

K.C. Cheung

Prior to the period of economic reform initiated in the 1980s, the budgetary system in China was based on the Soviet legacy whereby administrative and budgetary power was tightly controlled by the central government. Like many other Communist nations, China operated as a decision-making hierarchy in which authority was highly centralized. The budgetary system was one instrument of this central control. Initially seeking a viable budgetary model, the Chinese Communists replicated the Soviet's centralized system of budgeting. They were attracted to a 'unified income and unified expenditure' (*tongshou tongzhi*) budget as a rational and consolidated system.[1] According to a former cadre working in the Ministry of Finance in the 1950s, China not only adopted its budgetary system from the former Soviet Union, but also copied the Soviet's central finance ministry even down to such micro-details as the office and furniture layout (Yuqian 2001, pp. 188–89). This Soviet legacy would last for over three decades until a combination of economic reform and decentralization pressures gradually saw it superseded.

Although highly centralized, the administration of China was facilitated through a system of sub-national administrative units and the budgetary system reflected this structure. As Figure 10.1 indicates, the State Budget was divided into two principal levels – a central budget and various local budgets. The local budget level included semi-autonomous districts, large administrative regions, and provincial governments (which provided for municipalities and prefectures). However, neither the administrative regions nor the provincial governments had much influence in financial arrangements. This basic administrative structure still survives today although, as will become evident in the chapter, the way budgeting operates has changed remarkably since the onset of economic reform.

The main principles of the pre-reform budgetary system were four-fold:

1.   Unless specifically authorized all the revenues had to be remitted to the central government. Local governments had no authority to use revenues;
2.   All expenditures were appropriated by the central government on a monthly basis;
3.   Taxation, resource supplies, wage rates, personnel establishment and the State Budget were prepared and determined by the central government; and
4.   Local governments were only allowed to keep certain minor taxes and some of the agricultural, industrial and commercial taxes beyond a certain quota.

The need for such a centralized system during the early days of communist rule was perhaps understandable. At the time of the establishment of the People's Republic of China (PRC) in 1949, the administrative system was in its infancy and the economy was devastated due to the long civil war. Production was extraordinarily low while inflation was extremely high. Financially, the first State Budget of the Communist government was difficult because total revenue remained small while expenditure (and the immediate demands) was considerably higher – consequently, the State Budget recorded a huge deficit.[2] Accordingly, it quickly became apparent that a powerful central budget agency was necessary to rescue the economy and eliminate budget deficits as quickly as possible, in order to restore the confidence of the people under the new Communist regime.

With the introduction of economic reform and the increased importance placed on economic growth, the budget process and budgetary management in PRC have remained basically unchanged. Some observers believe that the overriding aim of China's primitive budgetary system was to preserve political stability for the Communist government. On the other hand, the aim of economic reform after 1980 was primarily concerned with economic development, and paid little or no attention to reforming China's political system.

But today's budgetary environment is now quite different from the past. During the past 20 years, the private sector has grown at a remarkable rate and now occupies an important role in economic activities. State-owned enterprises (SOEs) gradually lost their monopoly position in resource allocation and production. They were outperformed by joint-venture enterprises and private firms, and eventually became less competitive and adaptive to the new market economy. These moves have had a tremendous impact on government revenues. Prior to economic reform, incomes from state-owned enterprises formed the major source of income for the central state but their importance has decreased as economic reform has reshaped the economy. Moreover, more than half of the SOEs have suffered annual losses since the 1990s, and have themselves become a financial burden on the state.

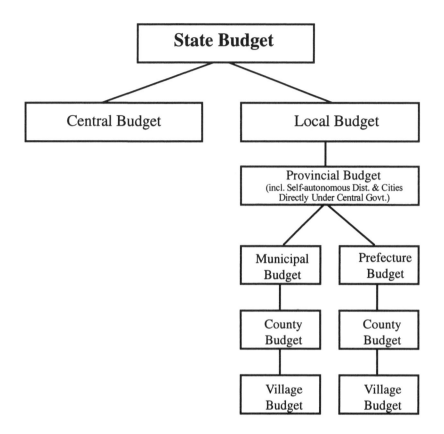

Figure 10.1   China's state budget system

Yet, the fiscal and taxation systems have not adapted sufficiently to cope with this dramatic change. Little effort was put into reforming the budgetary system to cope with this high change economic environment. The first major exercise in budgetary reform was conducted in 1994 and the resultant path-breaking *Budget Law* was enacted and implemented in 1995. This was the first legal document in China to define in specific terms the roles and responsibilities of the central and local budget agencies and the methods and processes of the budgetary system. However, despite these reforms focusing largely on processes and administrative procedures, the fundamental problems of China's budgetary system (i.e. to modify a centrally planned budgetary system to meet the needs of the new market economy) still remain unresolved.

Figure 10.2 characterizes the main problems that exist between the dynamism of the present economic system and the sedentary nature of the budgetary system.

PRINCIPAL CHARACTERISTICS OF THE BUDGETARY PROCESS IN CHINA

Decentralization with Remaining Vestiges of Strong Central Power

It took China 15 years to transform the State Budget from a Soviet-type unified revenue and unified expenditure system to a market based tax-sharing system in 1994. The principal objectives of the reformed budgetary system in China were, one the one hand, to grasp the benefits of fiscal decentralization and the rationalization of revenue sources, while at the same time strengthening and enforcing budget discipline and centralized budgetary power. Over the years, China has not had much success in establishing a system that can satisfactorily balance central-local fiscal relations. By having one dominant political party, however, China has been able to afford the luxury of searching for an acceptable way by the trial and error method in budgetary reform design. Hence, a number of experimental or transitional arrangements, such as a purchaser-provider 'contract system', were not retained as suitable devices for solving central-local conflicts as China moved toward fiscal decentralization. Indeed, dividing fiscal capacity on a contractual basis without first resolving the respective functions performed by different levels of government proved to be problematic

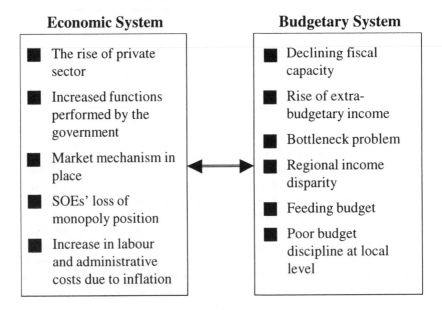

Economic System	**Budgetary System**
■ The rise of private sector	■ Declining fiscal capacity
■ Increased functions performed by the government	■ Rise of extra-budgetary income
■ Market mechanism in place	■ Bottleneck problem
■ SOEs' loss of monopoly position	■ Regional income disparity
■ Increase in labour and administrative costs due to inflation	■ Feeding budget
	■ Poor budget discipline at local level

Figure 10.2   High change in the economic system v. low change in the budgetary system

and ineffective. Although the terms of each individual 'contract' were mainly determined by political bargaining, the contract system failed to balance the income disparity among the regions in China. It also provided the opportunity for local governments to divert their attention to generating their own extra-budgetary revenue for local and private interests.

Executive-led without Public Scrutiny

State Council formally determines the policy directions expressed in the State Budget whilst administration rests with the Ministry of Finance (MoF). The power of the National People's Congress (NPC) in controlling public expenditure is merely cosmetic. Budget proposals are usually passed with few queries. Detailed budget figures are not usually presented during NPC meetings; rather only crude data is available for inspection. The role of the legislature is no more than a rubber-stamp.

The implementation of the State Budget nominally operates according to a vertical hierarchy with centralized supervision operating through a strict chain of command. Each lower level of government is supervised by officials at a higher level. Financial and taxation policies are tightly held in the hands of the MoF. As head of the financial system, MoF directs its subordinate units (down to the lowest level finance bureaux) from the centre.

In an era of fiscal decline, the power of the centre has become more problematic. The influence of MoF is often expressed in terms of policy settings rather than fiscal policy or financial leverage. For instance, the area of environmental protection provides a good example. Local environmental protection bureaus are basically self-financing administrative units, with only 10 per cent of their funding derived from the State Budget. Most of their revenues come from extra-budgetary or off-budget income – mainly from pollutant discharge fees. Their reliance on the central state is more for *policy* that may empower them to generate additional income rather than for budgeted *income per se*. A change in state policy will eventually affect their power and ability to collect revenue. Hence, local bureau officials need to maintain good working relationships with central government while hoping to keep interference from the centre to a minimum. Chinese budgeters are therefore more interested in *policy opportunism* than budget maximization.

In brief, China's State Budget is basically executive-led and involves little, if any, public scrutiny. Concepts contained in the Western literature, such as conflict resolution, do not seem to have much value in explaining the making of the Chinese State Budget. The central level of government determines the budgets of subordinate governments, and these decisions are final. Conflicts over spending are mostly reconciled before the budget is passed to the legislature for formal approval. Maintaining good working relationships determines budgetary allocation and remains a crucial budgetary tactic for spending units.

Subsistence Budgets and Low Efficiency

Public expenditure in China expanded rapidly during the era of economic reform. As a socialist country, the Chinese government provides major, essential public services from the public purse. In the past most of these were delivered by SOEs. Due to the failure of many of the SOEs, this burden has been partially or wholly shifted to the central government. Hence, total budget outlays have grown rapidly. For instance, between 1979 and 1992, government expenditure increased from 128,179 billion yuan to 374,220 billion yuan (but at the same time fell as a proportion of GDP from 31 per cent to around 15 per cent).

On the other hand, administrative costs now absorb an increasingly larger proportion of the State Budget. Between 1978 to 1996, the total expenditure on government administration, mainly labour costs, increased at an annual rate of 11 per cent, much higher than any other country in the world. It should be noted that public services provided through the State Budget are not universal; these services may only be enjoyed free by a limited number of people, mainly cadres and people working in SOEs. The rest of the population must pay through user-pays contribution/purchasing. Most of the public services available free or at a nominal cost in OECD nations are not provided in China or are supplied with a price tag. Health care and education provide two examples.

Moreover, there is also evidence that the efficiency of public expenditure is extremely low in China, with a large part going to pay basic wages and salaries not on providing services. This is why Premier Zhu Rongji exclaimed that the majority of resources of the state budget merely funded subsistence to public sector employees – it had in his words become a 'rice-providing budget'.

Fiscal Decline and a Weakened Centre

Total revenue in China as a proportion of GDP has also been steadily declining since the onset of economic reform. By the year 2000, revenue was equal to just over 13 per cent of GDP – one of the lowest rates of taxation in the world. Fiscal decline is a natural consequence of the central government's intention to delegate some of the fiscal capacity to lower level governments to promote economic efficiency and/or productivity. In the past the focus of the MoF was on the distribution of the total revenue between the central and local governments. A number of sharing arrangements were employed (usually based on incremental adjustments) that were mainly determined through individual negotiation and compromise. The final result was seldom based on rational or objective criteria and therefore fiscal disparities between the provinces remained. Local governments each attempted to secure from the MoF a higher base of budgetary income and a favourable annual adjustment factor to secure what they believed was a fair share for their own government.

The power of the central budget agency was further weakened by the massive expansion of off-budgetary income in the 1980s. Off-budgetary income was initially envisaged as a source of supplementary income for ministries or local governments, and the amounts involved were quite small prior to 1980. But with the decentralization of fiscal power and the empowerment of local governments to generate income to support the administrative apparatus, the magnitude of off-budgetary income rapidly grew. In fact, in 1993 aggregate off-budgetary income was higher than total budgetary income. The magnitude greatly reduced the power of the central budget agency to impose budgetary control over local governments. Accordingly, MoF decided in 1994 to incorporate most of the off-budget income back into the State Budget. But by then off-budget income provided an important alternative source of revenue for local governments beyond the control of MoF. Budgetary decentralization contributed to the fiscal decline of central government.

The growth of off-budget incomes not only eroded central revenues but also distorted the direction of public service provision. For example, a number of studies of environmental governance within China (Chan *et al.* 1995; Cheung 1998; Lo and Tang 1994) have demonstrated that the environmental protection bureau (EPB) in Guangzhou was much more interested in pursuing off-budget revenue-generating activities than in performing its assigned administrative duties. The bureau acted as a political entrepreneur, seeking opportunities to secure income by making use of its regulatory and administrative power. Such motives prevented it from performing its duties in an impartial and effective manner. The local EPB was motivated more by charging pollutant discharge fees than by the total damage caused by pollution to the community.

Today it is estimated that unless MoF can generate total revenues equal to around 20 per cent of GDP, China will not be able to perform its functions to an acceptable scale and standard. Yet, if off-budgetary incomes are included as part of the state budget, the total size of public revenue is not small compared with other developing countries. Tax reform commenced in 1994 has begun to address the central-local financial relationships by clearly defining the resources and the functions of each level of government. Provided financial discipline is strengthened, fiscal decline could be averted.

FRAGMENTED AUTHORITARIANISM AND THE BUDGETARY SYSTEM

The Chinese bureaucracy has been characterized by a model of 'fragmented authoritarianism' (Lam 2001). Below the authoritarian peak, a series of fragmented and disjointed sub-systems can be found and the budget system is no exception. These fragmented sub-systems operate in their respective jurisdictions without much coordination for a common stake or goal. Each sub-system directs its energy and administrative effort to preserving its interests and power under the tolerance of the centre.

Unlike in many Western countries, the power over the expenditure budget in China is not vested solely in the hands of one ministry. At present, four central agencies retain some authority over budget allocation: the MoF; the State Development and Planning Commission (SDPC); the State Council Bureau on Government and Administrative Affairs; and the Ministry for Science and Technology. Although the MoF is formally responsible for preparing the State Budget, the resource allocation power of the other three agencies is, however, independent. The power of the purse exercised by MoF is partial at most and accordingly a system of horizontal specialization co-exists alongside the vertical hierarchy of government.

Furthermore, the fragmentation of power occurs not only on the expenditure side. Although revenue policy is under the jurisdiction of MoF, the central ministry is only responsible for making laws and regulations on taxation but is not responsible for tax administration. Revenue collection is the responsibility of other agencies, mainly the agencies of State Tax Administration and Customs. While many within MoF consider the State Tax Administration as an executive arm of MoF, administratively they operate as separate and parallel agencies and both have equal status under State Council.

The central State Budget is formulated according to two discrete principles. On the expenditure side, the budget is distributed according to *functions* whereas on the revenue side it is classified according to *types*. These principles are also used in determining the expenditures and revenues of each ministry and department (prior to 2000 there was no such thing as a global or one-line departmental budget). The consequence of these two principles means that if a ministry wishes to expand its recurrent operations (enhancing its functions) it must apply to and seek authorization not from MoF but from the Bureau of Government and Administrative Affairs – an organ directly under the State Council. If it wishes to undertake new investment projects, the appropriate authority for granting funds is the State Development and Planning Commission. Taken together, the resource allocation process is disjointed and involves many agencies each with different functional authority and with little coordination between them.

After some important criticism from the NPC, four ministries were chosen in 2000 to act as pilot studies for allocating budgets on a departmental basis. These four ministries (the Ministry of Education, Ministry of Agriculture, Ministry of Science and Technology, and Ministry of Labour and Social Security) were chosen on the basis that they were not revenue-generating agencies and relied on MoF for their resources. While it may be too early to make a definitive judgement on the outcomes of these pilot studies, judging from the experience it was clear that the allocation of a departmental budget did normalize the process of budget formulation. But the basic problem of a fragmented structure of agencies each able to allocate parts of the budget remains unsolved (MoF 2000).

A Non-transparent Budgetary Process

Government departments and bureaus in China work with confidential (non-transparent) budgetary information. They maintain a number of secretive practices and keep more than one set of accounts. One set of accounts is maintained for the inspection of MoF (only including budgetary income); another set of accounts is for internal use (including both budgetary and off-budgetary income); and a third set is produced only for the eyes of very senior officials (containing information on off-budgetary incomes). Moreover, there is no unitary accounting system at present (one is supposedly under construction), and funds for budget units are kept in various accounts for different purposes. The number of these separate accounts has increased dramatically in the post-reform years due to a more diverse range of functions performed by agencies of the central government. An audit check revealed in 1997 that MoF alone had a total of 104 bank accounts, including 19 budgetary accounts, 35 off-budgetary accounts, 23 transitional accounts, 24 financial adjustment fund accounts and three special funds accounts (Deputy Director of Audit 1997). Most of these ministerial accounts are kept with commercial banks rather than with state banks such as the People's Bank or other public banks. Indeed, out of the 1600 bank accounts operated by the 38 ministries and commissions under the State Council, only 1.1 per cent are held with the People's Bank while 91.6 per cent are with commercial banks (MoF 2000, pp. 75–76). Commercial banks, not being part of the state, are not obliged to supply information to the Audit Administration nor are they normally willing to do so. It is, therefore, extremely difficult to discover the full financial picture of a ministry within the short timeframe of auditing.[3]

Efficient budget management is further prevented by the unreasonable budget cycle and budgetary timelines. Each ministry is instructed to prepare its budget for the next financial (calendar) year as late as November of each year. By December, draft budgets are forwarded to MoF which collates the submissions and prepares a consolidated budget for submission to Congress. The NPC does not pass the state budget proposal until the end of March. Almost four months of the new financial year have elapsed before the budget is formally approved. Finalized budgets are then distributed to individual ministries beginning at the earliest in May but sometimes taking until October at the latest. It is possible that when a ministry receives its money for the current year, it is almost time to prepare the next round of the budget cycle. On the other hand, once budget allocations are agreed by MoF (subject to the fragmented authorizations) they are granted to each ministry on a lump-sum basis, there is no further itemization of spending (line items) or specifications about how the money should be spent. Hence, the CBA has no mechanism to monitor whether the funds are properly used in accordance with the budget plan, or whether intended outputs have been achieved/produced. The efficient use of funds is almost impossible to determine under China's present budgetary system.

FORMULATING BUDGETS: THE KEY ACTORS

The semblance of authoritarian control is maintained by the existence of a number of key central committees that each exercise budgetary power. These actors appear formally to enjoy unrivalled authority. However, as peak decision-making bodies they suffer from a lack of institutional or bureaucratic capacities to coordinate the financial system. The main central actors are shown in Figure 10.3 and discussed in turn below.

The Central Finance and Economic Leading Group (CFELG)

The Central Finance and Economic Leading Group (*Zhongyang caijing lingdao xiaozu*) is the highest authority in the Chinese bureaucracy for financial and economic matters. It is a joint organ of the Politburo of the Chinese Communist Party (CCP) and the State Council. The Group consists of a few select members and it makes decisions only on key policies, with responsibility for implementation and daily administration being entrusted to the State Planning Commission (SPC). The basic role of this Group involves steering rather than directing economic policy. As a political and policy-making body CFELG tends to make decisions without any direct involvement or interaction with the Finance Ministry – both occupy separate loci of decision-making. Major decisions, if any, are disseminated via the State Council (and the Standing Committee of State Council usually decides all major new budgetary items). The CFELG, however, holds the final say in economic and financial matters, should it decide to intervene.

The State Planning Commission (SPC)

The SPC is an important organ for administering economic planning and it leads the work of a number of national policy research institutes and centres,

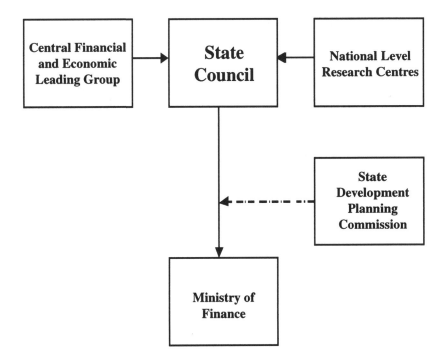

Figure 10.3   Key budgetary decision-making bodies

including the prestigious Planned Economy Research Centre. At one time, it employed over 7000 people of whom about 1400 were directly involved in planning work (Lixin and Fewsmith 1995). The SPC also oversees the work of the other major economic ministries, with which it has a professional leadership relationship (Lixin and Fewsmith 1995, p. 54). The financial section of the SPC's Financial and Monetary Division once oversaw the work of the Ministry of Finance but now no longer performs these functions.

In the past, as a centrally planned economy, the national economic plan was traditionally an important document in directing the flow of resources in the Chinese economy and in prioritizing national goals. The Economic Plan was first formulated by the SPC on the basis of the information available from economic forecasts and projections. The prime objective was to maintain stability and provide for balanced economic growth. Basic financial and economic parameters were presented to the provinces, municipalities and ministries for use in the preparation of their own plans. Upon receipt of all the drafts, the State Council would convene a National Planning Conference, normally in either November or December of each year.[4] This was an important meeting and crucial to the process of resource planning and allocation. All senior provincial members, ministries and party secretaries attended the conference, as it was the last opportunity to lobby for resources. Prior to economic reform, virtually all resources were under the control of the central state. The National Planning Conference was the most important battleground in securing money or gaining approval for large investment projects, capital construction works and new economic policies.

In recent years, the importance of this National Planning Conference has declined due to the financial independence of many newly-developed provincial areas as a result of rapid economic development at the local levels. The reliance on state resources has decreased, as has the influence of national economic plans; and accordingly the power of the SPC has also declined.

Despite the erosion of power in many important areas, the SPC still tightly controls the power for allocating central resources for large capital projects. Major capital investment decisions are made by the SPC rather than by MoF, and approved projects are included as part of the annual economic plan. Projects of strategic importance, such as the Three Gorges Dam project may even become individual items shown in the Five-Year Plan.

Capital works and other investment proposals are initiated by the ministries and provinces. They are then scrutinized and prioritized by the SPC on the basis of predetermined yardsticks, such as the level of resources available, the track record of the respective ministry and the overall goals of the economy. If they deem it necessary, a feasibility study will be carried out to assess a project's suitability and acceptability. Such a study, however, is only normally required in the case of large or highly controversial projects. The final proposals are taken to the annual National Planning Conference, which is convened by the SPC. The function of this Conference is mainly for the coordination and prioritizing of capital projects to be supported by the state. Normally at least a vice-premier of the State Council will attend to emphasize its importance, and the Ministry of Finance participates, along with other key ministries and provinces.

Conflicts between the Planners and the Budgeters

While the SPC has the sole responsibility for monitoring the economic situation during the planning period, MoF has the ultimate responsibility for determining the budgetary implications and consequences of the proposals. The formal communication between the planners in the SPC and the budget-makers in

MoF occurs at the annual National Finance Conference. As Lieberthal and Oksenberg (1998) have observed, SPC and MoF have somewhat different priorities. The planners are primarily concerned with what the country needs and whether the physical means are available to satisfy these needs, while the budget-makers are more concerned with what the nation can afford, without generating large budget deficits and/or inflation.

Understandably, there are often conflicts within the budgetary process. Most of these conflicts are eventually solved by compromise between the planners and the budgeters. Occasionally, conflicts that cannot be resolved at the level of the SPC are forwarded to the highest political level for reconciliation. Only once conflicts have been reconciled is the planning cycle complete and ready for submission to the National People's Congress to begin the legislative process.

The annual planning procedure and conferences constitute important steps in the adoption of projects and spending proposals, even though national planning now plays a reduced role. The SPC has gradually assumed the role of determining the broad strategic direction of the country instead of getting involvement in detailed implementation. On the other hand, MoF has taken up the important responsibility of controlling the public purse to reinforce its power in financial matters.

In the 1998 round of administrative reforms, SPC was renamed the State Development Planning Commission (SDPC) to reflect changes to its responsibilities and functions (Secretariat of the General Office, State Council 1998, pp. 109–12). Its role shifted from administering and controlling to supervising and overseeing major economic activities. Many of its former functions were transferred to other committees or ministries. Its staff establishment has been reduced to only 590 people including 68 people working for the new State Resources Reserve Bureau. This move was generally considered a major setback for the SPC, and evidence of the executive's aim to dilute the role of central planning. Wang and Fewsmith (1995) had earlier concluded that 'the essence of economic structural reform is precisely to reduce the concentration of authority at the centre, that is, to weaken the planning system and the authority of the SPC' (Secretariat of the General Office, State Council 1998, p. 59).

MoF was given the responsibility for the issuance and management of bonds from SDPC. Bonds are an essential means in balancing the State Budget in China. In the past, while bonds were issues by the SPC, it was MoF that had the responsibility for balancing the budget. MoF would usually attempt to seek an agreement from the SPC over the amount of bonds to be issued to cover China's financial deficits. Yet one of the senior members of MoF commented that the power of the SDPC with respect to the issuing of bonds was about the same. He highlighted that in the year 2000, bonds worth more than 170 billion yuan were issued by the Bonds Department of MoF. But all the money generated was spent by the SDPC for capital investment purposes and nothing was left for MoF.

In its own areas of spending the discretionary power of SDPC is high and there is no formal mechanism in the present budgetary system to monitor how they allocate and spend the money. Planners have maintained the practice of leaving a substantial part of their budget allocation undistributed when the budget is submitted to the National Planning Conference in March. In 2000, for instance, about 30 per cent of its budget fell under this category and MoF has no rights to query this amount. In many ways, SDPC operates as an insular 'village sub-culture' without much monitoring and interference from above or from other central budget agencies.

China's Expenditure CBA: the Ministry of Finance

MoF was established on 1 October 1949 in accordance with the *Law of Organization of the Central Government of the People's Republic of China*, the statute founding the People's Republic of China (Article 18). Headed by the Minster of Finance and five vice-ministers, the Finance Ministry is traditionally an important ministry in the administration of the PRC. Many senior cadres in the CCP have been appointed to this important position in the past, including Deng Xiaoping and Li Xiannian. MoF is directly responsible to the vice-premier in charge of economic and financial affairs. The present Premier, Zhu Rongji, because of his keen interest in this area, once being the vice-premier in charge of this area before his promotion to become Premier, has sometimes dealt with fiscal matters personally. Until very recently, a technocrat Xiang Huaicheng has been promoted to this important post under Zhu Rongji's administration.

Formally, the main duties of the MoF are as follows:

- to formulate and implement principles and policies in relation to finance and taxation;
- to carry out China's economic and social development strategy;
- to carry out macroeconomic policies;
- to organize and produce taxation laws and regulations on tax administration;
- to manage and control revenue and expenditure contained in the state budget, as well as other special funds;
- to manage public debts and other financial matters including borrowing requirements and negotiation with international financial organizations.

As at June 2001, MoF has a total of 21 departments that are organized mainly by function (http://www.mof.gov.cn/organizationalstructure and *Directory of*

China's Government Structure 1997, pp. 87–94). Each department is headed by a director and has two or three deputy directors. In addition, MoF also supervises a number of service organizations, as well as ten universities and colleges in financial and economic studies. Currently, the total establishment of MoF is 610 staff, most of whom are technocrats with formal training in finance and economics.[5]

As in many other countries, the Budget Management Department (BMD) is an elite department among all other departments in the MoF.[6] Within this department over 90 per cent are recruited from the ten colleges and universities directly under the supervision of MoF. The practice of 'closed shop' recruitment makes it very difficult for graduates from other institutions, even elite universities like Peking and Tsinghua, to penetrate this 'private village'. In recent years, however, in order to cope with fast-changing technological innovations, graduates from other disciplines have been recruited or transferred to this department, mainly from the discipline of economics, accounting and computing studies. Indeed, BMD is a much sought after agency by fresh finance and economics university graduates because of the superior position in the bureaucracy and perhaps because of its reputation of power over the purse.

While the Standing Committee of the State Council decides on any major adjustments to resource allocation, BMD officials are simply responsible for searching for resources to make these decisions possible. The BMD used to have the final say in spending decisions whenever there was a dispute with other departments. Senior officers in this department are also considered 'high-flyers' within MoF and usually have a good change of promotion to senior positions. For example, the present Minister of Finance, Xiang Huaicheng once worked in this prestigious department.

BUDGETARY BEHAVIOUR AND THE CUSTOMARY POLITICS OF THE BUDGETARY PROCESS

Budgetary behaviour in China is premised on historical allocations and incrementalism. There are many reasons that explain this continued reliance on incremental decision-making. First, the budgetary process still relies on the method of 'base + factor'. Last year's budget serves as a base for calculating the next year's allocation. Adjustments are sometimes made to cover known changes (for example, announced salary adjustments). But inevitably the base serves as the dominant factor in budget allocation. It is extremely difficult even for MoF to change this allocation, since the base represents the interests of a specific agency that is firmly backed by strong political forces within the Chinese bureaucracy. Any attempt to change an agency's base budget would involve shaking the balance of power in the bureaucratic game and very few cadres would dare or chose to do that. Zero-based budgeting has been proposed and discussed in recent years, but it does not occupy an important role in budget preparation.

Second, some of the expenditures, such as education, are directly linked by law with the growth of GDP, and accordingly there is little room for MoF to enforce its role as guardian of the public purse in these areas. Third, the importance of hierarchy and the emphasis on size in the Chinese bureaucracy increases the possibility of adopting incremental change as a working strategy in handling resource allocation and budget requests as Lindblom (1968) suggested. Incremental change is easy to justify and, hence, is easier for the senior cadres to accept and approve. It also has the advantage of preserving the stability of the relationships among different stakeholders. Fourth, the potential of conflict intensification between central and local authorities tends to underline the importance of incremental adjustments to base budgets. The strategy of local governments in budget formulation is to fight for a higher base for spending which is determined not necessarily by the genuine need but by the bargaining power of the localities. Every agency wants to reap its 'fair share' but given there is no objective way to determine this, the historical base serves as a default measure.

Incrementalism is not necessarily perceived as a problem by Chinese officials. The key concern in the political arena in China today is 'stability'. Budgetary politics reinforces this concern for stability, and agencies vehemently guard their own interests. Such motives enhance conservatism and entrench incrementalism in the budget formulation process.

In this context, the working relationship between MoF and other ministries is mainly a cooperative one since all formally share the same rank within the bureaucracy. MoF is generally highly respected by other ministries because of its centrality in the resource process. In China, relationships (*guanxi*) are an important dimension of politics and especially resource allocation. In the past, the power of the MoF and its ability to exercise its role as guardian depended on the influence of the 'key person' in charge of the ministry. While most Communist Party members are highly conscious of rank, the minister needs to be a strong man to resist unreasonable requests from most senior cadres, as well as powerful 'old men' in the party.

In practice, ministers might approach the director or deputy director to make requests for the use of public money. MoF officials scrutinize these requests, operating in similar ways to those in guardian agencies in western nations. The outcomes of budgetary requests are the product of compromise and negotiations. A director of the BMD said the following five factors are the basis for evaluation of spending requests:

1. how urgent and reasonable is the request?
2. how far does the request meet with the current needs of the country?
3. the customary relationship between the spending department and MoF;
4. the quality of the submission document;
5. the judgement of the cadre in charge of the request.

Cadres in MoF insisted that all requests were considered on a case-by-case basis and evaluated from a rational point of view. But BMD officials could be hard to persuade. Indeed, a line agency director of finance (from the Ministry of Public Health) confirmed she had only managed to convince the cadres in BMD to purchase certain new medical equipment after she personally visited MoF and explained the urgency to them more than ten times. Her view was that the bureaucrats in BMD were very skilled at negotiation but a little over-confident in the correctness of their judgements and about the primacy of their knowledge of financial matters. She concluded, therefore, that persistence and reasoning with strong evidence was the only means of getting money from the MoF, but even this tactic was not always successful.

Relationships or *guanxi* still play an important role, and the Chinese bureaucracy's ability to maintain and enforce *guanxi* is one of its main characteristics and key activities. However, Chinese officials are careful to use *guanxi* with care. Without trust relations and reliable *guanxi* very little could be done during fiscal difficulties. The abuse of *guanxi* (say over attempts to get a spending proposal accepted) would result in adverse effects on the cadres seeking to abuse their *guanxi*, probably leading to the damage of long-term working relationships. The usual way to proceed is to test the water by finding somebody to ask informally whether some spending latitude is possible and about the likelihood of success. If the answer is on the whole positive, then it would be appropriate to proceed formally with a request. Otherwise, if the answer is negative, the proposal will be shelved until a more fortuitous moment arrives.

THE COUNTERVAILING POWER OF AUDIT ADMINISTRATION

Audit did not perform an important role in China prior to economic reforms in the 1980s. Indeed, the first Audit Administration (AA) was only formally set up in 1983 with a small establishment. During the first few years, its role was cosmetic and it performed no substantial function in controlling public spending. In the late-1980s, countrywide corruption and the deterioration of discipline among cadres aroused the attention of the nation. The need for an independent body with suitable powers to oversee the discipline of state administrative organs became urgent and necessary. The power of Audit Administration has gradually expanded, both in its jurisdiction and staff size.[7]

On paper, the Audit Administration's right to access information is very wide. They have the right to see all relevant documents, search for bank accounts, scrutinize administrative files and even to access electronic financial transaction data. In addition, they also have the right to interview relevant staff for clarification and justification of budgetary items, should they deem it necessary. Audit reports are normally completed within three months of commencement, unless major difficulties are encountered. Draft reports normally contain detailed criticisms castigating cases of waste and unauthorized spending discovered in the course of the audit, or instances where an organization has failed to collect revenue and payments due to government or granted exemptions not in accordance with existing laws. All draft reports are first sent to the head of the concerned organization for comments, which should be made within 10 days of receipt of the report, otherwise it is assumed there are no objections to the content of the report.

From time to time staff in MoF complain about the criticisms raised by the AA with claims that they have misunderstood the workings of MoF. Minor disagreements are usually solved by negotiation and compromise. But if conflicts are severe, they may sometimes be referred to the State Council for arbitration. The final version of the audit report, once comments are assembled, is presented by the AA to the National People's Congress. The report will either be endorsed by the Executive Committee of the NPC or the Standing Committee on Finance and Economics. At the local level, the respective people's government may reconcile disagreement and conflicts between the local audit commission and the finance bureau in the same manner.

The audit report is published in China's most popular newspaper, the *People's Daily*, on the same day as the MoF publishes its report on the State Budget. Such publicity serves as a powerful tool for AA. The publication of the audit report usually arouses great interest amongst the general public over the extent of uncovered government malpractice. A senior official in MoF declared that such a news report exerted substantial pressure on the work of the Ministry of Finance. However, there remain a number of institutional constraints that inhibit the audit function in China. First, the quality of audit staff is not as high as those working in the MoF. While MoF recruits officials with exceptionally high talents and experience in financial management, the AA as a relatively new department in the State Council has considerably less experience in budgetary affairs. Second, the staff establishment of the AA is far too small to carry out the workload they are supposed to perform. It is well recognized that the accounting system in China is extremely complicated. Most ministries operate from more than one set of account books and bank accounts making audit work extremely difficult, especially in short timeframes.

The wastage and irregularities uncovered by the AA often do not amount to much of substance. In 1997, there were a total of 93,000 internal audit organizations in China, yet the total amount uncovered through the auditing process was only 24 billion yuan. In terms of figures that is less than 100,000 yuan per audit organization per year (Director of Audit 1997, p. 20). Most observers do not believe that this reflects the true picture of financial irregularity, given the less than satisfactory budgetary discipline in China. Some argue that the disappointing performance of AA is due to the authority structure of the Chinese bureaucracy. Local audit administrations are under the direct supervision of the local governments. They control the salary and the fringe benefits of the audit staff at the local level. Hence, it is both politically unwise and financially stupid to direct harsh criticisms at their supervisors. Moreover, as previously mentioned, only rough figures are provided in the State Budget on spending items. There is virtually no basis for an auditor to judge whether an item is spent appropriately.

In brief, the audit system in China does not provide a sufficient mechanism to safeguard the use of public funds due to many organizational and institutional constraints. Without public scrutiny as in the West and under one party rule, audit only performs a minimal role in the budgetary process.

CONCLUDING REMARKS

The budgetary process in China has remained relatively unchanged despite rapid changes in the remainder of the economy. The legislative process in China remains a simple formality, whereby the State Budget is passed with few problems. The State Budget is, therefore, determined mainly by the labyrinthine politics of the administration – divided between central and local nodes of power. The preparation of the State Budget is still largely based on incremental changes. Due to the fiscal decline of the central government in recent years, funds available at the centre have been reduced as a proportion of GDP, and MoF has little discretion in manipulating resources to achieve macroeconomic purposes.

The Chinese State Budget imposes soft budget constraints so that implementation according to hard budget estimates is not as rigorous as in the West. In the past, budget deficits could simply be covered by bank loans at the central level. At present, deficits are mainly provided for through government bonds. Budget discipline is low especially at the local level. Local budgets are often produced purely for cosmetic purposes and they are not strictly followed. A local cadre claimed that he prepared a budget only because MoF requests it.

Overall, the budgetary system in China is characterized by an administrative network of fragmented authoritarianism. Budget power is distributed amongst many semi-autonomous agencies without much coordination or powers to ensure that budget decisions are implemented. Each agency performs a specific function and works within its own sphere of responsibility independently, with the full picture not being known by anyone. Budgetary fragmentation also results in delays and frustration, endless bargaining, and low efficiency.

Within this precarious situation, the Ministry of Finance has gradually been transformed from a once political department to an executive-administrative department, whereby the talent of the technocrat is becoming more important than political connections or authority. Although some embryonic forms of budgetary reform have been undertaken in recent years, the evidence suggests that China needs to review its budgetary system comprehensively to adapt to the new economic order in the Chinese economy.

NOTES

1. Directive of the People's Government in March 1950, 'A Decision Regarding Unifying the Fiscal and Economic Activities'.
2. For example, in 1949 government revenue was recorded at 30.3 billion catty wheat (by that time, budgetary figures were still in physical terms as the currency has yet to be determined among different regions) and the expenditure was 56.7 billion catty – a deficit of 26.4 catty of wheat. The large expenditure was mainly due to high spending on the military during the wartime (see Zhengpeng *et al.* 1992, p. 2).
3. Audit has normally to be completed within one to at most two months duration.
4. For example, the 1998 National Planning Conference was held in 11 December 1998 to finalize the national economic and social development plan.
5. Before the major reform in July 1998, the total establishment was 1144, (see Huaicheng 1999, p. 297).
6. 'Treasuries in all democratic systems are considered to be elite departments' (Weller and Cutt 1976, p. 28).
7. The State Council announced the first *Audit Regulation of the People's Republic of China* in November 1988, to establish the formal administrative procedure for the auditing process (*Zhonghua renmin gongheguo shenji tiaoli* 1988). In 1995, the first *Audit Law* was enacted by the National People's Congress to lay the legal foundation for the audit institutions within China (*Zhonghua renmin gongheguo shenji fa* 1995). In a more recent round of civil service reform in 1998, the power and scope of the Audit Administration was further strengthened. The total establishment of staff as of 1998 was fixed at 450 and organized into 12 departments (Secretariat of the General Office, State Council 1998, p. 351). In addition, all the audit units previously set up within various ministries and organs are now under the supervision of the Audit Administration.

11. How do Sub-national Budget Agencies Operate? Experiences from Six Mid-west American States

Kurt Thurmaier

Unlike the rest of the works presented in this book, this chapter focuses attention on budgeting at the sub-national level, specifically in six mid-western state budget agencies (SBAs) in the US. Generally, the SBAs perform many of the tasks listed in the introductory chapter. This is not uniform across the American states by any means. The National Association of State Budget Officers (NASBO) annually surveys the states regarding functions and scope of activities, and reports the results in various publications, including their website.[1] The aim of this chapter is to explore beneath the superficial scope and functional descriptions to examine the relationships between the decision context of an SBA, the roles it implies for budgeteers, and the types of decision-making the decision context requires of them. This chapter posits the hypothesis that state budget agencies are becoming more rather than less involved in the policy assessment of the budgets they scrutinize. The roles performed by budgetary officials at the sub-national level have arguably become more complex over time, less oriented toward control and more toward aligning budgets to the policy orientation of political executives. Furthermore, to the extent that these trends are apparent, the skills of policy analysis will become more rather than less important in the budgetary process, calling for a new mix of policy analysts with more varied professional and educational trainings.

Defining the different contexts within which budgeteers make decisions is important for understanding budget rationality in SBAs. First, it explicitly recognizes that there are multiple decision contexts for budget decisions, taking us a step beyond the narrow 'budgeting as politics' or 'budgeting as economic rationality'. Second, it suggests that if decision contexts are different across SBAs, we might expect that budgeteers' roles may vary across SBAs as well. Third, we might expect to find different kinds of decision-making in different decision contexts. If decision contexts are more complex in some central budget agencies than others, we might expect that budgeteers' decision-making will be more complex in those agencies than in others. Finally, it is likely that budgeteer roles can reinforce or weaken the general SBA orientation that defines the decision context.

After identifying the different SBA decision contexts, this chapter explores the range and variety of roles identified by the budgeters; it then analyzes the relationship between SBA orientations (decision contexts) and budgeteer roles. In particular, it is shown that budgeteers who serve in an SBA with a policy orientation may be more likely to view their role in terms of advocacy for budget requests consonant with the governor's policies, and as an analyst (not necessarily guardian) of the public purse. Such analysts require a more complex decision-making calculus than those fulfilling a traditional controller role; and they must be much more adept at creatively investigating and analyzing public programs than a traditional controller when developing recommendations.

The analysis in this chapter is based on field study interviews of the individual budgeteers in six mid-west budget agencies: Minnesota, Wisconsin, Illinois, Iowa, Missouri and Kansas. The sample of 109 subjects includes most of the budgeteers and their team leaders (supervisors), and all of the state budget directors. The interviews used a loosely structured interview instrument of largely open-ended questions, and lasted about 45 minutes to an hour. The field study of mid-western SBAs was part of a larger study that included parallel methodology for SBAs in five southern states. Readers interested in the comparative data are encouraged to see Thurmaier and Willoughby (2001).[2]

BUDGET AGENCY ORIENTATIONS AS DECISION CONTEXTS

The field study explored the types of budget orientations found in mid-west SBAs. Schick (1966) suggested there were at least three central budget agency orientations (control, management and planning). Analysis of these orientations suggests each orientation represents a decision context in which budgeteers may approach budgeting problems with a particular viewpoint, and playing a particular role. Studies of US states suggest that some SBAs also have developed a policy orientation. When Gosling (1987) examined the orientations of state budget agencies in three mid-western states, he found that while Iowa maintained a control orientation, Wisconsin had evolved to a policy orientation and Minnesota was in transition to a policy orientation. Thurmaier and Gosling (1997) revisited the three states nearly ten years later and found the transition to a policy orientation nearly complete. In fact, the Iowa office had moved decisively from a control to a policy orientation as part of a general reorganization of Iowa government in the mid-1980s. Thurmaier and Gosling found little evidence that these three states had any significant management or planning orientation. The association of the governor's policy agenda with the development and execution of the budgets in these states was firmly in place in the mid-1990s.

Thurmaier and Gosling's findings are consonant with several other studies which suggest that a typology of SBA decision contexts can be narrowed to the degree to which the office has a *policy* orientation or a more traditional *control* orientation. Thurmaier (1995) found evidence of a continuum in three local governments in the metropolitan Kansas City area. One city had a strong policy orientation, while its neighboring city had a strong control orientation. Meanwhile, a neighboring county budget office was in transition from a traditional control orientation to a stronger policy orientation. Schick's analysis of budget reforms in OECD nations (1997) also identified a further policy orientation for central budget agencies. In the policy-oriented CBA 'budgeting shifts from items of expenditure to policy changes'. The CBA encouraged departments to initiate trade-offs among their programs – within prescribed constraints, and the trade-off became the main decision unit in budgeting.

Budget agency staff in the six mid-west SBAs were queried to determine the presence of any of the four orientations suggested by these studies, namely: control, management, planning, and policy. Table 11.1 presents their responses by state. The results suggest that it may be simpler to envision a 'more control' – 'more policy' continuum of orientations, but we should not rule out the management and planning orientations entirely. The total number of responses exceeds the number of budgeteers because many subjects identify more than a single orientation. This is consistent with Schick's (1966, 1973, 1997) arguments that while the primary orientation shifts over time, the multiple purposes of budgeting ensure the continued presence of each aspect, especially expenditure control, which is at the root of budgeting.

The number of unique responses and the total number of respondents to the question are presented for each state. About 71 per cent of the subjects (77 of 108) in the sample characterize their budget agency as having a policy orientation. The policy orientation is the modal response in five of the six states, and is the modal category among the unique responses, with 34 of 108 respondents identifying only a policy orientation for their agency. The strongest policy responses are found in Iowa and Wisconsin, where 100 per cent of the staff identified the budget agency as having a policy orientation. The lowest response for a policy orientation was found in Illinois, where only 29 per cent of the staff identified it as an orientation.

Budgeteers seldom (19 per cent) cited the management orientation, describing it as mainly the macro-management level of interagency coordination. The 19 per cent of the staff who noted a planning orientation were largely drawn from the budget directors and team leaders who saw this perspective as rather unique to their levels in the budget agency and their responsibility for financial management planning for the entire state.

Table 11.I   Distribution of orientation responses in mid-west State Budget Agencies

SBA Orientations	Iowa	Illinois	Kansas	Minnesota	Missouri	Wisconsin	Unique Responses	Total Responses
Numbers of Responses (n=163)								
Control	2	23	3	1	2	13	15	44
Management	0	5	4	2	8	2	2	21
Planning	3	6	0	3	7	2	5	21
Policy	11	8	13	16	11	18	34	77
Total Responses	16	42	20	22	28	35	56	
SBA Staff (n=108)	11	28	17	19	15	18		163
As a Percentage of SBA Staff:								
Control	18	82	18	5	13	72		40
Management	0	18	24	11	53	11		19
Planning	27	21	0	16	47	11		19
Policy	100	29	76	84	73	100		71
Total Responses	100%	100%	100%	100%	100%	100%		100%

Note: The number or responses to each question varied.

Source: Thurmaier and Willoughby (2001), p. 134.

Illinois (14 budgeteers) and Kansas (one budgeteer) were the only states where control was identified as the exclusive orientation of the budget agency. Moreover, Illinois was the only state in which a control orientation was the modal category (82 per cent). Of those budgeteers who identified control and another orientation for the agency, 17 also mentioned a policy orientation. This was particularly true of the only other state with a significant share of control responses, Wisconsin, where two-thirds of the staff cited control as an important emphasis of the budget agency. However, they mentioned this as a secondary orientation; and all of the budgeteers who identified control as an orientation in Wisconsin also identified a policy orientation. Almost every budgeteer in Iowa and Minnesota reported that their agency was moving away from control and toward something else (usually policy).

The Missouri SBA had the most diverse orientation, although it was strongly grounded in a policy orientation. A senior Missouri budgeteer even argued that

Missouri budgeteers should no longer be called by their official position title, 'budget and planning analysts':

> It would be fairer to call our analysts budget & policy analysts. We do not engage in planning in the sense of preparing a planning document that then sits on a shelf somewhere. When I first came to Budget & Planning, we had 40 folks appropriated to Budget & Planning. We had federal funds, and the planning and budgeting functions had relatively recently been merged and planning documents were prepared on a variety of topics. *But that is not something that takes place anymore.* It's much more policy-oriented. What does the governor want to accomplish with the budget or with legislative initiative? [Emphasis added].

In summary, 30 years after Schick's initial presentation, it is clear that few of the mid-west SBAs maintained a control or management emphasis, and that a policy orientation was the primary modality of most of the mid-west state budget agencies.

Overall, of the 163 total responses by the 108 staff in the mid-west SBAs, about 27 per cent identified a control orientation while 47 per cent identified a policy orientation, with only 13 per cent identifying management and 13 per cent planning. The striking exception to this pattern was the Illinois SBA. It was solidly grounded in the control orientation, with very few responses in the policy orientation. In fact, not one Illinois budgeteer identified policy as the unique Illinois orientation.

The diverse SBA orientations can be divided roughly into those that were policy-oriented and those that were control-oriented. The policy-oriented SBAs represented a decision context in which the SBA was dedicated to aligning the state budgets with the governor's policy priorities. The control-oriented SBAs represented a decision context in which the emphasis of the agency was on controlling line spending and not on the governor's policy agenda. Still, four of the six states had some responses in each orientation. These orientation weights are depicted graphically in Figure 11.1. While not plotted based on any mathematical or statistical algorithm, the ovals show the dominant policy orientation of the mid-west states, and the starkly contrasted control-orientation of the Illinois budget agency. The following section reviews the roles the mid-west budgeteers identified for themselves in the budget process, and analyzes the relationships between the roles and the SBA's orientations.

THE ROLES OF BUDGETEERS

The power of the budgeteers over line agency budgets has traditionally been a source of friction with agencies, leading to the traditional characterization of

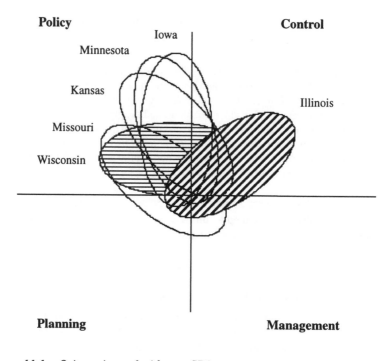

Figure 11.1   Orientations of mid-west SBAs

central budget examiners as being the 'naysayers' and 'cutters' in the executive budget process. Nationally, Tomkin (1998) identified at least four different roles for the Office of Management and Budget (OMB) examiners with respect to agencies. Cutters, absent a political imperative, emphasized holding back spending and growth in government. Neutral policy analysts strove to narrow 'the bounds of ignorance' for executive decisions by simplifying budgetary decisions to manageable dimensions for the CEO. Information conduits acted as translators, passing information back and forth between agencies and CEOs, and organizing the information for comprehensibility at the top and bottom of the bureaucratic hierarchy. Finally, Tomkin identified a relatively new role, policy advocates, seen by some as politicizing the examiner's role, and compromising the 'neutral competence' inherent in the conduit and 'neutral' policy analyst roles.

During the interviews for this study, the mid-west budgeteers were asked how they would characterize their role with respect to their assigned agencies, for example as being an agency's adversary, advocate or something else.

Responses to the role questions were grouped into five categories based on the frequency of a given type of role. For example, responses such as *antagonist*; *adversary*; *opponent*; or *bad guy* were coded as 'adversary'. Responses such as *conduit*; *liaison*; *facilitator*; *intermediary*; or *go-between* were coded as 'conduit'. Identified roles also included 'advocate', the 'policy analyst' and other. It is quickly apparent from Table 11.2 that almost half of the subjects (44 per cent) identified themselves as having roles in multiple categories. That is, a budgeteer could be recorded as indicating both a conduit and an adversarial role. There are only 60 unique responses for the 107 responding SBA staff.

Budgeteers often reported multiple roles that vary with the phase in the budget process or with different departments. For example, a Minnesota budgeteer described his role continuum. On the one end, agencies can have too much power and do not provide enough information. He had no problem playing the role of the 'antagonist' when an agency ended up running significant deficits without providing information to the SBA staff. On the other end, he can also serve as a 'protagonist, defender of the agency' when an administration gets 'into a chopping frenzy and will just snap at programs or administrative budgets without understanding the repercussions on the people that are ultimately getting served'.

As seen in Table 11.2, only 21 per cent of the sample (23 responses) identified with the traditional characterization of budgeteers as an agency antagonist or adversary and not a single budgeteer identified this as his or her singular role, even in Illinois. Many of them reported their adversarial role to be true only at certain periods of the process. The modal characterization (49 per cent) for the budgeteer's role appeared to be an information conduit for agency needs (52 responses). The conduit role incorporated a notion that the budgeteer was neither advocate nor adversary, but rather a liaison or facilitator for transmitting budget

Table 11.2   Budget analyst roles, by state

Budgeteer Role	Iowa	Kansas		Missouri			Unique Responses	Total Responses
		Illinois		Minnesota		Wisconsin		
Adversary/Cutter	3	6	2	4	6	2	0	23
Conduit*	6	17	11	5	7	6	29	52
Other	1	9	2	7	0	5	8	24
Policy Analyst	1	0	3	5	1	6	13	16
Advocate	9	6	3	6	12	11	10	47
Total SBA Staff (n=107)	11	28	17	18	15	18	60	
Total Responses	20	38	21	27	26	30		162

information between the departments and the budget director or governor's office. Information flowed both *from* the governor and budget director *to* agencies (especially regarding gubernatorial policies), and *to* the governor and budget director with information *from* agencies about problems and issues. Nearly half (48 per cent) of responses were in this category, and this was the dominant response category in the Illinois and Kansas SBAs. The Illinois staff overwhelmingly perceived a conduit role for the budgeteer; the Illinois staff accounted for 48 per cent of the conduit responses.

In stark contrast to the textbook role description, the next largest role category was as an advocate for agency needs, with 44 per cent of the 107 budgeteers identifying with that role. Within the states, the advocate role was most strongly present in Iowa, Missouri, and Wisconsin. A Missouri budgeteer made one of the strongest cases for this budgeteer role:

> I'm definitely an advocate ... Nobody wants to spend any money on the Public Defender or on criminals. That's just not a popular budget. So, if there are things that the department needs to do their job, I don't think they're going to get them *unless I can present their case for them*. I'm also critical. They frequently ask for things that I don't think are essential and if they can't convince me, I mean, that's their first job, to convince me that they really need something. *And if they can convince me, then I will advocate for them throughout the budget process.*

As the numbers in Table 11.2 suggest, this was not an isolated case, but it is also important to note that less than 10 per cent of the budgeteers claimed a unique advocate role. Most of the budgeteers who claimed an advocate role also claimed at least one other role. Still, this surprising result confirms that few budgeteers were wedded to the strictly traditional control role.

The modal response of Minnesota budget agency staff was 'other', reflecting some reluctance to classify themselves as adversaries and instead choosing 'critic'. As one budgeteer noted:

> I've always thought the thing I should be doing is asking the right questions at the right time ... It's never, ever to rubber stamp anything, but to critically assess any policy, existing or proposed, and try to take a big picture perspective and say, a) where is this going to get us and b) what are the unintended effects that may occur? What are the incentives that may or may not be operating here? And just what do we want to do?

Minnesota critics could also be interpreted as occupying a neutral policy analyst role (Tomkin 1998; Meltsner 1976; Snare 1995). This role category had the highest ratio of unique to total responses (13:16) and was dominated by budgeteers in Wisconsin and Minnesota (Table 11.2). Admittedly, there is a blurred line between being a neutral agency critic and an adversary. A Wisconsin budgeteer noted: 'we become a gatekeeper and control what agencies spend and what they spend it on. I personally try to work more as a policy analyst, to add to that at least a policy orientation'. Yet this budgeteer's role perception seems more closely akin to Tomkin's 'policy advocate' role. As a policy analyst, he tried:

to influence the direction of an agency's policies. We can send messages subtly or not so subtly, that the policy direction the agency's pursuing is acceptable or not. We can telegraph if you're going to do that, don't expect any extra money in the budget; that's not going to be looked upon favorably. Or, that something else will be looked upon very favorably. We can kind of push on the string, so to speak.

Those who identified a policy analyst role could subsume the role of 'agency critic' within it. A senior Wisconsin budgeteer expanded on the sometimes adversarial nature of a policy analyst's role in the Wisconsin budget agency:

In general, I think we have by design a somewhat adversarial relationship with the agency. And I mean adversarial in sort of a good sense of the word, not that we're bad mouthing each other, but I think that the agency ... is set up to make their best case for their budget initiatives and I think one of our jobs is to be as critical as possible of what the agency is asking for and seek alternatives and look for ways to reduce the cost. And I think somehow you hope out of that debate, good policy will emerge ... The best policy is going to emerge by me making the best case I can for this policy and then hoping [the agency] can make a better case. That if I can bring up, these are the reasons we need to do this, the reasons we need to get rid of this program, or the reason we need to put more funding into this program, and really think hard about it and make a good case, then that forces [the agency] to make a better case for why we should do something else. Hopefully the process works best if we're all doing our job as well as possible, then I think you get the best public policy ... In the long run, government's stronger for us playing our roles to the hilt.

This description of a policy analyst role is far removed from the 'number-crunchers' definition of policy analysis that was identified with the Planning, Programming and Budgeting Systems (PPBS) reform effort. One of the barriers inhibiting the inclusion of policy analysis into state budgeting under PPBS was the nature of policy analysis itself. Originating in operations research and systems theory, the policy analysis extolled by the advocates of PPBS was heavily quantitative (even 'mindless number crunching' to its detractors). Steeped in notions of benefit-cost analysis and other quantitative procedures, budget examiners were hard pressed to find time to add the data collection and analysis requirements onto their already full plate of traditional budget request reviews. In fact, among the Illinois budgeteers who identified other roles were several self-described 'number crunchers' who saw themselves fulfilling a largely neutral and technical role to 'find the number', and this was *not* perceived as policy analysis. The descriptions by these budgeteers bears striking parallels to those of OMB examiners working in the Stockman years (Tomkin 1998, pp. 89–113).

SBA Orientations and Roles

A correlation matrix of the SBA orientations and the budgeteers' role perceptions (Table 11.3) suggests that the new policy orientation of SBAs may be related to the expanded roles of budgeteers with respect to spending agencies.[3] The first interesting aspect of the matrix is that only four bivariate relationships are statistically significant, and they relate to the policy orientation and policy analyst role. The policy orientation is moderately related to both the policy analyst and advocate (rho=0.30 and rho=0.26 respectively). Those that identified a policy orientation were more likely to identify a policy analyst or advocate role with respect to their agencies. On the other hand, a policy orientation was moderately – but negatively – associated with a conduit role (rho=–0.285); those who saw themselves as a conduit between their agencies and the governor's administration tended *not* to identify their SBA as having a policy orientation.

Moreover, it is particularly noteworthy that a policy analyst role is moderately – and negatively – related to a control orientation (rho=–0.24), meaning that those who identified a control orientation for their agency tended *not* to see themselves as having a policy analyst role with respect to their agency assignments. Thus, the isolated position of Illinois in the orientation scheme (Figure 11.1) helps to explain why budgeteer roles in Illinois are substantively different from other states, especially the dearth of policy analyst and advocacy roles. As will be argued shortly, these relationships may be explained, in part, by the personal relationships between the governors and their budgeteers.

Still, Table 11.3 does not reveal a relationship between a control orientation and an adversary role. One explanation is that few budgeteers identified an adversary role, while quite a few saw both a control and policy orientation, coupled with a policy analyst or advocate role. (The bifurcated advocacy context is much influenced by the Wisconsin responses, as seen in Table 11.1). Consequently, the adversary role associated with a control orientation may be statistically washed out. This is supported by the lack of any unique adversary role responses by budgeteers. Meanwhile, 23 per cent identify an advocate perspective, even when they recognize a control orientation for their agency.

Relationship with the Governor

Budgeteer roles were also influenced by the personal budgeting style of the governor. The governor's involvement in the budget process varied across states,

Table 11.3   *Correlations of mid-west SBA responses on roles and orientations*

Spearman's rho (p=0.000)	Control	Management	Planning	Policy
Adversary	0.58	0.169	−0.063	−0.010
	(0.587)	(0.117)	(0.558)	(0.927)
Conduit	0.106	0.059	−0.044	−0.285
	(0.320)	(0.589)	(0.687)	(0.006)
Policy Analyst	−0.240	−0.057	−0.025	0.300
	(0.022)	(0.598)	(0.818)	(0.004)
Advocate	−0.054	0.025	0.027	0.259
	(0.611)	(0.817)	(0.805)	(0.012)
Other	0.086	−0.068	−0.015	−0.061
	(0.424)	(0.5297)	(0.887)	(0.567)

from person to person, and over time (Rosenthal 1990, p. 136). The importance of the budget process to a governor's political success depended on gubernatorial term limits, partisan alignments in the legislature, and other factors (Sabato 1983; Ransone 1982; Pilegge 1978). Thus, governors differed in how they wanted to use the budget agency with respect to their policy agenda, and even how much and what type of contact they wished to have with budgeteers.

In addition, these primary factors themselves may be subject to the influence of the political and fiscal climate in which any given state budget is developed and implemented; for example, a state's political culture may prohibit a governor from using the SBA vigorously to push the gubernatorial policy agenda (Axelrod 1995; Rosenthal 1990). Even within the same state, governors vary in their desire to use the SBA for policy and other objectives. Together, these factors may influence the degree of policy delegation given to the budgeteers. Thus, the quality and nature of the relationship between governors and budgeteers may also influence the role of budgeteers with respect to their agencies. The governor's policy demands and desires for budgeteer contact may also depend on the degree to which a particular spending agency's activities are high on the governor's policy agenda.

An important characteristic is how well the budgeteer becomes acquainted with the governor's policies and priorities. Thurmaier and Willoughby (2001) argued that budgeteers who have frequent and direct contact with their governor enjoyed a short 'policy distance' from their governor. Those with infrequent or no access to the governor had a long policy distance from their governor and were, therefore, detached from thinking about the public policy aspects of budget decisions. The mid-west budgeteers were asked how often they personally briefed the governor on budget decisions, and the degree to which they felt they 'worked for' the governor as opposed to citizens (or the state), their immediate supervisor, or the budget director. There was a stark contrast in briefing practices between the states. In Wisconsin and Kansas, nearly all of the staff briefed the governor often, resulting in a relatively short policy distance. Illinois and Minnesota presented nearly the opposite case. Typically these budgeteers met with the governor's policy staffs; even team leaders rarely briefed the governor. Contacts with the governor in these states were limited to the budget director and 'front office' staff, resulting in a relatively long policy distance between the budgeteers and their governors. In between these cases were Iowa and Missouri.

The increased contact/short policy distance from the governor led to a greater understanding of the governor's policies and priorities. This understanding enriched the budgeteers' decision context, but at the same time increases its complexity as well. Correlation analysis suggests that budgeteers were less inclined to anticipate the budget director's and governor's reactions to their budget recommendations if they perceived they worked for their supervisor instead of the governor (Spearman's rho=0.385) and were more inclined to anticipate reactions when they briefed the governor more frequently (rho=0.365).[4]

Staff in the Wisconsin budget agency revealed that briefing the governor was a key ingredient to ensure that budgeteers knew the governor's viewpoints. It was a way of learning what the governor's parameters were, and finding out how to develop well-thought options within those parameters. The budget director encouraged new budgeteers to sit through other briefings with the governor, because it was to their 'benefit to sit there and listen to the rest of the budgeteers brief. That's how you help get a feel'. Yet, Wisconsin staff remained clear about their political neutrality and the distinction between the governor's partisan policy staff and themselves. Still they valued the frequent interactions with the governor in various briefings and meetings because it kept them informed of priorities and policies. At the same time, they were comfortable enough in their relationship with the governor to present arguments with which they 'knew' he would not agree. That was their job, and they were strongly encouraged to present their independent and objective analyses of their assigned agencies and issues.[5]

The experience of Iowa and Missouri staff briefing the governor could be much weaker, depending upon the governor. Although the current governors have had more frequent interactions with the budgeteers, previous governors preferred that the budgeteers briefed the governor's chief of staff. Although they currently attended budget briefings and the monthly progress meetings, the Iowa and Missouri budgeteers were less participants and more observers. During the final stages of the budget cycle, the usual practice in Iowa was for the budget director and the Director of Management to present the budget agency recommendations to the governor, and the budgeteers attended the briefing to answer detailed questions. Certain budgeteers, especially senior staff, briefed the governor personally. The Missouri budgeteers spoke in terms of the governor's office and not the governor. As in Iowa, they sat in on the budget briefing meetings with the governor, but tended to act as information specialists for the discussions, participating when specific or technical information was requested.

The investment of the Missouri and Iowa budgeteers in the meetings was much smaller than their Wisconsin counterparts. They were prepared to answer questions, and sometimes would make presentations, but that was the exception rather than the rule. Still, this contact allowed them to listen to the governor express his views and concerns, and observe the politics of his inner circle. It gave them a foundation and context for their negotiations with their assigned agencies. This description from a budgeteer is typical of Iowa and Missouri:

> It just went like, 'well, Robert, you prepared this memo, I'm going up at 1:00, why don't you come up in case there's any questions'. I was very glad to see that because I had no problem taking responsibility for my work, but it also gave me the option. The governor's chief of staff or someone else said, 'well, what if we do this?' I had already looked at that option and we could tell them immediately instead of spending three days going back and forth trying to set up meetings.

Finding out the governor's position on an issue was more difficult for Minnesota and Illinois budgeteers, due in part to the absence of personal contact with the governor. Measured in terms of budgeteers' affiliation with the governor, the Minnesota staff had the most distant relationship, although the relationship with the governors has changed over time. Under one governor, 'there were meetings over in the mansion, over in his office in the Capitol. We were pretty much almost all on a first name basis. We were there. We were expected to be the person that did the briefing, made the recommendation, go through the budget'. But things were much different under the incumbent governor, and one staff member found 'we're pretty much free to put the budget together ourselves. We work with one of his staff'.

The Illinois staff were also far removed from the governor's briefings. The budget agency is located within the Office of the Governor, and the budgeteers are technically patronage appointments of the governor. Thus, it was surprising to find that only a third of the staff saw themselves as working for the governor.

Several reasons may account for this paradox. First, they rarely saw the governor personally, and so tended to view their function as one of controlling agencies and serving as technical number crunchers. Their decision-making context was relatively simple compared to their counterparts in Wisconsin. The Illinois budgeteers repeatedly spoke of their lack of policy input into budget decisions and their isolation from the governor's policy development. To the extent that they were involved in program or policy analyses, communications with the governor's policy staff were highly formalized and strictly channeled through the budget director and the division chiefs. Illinois budgeteers were not only isolated from the politics of budget issues, they were rarely given enough of the 'big picture' even to have a policy context within which to evaluate a department's request for alignment with the governor's priorities. The long policy distance between the governor and the budgeteers may reflect the political culture of Illinois, famous for the power of patronage in job selection and performance. Yet, budgeteers seemed to gain their positions through merit competition, perhaps reflecting a desire to maintain a group of technical budget experts with 'neutral competency' to balance the other political patronage appointments in the governor's office.

Further research on Illinois may discover a return to a policy orientation and a higher share of policy analyst roles among the budgeteers. The morale among the Illinois budgeteers at the time of the field study was very low, and many volunteered that they were actively looking for another job. A subsequent change of governor and a consequent change in budget director could very well result in a changed orientation in the SBA.

The staff in Iowa and Wisconsin more readily identified with the governor and his policies and priorities. About 56 per cent of the Iowa and 60 per cent of the Wisconsin budgeteers responded that they 'worked for' the governor. The utility of briefings in nurturing a policy orientation was supported by correlation analysis which indicated that frequency of briefings was positively correlated with a policy orientation of the budget agency (rho=0.479); a 'work for' the governor affiliation (rho=0.329); and a policy analyst role (rho=0.313). Working for the governor was also positively correlated with the policy orientation for the budget agency (rho=0.260).[6] Moreover, a budgeteer who 'worked for' the governor was more inclined to have a policy analyst's perspective, whereas a budgeteer who 'worked for' his/her supervisor was inclined toward a conduit or even adversary role.

These correlations between budgeteer roles and measures of policy distance contrasted to some degree with those reported by Tomkin in her study of OMB. Tomkin concluded that when feedback from political officials in OMB was slow or absent, examiners were able to increase their policy roles (1998, p. 78). A ready explanation for this discrepancy was not apparent, although the above-mentioned comment from a Minnesota budgeteer may provide a clue. The budgeteer believed the absence of the active involvement of the governor meant that 'we're pretty much free to put the budget together ourselves'. Yet, this statement was made in the context of an SBA with a strong policy orientation, and perhaps this budgeteer had gleaned enough policy cues about gubernatorial preferences to work with relative flexibility. The issue warrants further research.

Finally, the proportion of budgeteer recommendations affirmed by the budget director and governor were related to the policy distance between the budgeteers and governors. Affirmation rates were positively correlated with more frequent briefings of the governor (Pearson's r=0.279). Wisconsin staff estimated an average 90 per cent of their recommendations were affirmed by the budget director, although the averages in Missouri and Minnesota were somewhat lower (87 and 83 per cent respectively). The lowest estimate of affirmation rates was given by the Illinois staff (only 79 per cent). The overall average for the budgeteers and their supervisors was 83 per cent. Budget directors tended to agree with the self-assessment of the budgeteers and team leaders, sometimes even with higher estimates of budgeteer affirmation rates. This indicates that budgeteers have a substantial impact on the final shape of the budget.

Professional and Educational Backgrounds of SBA Staff

Extensive studies by Lee (1991) suggested there were substantial changes taking place in the professional and educational backgrounds of budgeteers. Lee found a significant increase in the number of budgeteers with broad social science and public administration educations. Meanwhile, a significant decrease in the number of budgeteers with accounting and business education degrees has occurred. Thurmaier and Gosling (1997) also found evidence linking budgeteer backgrounds to role and orientation perspectives.

Analysis of the educational and professional backgrounds of the mid-west budgeteers revealed several interesting findings. Undergraduate degrees were categorized as being in the social sciences, natural sciences, humanities, business, or accounting/finance. Graduate degrees were categorized as social sciences, public administration or public policy, business administration or accounting, or other professional degree (including social work or law). Professional backgrounds were categorized as being previously employed in the private sector, another state agency, another government or non-profit agency, a legislative position, or none (because they are coming directly from college). Chi-square analyses of each of these variables showed significant variations of backgrounds across the six states (p<0.05). Illinois and Minnesota were the only states where the budgeteers' most recent professional experience was in the private sector (about 25 per cent each), while Wisconsin had the highest share

(26 per cent) of budgeteers most recently employed in a legislative position (commonly the legislative budget office). Wisconsin also had the highest proportion of staff coming directly from college (47 per cent) followed by Kansas (36 per cent), with Iowa (18 per cent) and Missouri (13 per cent) the lowest. Missouri (with 40 per cent) and Iowa (with 82 per cent) had the highest proportion of staff with previous state agency experience, while Wisconsin and Kansas had the lowest (21 per cent each).

There is little evidence, however, to suggest that educational and professional backgrounds were related to budgeteer role perceptions. Chi-square analyses of contingency tables revealed no relationships (at $p \leqslant 0.05$) between a role category and the budgeteer's type of education degree or professional background. In sum, this data provides little support for the notion that professional and educational backgrounds are related to role perceptions. The overall SBA orientation and organizational culture appeared to dominate role perceptions, and budgeteers with professional backgrounds seem to have adapted to organizational expectations, diluting the influences of background experiences on role perceptions.

CHANGING ROLES AND BUDGETARY DECISION-MAKING

The multiple roles identified by budgeteers at the sub-national level are consistent with the historical emphasis of state budgeting on program implementation. A policy orientation by the SBA is firmly rooted in the need for state budgeteers to be able to evaluate various agency programs and policies to determine whether they are working well, facing obstacles, and most importantly, whether they are working in consonance with the governor's expressed policies and priorities. In this sense, the ability of budgeteers in policy-oriented SBAs to be both advocates and critics, even adversaries, of their assigned agencies reflects the tremendous delegation of discretion given them in the executive budget process at the state level. Governors rely upon them to help agencies 'do their job', at the same time depending upon the budgeteers 'to make sure the agencies are doing their job *my* way'.

The analysis presented here suggests that there is a relationship between the decision context created by the overall policy or control orientation of the SBA, and the types of roles budgeteers assume with respect to their assigned agencies. With the notable exception of Illinois, the SBAs were all taking on policy analysis and development in the course of their work for the governors. There has been a general evolution among the SBAs toward a policy-oriented decision context with budgeteers performing more advanced policy roles. In a policy-oriented SBA, the budgeteer's negative response to agency requests is more likely conditioned by a 'policy policing' role (Tomkin 1998) than the bias of the traditional controller role. Moreover, they are able to devote more attention to policy and management issues precisely because the budgets are relatively controlled.

The Illinois case underscores the importance of the governor's affiliation with the budgeteers as a factor conditioning their role perceptions and their budgetary decision-making. Illinois budgeteers with little regular contact with the governor perceive a role substantially different to their counterparts in a context that harkens back to Schick's control orientation of the 1920s–1950s. Isolated from the governor and external to the domain of policy development, they are 'number-crunching' technicians and conduits, unable to see the big picture the way their counterparts do in the other states. The lack of gubernatorial contact seems to reinforce a resistance to a stronger alignment with the governor's policies and priorities. In very many ways, the description of Illinois budgeting in the mid-1990s fits the archetype control orientation of the SBA in the literature and matches the situation in which OMB examiners found themselves when David Stockman became director (Tomkin 1998, pp. 89–113). By contrast, Wisconsin budgeteers met regularly with the governor to discuss decision-making strategies and provide acceptable policy alternatives for consideration. They enjoyed wide latitude in both the range of options they could field to the governor and in the scope of issues that might be developed for consideration.

Such stark differences may be attributed perhaps to the varying fiscal conditions of the states, but the interview data suggested that the decision structure of both states was related to how the governor chose to use the SBA – as a number-crunching machine or a policy analysis tool. But this conclusion is tentative, because role influence may be a function of the SBA's orientation or an antecedent to it. That is, budgeteers may have a particular relationship with governors because of the SBA orientation, or the role a governor chooses for the budgeteers may create or maintain a particular orientation.[7]

Implications for a Model of Budget Rationality

Ultimately, the theoretical issue is a question about the relationships between the decision contexts and budgeteer roles and whether these have any influence on the way in which budgeteers make budget decisions and recommendations to budget directors and governors. Thurmaier and Willoughby (2001) found a substantial relationship between decision contexts, budgeteer roles, and budgetary decision-making. They developed a micro-budgeting model of decision-making based on a notion of multiple rationalities. This 'multiple rationalities decision-making' model first identifies budget problems as multi-faceted policy problems that require funding. A budget problem is characterized by five aspects, each with its own attendant decision-making rationality. That is, each aspect can be thought of as a special type of problem, producing or requiring a unique rationality for resolution. *Social* aspects pertain to the underlying rationale of a public policy or program, the core public value that is fundamental to the policy or program. *Political* aspects relate to the process for garnering enough support for a policy or program, and the way in which the support and opposition is reflected in the character of the programs. *Legal* aspects pertain to the rights and obligations surrounding policies and programs and their funding, including intergovernmental aid restrictions and rights-based budgeting. *Economic* aspects of budget problems are carefully specified as the rationality of allocative efficiency, both across programs (across agencies) and within programs (internal to agencies). Finally, *technical* aspects are related to technical efficiency considerations in the production of public goods and services by agencies.[8]

Multiple rationalities decision-making varies in accord with whether the SBA is policy-oriented or control-oriented. The policy-oriented SBA is at the nexus of the policy process and the budget process, where budget rationality requires the examiners to incorporate these environmental factors into their budgetary decision-making. The complexity of this decision context requires the budgeteers to apply social, political, legal, technical and economic rationalities to the various budget problems that are presented to them as budget decision items. Including all five types of rationalities in budgetary decision-making has become an important condition of effective budget recommendations in a policy-oriented SBA. This level of decision-making complexity is not, and has not been, required of budgeteers in control-oriented SBAs. The decision context is much restricted in the control-oriented SBAs, where there is a large policy distance between the governor and the examiners which effectively removes the examiners from the policy process in those states. With little concern for policy complexity, budgeteers in control-oriented decision contexts seem to require a much simpler decision-making calculus. Their limited budgetary discretion is restricted to technical efficiency and legal rationality issues (Thurmaier and Willoughby 2001, pp. 153–70).

The Impact of Role Perceptions on SBA Decision-making

This exploration of decision contexts and budgeteer roles at the sub-national level provides an opportunity to compare their characteristics with national agencies. The presented evidence suggests an important relationship between decision contexts and budgeteer roles. The main aim of this chapter has been to define specific decision contexts that result from a particular SBA's policy or control orientation, and relate these decision contexts to budgeteer roles and decision-making. The evidence also points to a role-orientation feedback loop; that is, decision contexts condition budgeteer roles, but the degree to which the roles are assumed reinforces (or weakens) the strength of the SBA's orientation.

First, the analysis of the interview data suggests that many budgeteers assume multiple roles, but that the types of roles they assume are constrained or even promoted by the decision context – namely the general agency orientation with respect to either a control or policy emphasis. The results also suggest that a policy-oriented decision context requires more complex decision-making by budgeteers because the scope of their decision-making agenda is as wide as the policy issues generated from their agency programs, and they enjoy considerable latitude in deciding *which* alternatives to propose to the governor and *how* the arguments are to be framed for the governor's decision.[9] The results suggest that governors who wish to use the SBA to integrate budget and policy analysis to promote gubernatorial policy agendas ought to establish closer ties to budgeteers so they may become familiar with policies.

On the other hand, the budgeteers play multiple roles, and to the degree that they emphasize an active policy analyst role, they reinforce the SBA's policy orientation. But if there is a large policy distance between the budgeteer and governor, the budgeteers tend to choose a conduit or facilitator role that reinforces a control orientation for the SBA, diminishing its capacity to deliver relevant policy advice to the governor. To illustrate the point: were a new governor to take command of a control-oriented SBA and demand policy advice, it would seem from this evidence that the budget director would first have to change substantially the role perceptions of the budgeteers from conduits and adversaries to policy analysts and advocates in order to receive policy advice from the budgeteers. This study also suggests that an important step in the transformation of the roles and SBA orientation is to decrease the policy distance between the budgeteers and the governor by increasing the frequency of personal contacts between them.

These features mirror remarks made in the Introduction to the book about CBAs at the national level. In most cases, the mid-west budget agencies have reassessed their roles and basic purposes and have become more engaged in the policy aspects of agency budgets. This requires more reflexivity and it increases the complexity of the relationships between the agency and the SBA budgeteers. In many cases, the budgeteers have attempted to abandon their traditional adversarial roles to increase the ease with which they can work together with agency staff to create budget solutions that are consonant with the governor's policy priorities. In this sense, relinquishing traditional controls does not readily imply that the mid-west agencies are losing their traditional budgetary power. In fact, it would appear that they are moving from a traditional controller role into a policy control role, one that provides them with increased discretion in their dealings with agencies, but always within a policy context set by the governor.

NOTES

1. See www.nasbo.org and http://www.nasbo.org/Publications/PDFs/bupro99.pdf for a web version.
2. Readers interested in the field questionnaires may contact the author.
3. Recalling that subjects could have multiple responses on each dimension, Table 11.3 is based on the number of *responses*, not respondents.
4. These correlations exclude supervisors and budget directors, and are significant at $p = \leq 0.001$.
5. For further discussions about 'neutral competency' see Heclo (1975), Johnson (1984; 1989), and Hammond and Thomas (1989).
6. All reported correlations are statistically significant at $p \leq 0.05$ or better.
7. The influence of organizational context on budgeteer roles may be more complicated than has been discussed here. Other variables at the macro- and micro-budgetary level may also influence how budgeteers fashion their recommendations to the budget director and governor. For example, a superficial analysis comparing the state finances of the sample states with totals for all states revealed some interesting points which require further investigation. Fiscal 'hardship' may influence the control orientation of ILSBA budgeteers. Based on the State Finance Series of the US Census (1990–95), Illinois shows greater fiscal problems than the other states on two measures. First, its outstanding long-term debt as a share of total revenues is highest in the sample; and on a per capita basis, this debt grew faster (6 per cent annual rate) during 1990–95 than the sample average of the US (all states) average of 5 per cent. Second, its 'Other Cash' reserves (excluding insurance trusts, debt set-asides, etc.) fell 4 per cent over the period compared with the all state gain of 8 per cent; and it also fell as a share of general revenues. These measures alone do not identify fiscal stress, nor can we conclude that Illinois is more stressed than the other states. Such analysis is desirable, but beyond the scope of this study.
8. A complete presentation of the Multiple Rationalities Decisionmaking model is found in Thurmaier and Willoughby (2001), chapters 3 and 4.
9. See Thurmaier (2001) for an attempt to relate the political psychology literature to budgetary decision-making.

12. Conclusion: Better Guardians?

Lotte Jensen and John Wanna

The principal motivation behind this research project was to examine whether central budget agencies (CBAs) have changed or have begun to change their roles and responsibilities. Where we found evidence of change, then we were interested in analysing the nature of the changes and exploring what factors may have contributed to the changes in various countries, and whether identifiable patterns were found. It was apparent, for instance, that in a selection of OECD nations, the roles and responsibilities of their CBAs had changed in response to economic, fiscal and political imperatives affecting state decision-making from the 1980s onwards. We were interested to explore whether similar economic or fiscal influences had pushed these CBAs to react in similar ways or whether CBAs had responded differently to broadly similar contextual influences. It was also evident that a number of countries had been at the forefront of public sector reform, whereas others had not engaged with this agenda, and we were interested to see whether the degree of public sector reform was a vital factor in encouraging the CBA to adopt different roles and cultures. A related question involved the degree to which any CBAs had acted in anticipation of contextual changes or had pursued anticipatory strategies to reposition themselves relative to their counterparts. Given previous research into the entrenched 'village cultures' of CBAs, we were also interested to discover whether the cultural orientation of CBAs was changing and whether they were adopting different cultural styles through which to sustain their relationships.

The previous country-specific chapters have investigated these questions. They have highlighted the significance of different institutional structures and the various organizational dynamics of ten different CBAs. They have documented the various roles performed by the CBAs and whether these have changed in response to the changing environments. Some have explicitly discussed whether CBAs have 'learned from others' and attempted to emulate reforms or draw on prevailing ideas circulating internationally. Many contributors have particularly emphasized the extent to which the CBAs have extended their policy interests and sought to impose their preferences on the general directions of government policy or on the policy and administrative agendas of spending agencies. While some CBAs have been the initiators of major reforms and driven significant system-wide reform agendas, others have reacted with *ad hoc* changes as a result of some perceived threat or economic crisis. Most CBAs have attempted to remain active players in framing resource decisions and shaping budgetary politics within their jurisdictions, and have regularly changed their procedures or behaviours to enable them to maintain control over aggregate and departmental expenditure while preserving some formative influence in establishing priorities.

In this conclusion we seek to assess the relative importance of the factors driving change in CBAs. We discuss the various institutional configurations and organizational dynamics, and trace how budget procedures have recently evolved or been reshaped. From the evidence presented in the country studies, it is possible to point out general trends and patterns of behaviour, but equally it is possible to acknowledge significant points of divergence and departure. The various political arrangements, conventions and institutional constraints and the perceived appropriateness of reformist ideas have mitigated against any isomorphic pattern or global paradigm. Accordingly, we comment on some of the more unusual or particular findings contained in the preceding chapters. Finally, we discuss the wider points and implications of the research findings.

ECONOMIC CONDITIONS AND FISCAL STRINGENCY – DISCURSIVE CHALLENGES AND THE DRIVERS OF CHANGE

With the exception of China, the other nine OECD nations in this study all experienced constrained economic circumstances and fiscal stringency from the 1970s onwards. Whereas the ratio of public expenditure to GDP between 1960 and 1985 increased substantially in the nations of this study, thereafter the rates of increase tapered off with spending levels remaining flat. Across all OECD nations combined public expenditure was 28.5 per cent of GDP in 1960, but had risen to 39.7 per cent in 1985. For eight of the OECD countries in this study (all except New Zealand), their public sectors rose from 29.1 per cent in 1960 to 46.7 per cent in 1985. The combined percentage of spending then remained relatively constant until 1998 when it fell to 42.2 per cent, further declining to 41 per cent by 2001. Many attributed the 'fiscal crisis' or 'fiscal fatigue' in the West to the huge increases in social welfare spending and income transfers (see Foster and Plowden 1996).

Levels of economic growth also slackened after the 1970s with many countries facing recessions in the 1980s and early 1990s. Governments and their CBAs were caught in a vice between lower growth and rising spending pressures (and expectations) on public expenditure. Moreover, higher unemployment fuelled government spending even when governments (such as those in Canada, the UK, New Zealand and US) were concerned to reduce spending. With elections focusing on tax restraint (or promised cuts) and governments unwilling (or finding it impossible) to reduce spending, deficits and debt levels increased adding to a sense of fiscal crisis. Nowhere was this phenomenon more apparent than in Canada in the early 1980s, which after a decade of governments committed to expenditure control, had annual deficits of around $40 billion (or 20 per cent of outlays) and a public debt of over $700 billion (over 70 per cent of GDP). By 1994 the annual debt servicing cost was around 45 per cent of the annual budget. Many governments within the OECD began a period of 'deficit reduction' – with governments aiming to curb spending by focusing on 'the mix and severity of spending cuts and tax increases needed to bring the budget into balance' (Posner and Gordon 2001, p. 395). While the size of the deficits and debt burden differed between countries, the impact politically of the fiscal crisis of the late 1980s and early/mid-1990s was relatively universal.

Such fiscal conditions created a situation where the CBAs became more powerful and had more influence in decision-making over levels of spending and resource allocation issues. But while the conditions provided the potential for this to occur, the process did not occur automatically. When faced with fiscal stress and economic difficulties, senior officials in the CBAs were initially frustrated by expedient governments unable or unwilling to commit to remedial action. Examples of such situations are numerous – the Canadian Finance Ministry under the Mulroney governments in Canada (1984–93), the 'Dutch disease' most pronounced between 1979–82, the New Zealand Treasury prior to 1984, or the Danish case before 1983 when the Finance Ministry was relegated to a peripheral position by the unions and the Ministry of Labour. In all these cases governments at the time appeared to be merely 'tinkering around the edges'.

However, when economic imperatives have been successfully brought onto the policy agenda by committed governments, CBAs have played a central and powerful role in the politico-administrative landscape. They have each exploited the window of opportunity provided by the fiscal crisis and perceived need for budgetary discipline, but have been simultaneously unsure how long the window would remain open. Even in countries as disparate as the US, Germany and Sweden this phenomenon can be observed in the 1990s.

Hence, dire economic circumstances alone are not sufficient to shape policy direction or enhance the steering capacity of the CBA. Three factors must coincide: a sense of economic or fiscal stress, a sustained political drive from governments to take tough action (often responding to electoral pressures), and a preparedness by the CBA to increase its decision-making roles and pursue agendas of reform. These factors do not necessarily coincide in any given pattern, nor do they remain in place for lengthy or similar periods of time. There is much contingency involved in the particular constellation of factors present in each country under review.

With these forces impacting on each other, the budgetary system becomes a site of contest – not simply over winners and losers or allocative adjustments, but over the setting of the framework within which policy decisions will be taken. CBAs see themselves as the natural organizers and managers of those systems and as the main sources of advice in making cuts and delivering savings. Governments also tend to defer to or rely on the CBA's advice because of the perception that they are non-claimants in the process and are more likely to offer 'objective' and necessary advice, even if unpalatable. Moreover, the CBA's renewed central power and substantial legitimacy derived from being the 'responsible housekeeper' makes it harder for spending counterparts and line ministries to oppose their preferred directions. Yet, in practice, the success of this political strategy varies a little from place to place. In New Zealand, the Treasury became and remains the unquestioned 'power house' of reform, whereas in Canada the reforms adopted after 1994 further fragmented the institutional actors while centralizing decisions with the Prime Minister and effectively enervating the Treasury Board Secretariat.

In recent years, as economic conditions have improved, several countries have now achieved budget surpluses – some over multiple years (for example, Denmark recorded six surpluses in a row after 1996). These nations not only felt compelled to deliver surpluses, but also their actions in so doing reshaped the international political agenda. In their review of budget surplus in Australia, the US, New Zealand, Canada, Norway, Sweden and the UK, Posner and Gordon (2001) make reference to Schattschneider's observation that the winners of political conflict are those who successfully redefine what the conflict is about. They then pointed out that among these nations 'a "0" budget balance served as a strong claimant in the battle for agenda control during periods of deficits' (2001, p. 419). With the broader agenda settled, there was often little animated debate about deficit elimination. Indeed, the approach adopted tended to be 'no nonsense' and quantitative with debate only focusing on how fast the deficit should be reduced and where or by how much expenditure should be cut to reach the magic figure of a zero balance. The skills needed for this task were those of an economist with the 'jackboots' on, as the Australian chapter put it. Some other CBAs, such as the OMB in the USA, were accused of living up to their reputation as 'the abominable no-men' of budget restraint.

Nevertheless, once surpluses have been achieved and the cutback arguments for 'shared sacrifice' have begun to wear thin, the main budget claimants are likely to rebel and erode the consensus about budgetary restraint. This was the case in Canada where political pressure mounted to spend the 'fiscal dividend' (the projected surplus) as a reward for previous good behaviour. It was also true in the US in 1999–2002, both due to a generally tax-averse environment (coupled with Bush tax cuts of 2001) and then increasing demands for enhanced national security. Under such circumstances, the debate shifts from a hard-line 'no nonsense' set of quantitative edicts in which the CBA is central, to a fuzzy and qualitative debate that often marginalizes the CBA or condemns it to commentaries of caution. Political will tends to recede once politicians and agencies begin to ask questions such as how should the surplus be spent? Should it provide tax cuts, relieve the pressure on starving programs or allow governments to fund new initiatives? An improved economic situation will also influence the discussions of management further down within government. To paraphrase Al Gore's reform dictum: the focus moves from a 'government that costs less' to a 'government that works better'. The buzzword becomes 'value for money', opening a methodological can of worms over how 'value' is to be defined and assessed. The jackboots must be stored in the cupboard – at least for a while.

But other strategies are available for the CBA and other central actors who seek to keep the economy under control and continue to play the central part in this effort. Like the zero base strategy in times of deficits, these strategies are profoundly discursive, although they are more demanding. They are about creating a national 'stimmung' (or atmosphere) and promoting an agenda related to a 'healthy economic situation' and 'sound financial management'. In Sweden, Australia and New Zealand some CBAs have enshrined in legislation the need for governments to be focused on sound financial management – often intentionally leaving vague the precise definition of that term. Others have evoked the poor record of national savings or the existing debt as major issues of credibility with international financial markets. Yet others have attempted to bring the debate closer to the attention of the citizen, where 'sound financial management' operates as a moral imperative and is framed in an inter-generational discourse. Governments in surplus have insisted that 'we must pay off our debt now, otherwise it will be left for our children to pay it', and 'if we don't pay off the debt now, there will be no room for welfare services for the elderly when you, the voter, get old'. Both of these discourses were apparent in the Danish election campaign in November 2001. They were intended to keep the electorate and potential spenders in a restraint frame of mind, prolonging the existing centrality of the CBA which continued tried and trusted paternal arguments stressing it was the protector of the public interest.

A more adventurous way of addressing the issue of *spending* surpluses strategically is provided by the UK Treasury. This is the clearest example of a CBA standing for and developing distinct policy programs. The Treasury's

2001–2004 Public Service Agreement performance targets for each department, according to Parry and Deakin, 'range ambitiously wide into policy matters that go beyond Treasury organization' and also 'implicate other departments in the personal priorities of the Chancellor'. The permanent secretary, Terry Burns, as the British chapter reports, described the Treasury's new agenda by arguing that 'of course macro-economic policy is very boring at the moment because everybody agrees on it, there is nothing really to do, and micro-economic policy we have handed over to other people, so we are getting very interested in social policy'. Perhaps not coincidentally, it is also an area of policy that has substantial claim on the public purse.

THE SIGNIFICANCE OF INSTITUTIONAL CONFIGURATION AND ORGANIZATIONAL DYNAMICS

A major factor in explaining differences in the ways the CBAs have responded to changing economic and public sector imperatives was the fact that among the ten CBAs there was *no generic set of roles and functions that all performed*. The composite functions of the CBA are actually performed by different types of organizations across the countries included in this study. The institutional configuration does not appear to be dependent upon the size of the economy (GDP) or population, nor does it appear to be determined by the size and scope of government (that is, the extent of welfare state provisions). Nor does it seem to depend upon whether the country is federal or unitary, or monarchical or republican – both Germany and the UK have single composite finance ministries, China has a single ministry (but maintains other planning and financial committees) while the US and Canada both have multiple organizations. Rather, the composition of the CBA reflects the governmental traditions and administrative cultures that are framed within a legislative-bureaucratic context through which budgeting and expenditure are authorized and examined. While the individual differences are discussed in detail in the country chapters, from a comparative perspective these differences are important to the specific pressures faced and the perception of 'problems' to address. The institutional arrangements also provide the CBAs with different scope and skills to manoeuvre in their respective domains.

In the Canadian case, it is difficult to consider the CBA as a unitary actor; rather evidence suggests an *arena* where multiple actors compete and collaborate depending on the circumstances. Decision-making and the budget cycle are fragmented and episodic. Parts of the budgetary process are 'captured' or controlled by various agencies but these then tend not to exercise overarching or subsequent resource-related responsibilities over expenditure. Short of unilateral decisions from the Prime Minister it is difficult to consider the fragmented CBA as a quick and decisive actor or innovative player in the budgetary system. Indeed, the Canadian system 'works' on a system of shared norms of agreed windows and veto-points within which issues such as policy integrity are considered and the politics fought out. By contrast, the Australian case demonstrates that a 'fortuitously bifurcated' CBA can co-exist with two actors working in tandem, enabling Treasury to frame aggregate expenditure while the Department of Finance is able to specialize on business advice, expenditure controls (in-year and year-on-year), financial management and previously public sector reform. These dual agencies have separate but coordinated responsibilities and only rarely have they come into conflict or had to spend resources on bureaucratic battles over turf or agendas. In the US case, budgetary actors are deliberately split across the legislative and the executive branches to counterbalance one another – a process that initially saw the president's OMB rise in significance followed later (after 1974) by the CBO as legislators increased their attention to budget review and program performance.

At the other end of the spectrum Denmark, the UK, Holland, Germany, New Zealand and China have deliberately established and maintained unitary organizations. As single finance ministries or treasuries, their range of responsibilities and policy scope varies, as does their size. For example, the Dutch Ministry of Finance includes responsibility for revenue policy and collection, whereas the Danish and Swedish Finance ministries are responsible only for economic policy and budgetary expenditure (and not revenue collection). One consequence of this is that the Dutch Finance Ministry employs 33,000 staff, of whom some 31,000 work in the tax and customs agencies, whereas the Danish ministry employs 850 and Sweden just 420. Sweden is also of interest, in that while it has a central Ministry of Finance (with a Budget department within the ministry), it has deliberately chosen to fragment its broader budgetary and resourcing responsibilities among specialized and demarcated agencies. Most noticeably, Sweden operates with a separate agency managing pensions and other citizen entitlements, another for debt management, and one for financial management within government (separate from the Finance Ministry). Changing allocative decisions or policy on resource usage in government may involve a web of agencies and ministries, and some key decisions may not involve the budget department.

While there is no common pattern of institutional configuration, it is also worth noting that the various CBAs have resisted any change to their institutional form. Proposed or mooted institutional challenges to their domain have been contested and often rebuffed. Hence, the Australian Treasury resisted strenuously the attempt by a conservative government to divide the department into two in the mid-1970s. It had earlier resisted the establishment of a separate economic ministry. Similarly, in the UK an attempt to establish an economic ministry in the 1960s was resisted by Treasury, and a more recent parliamentary inquiry into whether the structures of Treasury were appropriate to the changing public sector environment was given short shrift by Treasury bureaucrats. The Canadian Treasury Board Secretariat has been attempting since the mid-1990s to create itself into a 'management board' over the whole of government, but without being able to define what this entails and with little outside support has not succeeded in this vision. Many in the Canadian government regard such overtures as an attempt by the TBS to reinvent a new role for itself once the Finance Ministry became more dominant in budget formulation. With more clearly segregated political masters, the two main CBAs in the US have worked out a *modus operandi* that allows them to focus their own input and priorities, while maintaining cordial relationships, described by Tanaka, O'Neill and Holen as 'friendly rivalry'.

FIRMING UP THE BUDGET PROCEDURES

All of the countries included have firmed up their budgetary procedures in the period considered. Budgetary and financial management reforms have differed in their comprehensiveness, timing and focus as well as the techniques and instruments used. Some, like New Zealand, have embarked on a virtual Odyssey of textbook reform composed by logical steps, guided by theory and enforced through legislation. Reformers made 'brave' assumptions about the behavioural consequences of institutional economics – and subsequently had to modify their approach (Schick 1996). Other countries were less programmatic and more selective in the pragmatic measures adopted. They often borrowed ideas and customized them to suit their own circumstances. Some countries, like Germany and China, have eschewed public sector reform to date but their CBAs have exploited their central position to maintain a strong influence over discretionary and extra-budgetary spending, in China's case after economic liberalization and in Germany's case especially after re-unification.

For a more complete picture, we discuss below the procedural reforms in relation to the three phases of the budget process – formulation, implementation and evaluation.

The Formulation Phase

Fiscal discipline through the medium-term setting and management of expenditure aggregates has become fundamental to the CBAs' control over budgetary formulation. To impose such controls, CBAs have promulgated new rules of the game designed to change the relationships between guardians and spenders and impose multi-year fiscal discipline on governments. CBAs have essentially attempted to force the various policy actors to operate within control frameworks with longer horizons, rather than the more immediate, one-off deals and bilateral arrangements of past eras of public budgeting.

The main rule change found in the budget processes of most countries was the imposition of an explicit *top-down framework*, based on aggregate ceilings or expenditure frames. In most cases these ceilings or frames were endorsed by cabinets and published to serve as accountability mechanisms and forms of self-discipline on governments. Some countries have rolled out 'hard forward estimates' that, in the words of Jensen writing on the New Zealand experience, shifts the burden of proof to the spenders who have to argue for changes in funds. The introduction of the 'Zalm budget norms' in Holland, the imposition of hard 'expenditure ceilings' three years out by Swedish governments, caps on spending in the US and the 'fiscal provisions framework' in New Zealand, all create top-down limits to what there is to play with in any annual budget round. Indeed, the New Zealand experience suggests that the old game-playing of the claimants has been replaced by the 'Zen of budget decision-making' where all actors now work to find robust solutions to shared problems. The Dutch chapter suggests that the highly centralized procedures of budget formulation now render the annual rounds essentially de-politicized exercises, involving results-oriented policy-managers socialized in the 'Zalm norm'.

Hence, budgetary politics has moved upwards to an elite strata of decision-makers inside government, often across political/administrative boundaries and always including finance ministers and top CBA actors as key advisors. Although finance ministers are not always 'Iron Chancellors', as Parry and Deakin put it, and although their formal position is no *primus inter pares*, they are increasingly powerful senior ministers who have been able to build strong positions within government and influence the core of economic and fiscal policy. Their role in imposing top-down frameworks is generally the key to their current influence. Many have also extended their budgetary roles to wider considerations of policy direction and performance assessment – a role often advocated by CBA officials in the new environment.

Most chapters have indicated that the CBAs have increasingly begun to gear their advice towards this top-down rationing, across government and policy assessment role, although how far this extends varies across countries. For example, the Swedish Finance Ministry has considerably expanded its policy purview in all areas except in the budget sections dealing with the direct budget analysis. The Danish Ministry of Finance now operates on the principle that staff members spend no more than 50 per cent of their time on routine control tasks leaving the other half to analysis and development. The Australian Department of Finance sees itself as 'far more a business analyst for government than a public sector spending controller'.

Reasons for the change of CBA focus in the formulation phase were that the detailed *ex ante* scrutiny created organizational overload at the centre, became a preoccupation and took up too much attention, and often made little difference in comparison with the cost of the exercise. Also detailed discussions with line agencies about the content side of each input made CBAs vulnerable to information asymmetry; it provided them with bottom-up rationales and, as one Danish executive put it, 'sucked people in', swamping the bigger picture and other structural priorities. Hence, the tendency has developed for CBAs to 'get out of the detail' and work instead on frame appropriations and budget ceilings for spending ministries. This also allows the responsibility for detailed distribution to 'cascade down', as the New Zealand chapter puts it, to ministries and agencies themselves. However, as many chapters have noted, getting out of the detail does not necessarily prevent the CBAs from selectively getting back in on a very detailed level. Such counter-trends (often related to specific problems or types of policy advice) have been apparent in Canada, Australia, New Zealand, Denmark and the US. Moreover, as Parry and Deakin remind us, the UK 'Treasury is no less confident than ever to hammer away disputatiously when a department is judged to be concealing possible savings'.

The decisions to shift attention away from detailed *ex ante* scrutiny has occurred as an increasing proportion of the budget is taken up by entitlements and mandatory expenditures that are not regulated directly by the annual budget round. This implies that the achievement of aggregate fiscal discipline now depends far more on strategic policy-making aimed at curtailing liabilities especially in the larger welfare states. The CBA's advice to government has been forced to become more policy strategic in order to alter the economic structures driving the main mandatory expenses such as tax expenditures and pension systems. With regard to 'new money' for policy activities, various experiments with 'budget margins' (icing on the cake) have been constructed in order to enable politicians to sponsor new programs and create a profile towards the electorate. And, in countries with perennial coalition governments (and occasional minority governments), such as Denmark, Sweden and the Netherlands, the Budget round has also been used to initiate other structural reforms (including non-financial) giving the impression of an institutionalized 'garbage can' process at work, tangentially related to annual expenditures.

An additional reason for the shift away from detailed *ex ante* budget scrutiny is an ideological shift in some countries towards managerialism with notions of 'letting the managers manage'. Under new public management discretionary responsibility for the budget of the ministry or agency is seen as a motivational driver and a precondition for managerial flexibility. It also means that, while the agency budget is open to the discretion of the managers and can be 'moved around' to best deliver the outputs intended, any cutbacks or 'sharing of the pain', as the New Zealand chapter indicates, can be more readily accepted.

The Implementation Phase

In contrast to the 'getting out of the detail' over existing expenditure estimates, CBAs have begun to insist on far more detail and regular reporting on in-year expenditure patterns. Holding agencies 'within budget' or programs under the declared caps in the implementation phase is crucial to reporting a balanced outcome. Given the imperatives of medium-term budgetary restraint, the OECD countries in this survey have all to some extent institutionalized different in-year reporting systems for line ministries and their agencies. The greater use of IT now enables the CBAs to scrutinize and if necessary follow up on the spending performance of agencies, and impose restrictions or sanctions if agencies are 'in deficit' or in the red. Typically CBAs release financial information every half-year or every quarter, although technology now makes it possible in some countries to check the balance of any agency any time, any day of the week. In most countries in-year financial reporting remains in cash terms, but in New Zealand, Australia and recently Holland and Sweden, that have now adopted accrual systems, such reviews are based on cash flows and balance sheet information. On advice from government accountants, Australia during 2000 pioneered the production of formal monthly reporting of the financial statements of agencies and across the whole of government, but discontinued this as the information was not regarded as particularly useful. Many CBAs now routinely produce half-yearly budgetary up-dates including revised fiscal balance figures and expenditure projections for the budget year.

The core point is that ministries and agencies have become obliged to report and explain any deviation from their appropriated funds continually to the CBA. The spending behaviour of agencies, once something of a 'black box' to the CBA, has become more transparent, and with more immediacy open to intervention from the CBA if required. In most countries, additional estimates or supplements in the budget year are still possible for spenders, but the CBAs are typically strong gatekeepers over these types of additional expenditures. Even in Canada, which regularly uses two or three sets of supplementary estimates and sometimes up to five, the government has of late restricted expenditure growth in these sources of funds, although within the budget margins many are still negotiated on a bilateral basis between the CBA and line agency. In multi-party systems with coalition governments, it may be possible for spending ministers and pressure groups to build parliamentary support in opposition to any CBA recommendations made over in-year controls.

The Evaluation Phase

The evaluation phase of the budgetary cycle is inevitably tied to accountability and it has become increasingly important for governments to be able to show performance to the electorate. Under conditions of budgetary stringency there has been a greater focus on improved performance and value for money. Performance measurement has developed from broader policy and program evaluation exercises to a much more economical focus on the costs (or value) of delivered outputs and outcomes. In countries like Australia where funds are appropriated by outcome (a broad economic or social priority area) and where CBA advice often focuses on the best purchase and investment to achieve the desired outcome, price evaluations were explicitly built into the logic of the system. In the UK the systematic comprehensive spending reviews based in the Treasury are now augmented by a 'delivery unit' in Number 10 which 'chases across departments' making sure that they 'deliver relentless progress', as the media was recently told.

In countries like Canada, the Netherlands, New Zealand, Sweden and Denmark, an extensive amount of non-financial performance information is now routinely produced by agencies and reported to the legislature. The main dilemma struck here by these governments is whether to integrate such information into the budget process, or treat it as separate information. Most countries have experienced some difficulties in linking non-financial performance information into the annual budget decision rounds (and most budget preparation exercises, as Paulsson argued for Sweden, principally remain 'rather number-oriented'). None of the countries surveyed has yet an integrated performance reporting system, and in many the process of specifying outputs appears a marginalized aspect of the process. The Dutch initiative starting out in late-2001 (the VBTB program) represents an ambitious attempt to create a useful dialogue between the substantial performance of the spenders and the financial requirements of the guardians. In the words of de Vries and Yesilkagit, the reform 'lays stress on the measurability of the policy goals, which means that goals should be presented in quantitative terms. The more quantitative this part is, the better departments can provide figures about performance and the better Parliament can control the achievements of each individual department'. Certainly, today's debate about linking budgetary numbers to performance results seems no less esoteric than the word games exchanged between CBAs and spending departments in days of line item input budgeting. It may, however, be important that the present debates are now actually about results-based information using such terminology as outputs, outcomes and value for money.

The evaluation phase, thus, exposes perennial questions about the language of accountability. In order to be accessible and digestible for decision-makers, evaluations must be simplified. In order to cover the range of activities, values and capacities maintained by the delivery organizations, it must be complex and take into account factors such as agendas, problem definition, flexibility and customization, human resource preservation, collective ethos and loyalty. This is no mere academic point, as Jensen's discussion of New Zealand attests. In the 'Review of the Centre' in New Zealand the question was raised whether contracts and performance measurements had led to a loss of collegiality and reduced the focus on the importance of maintaining long-term capability by running down human resources.

BUDGET LEGISLATION AND PRUDENT CONVENTIONS

Major changes to budget procedures sometimes take the form of budget legislation. New Zealand has opted to legislate its way though the reform program since it began in 1984. Other examples are the US *Budget and Emergency Deficit Control Act* of 1985 and the Swedish *Budget Act* of 1997. Elsewhere other prudent conventions have been adopted to the way budget rounds operate. A fundamental change in Denmark was the enhanced position of the economic committee of cabinet as the key government coordinating body in 1993. The Netherlands shows the importance of disseminated norms, especially the recent 'Zalm norm' stipulating guiding principles. The Canadian experience shows how in the early 1990s the Finance Minister, Paul Martin, was concerned to keep his 'butt out of the wringer' and retain his public credibility by meeting deficit targets 'come hell or high water'. Legislation was not altered, but the budgetary institutions and procedures of 'prudent budgeting' created a central organizational role for the Finance department.

Laws and conventions created in certain contexts can both empower and disempower the CBA because it binds actors to fixed rules and procedures. For example, spurred by governments of fiscal rectitude, many legislatures have attempted to bind future governments to expenditure constraints by inflexible statutory provisions. The New Zealand Treasury was anxious to contain the spending of future governments by the *Fiscal Responsibility Act 1994*. But it can be argued, as Jensen does, that the New Zealand legislation potentially *weakens* the position of Treasury because the basis of budget decision-making has changed from secrecy and internal rules determined by the Treasury itself, to openness business standards of good management. The Swedish statutory expenditure limits set three years out prevents the annual budget framers from establishing their own aggregate limits irrespective of the economic circumstances. In a similar vein, the Dutch VBTB program is premised on the view that this reform is 'nothing less than the strengthening of the position of the Parliament as the controller of the executive'. But does this also mean that the reforms make the politics of budgeting more transparent to all actors? Such fixed rules can curb the potential for the CBA to act creatively or address pressing exigencies, while in some ways enhancing the power of spending agencies and legislative overseers.

Fixed rules can also prove counterproductive in the longer run as other players work out ways to circumvent or get around them. This applies particularly to the spenders with a vested interest in the outcomes but little invested in the process of resource allocation. For example, the claim of greater honesty and transparency embedded in the Australian *Charter of Budget Honesty 1998* law led to the publication of three different sets of bottom-line figures. Initially, the Treasurer preferred the set that reflected best on his government's performance (the underlying fiscal balance) but as these figures became less flattering he swapped to a headline cash balance. Having promised to reduce central outlays in 1996 he also sought to exclude billions of dollars in Commonwealth revenues from the government's books because he argued much of it went back to the states as intergovernmental transfers. In other words, legislative measures that appear to strengthen the CBA's position at one point in time can become shackles in the next. CBA's have often recognized this feature by attempting to create and destroy rules and modify frameworks regularly. The Canadian case suggests that the Department of Finance has recently succeeded in this regard by increasingly controlling both the pertinent information and the timing.

But legislation and prudent conventions do not entirely remove power and politics from the budgetary arena – no system in which money is distributed across government can entirely remove these elements. But Wildavsky's (1975, p. 4) view that budgets record the outcome of the power struggle may not be as relevant today when, as Schick (2001c) puts it, 'budgets may be bigger, but budgeting weaker'. The main games and core decisions may gradually drift away from the budgetary process and congregate instead in discussions over the strategic framework, structural and economic reforms, political reforms and policy reviews. If this transpires, then transparency of the budgeting process itself may not be all that relevant for democracy.

TOWARDS NEW ROLES FOR THE CBAS – THE CULTURAL CONSEQUENCES

Few CBAs in this study have undergone extensive and deliberate transformations. However, it is possible to detect *silhouettes* of new roles emerging for the CBA, some of which are cultivated deliberately and explicitly in single countries whilst others exist as disjointed elements or as suggestions for possible future developments. Most of these new silhouette roles are connected to the different types of analysis that CBAs can offer.

In some countries, the role of the CBA is portrayed as fairly stable. In the US, the style of the OMB is still tied to the notion that it is the impartial professional *number-cruncher* for the President analysing budgets from a position of 'neutral competence'. It has paid but scant attention to new managerial fashions or new ways of delivering services. In Canada, there has been a long history of strong interest in improved management techniques, yet the more recent NPM reforms are not reported to have had much influence. The consequence of this diffidence has led to strife between the TBS and Finance – especially related to the desires of TBS to take on more responsibility for public management. But as in the US, management is not seen as an 'investment' in itself, rather Finance has tried to depict TBS as another claimant needing resources to begin its management role and invest in staff development programs. In this transition TBS is in a dilemma between trying to combat Finance to re-assert its former position as a co-guardian and becoming a more gentle and collaborative public manager.

As Pollitt and Bouckaert (2000) remark, the word 'management' has supplanted 'administration' in many countries. In some countries, this has resulted in a firm focus on financial management reforms with hoards of accountants entering government offices. In others, it has meant a more pragmatic import of performance models and a new kind of public management staff to soften up the 'can-do' head-kickers. Hence, one of the new silhouette roles that CBAs may adopt is that of the *public manager*. The legitimacy of the focus on management in the public sector is tied to the success of defining what are the values of the public sector and what social values is it attempting to achieve. It is, however, arguable whether the CBAs are the right actors in government to elaborate and measure the performance related to these values. Is there a real role here, which can add value to government performance and the quality of decision-making? To some, the new public management people are just 'smarties' in the jargon of the Dutch Ministry of Finance. Are they producing 'hot air in a ring binder' as it has been claimed about the Danish administrative politics? Or are they necessary parts of running modern government machines? Are they likely to enhance or damage the legitimacy of the CBA in the future? Certainly these are some of the questions the Canadian TSB has asked itself, as it considers swapping to the management specialist role.

A more explicit new role for the CBA is the *business or investor analyst* found in the antipodean examples. Although the Australian Department of Finance analyses the structural drivers of public expenditure just like other CBAs do, its own role is seen rather differently. Finance has repositioned itself as 'strategic investor' and it 'is now much more a business analyst than a public sector spending controller'. It has gone from 'nit picking' to providing analysis of options within the government's strategic priorities. It relates to the other stakeholders in the political environment as 'customers'. It has also toyed with the notion of making its own advice subject to market-testing, as other bidders are seen as competitors for the tasks of economic analysis, performance measurement and accounting. The Australian CBA now collaborates with private sector organizations in the field and 'contracts in' advice and services. A similar role is envisaged in the *New Zealand Fiscal Responsibility Act* where all government priorities must be costed, assessed and published, and the 'market situation' analysed. This is the explicit task of Treasury. The CBAs in Australia and New Zealand both increasingly deliver business advice to governments, and both organizations have championed extensive privatization programs. Thus, business and managerial skills have gained high priority. Moreover, in both these CBAs, and in stark contrast to the others, is the prevalence and influence of accountants initially engaged in order to run the accrual budgeting and reporting systems, but later relied on for business and policy advice. Their descriptive language has changed and now government activities are routinely talked of as 'outputs, outcomes, inputs, ownership, purchase interests, depreciation, cost of capital and baselines' – these terms have slipped almost unconsciously into the jargon of the antipodean CBAs. Also following a similar path, the Dutch introduction of NPM programs is still in the making and the cultural transformation remains less clear. The legitimacy of the business analyst role lies, as pointed out in the New Zealand and Australian chapters, in the CBA claim to intellectual superiority – the ability to deliver the best analysis in both the internal market (consisting of departments) and the external market (consisting of commercial competitors). The new legitimacy of these CBAs is fought for in a transparent and competitive environment. This is in contrast to the traditional situation where the CBA derived its power from monopolizing and selectively using information.

From a wider perspective, the legitimacy also hinges on the credibility of the business model itself. There is clearly a limit to the extent to which governments and the public sector can be viewed or operated as a 'business'. A business approach is not the only perspective that ought to be considered. Thus, the New Zealand 'Review of the Centre' highlights some unanticipated consequences of the business perspective such as the enervation of organizational capacities and the unnecessary fragmentation of the policy process. Similar debates have occurred in Sweden, where a 'Ministry of Democracy' has been created to extend the accountability perspective beyond a purely financial focus. De Vries and Yesilkagit comment that the financial management trend in the Netherlands has created a business-like technocratic environment and a void of politics. Such conditions are probably not sustainable.

These issues imply an alternative role silhouette may be available, with the CBA acting as a *meta-governor*. Most CBAs have been far less explicit than the UK Treasury about their policy role, which in the British case is stipulated publicly in the Public Service Agreements. But others have made similar moves. In Holland, the CBA role often extends beyond its 'conventional preoccupation with the financial-economic domain into more general areas of policy-making and the earlier stages of policy-decision making'. The Dutch Ministry of Finance, as de Vries and Yesilkagit argue (see chapter 7), is increasingly 'a policy-partner to be reckoned with', engaging with line ministries in setting policy frameworks. The Danish CBA has certainly played a crucial role in structural policy development in a range of issues over the past decade, as well as running several inter-ministerial think-tanks and intergovernmental networks and conducting negotiations with the local authorities. With such overt trends, the silhouette of the *meta-governor* emerges. The embryonic meta-governor role is to some extent a response to governmental fragmentation. It seeks, in the newspeak of the New Labour government of the UK, to 'join up government' or 'wire it up'. The CBA extends its domain into cross-cutting and substantial policy programs and builds institutions to support this new role. It also has to work through other players and combine abilities to act effectively within these new relationships. It has always been a natural quest for governments to seek better coordination; the new element is how the CBA has become the most crucial part of the apparatus of policy coordination, and often the leading part thereof.

Under this scenario, the CBA requires an organization and a staff profile tailored the task. The British example suggests that if the trend is continued, Treasury needs to import people with policy experience from line ministries in order to be able to develop good policy advice. In the case of Denmark and the Netherlands' political scientists and graduates of public administration have deliberately been recruited to enable the CBAs to perform policy and organizational analysis. The role of meta-governor (involving policy-producer and substantial policy-coordinator) is, however, bound to depend on the personalities of the Prime Minister and the Finance Minister and the relationship between them. The role can evaporate if the Prime Minister lacks trust in or feels over-shadowed by the Finance Minister. Evidence from the UK suggests that Number 10 develops parallel units to those embedded in the Treasury CSR institutions. Also the role of meta-governor can evaporate if the Finance Minister loses or lacks interest in policy areas. It is a role that demands a different sort of legitimacy than the guardian of the public purse, the effective public manager or the business analyst. It simply demands political legitimacy. The Danish case shows that this can be hard to first gain and then sustain in situations where meta-governing imposes costs on special groups (as in the case of pension reform); or in situations where the CBA has to juggle public investments such as its attempt to save the Copenhagen metro and the new metropolitan suburb.

Similarly, the UK Treasury has been criticized for having 'increasingly carried over into a very wide range of policy debates the special rights and privileges which it needs to have for the purpose of controlling public expenditure'. Nonetheless, comparative assessments show that several CBAs have taken on elements of the meta-governor role and begun to prepare for this role organizationally.

TRANSFORMING VILLAGE CULTURES?

The changing roles and *modus operandi* of the CBAs have to some extent impacted upon the 'village cultures'. While the US structure of government is too fragmented and turnover of executive positions too frequent to operate as a 'village culture', other nations arguably retained inner networks of officials that shaped budgetary decision-making. These have increasingly been dismantled by recent practices. De Vries and Yesilkagit report for the Netherlands that the old village culture of The Hague is no more. Today, they claim, young mobile policy managers travel between departments, and a rapid turnover of staff in the guardian and spending agencies makes the close contacts of a village network problematic. They insist however that this may make little difference as the policy managers are now homogeneously socialized under imposed budgetary norms. Shared information and shared understandings are now the medium of exchange.

In the business environment of New Zealand and Australian, the old cultures have changed significantly because the work of the CBAs is now exposed to scrutiny and competition. Much of the secrecy and in-house assumptions on which a village culture existed has been replaced with known frameworks and declared parameters. Much of the old-style detailed examination of budget formulation has been jettisoned or devolved out to the spending agencies. There has also been a high turnover of senior staff within these CBAs, with private sector professionals (attracted by market rates for their services) recruited in significant numbers. There are those in both Canberra and Wellington that worry whether the skills and single-mindedness of the accounting bean-counter have replaced (to the detriment) the previous skills of the policy analyst.

In the UK, the site of the original arguments over the Whitehall village conducting a 'private government of public money', there has been perhaps less challenge to the village community, possibly because the British civil service itself has changed less than other public services. Treasury is still able to pick the ablest recruits from the civil service entrance exams and remains predominantly a male bastion. There have been some developments in recent years with Treasury resorting to lateral recruitment of senior managers (with external advertising) and with senior Treasury officials departing to agencies – fearing little prospects for further promotion in the economic department.

In Denmark and Sweden, Finance staff members remain a coherent group and are content to be 'close to the centre of the political hurricane' rather than merely 'doing business' in the other ministries. Although there are notable changes in the cultures due to openness, competition, management fashions and policy-making, there has also been much stability. The Danish CBA still functions as an elite unit that is able to 'take its pick of the ablest recruits'. Although the CBAs are exposed to more competition and scrutiny, there is still a solid self-confidence that they are among 'the best'. But within a changed environment and new requirements, they may be the 'best' for new reasons. A preparedness to take on new agendas and maintain a toughness in negotiations remains its comparative advantage. Unlike other nations, the Scandinavian CBAs cannot attract staff with market rates of pay; instead employees see a career in the Ministry of Finance as a good investment for one's *curriculum vitae* which will be capitalized later.

Behind all the new jargon of public management, some fundamental aspects of CBA life are still evident. The 'Treasury Knights' of the UK Treasury are still in place; their standing and influence remains a perennial feature of the British state. In Denmark, the 'light blue shirts' are alive and well, while the 'suits' in Canberra still act as if they rule the roost. Despite the jargon of facilitation and partnership, what makes a budgetary official into a 'hero' in the Swedish Ministry of Finance is still finding somewhere to cut. The Dutch ministry still prizes a 'tough line' and the Australian Finance official's jackboots are close to hand. The tough 'nay-sayer' and devil's advocate is never likely to be popular, but equally never likely to be dispensable. Some of the classical functions of the CBA in preserving fiscal discipline and challenging spending patterns and the requests of others, remain fundamental to good government. And contrary to some attempts in the UK, Canada, the Netherlands and briefly in Australia, for the CBA to develop new 'partnerships' and closer relations with client spending agencies, there will always be limits to such co-habitation. It is not the role of the CBA to make itself loved; indeed, such attempts may cost it respect and credibility, and undermine its other important functions.

Hence, CBAs remain powerful organizations, but in the contemporary context power cannot be solely derived from what Parry and Deakin call 'organizational victories' or naked power demonstrations. Increasingly, the CBA's power derives from its arguments and quality of advice. It has to fight for 'intellectual victories' rather than institutional or procedural victories. Its advice today is far more open and contestable and, with the trend to present more consistent budgetary data and performance data, its credibility as a controller or manager of expenditure is more open to public scrutiny. In the final analysis, the CBA not only has to produce a superior economic and budgetary analysis, but also be the ablest agenda-setter, in both good times as well as in bad.

References

A Citizen's Guide to the Budget (2000), Washington: OMB, February.

AGC (Auditor-General of Canada) (1975), *Financial Management and Control Study: Interim Report on Department of Finance and the Treasury Board Secretariat*, Ottawa: Auditor General of Canada.

Administrationsudvalget af 1960 (1962), *1. Betænkning, Betænkning nr. 301*, København.

Andel, Norbert (1993), 'Die Rentenversicherung im Prozeß der Wiedervereinigung Deutschlands', in Hans-Heinrich Hansmeyer (ed.), *Finanzierungsprobleme der deutschen Einheit II: Aufbau und Finanzierung der sozialen Sicherung*, Berlin: Duncker und Humblot.

Andersen, Uwe (1992), 'Die Finanzierung der deutschen Einheit', in Hans-Hermann Hartwich and Göttrik Wewer (eds), *Regieren in der Bundesrepublik*, 4 Opladen: Leske und Budrich, pp. 227–43.

Andrews, Gwen, Stein Helgeby and John Wanna (1998), 'The Changing Role of the Central Budget Agency', paper presented to the 'Insight '98' Conference, 23–26 February, Canberra.

Aucoin, Peter and Donald Savoie (eds) (1998), *Managing Strategic Change: Learning from Program Review*, Ottawa: Canadian Centre for Management Development.

Audit Office NZ (1978), *Report of the Controller and Auditor-General on Financial Management in Administrative Government Departments (Shailes Report)*, Wellington.

Audit Office NZ (1996), *Governance Issues in Crown Entities*, Wellington.

Audit Office NZ (2000), *Government Departments – Results of the 1999–2000 Audits B.29*, Wellington.

Auditor-General (1999), *Management of Commonwealth Budgetary Processes: Preliminary Study, Efficiency Audit Report*, Canberra: Commonwealth of Australia.

Axelrod, Donald (1995), *Budgeting for Modern Government*, 2nd edition, USA: St. Martin's Press.

Badura, Peter (1995), 'Die Finanzverfassung im wiedervereinigten Deutschland', in Jörn Ipsen, Hans-Werner Rengeling, Jörg Manfred Mössner and Albrecht Weber (eds), *Verfassungs-recht im Wandel*, Köln: Carl Heymanns.

Ball, Ian (1990), 'Financial Management Reform of New Zealand's Public Sector: The Treasury's Role', Paper for IIR Conference, Sydney, June [Updated April 1991].

Ball, Ian (1993), 'New Zealand Public Sector Management', Paper presented to the 1993 National Accountants in Government Convention, Hobart, Australia, May.

Ball, Ian (1994), 'Reinventing Government: Lessons Learned from the New Zealand Treasury', *Government Accountants Journal*, Fall.

Ball, Ian (1995a), 'The New Zealand Experience with Accrual Budgeting, Accounting and Reporting', Presentation to the Joint ASCPA/RIPPA seminar, Hobart, March.

Ball, Ian (1995b), 'Whole of Government Reporting', Presentation to the Australasian Area Auditors-General, Hobart, March.

Ball, Ian (1996a), *Restructuring of the Estimates of Expenditure Presentation to the State Expenditure Conference – Expenditure Budget Reform: Essential Element for Improvement of Financial Management*, South Africa, April.

Ball, Ian (1996b), 'Success Factors in Implementing Resource Accounting and Budgeting in New Zealand', Presentation to the AIC Conference: Resource Accounting and Budgeting in Central, Local and Provincial Government, South Africa, March.

Ball, Ian and June Pallot (1996), 'Resource Accounting and Budgeting', in *The New Zealand Experience Public Administration*, Autumn 74 (3), 527–41.

Ball, Ian and June Pallot (1997), 'What Difference does Resource Accounting Make? The Case of New Zealand', in Dan Corry (ed.), *Public Expenditure – Effective Management and Control*, London: Dryden Press.

Barnes, Angela and Steve Leith (2001), *Budget Management that Counts: Recent Developments in Budget and Fiscal Management in New Zealand*, Treasury Working Paper 01/24, Wellington.

Bartos, Stephen (2000), 'The Application of Accruals in Australian Public Sector Budgeting and Reporting', *OECD International Symposium on Accrual Accounting and Budgeting*, Paris, 13–14 November.

Barzelay, Michael (2001), *The New Public Management: Improving Research and Policy Dialogue*, Berkeley: University of California Press.

Beck Jørgensen, Torben (1996), *Forvaltningspolitikken mellem Skylla og Karybdis*, København: Projekt Offentlig Sektor – Vilkår og fremtid.

Beck Jørgensen, Torben and Poul Erik Mourtizen (1997), *Udgiftspolitik og budgetlægning*, Viborg: Systime.

Beer, Samuel (1956), *Treasury Control*, Oxford: Clarendon Press.

Benson, E. J. (1966), 'Financial Administration Act: Amendments Respecting Functions of Treasury Board', in *House of Commons Debates Official Report*, First Session – Twenty-seventh Parliament Volume VII, Ottawa: Queen's Printer, pp. 6011–19.

Berlingske Tidende (28.11.1999), 'Kongen af Slotsholmen'.

Bille, Lars (2001), *Det politiske system*, København: Fakta ark til Udenrigs-ministeriet.

Birch, William (1995), 'Public Accounts – Accrual Accounting in Central Government – the New Zealand Experience', *The Parliamentarian*, April, 113–15.

Blom-Hansen, Jens (1996), 'Kan budgetsamarbejdet mellem staten og kommunerne forbedres?', *Nordisk Administrativt Tidsskrift*, 4, 285–303.

Bolger, Jim (1998), *A View from the Top: My Seven Years as Prime Minister*, Auckland: Viking.

Bollard, Alan (1999), 'Issues Facing the New Zealand Economy', An Address to a DMG Seminar for International Investors, March.

Bollard, Alan, Simon MacPherson and Alan Vandermolen (2000), *The Government's Fiscal Position and its Impact on the Public Sector Public Sector*, Finances Forum, Wellington, August.

Book of the States (1996), Lexington: Council of State Governments.

Borins, Sandford (1982), 'Ottawa's Expenditure "Envelopes": Workable Rationality at Last?', in G. Bruce Doern (ed.), *How Ottawa Spends 1982: National Policy and Economic Development*, Toronto: James Lorimer.

Børsen (10.03.1998), *Magtens minister*.

Boston, Jonathan (1992), 'The Treasury: its Role, Philosophy and Influence', in Hyam Gold (ed.), *New Zealand Politics in Perspective*, Auckland: Longman Paul.

Boston, Jonathan and Stephen Church (1999), 'The Impact of Electoral Reform on the Budget Process in New Zealand: Has MMP Made a Difference?', Paper to the 3rd Wellington Conference on World Affairs, European Union Studies Association – New Zealand Political Studies Association, Wellington, December.

Boston, Jonathan, John Martin, June Pallot and Pat Walsh (1991), *Reshaping the State: New Zealand's Bureaucratic Revolution*, Auckland: Oxford University Press.

Boston, Jonathan, John Martin, June Pallot and Pat Walsh (1996), *Public Management: The New Zealand Model*, Auckland: Oxford University Press.

Boxall, Peter (2000), 'Australia's Outcomes and Outputs Framework', Presentation to the OECD's Budget Committee, 30 May.

Bradbury, Simon, Jim Brumby and David Skilling (1997), 'Sovereign Net Worth: an Analytical Framework', Treasury Working Paper, Wellington, Treasury.

Bridges, Lord (1964), *The Treasury*, London: George Allen & Unwin.

Bryce, Robert B. (1986), *Maturing in Hard Times: Canada's Department of Finance through the Great Depression*, Toronto: Institute of Public Administration of Canada.

Budget Management Department, MoF (2000), *Zhongkuo yusuen bianzhi gaige (Reform on Budget Formulation in China)*, Beijing: Liberation Army Press.

Bundesminister für Verkehr (1992), *Bundesverkehrswegeplan 1992*, Bonn.

Bundesminister für Verkehr (ed.) (1993), *Gesamtwirtschaftliche Bewertung von Verkehrswegeinvestitionen, Bewertungsverfahren für den Bundesverkehrswegeplan 1992*, Bonn: BMV Schriftenreihe Heft 72.

Bundesministerium der Finanzen (1993–97), Finanzberichte 1994–1998, Bonn: Bundesanzeiger Verlagsgesellschaft.

Bundesministerium der Finanzen (1996), 'Die Finanzverteilung', in *Der Bundesrepublik Deutschland* (Bund, Länder, Gemeinden), Bonn.

Bundesministerium der Finanzen (1997), 'Deutsche Unterstützungsleistungen für den Reformprozeß', in *Den neuen unabhängigen Staaten der ehemaligen UdSSR*, IX B 5/prohUdSSR/roc vom 1, August, Bonn.

Bundesministerium für Wirtschaft (1997), *Die Beratung Mittel und Osteuropas beim Aufbau von Demokratie und sozialer Marktwirtschaft. Konzept und Beratungsprogramme der Bundesregierung*, Bonn: Transform.

Cabinet Office Circular (1994), Guidelines for Changes to Base-lines, New Zealand, December.

Chan, H., K. Wong, K. Cheung and J. Lo (1995), 'Implementation Gap in Environmental Management: The Case of Guangzhou, Nanjing and Zhengzhou', *Public Administration Review*, July/August, 55 (4).

Chapman, Richard (1997), *The Treasury in Public Policymaking*, London: Routledge.

Cheung, Kai-chee (1998), 'Environmental Challenge Facing China', in Joseph G. Jabbra and Onkar P. Dwivedi (eds), *Governmental Response to Environmental Challenges in Global Perspective*, Amsterdam: IOS Press.

Christensen, Jørgen Grønnegård (1998), 'Det kommunale førstekammer', Fordelingen af opgaver i den offentlige sektor. Debatindlæg, København: Opgavekommissionen.

Christensen, Jørgen Grønnegård (2000), 'Finansministeriets embedsmænd', *Administrativ Debat*, 2, 1–4.

Christensen, Jørgen Grønnegård (2001), 'Ministre forgår men embedsmænd består', *Politiken* (14.06.2001).

Clark, I. (1995), 'Restraint, Renewal, and the Treasury Board Secretariat', *Canadian Public Administration*, 37 (2).

Clynch, Edward, and Thomas Lauth (1991), *Governors, Legislatures, and Budgets: Diversity Across the American States*, Westport: Greenwood Press.

Cornett, Robert (1965), 'The Summing Up', in *The Budget Analyst in State Management, Partial Record of the First Budget Institute* (Lexington, 2–7 August 1964), Chicago: National Association of State Budget Officers.

Crosbie, John (1979), *The Budget Speech 1979–80*, Ottawa: Department of Finance.

Cullen, Michael (2001a), Financial Statement of the Government – Media Release, 13 September.

Cullen, Michael (2001b), Speech to Wellington Chamber of Commerce, 3 May.

Czada, Roland (1995), 'Der Kampf um die Finanzierung der deutschen Einheit', in Gerhard Lehmbruch (ed.), *Einigung und Zerfall*, Opladen: Leske und Budrich.

Dale, Tony (1995), Capital Planning and Budgeting in the New Zealand Government, Testimony to the House Committee on Government Reform and Oversight by John Wood, Ambassador of New Zealand, Washington, June.

Dale, Tony (1996), 'MMP and its Implication for the Budget Process', Presentation to the New Zealand Political Studies Research Group Seminar on Constitutional Implications of MMP, Wellington, May.

Dangerfield, Geoff (1997), 'Effectiveness, Efficiency and Accountability: Key Issues for the Future of Public Management', Paper Presented at the Future Issues in Public Sector Management Seminar, Wellington, March.

Danmarks Statistik (2000), *Statistisk tiårsoversigt*, København: Danmarks Statistik.

Davis, James and Randall Ripley (1969), 'The Bureau of the Budget and Executive Branch Agencies: Notes on Their Interaction', in James W. Davis, Jr. (ed.), *Politics, Programs, and Budgets: A Reader in Government Budgeting*, Englewood Cliffs: Prentice Hall.

Deakin, Nicholas and Richard Parry (2000), *The Treasury and Social Policy: the Contest for Control of Welfare Strategy*, London: Macmillan.

Deputy Director of Audit (1997), *Audit on Budgetary Units and Bank Accounts: Theory and Practice*, Beijing: China Audit Press.

Diamond, Lord (1975), *Public Expenditure in Practice*, London: Allen & Unwin.

Directive of State Council in the Establishing of Bureaus and Organs (1998), No. 5.

Directory of China's Government Structure (1997), Beijing.

Doern, G. Bruce (1979), 'The Cabinet and Central Agencies', in G.B. Doern and P. Aucoin (eds), *Public Policy in Canada*, Toronto: Macmillan.

Doern, G. Bruce (1980), 'Appendix A: The Federal Expenditure Budget Decision Process', in G. Bruce Doern (ed.), *Spending Tax Dollars: Federal Expenditure 1980–81*, Ottawa: Carleton University Press.

Doern, G. Bruce, Alan M. Maslove and Michael J. Prince (1988), *Public Budgeting in Canada: Organisation, Process and Management*, Ottawa: Carleton University Press.

DoF (Department of Finance) (1979), *The New Expenditure Management System*, Ottawa: Supplies and Services.

DoF (Department of Finance) (2000), *Budget Plan 2000–01*, Ottawa: Canadian Government.

DoF (Department of Finance) (2001), *Fiscal Reference Tables September 2001*, Canada: PWGSC.

DoFA (2001), *Annual Report 2000–01*, Canberra: Commonwealth of Australia.

Duncombe, S. and R. Kinney (1987), 'Agency Budget Success: How it is Defined by Budget Officials in Five Western States', *Public Budgeting and Finance*, Spring, 24–37.

Dunleavy, Patrick (1991), *Democracy, Bureaucracy and Public Choice: Economic Explanations in Political Science*, Hertfordshire: Harvester Wheatsheaf.

Eckertz, Rainer (1993a), 'Der gesamtdeutsche Finanzausgleich im System des geltenden Verfassungsrechts', in *Die Öffentliche Verwaltung*, 7, 281–91.

Eckertz, Rainer (1993b), 'Die Aufhebung der Teilung im gesamt-deutschen Finanzausgleich', in *Zeitschrift für Rechtspolitik*, 8, 297–301.

Eggleton, Arthur (1995), *The Expenditure Management System of the Government of Canada*, Ottawa: Treasury Board.

Ekonomistyrningsverket (2001), *Accrual Accounting in the Swedish Central Government*, ESV-rapport 2001: 8.

Eldrup, Anders (1988), 'Budgetdepartementet før og nu' in Finansministeriet, *Udviklinger 1975–88, Budgetdepartementet under Erling Jørgensen*, København: Finansministeriet, pp. 51–5.

Eldrup, Anders (1996), *Talemanuskript ved Nordisk Administrativt Forbund*, København.

Eldrup, Anders (1999), 'Resultatkontrakter og ledelse i staten', in Finansministeriet, *En ny tids ledelse*, København, pp. 19–32.

Evans, Lewis, Arthur Grimes, Boyce Wilkinson, with David Teece (1996), 'Economic Reform in New Zealand 1984–95: The Pursuit of Efficiency', *Journal of Economic Literature*, December, 34: 1856–902.

Fancy, Howard (1995), 'Budgeting in an MMP Environment', Seminar Paper, Institute of Policy Studies, Wellington: Victoria University.

Feldmeyer, Karl (1997), 'Waigel reagiert mimosenhaft und Kohl mit Achselzucken', in *FAZ*, 10 (9), 7.

Fiedler, Jürgen (1990), 'Die Regelung der bundesstaatlichen Finanzbeziehungen im Einigungsvertrag', in *Deutsches Verwaltungsblatt*, 1 December, pp. 1263–70.

Finance and Expenditure Committee (1994), *Report of the Finance and Expenditure Committee on the Fiscal Responsibility Bill*, Wellington: New Zealand Parliament.

Finansdepartementet (1995), *Fortsatt reformering av budget-processen*, Ds 1995: 73.

Finansdepartementet (2000), *Ekonomisk styrning för effektivitet och transparens*, Ds 2000: 63.

Finansministeriet (1979), *Budgetredegørelse 1979*, København.

Finansministeriet (1992), *Valg af velfærd – konkurrence med frit valg for borgerne*, Moderniseringsredegørelse, København.

Finansministeriet (1998), *Forholdet mellem minister og embedsmænd*, Betænkning 1354, København.

Finansministeriet (1999a), *Budgetanalyse af politiet*, København.

Finansministeriet (1999b), *Aftale om Finansloven år 2000*, København.

Finansministeriet (1999c), *Mål og midler i offentligt finansieret voksen-og efteruddannelse*, København.

Finansministeriet (1999d), *Effektive offentlige arbejdsprocesser*, København.

Finansministeriet (1999e), *Vejledning om nye lønsystemer i staten*, København.

Finansministeriet (1999f), *Resultatløn i staten*, København.

Finansministeriet (1999g), *Budgetredegørelse 1999*, København.

Finansministeriet (2000a), *Etik ansvar og værdier i den offentlige sektor*, København.

Finansministeriet (2000b), *Benchmarking i den offentlige sektor – nogle metoder og erfaringer*, København.

Finansministeriet (2000c), *Kontraktstyring i Staten*, København.

Finansministeriet (2001a), *Budgetredegørelse 2001*, København.

Finansministeriet (2001b), *Budgetvejledning 2001*, København.

Finansministeriet (2001c), *Brug for alle – Danmark år 2010 og et mere rummeligt arbejdsmarked*, København.

Finansministeriet (2001d), *En holdbar fremtid – Danmark 2001*, København.

Finansministeriet (2001e), *Budgetoversigt 2001*, København.

Forster, J. and J. Wanna (1990), 'Introduction', in John Forster and John Wanna (eds), *Budgetary Management and Control*, Melbourne: Macmillan.

Foster, J. and F.J. Plowden (1996), *The State under Stress: Can the Hollow State be Good Government?*, Buckingham: Open University Press.

Friauf, Karl Heinrich and Günter Püttner (eds) (1991), *Haus-haltsrecht. Vorschriftensammlung mit Sachregister und alphabetischem Schnellregister*, Heidelberg: C.F. Müller.

General Accounting Office (1999), 'Performance Budgeting: Initial Experiences under the Results Act in Linking Plans with Budgets', *GAO/AIMD/GGD-99-67*, April.

Gipper, Angelika (1996), 'Grundsätze der Investitionspolitik, Bundesverkehrswegeplanung und Bundesverkehrswegeplan 1992', Unpublished manuscript, Bonn.

Glassco, J. Grant (1963), *Report of the Royal Commission on Government Organisation*, Ottawa: Queen's Printer.

Gosling, J. (1985), 'Patterns of Influence and Choice in the Wisconsin Budgetary Process', *Legislative Studies Quarterly*, November, 10, 457–82.

Gosling, J. (1987), 'The State Budget Office and Policy Making', *Public Budgeting and Finance*, Spring, 7, 51–65.

Gottfried, Peter and Wolfgang Wiegard (1991), 'Finanzausgleich nach der Vereinigung: Gewinner sind die alten Länder', in *Wirtschaftsdienst*, 9, 453–61.

Gould, S.L., A.A. Oldall and F. Thompson (1979), 'Zero-Based Budgeting: Some Lessons from an Inconclusive Experiment', *Canadian Public Administration*, 22 (2), 251–60.

Government of Canada (1966), *Financial Management in Department and Agencies in the Government of Canada*, Ottawa: Queen's Printer.

Government of Canada (1973), *Organization of the Government of Canada*, 9th edition, Ottawa: Queen's Printer.

Greenspon, Edward and Anthony Wilson-Smith (1996), *Double Vision: The Inside Story of the Liberals in Power*, Toronto: Doubleday Canada.

Grimes, Arthur (2001), 'Crown Financial Asset Management: Objectives and Practice', Treasury Working Paper 01/12, Wellington.

Gustavsson, C.G. (1985), En ny struktur för statens budget, RRV 1995:54. Riksrevisionsverket, Stockholm.

Hamer, H.J. and A.T.L.M. van de Ven, (1993), Verzelstandiging nationaal en internationaal (Autonomisation national and international) in W.J.M. Kickert, N.P. Mol and A. Sorber (eds), *Verzelfstandiging van overheidsdiensten*, Den Haag: Vuga.

Hammer, Erik (1999), Det statslige budget og bevillingssystem, Frederiksberg: Danmarks Forvaltningshøjskoles Forlag.

Hammond, T. and P. Thomas (1989), 'The Impossibility of a Neutral Hierarchy', *Journal of Law, Economics, and Organization*, Spring, 5 (1), 155–84.

Hawker, Geoffrey, R.F.I. Smith and Patrick Weller (1979), *Politics and Policy in Australia*, St. Lucia: University of Queensland Press.

Heclo, Hugh (1975), 'OMB and the Presidency – the Problem of "Neutral Competence"', *Public Interest*, Winter, 38, 80–98.

Heclo, Hugh and Aaron Wildavsky (1974), *The Private Government of Public Money*, London: Macmillan.

Henneke, Hans-Günter (1991), 'Finanzverfassung im geeinten Deutschland. Einheitsfonds, Einigungsvertrag und Finanz-ausgleichssystem', in *Jura*, 5, 230–41.

Heun, Werner (1992), 'Strukturprobleme des Finanzausgleichs, Finanzverfassungsrechtliche Integration der neuen Bundesländer und die Frage einer Reform der grundgesetzlichen Finanzverfassung', in *Der Staat*, 205–32.

HM Treasury (2001a), *Departmental Report of the Chancellor of the Exchequer's Department*, London: HMSO, Cm 5116.

HM Treasury (2001b), *Public Expenditure 2001–01 Provisional Outturn*, London: HMSO, Cm 5243.

HM Treasury Committee (House of Commons) (2001), *Third Report: HM Treasury*, HMSO: HC 73-II 2000–01.

Horst, Patrick (1995), *Haushaltspolitik und Regierungspraxis in den USA und der Bundesrepublik Deutschland*, Frankfurt am Main: Peter Lang.

House of Representatives Standing Committee on Finance and Public Administration (1990), *Not Dollars Alone – Review of the Financial Management Improvement Program*, Canberra: Australian Government Publishing Service.

Howard, S. Kenneth (1973), *Changing State Budgeting*, Lexington: Council of State Governments.

Huaicheng, Xiang (ed.) (1999), *1999 Zhongguo caizheng baogao (China Finance Report)*, Beijing: China Financial and Economic Publishing House.

Huther, Jeff (1999), *An Integrated Approach to Government Financial Policy*, Treasury Working Paper 99/8, Wellington: Treasury.

Information (19.12.1998), *Danmark på vej til nyt enevælde*, København.

Information (23.12.1998), *Danmark på vej til nyt enevælde*, København.

Information (24.09.1999), *Holdningspolitikeren er død*, København.

James, Colin (1995), 'Potential, Possibilities, Pitfalls and Perils', Paper presented at the Pursuing Further Innovation in Public Sector Management, New Zealand Society of Accountants, 5–8 November, Wellington.

Janssen, John (2001), *New Zealand's Fiscal Policy Framework: Experience and Evolution*, Treasury Working Paper 01/25, Wellington: Treasury.

Jenkins, Roy (1998), *The Chancellors*, London: Macmillan.

Jensen, Lotte (2000a), 'Constructing the Image of Accountability in Danish Public Sector Reform', in Larry Jones, James Guthrie, and Peter Steane (eds), *Learning from International Public Management Reform*, Oxford: Elsevier.

Jensen, Lotte (2000b), 'Finansministeriet', in Tim Knudsen (ed.), *Regering og embedsmænd: Om magt og demokrati i centraladministrationen*, Århus: Systime.

Jensen, Lotte (2001a), 'Etik, kultur og værdier i Finansministeriet', in Anders Berg-Sørensen (ed.), *Etik til debat*, København: DJØF.

Jensen, Lotte (2001b), 'Denmark – The Island Culture', in R.A.W. Rhodes and Patrick Weller (eds), *The Changing World of Top Officials. Mandarins or Valets*, Buckingham: Open University Press.

Johnson, A.W. (1971), 'The Treasury Board of Canada and the Machinery of Government of the 1970s', *Canadian Journal of Political Science*, 4 (3), 240–59.

Johnson, B. (1984), 'From Analyst to Negotiator: the OMB's New Role', *Journal of Policy Analysis and Management*, Summer, 3, 501–15.

Johnson, B. (1989), 'The OMB Budget Examiner and the Congressional Budget Process', *Public Budgeting and Finance*, Spring, 9, 5–14.

Jyllandsposten (01.11.1998), *Budgetbisserne*.

Kelly, Joanne (2000), 'Managing the Politics of Expenditure Control: Cabinet Budget Committees in Australia and Canada', PhD dissertation, Brisbane: Griffith University.

Kibblewhite, Andrew and Chris Usher (2001), *Outcomes Focused Management in New Zealand*, Treasury Working Paper 01/05, Wellington: Treasury.

Kickert, W.J.M. and F.O.M. Verhaak (1995), 'Autonomizing Executive Tasks in Dutch Central Government', in *International Review of Administrative Sciences*, 61 (4), 531–48.

Kilian, Michael (1991), 'Das System des Länderfinanzausgleichs und die Finanzierung der neuen Bundesländer', in *Juristenzeitung*, 46 (9), 425–31.

Kilian, Michael (1993), *Nebenhaushalte des Bundes*, Berlin: Duncker und Humblot.

Kirste, Ulrike (1995), *Die Finanzhilfen des Bundes an die neuen Länder nach Artikel 104a Absatz 4 Grundgesetz*, Sinsheim: Pro Universitate.

Klijn, Erik-Hans (1996), 'Analyzing and Managing Policy Processes in Complex Networks: A Theoretical Examination of the Concept of Policy Networks and its Problems', *Administration and Society*, 28 (1), 90–119.

Knudsen, Tim (1995), *Dansk statsbygning*, København: DJØF.

Knudsen, Tim (1999), 'How Informal Can You Be?' in B. Guy Peters, R.A.W. Rhodes and Vincent Wright (eds), *Administering the Summit*, London: Macmillan.

Knudsen, Tim (2000), *Regering og embedsmænd. Om magt og demokrati i centraladministrationen*, Århus: Systime.

Kohl, Helmut, Theo Waigel and Klaus Kinkel (1994), *Koalition-svereinbarung für die 13*, Legislaturperiode des Deutschen Bundestages, Bonn.

Kooiman, Jan (2000), 'Societal Governance: Levels, Models and Orders of Social-Political Interaction', in Jon Pierre (ed.), *Debating Governance*, London: Oxford University Press.

Korff, Hans Clausen (1975), *Haushaltspolitik. Instrument öffentlicher Macht*, Stuttgart: Kohlhammer.

Kortmann, C.A.J.M. (1990), *Constitioneel Recht (Constitutional Law)*, Deventer: Kluwer.

Kunas, Siegmar (1982), 'The Budget of the Federal Republic of Germany', in *Public Budgeting and Finance*, 2, 43–52.

Lalley, Martin (1995), 'The Cost of Capital for Government Entities: An Evaluation of the New Zealand Government's Capital Charge Model', *Accounting Research Journal*, 8 (1), 15–26.

Lam, T.C. (2001), 'Department of Management, Hong Kong Polytechnic University, May', Unpublished Manuscript.

Lane, Steve (1995), Interview with Steve Lane, Treasury Board Sectetariat, Ottawa (Joanne Kelly).

Lange, D. (1998) 'With the Benefit of Foresight and a Little Help from Hindsight', in *Australian Journal of Administration*, March, 57 (1), 12–18.

Larsson, T. (1986), *Regeringen och dess kansli – Samordning och byrakrati i maktens centrum (The Government and its Offices – Coordination and the Bureaucracy in the Centre of Power)*, Lund: Studentlitteratur.

Larsson, T. (2001), 'The Swedish Central Administration – A Dual Nature', Paper presented at the Governance of State Agencies and Authorities, Expert Meeting in Paris, April.

Lawson, Nigel (1992), *The View from No. 11*, London: Bantam Press.

Lee, R. (1991), 'Developments in State Budgeting: Trends of Two Decades', *Public Administration Review*, 51, 254–62.

Lehmbruch, Gerhard (1991), 'Die deutsche Vereinigung, Strukturen und Strategien', in *Politische Vierteljahresschrift*, 32 (4), 585–604.

Lieberthal, Kenneth and Michel Oksenberg (1998), *Policy Making in China: Leaders, Structures, and Processes*, New Jersey: Princeton University Press.

Lindblom, C. (1968), *The Policy-making Process*, New Jersey: Prentice Hall.

Lindquist, Evert (1996), 'On the Cutting Edge: Program Review, Government Restructuring and the Treasury Board of Canada', in Gene Swimmer (ed.), *How Ottawa Spends 1996–97: Life under the Knife*, Ottawa: Carleton University Press.

Lindquist, Evert (2001), 'How Ottawa Plans: the Evolution of Strategic Planning', in Leslie Pal (ed.), *How Ottawa Spends 2001–02: Power in Transition*, Ottawa: Carleton University Press.

Lipsey, David (2000), *The Secret Treasury*, London: Viking.

Lixin, Wang and Joseph Fewsmith (1995), 'Bulwark of the Planned Economy: The Structure and Role of the State Planning Commission', in Carol Lee Harmrin and Suiheng Zhao (eds), *Decision-making in Deng's China: Perspective from Insiders*, New York: M.E. Sharpe.

Lo, C. and S. Tang (1994), 'Institutional Contexts of Environmental Management: Water Pollution Control in Guangzhou', *Public Administration and Development*, 14 (1).

Lye, Joanne (1996), 'An Analysis of the Evolution of Crown Financial Statements in New Zealand: A Grounded Theory Approach', Masters Thesis, Palmerston North: Massey University.

Lykketoft, Mogens (1999), 'Udlicitering er i virkeligheden ofte en måde at få en bedre ledelse på', *Administrativ Debat*, 3, 1–3.

Lynch, Thomas D. (1995), *Public Budgeting in America*, Englewood Cliffs: Prentice Hall.

MAB/MIAC (1992), *Australian Public Service Reformed: An Evaluation of a Decade of Management Reform*, Canberra: Australian Government Publishing Service.

Mallard, Trevor (2001), *Review of the Centre Advisory Board and Second Standards Board Report Official Announcement*, 21 August.

Mallory, J.R. (1979), 'The Lambert Report: Central Roles and Responsibilities', *Canadian Public Administration*, 22 (4), 517–29.

Manow, Philip (1996), 'Informalisierung und Parteipolitisierung – Zum Wandel exekutiver Entscheidungsprozesse in der Bundesrepublik', in *Zeitschrift für Parlamentsfragen*, 27 (1), 96–107.

Mansbridge, S.H. (1979), 'The Lambert Report: Recommendations to Departments', *Canadian Public Administration*, 22 (4), 530–40.

Martin, Paul (1994), 'Minister of Finance Disappointed with Moody's Downgrade', *News Release*, Finance Canada, 2 June.

Mattsson, I. (1998), *Den statliga budgetprocessen – Rationell resursfördelning eller meningslös ritual?*, Stockholm: SNS Förlag.

Mazankowski, Donald (1992), *Cost of Government and Expenditure Management Survey: Review of Federal and Provincial Cost Containment Initiatives*, Ottawa: Department of Finance.

McCready, D.J. (1984), 'Treasury Board: Lost Influence?' in Alan M. Maslove (ed.), *How Ottawa Spends 1984–85: The New Agenda*, Toronto: Methuen.

McCulloch, B. (1991), 'A Capital Charge for Government Departments', *Accountants Journal*, October.

McCulloch, B. and I. Ball (1992), 'Accounting in the Context of Public Sector Management Reform', *Financial Accountability & Management*, Spring 8 (1), 7–12.

Meer, F.M. and L.J. Roborgh (1993), *Ambtenaren in Nederland: Omvang, bureaucratisering en representativiteit van het ambtelijk apparaat* (Civil Servants in the Netherlands: Size, Bureaucratisation and Representativeness of the Civil Service), Alphen a/d Rijn: Tjeenk Willink.

Meltsner, Arnold (1976), *Policy Analysts in the Bureaucracy*, Berkeley: University of California Press.

'Message of the President' to the Congress of the United States Accompanying Reorganization Plan No. 2 of 1970, 12 March, 1970.

Ministerie van Financiën (1997), *Aansturen op Resultant (Towards Results)*, Den Haag.

Ministry of Finance (2001a), *This is The Ministry of Finance*, Stockholm.

Ministry of Finance (2001b), *Sweden's Economy*, Appendices to the Spring Budget Bill of 2001, Stockholm.

MoF (Ministry of Finance) (2000), *Reform on Budget Formulation in China*, Beijing: Liberation Army Press.

Monck, Nick (1997), 'The Need for a Strong Treasury, and How to Make it Work', in Dan Corry (ed.), *Public Expenditure: Effective Management and Control*, London: Dryden Press.

Morris, Richard (1994a), *Pre-budget Media Briefing on Advantages of Accrual Accounting*, June.

Morris, Richard (1994b), 'The New Zealand Experience with Accrual Reporting', Speech to the Australian Standing Treasuries Liaison Committee, Melbourne, November.

Muhlen, Norbert (1938), *Hitler's Magician: Schacht*, London: George Routledge.

National Audit Office (1998), *The Swedish State Budget – An Instrument for Governance and Management*, Riksrevisionsverket Report.

Naughtie, James (2001), *The Rivals*, London: Fourth Estate.

Nethercote, John, Brian Galligan and Cliff Walsh (eds) (1993), *Decision Making in New Zealand Government*, Canberra: Australian National University.

New Zealand Institute for the Study of Competition and Regulation (2000), *The Economic Performance of Five State Owned Enterprises 1989 to 1998*, Report to the New Zealand Treasury, Wellington.

New Zealand Parliament (1994), *Second Reading of the Fiscal Responsibility Bill*, May.

New Zealand Parliament (2001), *Budget 2001 – The Hon Michael Cullen Treasurer Minister of Finance Speech*, 24 May.

Nørgård, Asbjørn Sonne (2001), 'Det institutionelle valg og dets konsekvenser: et forsvar for en ærlig og mådeholden hierarkisk styring', in Anders Berg-Sørensen (ed.), *Etik til debat*, København: DJØF Forlag.

Norman, Richard (1997), *Accounting for Government Cases in Public Sector Innovation*, Wellington: Victoria University Press.

Norman, Richard (2000), 'Letting and Making Managers Manage — the Effect of Control Systems on Management Action in New Zealand's Central Government', *Public Sector*, 24 (2), 2–7.

O'Neill, June (2000), 'The Story of the Surplus', *Policy Review*, June and July, 101.

O'Neill, Paul H. (1988), 'Presentation to Office of Management and Budget Staff', 6 September.

OCG (Office of the Comptroller General) (1988), *Estimates 1988–89 Part III Expenditure Plan*, Ottawa: Minister of Supply and Services.

OECD (1993), *Wirtschaftsbericht Deutschland*, Paris: OECD.

Office of Management and Budget (2001), *The President's Management Agenda – Fiscal Year 2002*, August.

Økonomistyrelsen (1998), *Vejledning i virksomhedsregnskaber*, København.

Økonomistyrelsen (2000), *Økonomistyring med balance og fokus*, København.

Olsen, Karsten (1988), 'Fra rammebevillinger til totalrammer; budgetreform-arbejdet', in Finansministeriet, *Udviklinger 1975–88, Budgetdepart-ementet under Erling Jørgensen*, København: Finansministeriet, pp. 31–7.

Osbaldeston, Gordon R. (1990), *Organizing to Govern* (Vol. 2), Toronto: McGraw-Hill Ryerson.

Osbourne, D. (1999), 'Strategic Management in Government: The Challenges Ahead', *Public Sector*, November, 22 (4).

Østergaard, Hans Henrik H. (1998), *At tjene og forme den nye tid, Finans-ministeriet 1848–1998*, København: Finansministeriet.

Page, Ed (1991), *Localism and Centralism in Europe*, New York: Oxford University Press.

Palmer, J. (1995), 'Reflections on Reform of the New Zealand Public Sector', Paper presented at the Pursuing Further Innovation in Public Sector Management, New Zealand Society of Accountants, 5–8 November, Wellington.

Paquet, G. and R. Shepherd (1997), 'The Program Review Process: a Deconstruction', in G. Swimmer (ed.), *How Ottawa Spends 1996–97: Life under the Knife*, Ottawa: Carleton University Press.

Patzig, Werner (1991), 'Zwischen Solidität und Solidarität: die bundesstaatliche Finanzverfassung in der Übergangszeit', in *Die Öffentliche Verwaltung*, 14, 578–86.

PCO (Privy Council Office) (1980), *A Guide to the Expenditure Management System*, Ottawa: Supplies and Services.

PCO (Privy Council Office) (1981), *The Policy and Expenditure Management System*, Ottawa: Supplies and Services.

PCO (Privy Council Office) (1998), *Decision Making Processes and Central Agencies in Canada: Federal, Provincial and Territorial Practices*, Ottawa: Government of Canada.

Pearson, Lester B. (1966), 'Government Organisation: Provision for Establish-ment of New Departments', *House of Commons Debates: Official Report*, First Session – 27th Parliament Vol. V, Ottawa: Queen's Printer, pp. 4870–911.

Petrie, Murray and David Webber (2001), *Review of Evidence on Broad Outcome of Public Sector Management Regime*, Treasury Working Paper 01/06, Wellington.

Pilegge, Joseph (1978), *Taxing and Spending: Alabama's Budget in Transition*, Montgomery: University of Alabama Press.

Pittelkow, Ralf (2001), *Det personlige samfund*, København: Lindhardt og Ringhof.

Pollitt, C. and G. Bouckaert (2000), *Public Management Reform: A Comparative Analysis*, Oxford: Oxford University Press.

Posner, P. and B. Gordon (2001), 'Can Nations Save? Experiences with Budget Surpluses', in L. Jones, J. Guthrie and P. Steane (eds), *Learning from Public Management Reform*, Amsterdam: Elsevier.

Pot, C.W. van der and A.M. Donner (1983), *Handboek van het Nederlandse Staatsrecht* (Handbook Dutch Constitutional Law), Zwolle: Tjeenk Willink.

Potter, Evan (2000), 'Treasury Board as Management Board: the Re-invention of a Central Agency', in Leslie Pal (ed.), *How Ottawa Spends 2000–01: Past Imperfect, Future Tense*, Toronto: Oxford University Press.

Pradhan, S. and E. Campos (1996), 'Budget Institutions and Expenditure Outcomes: Binding Governments to Fiscal Performance', *World Bank Policy Research Working Paper*, No. 1646.

Presse und Informationsamt der Bundesregierung (1990), *Bulletin*, 17 October. No. 123, Bonn.

Public Law 93–344, 12 July 1974.

Public Law 99–177, 12 December 1985.

Public Law 100–119, 29 September 1987.

Public Law 101–508, 5 November 1990.

Ransone, Coleman (1982), *The American Governorship*, Westport: Greenwood Press.

Rawnsley, Andrew (2000), *Servants of the People: the Inside Story of New Labour*, London: Hamish Hamilton; revised edition 2001, London: Penguin.

Regeringskansliet (2001), *Regeringskansliets årsbok 2000*, Stockholm.

Report of the President's Commission on Budget Concepts (1967), October.

Rhodes, R.A.W. (ed.) (2000), *Transforming British Government*, Volumes I and II, London: Macmillan.

Rhodes, R.A.W. and Patrick Dunleavy (1999), *Prime Minister, Cabinet and the Core Executive*, London: St. Martin's Press.

Richardson, Ruth (1994), 'Opening and Balancing the Books, the New Zealand Experience', *The Parliamentarian*, October, 244–46.

Richardson, Ruth (1995), *Making a Difference*, Christchurch: Shoal Bay Press.

Robinson, Geoffrey (2000), *An Unconventional Minister: My Life Inside New Labour*, London: Michael Joseph.

Robson, Steve (2001), 'A Manifesto for Inescapable Change', *Financial Times*, 17 May.

Rosenthal, Alan (1990), *Governors & Legislatures: Contending Powers*, Washington: Congressional Quarterly Press.

Roseveare, H. (1969), *The Treasury: the Evolution of a British Institution*, London: Allen Lane.

Sabato, Larry (1983), *Goodbye to Good-time Charlie: The American Governorship Transformed*, 2nd edition, Washington: Congressional Quarterly Press.

Savoie, Donald (1990), *The Politics of Public Spending in Canada*, Toronto: University of Toronto Press.

Savoie, Donald (1999), *Governing from the Centre: The Concentration of Power in Canadian Politics*, Toronto: University of Toronto Press.

Scharpf, Fritz (1993), 'Coordination in Hierarchies and Networks', in Fritz Scharpf (ed.), *Games in Hierarchies and Networks: Analytical and Empirical Approaches to the Study of Governance Institutions*, Frankfurt am Main: Campus Verlag, pp. 471–94.

Schäuble, Wolfgang (1991), *Der Vertrag, Wie ich über die deutsche Einheit verhandelte*, Stuttgart: Deutsche Verlags-Anstalt.

Schick, Allen (1966), 'The Road to PPB: The Stages of Budget Reform', *Public Administration Review*, December, 26, 243–58.

Schick, Allen (1973) 'A Death in the Bureaucracy: The Demise of Federal PPB', *Public Administration Review*, March/April, 146–56.

Schick, Allen (1990) *The Capacity to Budget*, Washington: Urban Institute Press.

Schick, Allen (1996), *The Spirit of Reform: Managing the New Zealand State Sector in a Time of Change*, Wellington: State Services Commission.

Schick, Allen (1997), 'The Changing Role of the Central Budget Office', Discussion Paper, Organization for Economic Cooperation and Development, Paris (OECD/GD 97/109).

Schick, Allen (1998), *A Contemporary Approach to Public Expenditure Management*, International Bank for Reconstruction and Development, Washington: The World Bank.

Schick, Allen (2001a), *Budgeting and Management in the Netherlands*, 22nd Annual Meeting of Senior Budget Officials, Paris, 21–2 May.

Schick, Allen (2001b), 'The Changing Role of the Central Budget Office', in *OECD Journal on Budgeting*, Issue 1, Vol. 1, Paris: Public Management Service OECD.

Schick, Allen (2001c), 'Does Budgeting Have a Future?', Paper for 22nd Meeting of Senior Budget Officials, Paris: Public Management Service (OECD/SBO 2001/4).

Schieber, G. and A. Maeda (1999), 'Health Care Financing and Delivery in Developing Countries', *Health Affairs*, May/June, 18 (3).

Schmitz, Gerald (1989), 'The Expenditure Management System Revisited', Parliamentary Research Branch Background Paper 108E, Ottawa: Minister of Supply and Services.

Schwinn, Oliver (1997), *Die Finanzierung der deutschen Einheit. Eine Untersuchung aus politisch-institutionalistischer Perspektive*, Opladen: Leske und Budrich.

Scott, Graham (1995), 'The Goals of Reform', Paper to the Pursuing Further Innovation in Public Sector Management, New Zealand Society of Accountants, 5–8 November, Wellington.

Scott, Graham (1996), *Government Reform in New Zealand*, International Monetary Fund Occasional Paper 140, Washington, October.

Scott, Graham (2001), *Public Management in New Zealand Lessons and Challenges*, New Zealand: New Zealand Business Roundtable.

Scott, Graham and Peter Gorringe (1989), 'Reform of the Core Public Sector: The New Zealand Experience', in *Australian Journal of Public Administration*, March 48 (1).

Secretariat of the General Office, State Council (1998), *Zhongyang zhengfu zuzhi jigou (Organizational Structure of the Central Government)*, Beijing: Reform Press.

Shand, David (2001), *Towards a Better Public Sector*, Presentation to CPA Australia, National Public Sector Convention, Gold Coast, Australia, 27 March.

Sharp, Mitchell (1966), 'Text of Address by the Honourable Mitchell Sharp, Minister of Finance, at a Luncheon Meeting of the Women's Canadian Club of Ottawa', Press Release Office of the Minister of Finance, 21 April.

Siegal, Don (1982), 'Evolution of the Expenditure Budget', in Kenneth Kernaghen (ed.), *Public Administration in Canada*, 4th edition, Toronto: Methuen.

Simpkins, Kevin (1998), 'Budgeting and Accounting Issues – New Zealand', Speech to the International Federation of Accountants, Public Sector Committee, April.

Skærbæk, Peter (1999), 'Giver det industrielle virksomhedsregn-skab mening i staten?', *Samfundsøkonomen*, 5, 33–42.

Snare, C. (1995), 'Windows of Opportunity: When and How can the Policy Analyst Influence the Policymaker during the Policy Process', *Policy Studies Review*, 14 (3/4), 407–30.

Sowden, Mark and Louise Young (2000a), 'Introduction to Financial Analysis', Pre-workshop Reading to Victoria University of Wellington, Wellington: The Treasury.

Sowden, Mark and Louise Young (2000b), 'Monthly Monitoring of Departments', Lecture Material to Victoria University of Wellington, Wellington: The Treasury.

Special Report (1985), 'Congress and OMB', *Congressional Quarterly*, 14 September, pp. 1809–18.

State Services Commission (1991), *Review of State Sector Reforms – Logan Review*, Wellington: State Services Commission.

State Services Commission (1996), *New Zealand's State Sector Reform: A Decade of Change State Services Commission*, Wellington: State Services Commission.

State Services Commission (1999a), *Crown Entities Initiative*, Wellington: State Services Commission.

State Services Commission (1999b), *Medium-Term Fiscal Modeling: Update Report*, Occasional Paper No.14, Wellington: State Services Commission.

Statskontoret (2000), *Staten i omvandling 2000*, Rapport 2000:15.

Statsministeriet (1924), *Cirkulære nr. 98 af 25, Juni 1924*, København.

Sterns, A.A. (1965), *A History of the Department of Finance*, Ottawa: Department of Finance.

Sturm, Roland (1988), *Der Haushaltsausschuß des Deutschen Bundestages*, Opladen: Leske und Budrich.

Sturm, Roland (1989), *Haushaltspolitik in westlichen Demokratien*, Baden-Baden: Nomos.

Sturm, Roland (1991), 'Die Zukunft des deutschen Föderalismus', in Ulrike Liebert and Wolfgang Merkel (eds.), *Die Politik zur deutschen Einheit*, Opladen: Leske und Budrich, pp. 161–82.

Sturm, Roland (1993), *Staatsverschuldung*, Opladen: Leske und Budrich.

Sturm, Roland (1994), 'Budgeting as Informed Guess Work: Has the German Budgetary Process Lost Direction?', in *Public Budgeting and Financial Management*, 6 (1), 130–53.

Sturm, Roland with Markus M. Müller (1999), *Public Deficits: A Comparative Study of their Economic and Political Consequences in Britain, Canada, Germany and the United States*, London: Longman.

Swimmer, Gene (ed.) (1996), *How Ottawa Spends 1996–96: Life Under the Knife*, Ottawa: Carleton University Press.

TBS (Treasury Board Secretariat) (1989), *Backgrounder: Federal Expenditure Reduction and Management Improvements*, Ottawa: Treasury Board Secretariat.

TBS (Treasury Board Secretariat) (2000), *Results for Canadians: a Management Framework for the Government of Canada*, Ottawa: Treasury Board Secretariat.

Thain, Colin and Maurice Wright (1995), *The Treasury and Whitehall: the Planning and Control of Public Expenditure 1976–93*, Oxford: Clarendon Press.

The Research Institute of the Audit Administration (ed.) (1997), *Yuxuan danwei yinhang zhanghu shenzi: lilun yu shijian (Audit on Budgetary Units and Bank Accounts: Theory and Practice)*, Beijing: China Audit Press.

The Wall Street Journal (1984), 'Budget Process Is Just Fine, Thank You', 3 September.

Thurmaier, Kurt (1995), 'The Multiple Facets of Budget Analysis: Focusing on Budget Execution in Local Governments', *State and Local Government Review*, 27 (2), 102–17.

Thurmaier, Kurt (2001), 'A Recursive Problem Framing Model of Decision-making in Policy Oriented State Budget Offices', Paper Presented at the Midwest Political Science Association Annual Meeting, Chicago, April.

Thurmaier, Kurt and James Gosling (1997), 'The Shifting Roles of State Budget Offices in the Midwest: Gosling Revisited', *Public Budgeting and Finance*, Winter, 17 (4).

Thurmaier, Kurt and Katherine Willoughby (2001), *Policy and Politics in State Budgeting*, Armonk: M.E. Sharpe Press.

Timmons, Bascom (1953), *Portrait of an American: Charles G. Dawes*, New York: Henry Holt and Company.

Togsverd, Tom (1988), 'Fra statsbudget til samlet offentlig udgiftspolitik', in Finansministeriet, *Udviklinger 1975–88. Budgetdepartementet under Erling Jørgensens ledelse*, København: Finansministeriet, pp. 37–43.

Toirkens, Jose (1988), *Schijn en werkelijkheid van het bezuinigingsbeleid 1975–1986: een onderzoek naar de besluitvorming over bezuinigen in de ministerraad en het gedrag van individuele ministers (Appearance and Reality of the Austerity Policy: A Research on Decision-making in the Council of Ministers and the Behaviour of Individual Ministers)*, Deventer: Kluwer.

Tomkin, Shelley (1998), *Inside OMB: Politics and Process in the President's Budget Office*, New York: M.E. Sharpe Press.

Treasury – New Zealand (1984), *Economic Management*, Wellington: Government Printer.

Treasury – New Zealand (1987), *Government Management: Brief to the Incoming Government*, vol. 1, Wellington: Government Printer.

Treasury – New Zealand (1989a), *Putting it Simply: An Explanatory Guide to Financial Management Reform*, Wellington: Treasury.

Treasury – New Zealand (1989b), *Putting it Together: An Explanatory Guide to the New Zealand Public Sector Management System*, Wellington: Treasury.

Treasury – New Zealand (1990), *Treasury Advice to the Incoming Government*, Wellington: Treasury.

Treasury – New Zealand (1990–2001), *The Treasury's Annual Reports 1989/90–2000/01*, Wellington: Treasury.

Treasury – New Zealand (1993), *Briefing to the Incoming Government*, Wellington: Treasury.

Treasury – New Zealand (1995), *Fiscal Responsibility Act 1994 – An Explanation* (Amended version 1996), Wellington: Treasury.

Treasury – New Zealand (1999a), *Briefing to the Incoming Government*, Wellington: Treasury.

Treasury – New Zealand (1999b), *Guide to Incoming Vote Ministers*, Treasury Circular, Wellington: Treasury.

Treasury – New Zealand (1999c), *New Zealand Government Asset Sales as at 30 September 1999*, Treasury website http://www.treasury.govt.nz/assetsales/default.asp.

Treasury (1999d), *Overview of the Budget Process*, Wellington: Treasury.

Treasury (2001a), *Relationship Protocols 2001/02*, at http://www. treasury.govt.nz/relationshipprotocols.

Treasury (2001b), 'Role of the Vote Analyst', Notes for Internal Treasury Seminar.

Treasury – New Zealand Debt Management Office (2001), *New Zealand Economic and Financial Overview*, July.

Tweede Kamer (1996–2000), 25396, nr. 3; 25238, nr. 2; 25257, nr. 1; 25396, nr. 2; 25396, nr. 7; 26974, nr. 3.

United States, Bureau of the Census, *County Business Patterns* (1993–94), data available at http://www.census.gov/ftp/pub/prod/1/bus/93cbp/cbp93.htm and http://www.census. gov/prod/2/bus/cbp94/cbp94-1.pdf.

van de Ven, A.H. and R. Drazin (1985), 'The Concept of Fit in Contingency Theory', *Organizational Behavior*, 7, 333–65.

van Loon, Richard (1981), 'Stop the Music: the Current Policy and Expenditure Management System in Ottawa', *Canadian Public Administration*, 22 (2), 251–60.

van Loon, Richard (1983a), 'Ottawa's Expenditure Process: Four Systems in Search of Coordination', in G. Bruce Doern (ed.), *How Ottawa Spends 1983: Liberals, the Opposition and Federal Priorities*, Toronto: James Lorimer.

van Loon, Richard (1983b), 'The Policy and Expenditure Management System in the Federal Government: the First Three Years', *Canadian Public Administration*, 26 (1), 255–85.

Vertigan, Michael (1999), *Review of Budget Estimates Production Arrangements – Vertigan Report*, Canberra: DoFA, 28 July.

Vielleux, G. and D.J. Savoie (1988), 'Kafka's Castle: the Treasury Board of Canada Revisited', *Canadian Public Administration*, 31 (4), 517–38.

Vries, J. de and A.K. Yesilkagit (1999), 'Core Executives and Party Politics: Privatisation in the Netherlands', *West European Politics*, 22 (1), 115–37.

Waigel, Theo and Manfred Schell (1994), *Tage, die Deutschland und die Welt veränderten, Vom Mauerfall zum Kaukasus, Die Deutsche Währungs-union*, München: Bruckmann.

Wang Lixin and Joseph Fewsmith (1995), 'Bulwark of the Planned Economy: the Structure and Role of the State Planning Commission', in C. Hamrin and S. Zhao (eds), *Decision-making in Deng's China*, New York: Sharpe.

Wanna, John and Joanne Kelly (1998), 'Same Means, Different Ends: Expenditure Management in Australia and Canada', *Financial Management Institute Journal*, 9 (3).

Wanna, John, Joanne Kelly and John Forster (2000), *Managing Public Expenditure in Australia*, Sydney: Allen and Unwin.

Warren, Ken (1993), 'Accrual Accounting in the Public Sector: The New Zealand Experience', Presented to IIR Conference – Implementing Accrual Accounting in the Public Sector, Canberra, April.

Warren, Ken (1995), 'Managing the Migration to Accrual Accounting and Budgeting', AIC Conference Paper Financial Management and Budgeting in the Public Sector Conference, June.

Warren, Ken (1996a), *Directions in Using Accrual Accounting*, Wellington: Treasury.

Warren, Ken (1996b), *Implementing Accrual Accounting in Government: The New Zealand Experience*, International Federation of Accountants Public Sector Committee, New Zealand.

Warren, Ken (2000), *The Impact of GAAP on Fiscal Decision Making: A Review of Ten Years Experience with Accrual and Output-Based Budgets in New Zealand*, ATO Conference Paper.

Weber, Max (1948), *Economy and Society*, Berkeley: University of California Press.

Weller, Patrick and James Cutt (1976), *Treasury Control in Australia: A Study in Bureaucratic Politics*, Sydney: Ian Novak.

White, Walter and John Strick (1970), *Policy, Politics and the Treasury Board in Canadian Government*, Ontario: SRA Canada.

Whitwell, Greg (1986), *The Treasury Line*, Sydney: Allen and Unwin.

Wieland, Joachim (1992), 'Einen und Teilen, Grundsätze der Finanzverfassung des vereinten Deutschlands', in *Deutsches Verwaltungsblatt*, 107 (18), 1181–193.

Wildavsky, Aaron (1964), *The Politics of the Budgetary Process*, Boston: Little & Brown.

Wildavsky, Aaron (1975), *Budgeting: a Comparative Theory of Budgetary Processes*, Boston: Little, Brown.

Wildavsky, Aaron (1988), *The New Politics of the Budgetary Process*, New York: Harper Collins.

Yuqian, Guan (2001), *Lang (Wave)*, Beijing: People Literature Press, pp. 188–9.

Zhengpeng, Ye, Wang Zhongfa and Liu Jing (1992), *Zhongguo caizheng Gaige yu fazhan (Reform and Development in China's Public Finance)*, Guangdong: High Education Press.

Zhonghua renmin gongheguo shenji fa (1995), 1 January.

Zhonghua renmin gongheguo shenji tiaoli (1998), November.

Index